HISTORY OF
THE FREE METHODIST CHURCH
OF NORTH AMERICA

VOL. 1

BY

WILSON T. HOGUE

First Fruits Press
Wilmore, Kentucky
c2016

History of the Free Methodist Church of North America By Wilson T. Hogue

First Fruits Press, © 2016
Previously published by the Free Methodist Publishing House, ©1915.

ISBN: 9781621714736 (volume.1), (print), 9781621714743 (digital),
9781621714750 (kindle)

Digital version at http://place.asburyseminary.edu/freemethodistbooks/6/

For all other uses, contact:

First Fruits Press
B.L. Fisher Library
Asbury Theological Seminary
204 N. Lexington Ave.
Wilmore, KY 40390
http://place.asburyseminary.edu/firstfruits

Hogue, Wilson T. (Wilson Thomas), 1852-1920

History of the Free Methodist Church of North America / by Wilson T. Hogue ; introduction by Edward P. Hart.

2 volumes : illustrations, portraits ; 21 cm.

Wilmore, Ky. : First Fruits Press, © 2016.

Reprint. Previously published: Chicago : Free Methodist Publishing House, ©1915. Includes bibliographical references and index.

ISBN - 13: 9781621714736 (v.1 : paperback)

1. Free Methodist Church of North America--History. I. Title.

BX 8413 .H6 2016 287.9709

Cover design by Jonathan Ramsay

asburyseminary.edu
800.2ASBURY
204 North Lexington Avenue
Wilmore, Kentucky 40390

First Fruits Press
The Academic Open Press of Asbury Theological Seminary
204 N. Lexington Ave., Wilmore, KY 40390
859-858-2236
first.fruits@asburyseminary.edu
asbury.to/firstfruits

THE GENERAL CONFERENCE OF 1870

1 Joseph Jones. 2 John Plues. 3 M. N. Velzey. 4 G. W. Holmes. 5 O. P. Rogers. 6 B. Hackney. 7 J. W. Reddy. 8 F. C. Tritle. 9 B. R. Mosier. 10 Levi Wood. 11 F. J. Ewell. 12 Joseph Mackey. 13 W. W. Kelley. 14 J. B. Freeland. 15 M. N. Downing. 16 J. Leisering. 17 C. Brainerd. 18 Asa Abell. 19 Lewis Bailey. 20 John Ellison. 22 C. S. Gitchell. 23 A. H. Greene. 24 T. Corliss. 25 F. A. Town. 26 C. H. Lovejoy. 27 Lucien Woodruff. 28 Wm. Gould. 29 E. Owen. 30 D. M. Sinclair. 31 J. Mathews. 32 J. Travis. 33 E. P. Hart. 34 B. T. Roberts.

Yours affectionately
B T Roberts

[Plate One]

HISTORY

OF THE

FREE METHODIST CHURCH

OF NORTH AMERICA

By

BISHOP WILSON T. HOGUE, PH. D.

Introduction by

BISHOP EDWARD P. HART

VOLUME I

"*All history is an inarticulate Bible.*"—*Carlyle.*

CHICAGO

THE FREE METHODIST PUBLISHING HOUSE

1915

TO THE MEMORY

OF

MY FATHER AND MOTHER

CONTENTS

VOLUME I

CONTENTS

LIST OF ILLUSTRATIONS

LIST OF ILLUSTRATIONS

INTRODUCTION

"The Free Methodist Church had its origin in necessity and not in choice." Its existence is not due to the efforts of ambitious men who sought notoriety by founding a new sect, but rather to the self-denying labors of those who obeyed their conscience and left results with God. What are usually referred to as "her issues" are incidental rather than fundamental.

The men providentially raised up as the founders of this movement stood solidly upon the platform of Scriptural Holiness, and were jealous only for moral purity. But the righteousness for which they contended was the same in character as that ascribed to the Son of God: "Thou hast loved righteousness and hated iniquity; therefore God, even Thy God, hath anointed Thee with the oil of gladness above Thy fellows." Heb. 1:9. The holiness they demanded was not of that sentimental kind which, baptized in the name of Christianity, is loud in its protestations of love for righteousness, but dares not strike one effectual blow at iniquity. These bold reformers, in their uncompromising opposition to iniquity, soon came to questions involving moral issues, and they were not slow in taking their stand, nor equivocal in defending their position.

Early in the latter half of the nineteenth century the Rev. B. T. Roberts, the Rev. Loren Stiles and other members of the Genesee Conference of the Methodist Episcopal Church, saw, as they believed, evidences of a growing departure from Scriptural Christianity and original Methodism. By a heaven-quickened, spiritual intuition these men felt and saw the oncoming flood of worldliness, and by the help of God were enabled to raise up a standard against it.

INTRODUCTION

With careful and painstaking research the author has, in the following pages, been successful in giving a true and impartial account of the self-sacrificing labors of the men who, under God, were instrumental in originating the movement which resulted in the formation of the Free Methodist Church. With equal impartiality he has traced throughout its existence of over half a century the development and growth of the Church thus organized.

The Free Methodist Church is fortunate in having for its historian a man so eminently qualified for his work as Bishop Hogue. He was personally acquainted with many of its founders, and has spent much of his life traveling throughout its boundaries. He therefore writes with a personal knowledge of his subject. He is also qualified for his task by his balanced judgment and by his mastery of the English language. Nine years in the editorial chair of the *Free Methodist* cultivated his natural facility for elegant English, so that he undertakes the present work with a mastery of style which is both charming and forceful.

Some one has said that a reform seldom outlives the lives of the reformers. We are glad to note that, while all of those who were most prominent in the beginning of this movement have passed away, other hearts and hands are actively engaged in maintaining the same standard of unworldly and aggressive Christianity. For this there is an imperative need. For while many, in a spirit of Laodicean boasting, are saying, "We are rich, and increased with goods, and have need of nothing," there are those with anointed vision who are grieving over the departure not only from sound doctrine, but from practical Christianity as well. Many still have the form of godliness who deny the power thereof.

If, in the perusal of this work, the arraignment of some of the characters seems severe, the reader must remember that this is to be charged up not to the author but to the facts.

EDWARD P. HART.

Alameda, California.

PREFACE

The demand for such a work as the following is the author's chief apology for having written it. The Free Methodist Church has been in existence for about fifty-five years, and nothing like a complete history of the organization has heretofore been undertaken. Bowen's "History of the Origin of the Free Methodist Church," as suggested by its title, deals exclusively with the *origin* of the movement. Roberts's "Why Another Sect?" though containing much valuable historical information, was written chiefly as an apology for the existence of the denomination, and also deals almost exclusively with matters pertaining to its origin. MacGeary's "Outline History of the Free Methodist Church" was intended *merely* as an outline, and was particularly designed for use in "The Sunday-school Teachers' Training Course."

Dr. Bowen's work and that of General Superintendent B. T. Roberts are both out of print, and have been for a considerable time; and MacGeary's "Outline" is so brief as of necessity to omit the greater part of the history connected with the origin of the Church, and as to forbid any extended discussion of those matters of controversy in the Genesee Conference of the Methodist Episcopal Church which preceded and finally led to the organization of the new denomination. Moreover, the first generation of Free Methodists has nearly all passed away, and a new generation has taken its place. Hence there is the greater need for such a history of the movement as will give the new generation, and those who will succeed it, a broadly intelligent idea of what the fathers of Free Methodism were contending for in the conflict amid which the movement originated—a clear and intelligent idea of what the

Free Methodist Church stands for, and should stand for to the end of time.

Moreover, many important things in the earlier history of the Church would likely be forgotten—things, too, which it is very desirable to preserve in proper form for ready reference—were they not gathered up in some such form as this for preservation. As an illustration of how such matters may become lost to the Church, the author desired to secure a copy of a certain historic pamphlet published about fifty years ago, and advertised throughout the whole Church for a copy, without getting a single response. Fortunately he found a copy that had been bound with an old magazine file, and had been turned in to the library of the Free Methodist Publishing House. Perhaps there is not another copy in existence, and the old volume containing that will not be long-lived. To rescue such things from oblivion is no small consideration.

In the prosecution of his task the author has generally obtained his information from original sources. Where other authors have been quoted full credit has usually been given in the body of the work. A more free use has been made of Bowen's "Origin of the Free Methodist Church" and Roberts's "Why Another Sect?" than of other works, inasmuch as they substantially agree regarding those early controversies which issued in the origin of Free Methodism, and during the years that have elapsed since their publication they have never been contradicted. The silence of those authors, to the day of their death, whose statements regarding the Free Methodist Church are challenged in "Why Another Sect?" certainly appears to have been a tacit acknowledgment that the challenge was unanswerable.

At least a dozen competent persons have had the reading of this work, in advance sheets, some of whom were in the midst of the conflict of over fifty years ago, and all of whom have been familiar with the entire subsequent history of Free Methodism; and these all attest the general correctness of what is herein written. The author has also received many valuable suggestions from these persons, which have helped materially in producing what he trusts will prove to be a readable and reliable history.

Acknowledgement is made of the valuable service rendered by the Rev. J. T. Logan, Editor of the *Free Methodist,* in preparing the Index to the contents of these volumes.

The publisher, and also the readers, are to be congratulated on the excellence of the mechanical part of the work, especially of the illustrations accompanying it. The aim has been to present, so far as practicable, photogravures of principal actors in the movement whose history is herein related, and of some of the chief institutions of the Church, as well. It has been necessary, however, to limit portraits of living persons almost wholly to those of General Conference officers and officers of the Woman's Foreign Missionary Society, and in a few cases even these have had to be omitted.

The preparation of this work has been a long, but far from a tedious task. It has been conscientiously performed, but with the full realization that conscientiousness in its performance is no guaranty of perfection. It is hoped, however, that no imperfections will be found of such a character as to depreciate the work as history, and that no errors will have escaped notice except such as are of minor significance, and can be corrected in a future edition.

WILSON T. HOGUE.

Chicago, Illinois.

HISTORY OF THE FREE METHODIST CHURCH
VOLUME I

CHAPTER I

PRELIMINARY OBSERVATIONS

The Free Methodist Church came into existence as a result of spiritual declension in the parent body—the Methodist Episcopal Church. Unlike other branches of Methodism its rise was not due either to discontent with an episcopal form of government, to any alleged discrimination against laymen in the Conferences, to any system of caste based on nationality, color, or social condition, or to anything then conceived of as fundamentally wrong with the general polity of the Church.

That there were abuses of Methodist polity, growing out of the Church's spiritual decline, was generally recognized, but even these abuses were never regarded by the founders of the Free Methodist Church as sufficient grounds for secession from the Methodist Episcopal Church, nor as justifying a warfare against her polity and usages.

John Alfred Faulkner, D. D., of Drew Theological Seminary, in his "Story of the Churches," a series of 12mo. volumes on the history of the leading religious denominations, says:

"The only Church that has sprung out of Methodist ground by reason of dissatisfaction with the worldliness of the Church and with its abandonment of the heroic ideals of the elder time, is the Free Methodist Church, which was organized in Pekin, New York, in 1860. It was the outgrowth of a profound agitation in Western New York in the fifth and sixth decades of the nineteenth century, and was occasioned by the alleged lapse of the Church from its primitive testimony, (1) as to slavery,

(2) as to holiness, (3) as to non-conformity with the world, and (4) as to evangelical conception of doctrine."*

The foregoing is a correct statement of the case, with one exception. In naming the items regarding which the Methodist Episcopal Church was conceived of as having departed from its primitive testimony, "(1)" and "(2)" should be transposed. It was the "lapse of the Church from its primitive testimony" concerning holiness, first of all, that occasioned the "profound agitation" of which Dr. Faulkner writes. The agitation as to its testimony regarding slavery, non-conformity to the world, and evangelical conception of doctrine, grew out of the agitation regarding the Church's attitude on the subject of holiness, or entire sanctification, and was altogether subordinate thereto.

It should be particularly noted that the Free Methodist Church did not originate in a secession from the parent body. This is another respect in which it differs from all other bodies of American Methodism. Others seceded, on various grounds, and for various reasons; but those who were instrumental in forming the Free Methodist Church were loyal to the parent Church to the very last, as the sequel will show, and sought in good faith and by most earnest effort to conserve and promote its purity and integrity. Not until they were (as they believed, unjustly and unlawfully) excluded from its pale, and even denied the right of appeal to the General Conference, guaranteed them by the Discipline of the Church, did they entertain the idea of forming a separate branch of Methodism. The following paragraphs, from the Introduction to the Discipline adopted at the time the Free Methodist Church was organized, and which, during more than half a century, have never been refuted, corroborate the foregoing statement:

"The Free Methodist Church had its origin in necessity, and not in choice. It did not grow out of a secession, nor out of an unsuccessful attempt to bring about a reform in

*Volume on "The Methodists," p. 175.

the government of the Church. Those concerned in its formation never expected a separation from the Methodist Episcopal Church, until they were unjustly excluded from its pale. They sought redress at the proper tribunal. It was not granted. Even a candid hearing was denied them. Thus thrown out, and the possibility of a restoration being cut off, and believing that God still called them to labor for the salvation of souls, they had no alternative but to form a new organization. In doctrine, discipline, and spirit they were Methodists, and hence they could not offer themselves to any other denomination.

"The issue on which they were thrust out was between dead formalism, and the life and power of godliness, and so they could not feel at home with those branches of the Methodist family into whose formation other questions mainly entered."

The Free Methodist Church is not a schismatic organization, although it came into existence as a result of schism in the Methodist Episcopal Church. Its originators did not produce the schism, however, which led to its formation. The parent body must be held responsible for that. We believe, with the late Rev. A. A. Hodge, D. D., that, "If the Church be an external society, then all deviation from that society is of the nature of schism; but if the Church be, in its essence, a great spiritual body, constituted by the indwelling of the Holy Ghost through all the ages and nations, uniting all in Christ, and if its external organization is only accidental and temporary, and subject to change and variation (which is the Protestant doctrine), then deviation from organization, unless touched with the spirit of schism, is not detrimental to the Church." We still further believe, with the same celebrated writer, that "under this dispensation God has left us free to form organizations. He has left us free to experience Christianity under all the conditions in which He has placed us; and the Christian religion which we receive takes various colors and tones from the nationality, from the tribe, and from the race. Undoubtedly, there is such a thing as schism. Schism is a great sin. But if the Church is a spiritual body, the sin is against spiritual unity."*

So far were the founders of the Free Methodist Church from being schismatics that they were generally acknowledged to be devout and spiritual men, who contended with much earnestness and power for "the unity of the Spirit;" and, in their devotion to even the organic unity of the Methodist Episcopal Church, they endured severe persecution to the last from their less spiritual brethren rather than voluntarily to withdraw themselves from the organization. They remained within the pale of the Church until placed outside by excommunication. Therefore, whichever of the foregoing views regarding the nature of the Church one may entertain, it must be acknowledged that they were not schismatic in any proper sense of the word. They lived in closest fellowship with all that was spiritual in the Methodism of their time, and were so devoted to its integrity as an external society that they chose to suffer misrepresentation, defamation, malignity, and cruel abuse, rather than break from its organic unity.

Moreover, when finally expelled, some of them again united with the Church on probation, while all save one appealed to the General Conference, in hope that the verdict of expulsion would be set aside, thereby admitting of their continuance within its pale. Not until the Supreme Court of the Church refused to entertain their appeals did it become manifest that their enforced separation from their ecclesiastical mother must be final.

The Free Methodist Church is an organization designed to conserve and promote that type of Christianity which primitive Methodism so admirably illustrated. Dr. Chalmers defined the Methodism of his time as "Christianity in earnest." This was its essential character. This also is the essential character of the Free Methodist Church.

*"Popular Lectures on Theological Themes," pp. 211-213.

The most essential thing in all true Methodism is its principle of intense spirituality, of uncompromising righteousness, of experimental and practical holiness, of whole-hearted and unswerving devotion to the advancement of the kingdom of God among men. As a principle, or a system of truth and righteousness, Methodism is as old as Christianity itself; as an ecclesiastical polity it dates from the early part of the eighteenth century, when, under John Wesley, the United Societies of Methodism were founded. As to its chief essentials Methodism, when true to the original type, is one and the same everywhere. Its polity may change, but its principles never, unless by such deviation from type as leaves it no longer Methodism in any true and proper sense.

"It does not follow, however, that because Methodism is always the same," wrote Rev. Elias Bowen, D. D., in 1864, at that time a member of the Methodist Episcopal Church, "that, therefore, it is always known by the same name, or is always found with the same denomination of people. Adaptation is an essential element of the system; and from the wonderful facility with which it accommodates itself to time, place, and circumstance, it finds no difficulty in taking on a new name, or passing from one association of people to another, whenever there is occasion for it, or the offer of more eligible means for the accomplishment of its legitimate ends requires such a change.

"As the mountain turtle casts off its old shell, upon occasion, and takes on a new covering more suitable to the purposes of its being; and as the rushing stream, when too much obstructed in its course, leaves the old channel for a new one, where it can pursue its ocean-bound course with more freedom; so Methodism, tied up and embarrassed in its soul-saving operations by an unscrupulous and almost universal conformity to the world in the old Church, has been compelled, in order to fulfil its appropriate mission of 'spreading Scriptural holiness over the land,' to leave its accustomed pulpits and altars, so terribly desecrated latterly by worldliness and Churchism, and carry on its work through the newly organized medium of the Free Methodist Church."*

Finally, the Free Methodist Church claims to have been providentially raised up, as Wesley said of the Methodists of his day, "to reform the nation, particularly the Church; and to spread Scriptural holiness over the land." "Holiness unto the Lord" has been their watchword and the inspiration of the movement from the beginning. In the Prefatory Address to their Book of Discipline,† on the "Origin and Character" of the movement, they expressed themselves regarding the character of Free Methodism in the following paragraphs:

> The Free Methodists are a body of Christians who profess to be in earnest to get to heaven, by conforming to all the will of God, as made known in His Word. They do not believe that either God or the Bible has changed to accommodate the fashionable tendencies of the age. They solemnly protest against the union of the Church and the world. The conditions of salvation, as they teach, are the same now that they were eighteen hundred years ago. He who would be a Christian in reality, as well as in name, must deny himself, take up his cross daily, and follow Jesus. He must come out from the world and be separate, and touch not the unclean thing.
>
> In doctrine they are Methodists. They believe in the doctrine of the Holy Trinity, in a general atonement, in the necessity of the new birth, in the witness of the Spirit, and in future rewards and punishments. They insist that it is the duty and privilege of every believer to be sanctified wholly, and to be preserved blameless unto the coming of the Lord Jesus Christ. Every one who is received into full connection, either professes to enjoy that perfect love which casts out fear, or promises diligently to seek until he obtains it.
>
> They look upon practical godliness as the never failing result of a genuine religious experience. "By their fruits ye shall know them." Hence they insist that those who profess to be the disciples of Christ should come out from unbelievers and be separate, abstaining from connection with all secret societies, renouncing all vain pomp and glory, adorning themselves with modest apparel,

*Preface to "History of Origin of the Free Methodist Church," pp. ix. and x.
†Ed. 1866.

REV. E. BOWEN, D. D.

REV. WILLIAM C. KENDALL

REV. LOREN STILES, JR.

REV. JOSEPH McCREERY

[Plate Two]

and not with gold, or pearls, or costly array. We have no right to abolish any of the requirements made by Christ and the apostles; or to make obedience to them a matter of small consequence. The Golden Rule, they hold, applies equally to all mankind.

The government is not aristocratic, but the members have an equal voice with the ministers in all the councils of the Church. Both the Annual and the General Conferences are composed of as many lay as ministerial delegates, who have an equal voice and vote in all the proceedings. The Stationing Committee, by which the appointments are made, is composed of the General Superintendent, the District Chairmen and an equal number of laymen chosen for that purpose. The Official Boards are selected by the members of circuits, and not appointed by the preachers. They have District Chairmen, who may be appointed to circuits the same as the rest of the preachers. They have General Superintendents, elected once in four years, whose duty it is to preside at the Annual Conferences, and travel through the connection at large. The rights of the members are carefully guarded.

They endeavor to promote spirituality and simplicity in worship. Congregational singing is universal, and performances upon musical instruments and singing by choirs in public worship are prohibited. They believe in the Holy Ghost. If men are really converted and sanctified, it is through the Spirit of God. When He works there is a stir. As President Edwards says, "Eternal things are so great, and of such vast concern, that there is great absurdity in men being but moderately moved and affected by them." "Where the Spirit of the Lord is, there is liberty." The Free Methodists, while they do not believe in any mere formal noise, yet, when the Spirit comes like "a rushing mighty wind," as on the day of Pentecost, do not dare to oppose the manifestations of His presence. As Edwards says, "Whenever there is any considerable degree of the Spirit's influence upon a mixed multitude, it will produce, in some way, a great visible commotion." To resist His operations is to hinder the work of God.

They do not believe in resorting to worldly policy to sustain the Gospel. Christ has said, that whosoever giveth a cup of cold water in His name, shall in no wise lose his reward. But it is the motive, and not the amount done, that secures the divine approbation. There is no more virtue in giving to the cause of God for carnal pleasure, than there is in any other purely selfish action. Hence they give no countenance to modern expedients for promoting Christianity, such as selling or renting pews, festivals, lotteries, fairs, and donation parties. To say that the Church cannot be sustained without these contrivances to beguile the world into its support, is to confess that professing Christians are "lovers of pleasure more than lovers of God." It is to pronounce Christianity a failure. The Gospel possesses an inherent power that will not only sustain itself, but make its way through all opposition, wherever its advocates live up to its requirements and rely upon its promises.

All their Churches are required to be as free as the grace they preach. They believe that their mission is twofold—to maintain the Bible standard of Christianity, and to preach the Gospel to the poor. Hence they require that all seats in their houses of worship shall be free. No pews can be rented or sold among them. The world will never be converted to Christ, so long as the Churches are conducted upon the exclusive system. It has always been contrary to the economy of the Christian Church to build houses of worship with pews to rent. But the spirit of the world has encroached, by little and little, until, in many parts of the United States, not a single free Church can be found in any of the cities or larger villages. The pew system prevails among nearly all denominations. They are thoroughly convinced that this system is wrong in principle and bad in tendency. It is a corruption of Christianity. Free Churches are essential to reach the masses. The provisions of the Gospel are for all. The "glad tidings" must be proclaimed to every individual of the human race. God sends the true light to illuminate and melt every heart. To savage and civilized, bond and free, black and white, the ignorant and the learned, is freely offered the great salvation.

But for whose benefit are special efforts to be put forth? Who must be particularly cared for? Jesus settles this question. "The blind receive their sight, and the lame walk, the lepers are cleansed, and the deaf hear, the dead are raised up," and, as if all this would be insufficient to satisfy John of the validity of His claims, He adds, "and the poor have the Gospel preached to them." This was the crowning proof that He was the One that should come. In this respect the Church must follow in the footsteps of Jesus. She must see to it that the Gospel is preached to the poor. Thus this duty is enjoined by the plainest precepts and examples. If the Gospel is to be preached to all, then it follows, as a necessary consequence, that all the arrangements for preaching the Gospel should be so made as to secure this object. If it be said that seats would be freely given to those who are unable to pay for them, they answer, this does not meet the case. Few are willing, so long as they are able to appear at Church, to be publicly treated as paupers.

CHAPTER II

SPIRITUAL DECLINE OF AMERICAN METHODISM—THE ZINZENDORFIAN HERESY

There has always been a tendency in the Church, considered as an earthly institution, toward backsliding. It was so with ancient Israel. God said of them, "My people are bent to backsliding from me." Hos. 11:7. It is so with the Church of to-day.

"The Churches of Galatia" manifested this tendency, even under the ministry of inspired men. In his Epistle to those Churches St. Paul found it necessary to say to them, "I marvel that ye are so soon removed from Him that called you into the grace of Christ unto another Gospel: which is not another; but there be some that trouble you, and would pervert the Gospel of Christ. But though we, or an angel from heaven, preach any other Gospel unto you than that which we have preached unto you, let him be accursed." Gal. 1: 6-8.

The Epistle to the Hebrews was evidently written to safeguard those to whom it is addressed from this well-nigh universal tendency. They, having been accustomed to a religion that continuously appealed spectacularly to the senses, and which consisted largely in impressive rites and ceremonies, as also in "the works of the law," were peculiarly in danger of turning again to "the beggarly elements" from which Christ had delivered them.

The tendency to spiritual declension is occasioned by the natural weakness of humanity; by the spiritual sluggishness of even Christian men and women; by the prevailing lack of principle among the rank and file of those who compose the nominal Church; by the susceptibility of human beings to being influenced by those worldly excitements which are unfriendly to spiritual religion; by the fact that "struggle for existence" is the law of the spirit-life as well as of the physical; by the law of "reversion to type," which operates in the spiritual as well as in the natural realm; by the inculcation of error through false teachers; and by the tendency of all carnal traits among God's professed people to work throughout the entire body, like leaven in the meal, until the whole is leavened, or corrupted, by carnal principles.

So clearly did President Finney recognize this tendency of the Church to backsliding that, in the first of his "Lectures on Revivals of Religion," he says: "A revival of religion presupposes a declension. Almost all the religion in the world has been produced by revivals. God has found it necessary to take advantage of the excitability there is in mankind to produce powerful excitements among them, before He can lead them to obey. Men are spiritually so sluggish, and there are so many things to lead their minds off from religion, and to oppose the influence of the Gospel, that it is necessary to raise an excitement among them, till the tide rises so high as to sweep away opposing obstacles. They must be so excited that they will break over these counteracting influences, before they will obey God. Not that the excited feeling is religion, for it is not; but it is excited desire, appetite, and feeling that prevents religion. * * *

"The great political, and other worldly excitements that agitate Christendom, are all unfriendly to religion, and divert the mind from the interests of the soul. Now these excitements can only be counteracted by *religious* excitements. And until there is religious principle in the world to put down irreligious excitements, it is vain to try to promote religion, except by counteracting excitements. This is true in philosophy, and it is a historical fact."*

*Pages 1 and 2.

FIRST FREE METHODIST CHURCH BUILDING ERECTED AFTER THE CHURCH WAS FORMED

Located at Clintonville, Illinois

[Plate Three]

THE GENERAL CONFERENCE OF 1870

1 Joseph Jones. 2 John Plues. 3 M. N. Velzey. 4 G. W. Holmes. 5 O. P. Rogers. 6 B. Hackney. 7 J. W. Reddy. 8 F. C. Tritle. 9 B. R. Mosier. 10 Levi Wood. 11 F. J. Ewell. 12 Joseph Mackey. 13 W. W. Kelley. 14 J. B. Freeland. 15 M. N. Downing. 16 J. Leisering. 17 C. Brainerd. 18 Asa Abell. 19 Lewis Bailey. 20 John Ellison. 22 C. S. Gitchell. 23 A. H. Greene. 24 T. Corliss. 25 F. A. Town. 26 C. H. Lovejoy. 27 Lucien Woodruff. 28 Wm. Gould. 29 E. Owen. 30 D. M. Sinclair. 31 J. Mathews. 32 J. Travis. 33 E. P. Hart. 34 B. T. Roberts.

[Plate Four]

Toward the middle of the nineteenth century Methodism in the United States had begun to manifest "its abandonment of the heroic ideals of the elder time" in a most lamentable degree, and well-nigh universally.

The Methodist Episcopal Church of that day had come to accept very largely the Moravian view of holiness, or sanctification, as taught by Count Zinzendorf, the gist of which is, as stated by Mr. Wesley, that "We are sanctified wholly the moment we are justified, and are neither more nor less holy to the day of our death; entire sanctification, and justification, being in one and the same instant."*

The original teaching of Methodism on this point is set forth by Mr. Wesley as follows:

"Q. When does inward sanctification begin?"

"A. The moment a man is justified. (Yet sin remains in him, yea, the seed of all sin, till he is sanctified throughout.) From that moment a believer gradually dies to sin, and grows in grace."†

"Q. Is this death to sin, and renewal in love, gradual or instantaneous?

"A. A man may be dying for some time; yet he does not, properly speaking, die, till the instant the soul is separated from the body; and in that instant he lives the life of eternity. In like manner, he may be dying to sin for some time; yet he is not dead to sin, till sin is separated from his soul; and in that instant he lives the full life of love. And as the change undergone, when the body dies, is of a different kind, and infinitely greater than any we had known before, yea, such as till then it is impossible to conceive; so the change wrought, when the soul dies to sin, is of a different kind, and infinitely greater than any before, and than any one can conceive till he experiences it. Yet he still grows in grace, and in the knowledge of Christ, in the love and image of God; and will do so, not only till death, but to all eternity."‡

---

*"Wesley's Works," Vol. vi, p. 22. †Do Vol. vi, p. 496.
‡Works, Vol. vi., p. 505.

Here we have a clear and definite statement from the immortal founder of Methodism himself of that doctrine which, more than any other, has ever distinguished the creed of Methodism from the creeds of all other evangelical bodies. In her doctrinal standards the Methodist Church still retained this doctrine, in its verbal form; but, while the doctrine remained unchanged in the various standards of the Church, there had been a general practical drift from the same throughout her pale, and especially among her ministry.

In preaching the semi-centennial sermon before the Oneida Annual Conference of the Methodist Episcopal Church, at the celebration of its fiftieth anniversary, in April, 1864, the Rev. E. Bowen, D. D., speaking of the changes which had occurred latterly among Methodists, said:

"But now, the old Moravian heresy of the identity of the two states [i. e., of justification and entire sanctification] is pretty generally embraced among us; and its advocates, we are sorry to say, exhibit a virulence in their opposition to the Wesleyan view of sanctification which but too clearly betrays the cause of the change they have undergone—a manifest want of the Spirit of Christ, and the aversion they feel for the subjects of a living piety."

This was the testimony of one of the most venerable men of Methodism in his day, a man not given to rashness of statement, but who weighed well his words, and kept within the bounds of truth and sobriety. Moreover, the foregoing statement has never been successfully challenged during the more than fifty years that have since passed away. It is cited here in proof of the allegation made that, while Methodism held nominally to the primitive Wesleyan standard of doctrine regarding sanctification, there had been a general practical drifting toward the Zinzendorfian view, that sanctification and justification are identical. Further proof of this fact will appear in abundance in subsequent chapters of this work.

With this practical drift away from her most distinguishing doctrine and experience, came, as a consequence, the lowering of the tone of Methodism regarding all that is vital to Christian experience, discipline, character, and fruitfulness. So great and general was the spiritual desolation that spiritually-minded men and women found Jeremiah's lamentation expressing the feeling that burdened and oppressed them:

> "How is the gold become dim! how is the most pure gold changed!
> The stones of the sanctuary are poured out at the head of every street.
> The precious sons of Zion, comparable to fine gold,
> How are they esteemed as earthen pitchers, the work of the hands of the potter!" etc. Lam. 4:1, 2.

In its primitive purity Methodism had been Scriptural and strict in its attention to matters of Church discipline. The General Rules, the Baptismal Vow, the Church Covenant, and the Rules for a Preacher's Conduct; the directions of the Church concerning dress, class-meetings, and attendance at the sanctuary services; and also the advices regarding free seats in Church buildings, as well as regarding economy and plainness in the erection of such structures; were generally regarded as parts of the Book of Discipline to be observed, and, where not otherwise observed, to be enforced in a Scriptural and disciplinary way. In fact, the Discipline was looked upon generally, not merely as a monument of "heroic ideals of the elder time," but as a book of rules for holy living, applicable alike to both preachers and laymen, and which could be grievous only to the unregenerate and the backslidden. These were things, which, according to the primitive idea of Methodism, made for the strengthening and upbuilding of Christian character in the individual and in the Church collectively—fruits of holiness, the absence of which, or indifference to which, indicated defection of the heart from God.

Whether these principles were Scriptural or unscriptural, whether right or wrong, whether wise or unwise, Methodism was originally built up, and also won those illustrious victories of "the elder time," on such views of Christian experience and discipline as the foregoing; and the Methodisms of later generations are obligated, by virtue of their claim to be in the line of direct succession from original Methodism, as also by their professed belief that "all these things His Spirit writes on truly awakened hearts," to treat them with the utmost seriousness, and to "walk by the same rule and mind the same thing."

However, at the period of which we write Methodism, as illustrated by the Methodist Episcopal Church, was very far gone from original righteousness in regard to these particulars. The Wesleyan doctrine of entire sanctification as a second work of grace attainable and obligatory in the present life to all believers, was generally ignored, and by not a few even in the ministry was treated with ridicule and contempt. This naturally led to great looseness regarding the doctrines of the new birth, the witness of the Spirit, and practical holiness in many of its most important details. The prevailing type of Christian experience became decidedly shallow, and the fervor and spirituality which had once been chief characteristics of Methodist worship were so uncommon that, when now and then they would be manifest, they were generally regarded and treated as outbursts of fanaticism, which it was dangerous to allow and wise to disparage and oppose. Such manifestations were more liable to be the occasion of Church discipline than were the plainest violations of the General Rules.

Moreover, the worst feature of the case was, that not only the Bishops generally, but the General Conference as well, notwithstanding the fact that every ordained Methodist preacher was solemnly pledged to do all in his power "to banish and drive away all erroneous and strange doctrines contrary to God's Word," allowed themselves to sanction the rise of the Zinzendorfian heresy within the pale of Methodism, and even to regard with complacency the consequent defection of the Church from her primitive standards of discipline, experience, and unworldliness of life. The condition was at least an approach toward that of Judah in Jeremiah's time, regarding which the prophet testified, "A wonderful and horrible thing is come to pass in the land: the prophets prophesy falsely, and the priests bear rule by their means; and my people love to have it so." Jer. 5:31.

The period of which we write was a transitional period in the history of the Methodist Episcopal Church. It still retained, in various localities, a goodly degree of that vital religion, fervor, simplicity, plainness, and general non-conformity to the world which characterized it in primitive days, and were the only justification of its existence as a separate religious denomination. But early in the period spiritual declension set in, and a world-ward trend began. This defection "was accelerated when the United States census disclosed the fact that the Methodist Episcopal Church was the largest Protestant denomination in the country, and had the greatest amount of Church property. This gratifying intelligence was often dwelt upon in the Church periodicals, and in addresses at the Conferences, and at other large gatherings."

Self-gratulation soon made its evil effects visible. Why should a people who had become so numerous, strong, wealthy and influential continue to be so singular? Why erect such plain houses of worship as they had done in the former times? Why insist upon modesty and plainness of attire? Why continue to be so unlike the nations round about them? Why incur the displeasure of those in lofty stations, of those who abounded in wealth, of those who were the *élite* of society, who otherwise might patronize their services and be drawn into their communion? Had they not hitherto been too narrow and exclusive? Would it not be wise to broaden Methodism so as better to adapt it to the higher social classes? Such appears to have been the tacit reasonings of prominent and influential leaders in the Methodist ranks, judging from the changes that soon occurred.

So late as 1846 the Methodist Episcopal Discipline contained the following questions and answers:

"Is anything advisable in regard to building Churches?"

"Let all our Churches be built plain and decent, and with free seats; but not more expensive than is absolutely unavoidable; otherwise the necessity of raising money will make rich men necessary to us. But if so, we must be dependent on them, yea, and governed by them. And then, farewell to Methodist Discipline if not doctrine too."

The directions regarding dress were as explicit and positive as those concerning the erection of Churches:

"Should we insist on the rules concerning dress?"

"By all means. This is no time to give encouragement to superfluity of apparel. Therefore, receive none into the Church till they have left off superfluous ornaments." "In visiting the classes be very mild, but very strict." "Allow of no exempt case: better one suffer than many."

While the Discipline was thus plain, positive, and mandatory regarding these things, it soon began to be practically ignored by influential ministers and laymen as out of date in these requirements; whereupon worldly conformity in these and other directions rapidly increased, until, at length, those changes in the Discipline were easily effected which made such sections as the foregoing no longer mandatory, but merely advisory, and that without possibility of enforcing the advices given. The effect of these changes was "to paralyze the arm of the Church in the training of her children for heaven, and to open the door of spiritual licentiousness and pride," so that, as Dr. Bowen put it in his semi-centennial sermon, " 'The world, the flesh, and the devil' might now make their onslaught upon us, and riot upon our sacred altars, with no penal inhibition to arrest their depredations."

CHAPTER III

SPIRITUAL DECLINE OF AMERICAN METHODISM—TOLERATION OF SLAVERY

Another indication of the Methodist Church's departure from first principles was its change of attitude respecting what John Wesley designated as "that execrable sum of all villainies commonly called the slave trade."

During his entire public career Mr. Wesley was intensely hostile to slavery in all its forms; and perhaps nothing ever written has dealt with the subject more thoroughly, or exposed its diabolical character more clearly and vigorously, especially within the same limits, than his tract entitled, "Thoughts on Slavery." He wrote it in 1774, before the first society for the suppression of slavery was formed, and seventeen years before the efforts made by Wilberforce and others to abolish the system under British rule. Its publication brought upon him much censure and opposition, and also subjected him to great ridicule in the various publications of the time. The tract proved decidedly effective, however, in England, and was finally published in America by Mr. Benezet, "who sent him a friendly letter by William Dillwyn, whom he refers to as 'a valuable religiously-minded person who is going a voyage to your country.' "

As a fitting climax to his life-long hatred of the system and testimony against it, Wesley addressed a dying exhortation to Wilberforce, the British Abolitionist, on the occasion of the latter having introduced before Parliament a bill, or resolutions, for the suppression of slavery in the West India Islands. It was written February 26, 1791, just four days before Mr. Wesley's death, in his eighty-eighth year. In that exhortation he expressed himself with characteristic vigor and earnestness as follows:

"Unless the Divine power has raised you up to be as Athanasius against the world, I see not how you can go through your glorious enterprise, in opposition to that execrable villainy, which is the scandal of religion, of England, and of human nature. Unless God has raised you up for this very thing, you will be worn out by the opposition of men and devils. But, 'If God be for you, who can be against you?' Are all of them together stronger than God? 'O, be not weary in well doing!' Go on, in the name of God, and in the power of His might, till even American slavery (the vilest that ever saw the sun) shall vanish away before it."*

Methodism in England appears to have been generally, perhaps it might be said universally, in accord with Mr. Wesley on this subject; and the same was true of Methodism in America during its earlier history. In fact, there appears to have been no necessity to legislate against the buying, selling, or holding of human beings as slaves by Methodists of this country before the War of the Revolution, inasmuch as the system of chattel slavery was so uniformly, strongly, and persistently denounced from Methodist pulpits that the converts and members of Methodist societies would no more have entered into complicity with such an iniquitous system than with highway robbery or murder.

Notwithstanding the changes that occurred during the period of Revolutionary struggle, whereby quite a percentage of slave owners obtained membership in the Methodist societies, still American Methodism testified in most unequivocal terms against the moral turpitude of the system, and from time to time passed resolutions condemning in strong terms all complicity with it. But about the beginning of the nineteenth century the Church began

*Works, Vol. vii., p. 237.

to assume a compromising attitude and a softened tone respecting this great evil.

Says Dr. James M. Buckley: "From its foundation in the United States until the year 1800 Methodism had testified against slavery as a moral evil. Many of its enactments were uncompromising, and all were beyond the position taken by other Churches and in advance of public sentiment; although very soon after the Methodist Church was organized concessions began to be made in view of the necessities of the South.

"The tone of condemnation was softened in 1804, and in 1808 all that relates to slaveholding among private members was stricken out, and no rule on the subject has existed since."*

Writing of the organization of the Wesleyan Methodist Connection, or Church, in 1843, Dr. John Alfred Faulkner says:

"From the point of view of an anti-slavery reformer the position of the Methodist Episcopal Church on the subject [of slavery], * * * especially after 1800, must be considered disappointing and untenable. There had not only been a constant recession of testimony, but active participation in anti-slavery measures, or even the holding of pronounced views on freedom, on the part of ministers, made them liable to the loss of reputation and standing, or even to discipline. Northern Conferences frequently passed resolutions condemning Abolition and ministers who in any way connected themselves with anti-slavery movements. Matlack was denied admission to Conference because of his views on slavery, and Charles K. True, James Floy, and Paul R. Brown, of the New York Conference, were tried and suspended for alleged aiding in the circulation of an anti-slavery tract (was it one of Wesley's?), and attending an anti-slavery convention."†

The Wesleyan Methodist Church was organized chiefly

*Hist. of Methodism in the U. S., Vol. II., p. 1.
†Story of the Churches, Vol. on "The Methodists," pp. 165, 166.

as a protest against the complicity of the Methodist Episcopal Church with the abomination of slavery, and against her abuse of the Episcopacy to oppress those among her members and ministers whose consciences led them to speak out plainly against the iniquitous system and to unite in efforts toward its suppression. Many strong men, both ministerial and lay, separated from the parent body and connected themselves with the new organization. No more heroic band of reformers than those who composed the newly organized Church were ever enlisted in defense of human rights and liberties. The organization proved a mighty factor in the agitation and action which finally led to the overthrow of American slavery. Honor to whom honor is due.

The Methodist Episcopal Church was not reformed, however, by the efforts of either those Abolitionists who remained within her pale or those who seceded and formed themselves into the new denomination. She continued her policy of compromise with the slave-power, and increased in her hostility toward Abolition and those in sympathy with it. In 1856, after 500,000 southern Methodists had seceded and organized the Methodist Episcopal Church, South, on account of the action of the General Conference in deciding that Bishop Andrews, who had married a slaveholding wife, "should desist from the exercise of his office until the impediments should be removed," the Methodist Episcopal Church inserted a new chapter in its Discipline on the subject of slavery, declaring against slaveholding in all its forms; but the General Rule which favored the system remained unchanged until 1864.

During the period of the agitation which led up to the formation of the Free Methodist Church slavery was the all-absorbing question in the Methodist Episcopal Church, as it was in the nation. The Church for years had been divided on the slavery issue, but, strangely enough, the division was over the right of *ministers* to hold slaves. The right of members to hold them was conceded by the

Discipline. By the action of the General Conference of 1860 on the subject of Church slavery "the last vestige of mandatory prohibition of the evil was toned down to a mere matter of advice," with no penalty attached for violation of the advisory section. "Up to the day that slavery was abolished by the sword there were thousands of slaveholders in good standing in the Methodist Episcopal Church. The Methodist Episcopal Discipline tolerated slavery to the last."*

The attitude of the Church on a question so vitally affecting both religion and the national weal, and that at a time of such general excitement over the slavery question everywhere, was certainly a grievous lapse "from the heroic ideals of the elder time."

*Roberts's "Why Another Sect?" p. 46.

CHAPTER IV

SPIRITUAL DECLINE OF AMERICAN METHODISM—SECRET SOCIETIES

Still another evidence that Methodism had departed from her original unworldliness and purity was manifest in the extent to which her members, and her ministers in particular, had become "unequally yoked" with Freemasonry and Odd-Fellowship. In the excitement which followed the abduction and murder of William Morgan, of Batavia, New York, in 1826, the Masonic lodges had quite generally disbanded. But at length a revival of Freemasonry, for which Odd-Fellowship had largely prepared the way, led to their reorganization. A number of ministers in the Genesee Conference had become identified with one or both of these fraternities. Sharp collisions had occurred between these preachers and some of the older and more conscientious brethren in the Churches which they had been appointed to serve. "Men of God, in whose minds the remembrance of the Morgan tragedy was fresh, felt that they could not, in conscience, support men who took upon them oaths which required them to commit similar crimes, should occasion demand it. Such men were often put out of the Church. But this action brought about dissatisfaction and division."*

Confirmatory of the foregoing statement of the case is the following, from a pamphlet written and published by the Rev. C. D. Burlingham, of the Genesee conference, in 1860, entitled: "An Outline History of the Genesee Conference Difficulties":

Some sixteen or eighteen years since a disturbing element was

*Roberts's "Why Another Sect?" p. 48.

introduced into the Genesee Conference. Our Church, as well as the community in general, had for a number of years been much agitated by the *Masonic question*, and the anti-Masonic excitement consequent upon the abduction and murder of William Morgan, of Batavia, in 1826. As the tumultuous waves were gradually subsiding into a calm, this new element of discord began to introduce itself in our Church, professedly as a mutual insurance company against temporal want, and a newly discovered and remarkably successful Gospel appliance for bringing the *world, reformed and saved, into the Church.* But our people very naturally looked upon it with suspicion. Dreading its power as a *secret agency* acting through *affiliated societies*, and doubting its utility as a financial scheme, they feared that it would *drag the Church, debased and corrupted, into the world.*

Not only in the Genesee Conference had Methodist ministers in considerable numbers identified themselves with Odd-Fellowship and Masonry, but similar conditions prevailed quite generally throughout the country. It became very noticeable also that among the secret-society preachers the bond of Lodge fellowship became stronger than the bond of Christian fellowship and of Church fellowship. The preachers who had joined the Lodges and those who were of a time-serving and timid character naturally drew together, and in such a manner as enabled the former to acquire leadership of the latter and use them as tools for the accomplishment of their purposes. Especially was this true as respected the Genesee Conference; and there can be little doubt that the division in that body which finally spread through various parts of Methodism and resulted in the formation of the Free Methodist Church had its real origin in these very circumstances.

There were many in the Conference who, with prophetic vision, foresaw the evil consequences likely to arise from the alliance of the Church through her ministers with the system of oath-bound secrecy, and who consequently strove earnestly to resist the encroachments of the Lodge upon the Church. They knew full well that, in the days of her greater purity and power, Methodism could not have been betrayed into such an enervating and corrupting amalgamation with the world. As simple-minded Christians, who had been taught and who believed the truth expressed in the dictum of the Apostle Paul, "Christ is all and in all," they felt no need of buttressing their faith in Christ with membership in and devotion to any other society than that of the Christian Church, and saw only spiritual defection as the inevitable result of sworn fellowship with men of the world in Christ-rejecting Lodges, even for purposes of mutual insurance against temporal want.

These men were Methodists from deep and abiding conviction that Methodism was providentially raised up to "spread Scriptural holiness over these lands." They also believed that this end could be accomplished only by holy men, and in the use of holy means and methods. They believed the doctrines of Methodism from their hearts, as they also believed in her primitive attitude of unworldliness and her original uncompromising testimony against a worldly-conformed type of religion. True to the solemn responsibility imposed on them by their ordination vows, they faithfully endeavored to bring themselves to the standard set by the fathers in accordance with the Holy Scriptures, both as to experience and practise, and also to bring all under their ministry into conformity to the same standard, that they might "present every man perfect in Christ Jesus." They believed in the Methodist Episcopal Discipline as a book of rules for holy living, which they had solemnly promised to enforce, and were unremitting in their efforts wisely and effectively to carry that promise into effect.

"These men, calm, trustful, and ignorant of the tactics of the Lodge, received their appointments as from the Lord, not knowing that there was a power at work, secretly, to fill the chief places of the Conference with those who at least were not opposed to the workings of the Lodge." Such appears to have been the case, however, as will be shown in a subsequent chapter. Under such conditions these loyal sons of Methodism were, by virtue of like experiences in devotion to Christ and in suffering for Him, brought into closest sympathy and fellowship, and into glorious Christian brotherhood.

It will now be seen, from the things related in this and the two preceding chapters, that an issue had arisen in the Genesee Conference of the Methodist Episcopal Church, which gradually became more and more clearly defined, and that said issue, occasioned by the lapse of the Church from her earlier and more exalted ideals was on Scriptural holiness, slavery, non-conformity to and separation from the world, the latter involving the question of secret societies. In fact, to sum it all up more briefly, the issue was on holiness, since the other items mentioned are all involved in holiness of the Scriptural type.

The effort was honestly made to reform these abuses without a separation from the Methodist Episcopal Church being necessary, but in vain. These efforts only revealed more fully the hopelessness of the situation, and hastened those developments by which those who diligently sought to restore the Church to her primitive simplicity and purity were forced to a separation.

"He who studies the Reformation attentively," says John Clark Ridpath, the eminent historian, "will not fail to perceive that the success of the movement in Germany under the leadership of Luther followed two other efforts, *not* successful, to reach the same result. The first of these—first in time and first in natural sequence—was the effort of the Church to work a reform inside her own organization. Vain chimera! Fond and childish credulity to suppose that the thing to be reformed could mend itself, that the abusers should abolish the abuse! The history of the world has not yet presented an example of an organization, gone sleek and fat and conscienceless by the destruction of human freedom and the spoilation of mankind that has had the virtue and honesty to make restitution and return to an exemplary life; nor will such a phenomenon ever be seen under the sun. Whether the organization be religious, political, or social, that law is equally irreversible, by which Ephraim is joined to his idols. He and they are bound by an indissoluble tie and will perish together."*

*Cyclopedia of Universal History, Vol. II., p. 570.

CHAPTER V

A CRISIS APPROACHING IN GENESEE CONFERENCE

Those ministers and laymen within the Genesee conference who remained loyal to the "heroic ideals of the elder time" and contended earnestly for "the old paths" of Christianity as illustrated by primitive Methodism, were not only committed to the Wesleyan view of holiness, or entire sanctification, and to the maintenance of the original plainness, simplicity and spirituality of Methodism, but they were all Abolitionists of the most pronounced type, and were also unitedly opposed to secret societies.

At the General Conference of 1856, the Rev. F. G. Hibbard had been elected editor of the *Northern Christian Advocate* over the former editor, the Rev. William Hosmer, by the pro-slavery men, who appear to have been in the majority, although Hosmer was the choice of those Conferences which chiefly patronized that publication. This was regarded by the anti-slavery men as an unwarranted usurpation on the part of the pro-slavery delegates, and as too much of an outrage to win their tame submission. Accordingly they started a new publication known as the *Northern Independent,* and elected Hosmer as its editor.

This paper soon obtained a wide circulation and exerted a powerful influence. Its editor was a broad-minded, whole-souled, but uncompromising man of God, who made his influence widely felt on all those lines of truth which center in and radiate from Scriptural holiness. He ranked among the foremost of reformers. It has been said of him, "In intellect and courage, Hosmer was the John Knox of his day. His anti-slaveryism was not of that sentimental kind which opposed slavery at the South and defended tyranny at home. With true nobility of soul he hated injustice and oppression everywhere, and condemned it just as strongly when found in the North as in the South, in his own Church as in the world. He not only opened his columns for those whom the dominant party of the Genesee Conference proscribed, but spoke out editorially in vigorous condemnation of the oppressive acts of the majority of the Conference."

It was becoming more and more evident that matters were verging toward a crisis in the Genesee Conference. Since the early forties a conflict had been on in which holiness was the principal issue, but involving other questions, particularly slavery and secret societies. The line of battle became more definitely drawn at the Conference session held in Buffalo in 1848. At one of the sittings the Rev. Eleazer Thomas, D. D., presented each preacher in his seat with a copy of a well-written pamphlet, of which the Rev. C. D. Burlingham was the author, exposing the infidel character of Freemasonry and Odd-Fellowship. With the vision of a seer the author had pointed out the evil consequences that would ensue from the union of Methodist preachers with such societies. The following is an extract:

It is believed that the *direct tendency* of Odd-Fellowism is the formation of parties in the *Conference*, in the *Church*, and in *Civil Society;* parties injurious to the cause of God and dangerous to the State. As all the operations and movements of the order are arranged in secret conclave, all persons, except the initiated, are supposed to be ignorant of its nightly transactions. It must be well known, that a *small party*, acting in perfect *concert* and in *secret*, bound together by strong *partisan* feeling, and under the influence of an obligation imposed upon its members, deemed by them as *sacred*, perhaps as an oath, is able to control, in almost any given case, a *multitude* of unsuspecting men, who are not under the influence of such affinities. And may we not justly fear, when a score or two of the members of our Conference, embracing the various *intellectual* grades in the ministry, shall combine under such influences as above named, that a *favoritism* (if nothing

REV. LEVI WOOD
Founder and first Editor of the "Free Methodist"

REV. HENRY HORNSBY

REV. T. B. CATTON

REV. CLAUDIUS BRAINERD

[Plate Five]

more) will be practised, *on account of attachment to the Order*, which will create envyings and jealousies in the Ministry, and very much injure all the interests in the Church?"

The introduction of this pamphlet among the preachers created a furore of excitement in the Conference. Those who were Masons and Odd-Fellows insisted that Brethren Burlingham and Thomas had accused them of being infidels. One of them, Thomas Carlton, openly declared, and with much emphasis, that, if "compelled to leave either, he would leave the Church before he would the Lodge." "The conservatives were greatly alarmed. They begged the offended brethren not to rend the Church in pieces. The secret society men were [finally] appeased by a compromise resolution, which, as they construed it, conceded all they wished." The purport of that resolution was to the effect that neither party should do anything in the future calculated to perpetuate the agitation. The secret society men construed this to mean that their membership in the Lodge should not be interfered with, nor their efforts to induce as many others to join as possible, and that, in face of such a course on their part, the others must do or say nothing that would tend to continue the agitation. The opponents of secret societies construed it as meaning that those who were members of secret Lodges must detach themselves therefrom as quickly as possible, and that others must not join.

Thus the issue was joined, and a breach was begun which could never be healed. Already the prophetic words of the foregoing extract from Burlingham's pamphlet were having their fulfilment, and that with more dire consequences than their writer had imagined, as the sequel shows. The secret society men applied themselves with diligence to the recruiting of their forces, from both the ranks of the ministry and of the laity. "They used every inducement to persuade the young preachers to join, giving them to understand that their position in the conference would depend upon the party with which they affiliated. As fast as they could, they took the Church into the Lodge and the Lodge into the Church. In a few years the power of the Lodge was exercised to control the affairs of the Church."*

The following instance is one among many that might be cited in proof of the foregoing statement. The Rev. J. B. Alverson, a venerable, respected and influential member of the Conference, endeavored to dissuade Thomas Carlton from becoming candidate for Agent of the Book Concern, on the ground that he could not be elected. Carlton replied: "I can command sufficient secret society influence in the General Conference to secure my election." The sequel showed that he knew his reckoning. He was not only elected, but re-elected, "and—*became a wealthy man!*"

For a few years matters went on without open collision in the Conference, although the fire was smoldering out of sight. Secret society preachers and those opposed to secrecy labored in their respective ways without seriously crossing each other's views, the former class catering generally to public opinion and seeking popularity along lines of compromise, and the latter seeking to promote pure and undefiled religion by the uncompromising proclamation of most radical truth "in demonstration of the Spirit and in power." The people generally began to perceive the difference between these two classes. They saw that the charges served by the more radical brethren usually had gracious revivals and were built up both in spirituality and in numerical strength, while those served by the more liberal ministers had few if any gracious visitations from on high, and were not built up spiritually, even if occasionally there was numerical increase. Hence those preachers whose ministry brought spiritual results came to be in such demand that the charges which they had filled would, with much reluctance, accept the appointment of a secret society man, while those which

*"Why Another Sect?" p. 52.

had been filled by secret society men would most gladly welcome a change, in the hope of obtaining more spiritual and efficient pastors.

A few words respecting those who, at this time, were chiefly enlisted in the work of endeavoring to restore Methodism in the Genesee Conference to its primitive purity and power seem here to be in place. We quote from Roberts's "Why Another Sect?" inasmuch as its author was associated with those men, knew them intimately, as also the facts connected with the history of those eventful days, and could write with a degree of intelligence regarding them denied to one who is compelled to write more than half a century after the events in question occurred:

> Those opposed to this union of the Church and the world went out to promote, as best they could, the life and power of religion. They endeavored to enforce the Discipline,—and they preached plainly and clearly the doctrine of holiness.
>
> Prominent among these were Asa Abell, Eleazer Thomas, and William C. Kendall. Asa Abell made a distinct profession of the blessing of entire sanctification at the Byron Camp Meeting, in 1851. He preached it on his district, and secured at different times the services of Fay H. Purdy, then in his early prime, a lawyer, who had received a mighty baptism of the Spirit, and whose efforts for the awakening of formal Churches met with remarkable success. Deep and powerful revivals broke out in Parma, Kendall, and other places, and the district generally was in a prosperous, spiritual condition.
>
> Rev. Eleazer Thomas kept the Cattaraugus district, to which he was appointed, in a flame of revival. He said that, like Asbury, he felt divinely commissioned to preach holiness in every sermon. At a camp-meeting which he held in Collins, Erie Co., N. Y., at which Dr. and Mrs. Palmer were present, we received the blessing of holiness: and from that time our troubles in the Conference commenced. Brother Thomas introduced at each of his Quarterly Conferences and secured the passage of resolutions against choir singing and instrumental music in worship. His camp-meetings were seasons of great power. The lines were as closely drawn, and the truth as plainly preached as now among the Free Methodists.
>
> Rev. William C. Kendall had extensive and powerful revivals on his charges; and, under his labors, many came out in the enjoyment and the profession of the blessing of holiness. Other

preachers—especially on the districts named, entered heartily into the work of soul-saving, and there was a steady increase, both in the number of members and their spirituality, on many of the charges.

Meanwhile, the secret society men and their adherents were busy, seeking to build up the Church in external splendor. They read fine sermons—sometimes without being particular as to the source where they were obtained.

"Was not that an eloquent sermon which our preacher delivered yesterday?" said one of the stewards to John A. Latta, one Monday morning.

"Perhaps you enjoyed it so much you would like to hear it again," replied Mr. Latta. He then took down a book and read him the identical sermon, word for word.

* * * * * * *

Under a specious pretext, Rev. Eleazer Thomas, the acknowledged leader of the salvation party, was sent to California, and, as is well known, was afterwards killed by the Modocs. The venerable Dr. Samuel Luckey was appointed to the Genesee district. Though great efforts had been made to stigmatize the work as fanatical, this veteran preacher recognized it at once as the work of God; and with all his great ability helped it on. The Bergen Camp Meetings had become famous for their remarkable manifestations of saving power. The religious interest did not decline under his administration. He encouraged what was called the fanaticism of the district, and was not reappointed Presiding Elder.

He was succeeded by the Rev. Loren Stiles. Mr. Stiles was a young man, a graduate of the Methodist Theological Seminary at Concord, N. H. He had already become celebrated in Western New York as a pulpit orator. Amiable in his disposition, pleasing in his manners, and a thorough gentleman in all his bearing, it was taken for granted that he would instinctively recoil from what was branded as the "coarse fanaticism" prevalent in the district. It was supposed that he would win the hearts of the people, and gradually turn them, without friction, back to the respectable quiet of spiritual death. But never were men more grievously disappointed. His prejudices were based solely upon the reports which he had heard and read. Thoroughly sincere, he recognized as soon as he came on the district the marks of the work of God. He saw that many had a spiritual power which he as yet had never received. He sought it at once; and he who was sent to put down the work of holiness, helped it on with all the influence he possessed. His quarterly meetings were thronged, and many of the people consecrated themselves wholly to God.

On the Niagara District a similar disappointment was experienced. The Rev. Isaac C. Kingsley, the Presiding Elder, was a graduate of an Ohio college. He had been brought up a Presbyterian, and still retained many of his Presbyterian ways. He sometimes read his sermons, and was rather stiff in his manners, and precise in his way of doing things. He was intellectually a strong man, examined things for himself, and when he came to a conclusion had the honesty and the courage to avow it, though he might differ from others. After a careful survey of the work he decided that what was branded as "fanaticism" was only the vital godliness which he had expected to find when he joined the Methodist Church. So, instead of opposing it, he gave it his cordial support.

The Rev. Charles D. Burlingham was pushing on the work of God on the Olean District with a hearty zeal and abundant success. The interest on the subject of holiness was kept up, and the quarterly meetings were lively and interesting.

The secret society men, stirred up by this state of things, began to publish unfavorable criticisms upon those prominent in the holiness movement, and to throw out insinuations against them. Their accredited organ was the *Buffalo Advocate.*

One of the first direct attacks made by the *Buffalo Advocate* was in an editorial reflecting upon Ex-Bishop Hamline. It was as follows:

"An article is going the rounds of the papers which states that Bishop Hamline has donated $25,000 to a Western College. We don't believe a word of it. He who was once Bishop, is, if we are correctly informed, as snug and keen in the management of his finances as any other property-famed man. He may have given something nevertheless."—*The Advocate*, April 12th, 1855.

After several efforts from the friends of the Bishop to have the above corrected, the editor finally admitted he stood corrected, that the Bishop had given the above sum, and added the sneer:

"Noble man! he shall have all our praise, if it will do him any good."

Other articles reflecting still more severely upon the Bishop were published from time to time in *The Advocate.* Why all this? "*Bishop Hamline was eminent for the advocacy of the doctrine of holiness.*"

The foregoing extract, which can be attested by men of unimpeachable character who are still living (1915), throws much light on the real nature of the issue over which the conflict raged, as also on the characters of those who were the chief participants therein.

CHAPTER VI

HISTORICAL MISREPRESENTATIONS—THREE AUTHORS REVIEWED

Three literary productions of importance have appeared during the last third of a century, from as many different authors, all representing the Methodist Episcopal Church, in which the reading public has been furnished with what assumes in each case to be a historical sketch of the origin of the Free Methodist Church.

The first of these works is the "History of the Genesee Annual Conference of the Methodist Episcopal Church," by the late Rev. F. W. Conable, for many years a member of that Conference. We were unable to determine the exact year in which the first edition was published, as there is nothing in the volume before us (second edition) to indicate when the first edition made its appearance, save that the Preface to the volume is dated March, 1876. The author has devoted between thirty and forty octavo pages to setting forth what purports to be the history of "Nazaritism" until its alleged culmination in the formation of the Free Methodist Church.

Next we have the "Cyclopedia of Methodism," a quarto volume of 1,031 double-column pages, edited by the late Bishop Matthew Simpson, D. D., LL. D., and first published in 1878. This is a much more important work than Mr. Conable's history, inasmuch as the latter work deals chiefly with matters of a more local nature, while the "Cyclopedia" deals with universal Methodism, and is for general use on the part of English-speaking people throughout the world. In this large volume about a page is devoted to the "Free Methodists." Apparently the author of the article has drawn his information from Conable's "History of the Genesee Conference," though he has presented it in a greatly abridged form. If the article was not substantially drawn from Mr. Conable's book, then it must have been written by some one in close sympathy with the views of that author, and of the faction in the Genesee Conference which he represented.

In 1897 the "History of Methodism in the United States," by Dr. James M. Buckley, appeared. It is in two large octavo volumes, together containing in the neighborhood of one thousand pages. The author of this work devotes a little over two pages to the "Origin of the Free Methodist Church," and appears to have borrowed his information from one or both of the volumes just mentioned. If such be not the case, he must have obtained it from the same traditional sources. He has given us no authority for his statements, except a single reference to the Journal of the General Conference of 1860, touching the appeals of B. T. Roberts and William Cooley, which that body refused to entertain.

Now, unpleasant as is the task, it becomes our duty to say, and then at some length to show, that a person reading any or all of the above-mentioned works touching the Origin of the Free Methodist Church, had he no other source of information, would be utterly misinformed and misled with reference to that subject. Where, in works of such importance as ecclesiastical histories and Cyclopedias, authors and editors have, whether intentionally or unintentionally, allowed gross misrepresentations of historical facts to occur, it becomes the duty of such as write history later, and who have the proofs of such literary distortion and misrepresentation, to produce such proofs for the better enlightenment of the reading public. It is in no invidious spirit, however, but rather in a spirit of unswerving loyalty to truth and right, that the author now proceeds to deal with the historical misrepresentations regarding the Origin of the Free Methodist Church, to which he has referred. It is unfortunate that such grave errors should have been allowed to remain in the volumes referred to so long.

The three works under consideration alike ascribe the remote origin of Free Methodism to the disaffection of certain ministers of the Genesee Conference of the Methodist Episcopal Church because they were not treated as well as they thought their characters and abilities deserved. These men, so it is alleged, formed an association, *secret* in character and workings, in hope of thereby obtaining control of the Conference, and under pretense of endeavoring to bring about a much-needed reform in the Methodist Church. That association, we are told, was variously known as the "Nazarite Union," "Nazarite Band," "Nazarite Association;" and those who belonged to it or who sympathized with its objects were commonly designated as "Nazarites." All three writers assert with much positiveness the existence of such an association; all alike declare it to have been of a secret character; and all are alike in connecting the remote origin of the Free Methodist Church with the aforesaid "Nazarite Union," or "Association."

Mr. Conable's presentation of this phase of the matter is much too lengthy for reproduction here. It contains the "Documents" of the so-called "Nazarite Union," which are lengthy. These and also a review of Mr. Conable's book, will appear in the Appendix to this volume.* Inasmuch as the "Cyclopedia of Methodism" and the "History of Methodism in the United States" give in much more concise form the gist of what Mr. Conable's work contains on the subject, it has been decided to insert the full text (except statistics) of what those two works say regarding it, and let that here answer for all.

The following is the article from the first edition of the "Cyclopedia," which remains unchanged in the second edition as to all its more important particulars:

---

*See Appendix A.

BISHOP EDWARD P. HART
Retired

[Plate Six]

MRS. MARTHA B. HART

[Plate Seven]

THE FREE METHODIST CHURCH

The organization of the Free Methodist Church dates from August 23, 1860, at a Convention composed of ministers and laymen, who had been members of the Methodist Episcopal Church, but became dissatisfied with the workings of its government. Though organized at that date, the movement commenced several years earlier, within the bounds of the Genesee Conference, and originated in an association of ministers, who thought they had not been properly treated by the leading men of the Conference. They privately adopted a platform, and in this organization were known as "Nazarites." In their writings, and speeches, they complained of the decline of spirituality in the Church, charging the Church with tolerating, for the sake of gain, the worldly practises of its members, and its departure, both in doctrine and discipline, from the teachings of the fathers. They professed themselves to be moved by the Holy Spirit, and believed it was their duty to bear open testimony against what they alleged to be the sins of the Church. This organization, and its publications, containing such charges against the leading members of the Conference, led, in 1855, to a very unpleasant state of feeling, and resulted in various Church trials. In 1858, two of the leaders were expelled from the Conference; they appealed to the ensuing General Conference, held at Buffalo in 1860; but as they had declined to recognize the authority of the Church, and had continued to exercise their ministry, and to organize societies, the General Conference declined to entertain the appeal. Even previous to the trial, some of the ministers had established appointments, and organized societies in opposition to the regular Church services.

At the organization of this Church in 1860, they accepted the doctrines of Methodism, as contained in the Articles of Religion, and placed a special stress on Christian perfection, or sanctification. They added an additional article which says: "Those that are sanctified wholly are saved from all inward sin, from evil thoughts and evil tempers. No wrong temper, none contrary to love, remains in the soul. All their thoughts, words and actions, are governed by pure love.

"Entire sanctification takes place subsequently to justification, and is the work of God, wrought instantaneously upon the consecrated, believing soul. After a soul is cleansed from all sin, it is then fully prepared to grow in grace."

They also added a second article on future rewards and punishments.

In Church polity, the name of Bishop was abandoned, and a General Superintendency substituted. The Conference organiza-

*See Appendix D.

tions were retained as in the M. E. Church, and laymen, in numbers equal to the ministers, were admitted into each of these bodies. The name of Presiding Elder was changed to that of District Chairman. No one is admitted as a member, even after [on] probation, without a confession of saving faith in Christ. The reason alleged by them is, that much of the defection in other Methodist Churches, is due to the fact that multitudes who have joined the Church as inquirers have failed to pursue a strictly spiritual life. They also require their members to be exceedingly plain in their dress, and they prohibit any one connected with the Church from being a member of any secret society. They require not only abstinence from intoxicating liquors, but also from the use of tobacco, except as a medicine.

In its early history, some of its leaders encouraged a spirit of wild fanaticism, claiming the power of healing by the laying on of hands. In many cases the excitement connected with their meetings passed into extravagance, which was sanctioned by their leading men, as being evidence of the influence of the Holy Spirit. As the denomination has progressed, and has extended its boundaries, though their services are still characterized by much fervor, there is less of these manifestations. The Free Methodist Church is confined almost exclusively to the Northern states. There are at present [1878] ten Annual Conferences.

DR. BUCKLEY ON THE ORIGIN OF THE FREE METHODIST CHURCH

In writing of the General Conference of 1860 he says: "This Conference had to consider the appeals of the Rev. Benjamin T. Roberts and others, growing out of an agitation in Western New York, the germs of which appeared as early as 1850, but did not attract general attention till some years later, when an association of ministers was formed within the bounds of the Genesee Conference. They claimed that they had not been properly treated by the leading members of that body; that on account of their principles on certain subjects they were ostracised, and did not receive the personal or official consideration to which their characters and abilities entitled them. They were known as 'Nazarites,' and their association was at first secret.

"So long as they confined themselves in their publications and addresses to complaining of the decline of spirituality in the Church, or neglect of the Discipline, and of the ignoring of some of the fundamental doctrines of Methodism, and to bearing testimony against the sins of the Church, they were not amenable to Discipline. But when they made specific charges against prominent members of the Conference they became subjects of investigation.

The Rev. Benjamin T. Roberts was adjudged guilty, in 1857, of immoral and unchristian conduct growing out of these charges, and sentenced to be reprimanded by the Bishop presiding. As he made no change in his course during the intervening year, at the next Conference he was charged with contumacy and expelled from the Church. Similar proceedings were taken against others.

"Against both these decisions Roberts appealed to the General Conference. This action was taken:

" 'The committee having heard and considered the minutes, documents, and pleading of the first appeal case of Benjamin T. Roberts, who appeals from the decision of the Genesee Conference whereby he was adjudged to be reprimanded before the Conference, proceeded to vote in the case with the following result: On the question of affirming, nineteen voted in favor and nineteen against it. On the question of remanding the case for a new trial, the committee voted almost unanimously in the negative. On the question of reversing the action of the Conference, eighteen voted in favor and twenty-eight against, a result which, as the General Conference has decided, leaves the decision of the Genesee Conference as the final adjudication of the case. J. T. CRANE, Secretary.

" 'The committee have considered the second appeal of B. T. Roberts, who appeals from the action of the Genesee Conference whereby he was expelled from the ministry and the Church.

" 'The representatives of the Genesee Conference objected to the admission of the appeal on the ground:

" '1. That B. T. Roberts subsequently to his trial and condemnation joined the Methodist Episcopal Church as a probationer, and thus, tacitly at least, confessed the justice of the action of the Conference in his case.

" '2. That B. T. Roberts since he was deprived by his expulsion of his ministerial authority and standing has continued to preach and thus rebelled against the authority of the Conference and the Church.

" '3. That B. T. Roberts since he declared his intention of appealing to the General Conference has connected himself with another organization, contemplating Church ends independent [of] and hostile to the Church to whose General Conference he now appeals.

" 'The committee, after hearing the statements and pleadings of the representatives of the parties,

" '*Resolved*, That the appeal of B. T. Roberts be not admitted.'

"Similar action was taken in the case of William Cooley (Journal of the General Conference of 1860).

"The ministers and members of the Methodist Episcopal Church who sympathized with them met in Pekin, Niagara County, N. Y., on the 23rd of August, 1860, and organized the Free Methodist Church, adopting, with slight modifications, the Articles of Religion of the Methodist Episcopal Church, but in government provided that the members should have an equal voice with the ministers in the councils of the Church."*

The foregoing extracts are given at length, first, in order that the reader may have the complete statements of these authors for comparison with what we shall have to offer regarding them by way of criticism and dissent; and, second, because of the several occasions we shall have for referring to the different parts of those statements.

In the book entitled, "Why Another Sect?" written and published by the Rev. B. T. Roberts in 1879, that author, who writes in review of the article on "The Free Methodist Church" in Bishop Simpson's "Cyclopedia of Methodism," says: "In this article there are some fifteen statements or re-statements, which are utterly untrue, and some five or six statements which, though in a sense true, are from the manner in which they are made, misleading."† Mr. Roberts seems to furnish abundant proof of his statements before concluding his review. Moreover, we do not hesitate to state that at least half a dozen of the most important statements in the foregoing extract from Dr. Buckley's version of "The Origin of the Free Methodist Church" are also utterly incorrect.

The only items from the foregoing extracts, however, with which we shall be immediately concerned, are those in which the remote origin of the Free Methodist Church is ascribed to a "Nazarite Organization," "Union," or "Band," formed within the Genesee Conference some years before the organization of the Free Methodist Church, as a sort of secret society. Statements to this effect had been commonly made, and for so long a time, both privately and through the Methodist Episcopal press, that the Bishop who edited the "Cyclopedia of

*"History of Methodism in the United States," pp. 168-170. †Page 17.

Methodism," and the eminent author of the "History of Methodism in the United States," may have come to believe them true; although it is difficult to see how those who were originally responsible for such unauthorized statements could have made them otherwise than with the intention to deceive the uninformed. Moreover, it is equally difficult to conceive of how such honored men as the two last named authors could have been betrayed into giving general currency to such unauthorized, inaccurate and harmful statements, especially when they both knew of the fact that those statements had been challenged and denied by as respectable and credible men as Methodism had ever produced, many of whom were then living, and all of whose challenges and denials had been printed over their own signatures. The most charitable view that can be taken of their action in this matter is to attribute it to prejudice on their part. But even this is a reflection upon their credibility as historians.

CHAPTER VII

HISTORICAL MISREPRESENTATIONS—GENERAL SUPERINTENDENT ROBERTS VERSUS BISHOP SIMPSON

So far as the author has been able to ascertain no history put forth by any member of the Methodist Episcopal Church until this day, covering the period of the difficulties in the Genesee Conference which led to the organization of the Free Methodist Church, has fairly and truthfully stated the facts in the case. On the other hand those writers who have dealt with these matters have appeared with one consent determined to put the brand of reproach and disgrace upon the Free Methodist movement by the uniform misstatement of facts. When Roberts's appeal from the verdict by which he was expelled from the Genesee Conference and the Church was refused consideration by the General Conference of 1860, that good man turned away saying, "*I appeal to God and the people.*" Referring to the matter in the Preface to "Why Another Sect?" about twenty years later, he said:

> Here we should have let the matter rest, but those opposed to us will not permit it. They have published and sanctioned the most bare-faced, flagrant falsehoods, which they intend shall pass as a history of the affair. We should be wanting in our duty to the cause which is dearer to us than life, and to the noble men and women who have given us their confidence, if we allowed these falsehoods to pass uncontradicted.*

The volume from which the foregoing extract is made was called forth by the gross misrepresentations contained in the "Cyclopedia of Methodism," but not without a candid effort on the part of its author to have the needful cor-

*Page vi.

rections made in the periodicals of the Methodist Episcopal Church, and in future editions of the book, and so to avoid the necessity for its publication. This the following letter from his pen will show:

ROCHESTER, N. Y., Sept. 13, 1878.

REV. M. SIMPSON, D. D.,
Bishop of the M. E. Church.

Dear Sir: I think when one makes incorrect statements, he should have the privilege of correcting them. I therefore take the liberty to address you in reference to the article in your "Cyclopedia of Methodism," on the Free Methodist Church. In your Preface you say: "The aim has been to give a fair, and impartial view of every branch of the Methodist family. For this purpose, contributors and correspondents were selected, as far as practicable, who were identified with the several branches, and who, from their position, were best qualified to furnish information as to their respective bodies."

Either no such selection was made from the Free Methodists, or the information which they furnished, with the exception of the bare statistics, was not given to the public in that article. In either case, what becomes of the claim of fairness?

In this article there are some fifteen statements or re-statements, which are utterly untrue, and some five or six statements which, though in a sense true, yet are, from the manner in which they are made, misleading.

If furnished with proof, satisfactory to candid minds, that these statements referred to are untrue, and misleading, will you correct them in the Church periodicals, and in future editions of your book? If not, will you give the authority upon which the statements complained of, are made?

Yours most respectfully,

B. T. ROBERTS.

To this letter the Bishop returned the following reply:

PHILADELPHIA, Oct. 23, 1878.

REV. B. T. ROBERTS,

Dear Sir: Returning home from a long tour in the West, I find your letter of September 13th, complaining of inaccuracies in the article on Free Methodism, but without specifying what those inaccuracies are.

I am not aware of any incorrect statements in the article, but if you will furnish me with corrections and the accompanying proofs, I will gladly make any alterations in a future edition, should such edition be called for. I desire to have perfect accuracy in every article, and it will give me as much pleasure to correct, as it can you to furnish the corrections.

Yours truly,

M. SIMPSON.

The foregoing letters are worthy of careful perusal and comparison. Careful attention to their contents will disclose to the intelligent reader the following points:

1. Mr. Roberts proposes to the Bishop, (a) To furnish "proof, satisfactory to candid minds, that the statements complained of are untrue and misleading;" (b) That he (the Bishop), in case he is furnished with such proof, "correct them in the Church periodicals, and in future editions of [his] book;" (c) That, if unwilling to do this, he "give the authority upon which the statements complained of are made."

2. Bishop Simpson's letter discloses the following facts: (a) That he fully assumes all responsibility for the contents of the article in question. (b) That he shows no disposition, however convincing the proof of their inaccuracy may be, to make any corrections, through the Church periodicals, or otherwise until and unless a future edition of his book be called for. In other words, he proposes to leave the article, however inaccurate, to create whatever prejudice it may, and to do all the injustice of which it is capable, until a second edition of his book is demanded, and for all time, should no such demand arise. (c) That he is utterly silent with reference to giving authority for the offensive statements. (d) That he does not claim here, as in the Preface to his book, that, in order "to give a fair and impartial view" of this "branch of the Methodist family," he had selected a "contributor" from the Free Methodist Church who was identified with the movement, and who, "from his position, was best qualified to give information" as to this particular body. Neither does he assign any reason why this was not considered "practicable." Right in the city where he lived were men

fully informed on the subject, and every way qualified to give an accurate and trustworthy statement of the case.

Mr. Roberts's letter does not charge the Bishop with the *wilful* misrepresentation of a single fact, but on the contrary assumes that the errors had crept into the book unwittingly on his part, and that, on being satisfied of their inaccuracy, he would be glad to make the proper corrections. This the Bishop would not consent to, except in a second edition of his book, should one be called for. Inasmuch as that might never be, Mr. Roberts proceeded to write and publish, upon the request of the General Conference of the Free Methodist Church, "Why Another Sect?" a volume of 333 pages. Regarding the production of this work he writes as follows in the Preface:

> With the leading facts which I narrate in this volume, I was personally acquainted. I have endeavored to state them plainly, in a Christian spirit, and without the slightest exaggeration. I have given proofs which can not be set aside without practically denying the validity of human testimony. But I am conscious of laboring under this great disadvantage: the action of the Genesee Conference, sustained by the General Conference, was so unjust and unprovoked—so contrary to anything which we might look for in a body of respectable men, even though they laid no claim to piety, that the plainest narrative of the events looks like wild exaggeration. But I have endeavored to give the simple truth, without the slightest coloring. I have read my manuscript to several intelligent, judicious brethren, familiar with the facts, and they give it their hearty indorsement.

Dr. Buckley's "History of Methodism in the United States" did not appear until eighteen years after Mr. Roberts's "Why Another Sect?" was published. Either its author knew of the existence and character of that work, or he did not know thereof. If he did know of these things, and refused to recognize the charges made by Mr. Roberts, and the abundance of proof furnished to sustain those charges, it would seem to be a grave reflection upon his boasted love of historical accuracy and his loyalty to truth; and if he did not know of "Why Another Sect?"

and its contents, then we submit that he must have written this particular part of his "History of Methodism in the United States" without that fulness of research which a work of such importance demands, and for the making of which a reputable writer of history should spare no pains.

Now, with reference to the statement made in the "Cyclopedia of Methodism," and reiterated by Dr. Buckley, which identifies the remote origin of the Free Methodist movement with "an association of ministers" in the Genesee Conference who "privately adopted a platform, and in this organization were known as 'Nazarites,'" the author is prepared to show that the alleged "Nazarite Organization," "Union" or "Band," never had any existence, but was wholly a fictitious affair. Still, upon the authority of such pretentious volumes as Bishop Simpson's "Cyclopedia of Methodism," and Dr. Buckley's "History of Methodism in the United States," it has been written of as a matter of historical verity, and as partaking the character of *a secret society,* in which the movement originated which resulted in the formation of the Free Methodist Church. During all the intervening years the erroneous and damaging statements have been spreading, and their harmful influence has been increasing.

During the troubles in the Genesee Conference back in the fifties those ministers who were opposed to the distinctive work of holiness then in progress confidently affirmed, both privately and through the press, that a "Nazarite Union" or "Band" existed within their bounds, and that those preachers who were identified with the work of holiness were members of the alleged organization, and especially advocated it with a view to accomplishing the desired reformation in the Methodist Episcopal Church. Official papers gave room to statements specially intended to helping the delusion on.

Although repeated denials were made, of the most emphatic character, regarding the existence of any such organization, and made by those ministers of the Genesee

BISHOP GEORGE W. COLEMAN
Deceased

[Plate Eight]

Conference who were in a position to know the facts, and who were supposed to be members of the "Nazarite Band," their denials were ignored, and their opponents continued persistently to affirm the existence of such a society; and it is difficult for the broadest charity to credit them with sincerity and honesty in those affirmations.

Great as is this difficulty, however, it is much more difficult to understand how honest and unprejudiced men, writing from twenty to forty years later, and with all the historic facts available which have been committed to the general public since that time, and which abundantly refute those earlier allegations regarding the existence of a "Nazarite Band," should feel bound to perpetuate these misstatements.

"Is it on the principle that a story often told is at last believed? Or is it because it is the only shadow of an excuse that can be made for an act of ecclesiastical tyranny and proscription which, looking back upon after the lapse of twenty years, we deliberately pronounce to be without a parallel in modern times, for its injustice?"

In further discussing this question frequent extracts from Mr. Roberts's "Why Another Sect?" will be made, because of the undoubted honesty and integrity of its author, his personal, undisputed, and comprehensive knowledge of the facts, the abundance of the evidence he furnishes to substantiate his positions, and the general spirit of fairness and justice with which he writes. Moreover, the author hopes to present such proofs of the wholly fictitious character of the alleged "Nazarite Band" as will abundantly satisfy any candid reader that what has been written by various authors assuming to connect the remote origin of Free Methodism with such an organization is utterly without foundation.

CHAPTER VIII

HISTORICAL MISREPRESENTATIONS CONTINUED—ALLEGED "NAZARITE UNION" DENIED

We now present the following paper, which was prepared and signed by seventeen ministers of the Genesee Conference who were supposed to be prominent members of the "Nazarite organization," in which they emphatically deny that any such organization had an existence. The paper was published at the time in the *Northern Independent,* and also in fly-sheet form. A copy of the same was also presented to Bishop Simpson.

GENESEE CONFERENCE MATTERS

Read and Then Judge

Certain reports having been put into circulation, charging a portion of the ministers of the Genesee Conference of the Methodist Episcopal Church with the disreputable and unworthy act of having organized a society "bearing certain marks of secrecy" under the name of the "Nazarite Band or Union," the object of which, it has been reported, is to control the appointments, and direct the affairs of the Conference; and this charge implicating many of our ministers as taking steps unworthy the Christian, and derogatory to the ministerial character:

Therefore, We, the undersigned, members of the Genesee Conference, hereby declare, that after careful inquiry, we are fully convinced that no such society has ever existed in the bounds of this Conference. The whole excitement with reference to the supposed organization grew out of certain letters, indicating the existence of such a society, written by a single individual, who, on the floor of the Olean Conference in 1855, publicly declared, that he alone was responsible for the whole affair. These letters were written without our knowledge, and have never received our approval. Though the existence of such a society has been repeatedly denied, in various ways and on numerous occasions, yet in public and in private, and especially through the columns of the *Buffalo Christian Advocate*, these reports have been spread abroad, to the injury of the ministerial reputation, and Christian influence and usefulness of numbers of our ministers, by creating an unjust prejudice against them; among whom are some of our most able and efficient men.

Connected with the charge of association, is that of encouraging fanaticism, and extravagance in religious exercises and worship. This charge we declare to be as groundless as the other. We have never encouraged excesses, and with them we have not the *least* sympathy. But while we stand opposed to all improprieties in religious exercises and worship, we declare ourselves in favor of a *consistent* and *vitalized* religion; not a dead formalism, but the power of godliness. Not that form of religion that expresses itself in confused irregularities on the one hand, or on the other, in sermons without life and without adaptation,—the abandonment of social meetings, and the neglect of family and private prayer; but in a religion that moves the heart, and prompts to every good work; not of beneficence alone, but also of devotion.

These charges then, of forming an association or encouraging fanaticism, having their origin, in the opinion of some, in ambition and jealousy, made and reiterated, it has been feared, with a design and for effect—*if applied to us*, we unhesitatingly pronounce to be unjust, iniquitous, *slanderous* and FALSE.

A. ABELL,
JOHN P. KENT,
SAMUEL C. CHURCH,
LOREN STILES, JR.,
JOHN B. JENKINS,
W. GORDON,
A. W. LUCE,
J. MILLER,
ISAAC C. KINGSLEY,
C. D. BURLINGHAM,
A. HARD,
B. T. ROBERTS,
E. S. FURMAN,
R. E. THOMAS,
DANIEL B. LAWTON,
WM. KELLOGG,
J. BOWMAN.

LeRoy, September, 1857.

The signers of the foregoing paper are the men of whom the "Nazarite Association" was said to be chiefly composed. Had there been any such "Association" they were the men who would have known it. Their united testimony, however, is: "We are fully convinced that no such society has ever existed in the bounds of this [the Genesee] Conference."

The standing and character of these witnesses were

such as to afford the strongest guaranty of their veracity. Five of them had served as Presiding Elders, and four of them as members of the General Conference. All were ministers of the Methodist Episcopal Church. Of the seventeen only three ever became members of the Free Methodist Church. One is said later to have become a Presbyterian, and another to have joined the United Brethren. The others all appear to have remained in the Methodist Episcopal fold, and some of them finally became decidedly hostile to Free Methodism. To this day, however, none of them, so far as we can learn, has ever retracted the statements of the foregoing paper, or made any statements inconsistent with its contents.

In view of the character and standing of these men, as well as of their undoubted knowledge of the facts, who will dare even to suggest that the paper in question, and to which they unitedly affixed their signatures, is false, or in any other way misleading? Had Bishop Simpson regarded any one of these men as guilty of deliberately signing his name to a glaring falsehood for publication, would he from time to time have appointed that man to the pastorate of Methodist Churches, to feed and care for the flock of God, and to guide the members of that flock in the way to heaven? Would he have been willing to have it appear that so gross a sin as deliberate and persistent falsehood was no disqualification for the ministry in the Methodist Episcopal Church? And yet, think of it! if the Bishop's version regarding the "Nazarite Association" is credited, it places those seventeen ministers of Jesus Christ, against whom no complaint had ever been brought, under the imputation of conspiring to write, sign, and publish an outrageous and deliberate falsehood, regarding a matter of which they had full knowledge and could not possibly have been mistaken! To fix such an imputation upon innocent men would be a sad comment on Christian charity indeed.

Yet here is the situation, let the reader make the best

of it he may be able to make by skill in the use of language. Bishop Simpson says of the Free Methodist movement, that it "originated in an association of ministers who thought they had not been properly treated by the leading men of the Conference. They privately adopted a platform, and in this organization were known as 'Nazarites.'" Dr. Buckley reiterates the statement in substance, and in a more aggravated form. Those seventeen ministers who signed the paper in question, say: "We are fully convinced that no such society ever has existed in the bounds of this Conference." These statements are plain and irreconcilable contradictions, and therefore one or the other must be false.

Those seventeen men said of the statement which alleged the existence of a "Nazarite Band" at the time it first became current within the Genesee Conference, "This charge of forming an association to encourage fanaticism, *if applied to us,* we unhesitatingly pronounce to be unjust, iniquitous, *slanderous,* and FALSE." A more specific denial could not well be framed. Both statements—that signed by the seventeen ministers and that made by Bishop Simpson and by Dr. Buckley—can not possibly be true. Either the denial by the seventeen or the affirmation by the Bishop and the Doctor must be false. If the affirmation was "unjust, iniquitous, slanderous, and false," when it first obtained currency, it of necessity is equally so when made from twenty years to a generation later, and by whomsoever made. Those seventeen men spoke from personal knowledge; and, if what they uttered was untrue, it was the deliberate utterance of untruth, and would classify them as belonging to the Ananias Association. Bishop Simpson and Dr. Buckley do not profess to have spoken from personal knowledge; and, since they evidently relied upon information given them by others, they may have been deceived. The statements are made, however, with as much positiveness as though made from personal knowledge, and thus, if untrue, they are left to do all the harm of which they are capable. It would seem that these authors should have given some authority for their statements, at least.

In addition to signing the statement denying the existence of a "Nazarite Organization" within the bounds of the Genesee Conference, which has been under discussion in this chapter, the Rev. Asa Abell, one of the most godly men produced by American Methodism, in an article published in the *Northern Independent* of March 10, 1859, gave his further personal testimony regarding the matter in the following paragraphs:

> It does seem to me that I have been so circumstanced, that had there really been any such Union or Society, it could not have failed to come to my knowledge; and I solemnly declare that I neither know *now*, nor have ever known of any society called by the name in question, neither in form nor in fact: nor of any association like to the one whose existence is so boldly and positively asserted; nor of any such league or combination whatever, by any name whatever.
>
> All this I intend to assert, without any such mental reservation as would leave what I say to be true, and yet in some hidden and mysterious sense true, [so] that there is, or has been such an organization or society. No man has yet proved, and I am sure no one ever can prove, the existence of such a league or society, for the reason that no one can prove a *non*-entity to be an entity. I never knew or heard of any meeting for the purpose of forming such a society, or league, or union, nor of any meeting of any such society; nor of any meeting of reputed officers of any such society.

Asa Abell was one of the noble pioneers of Western New York Methodism. He had been a member of the Methodist Episcopal Church since 1821. His career in the ministry had been a long one, and during eighteen years of this time he had served in the office of Presiding Elder. He was elected four times in succession as delegate to the General Conference of his Church, and filled the position with credit to himself and his constituency. When the Free Methodist Church was finally organized, he showed his disapproval of the action of the Genesee Conference in its policy of proscription and expulsion of the so-called "Nazarite" preachers, and of the action of the General Conference in refusing to entertain their appeals; and also exhibited his devotion to the principles which he had advocated throughout his entire ministry; by severing his connection with the Church which had been his spiritual mother, and to which his best energies had been given for many years, and uniting with the proscribed and persecuted few who composed the newly organized sect. Nor did he wait before taking this step until it was manifest that the new venture was likely to be a success, but entered at the beginning, willing to share the fortunes of his persecuted brethren, whatever those fortunes might be. He was loyal to his convictions to the end, and no breath of scandal or of calumny ever detracted from his spotless record. Surely the testimony of such a man should be regarded as unimpeachable and every way convincing.

The men who signed the denial of a "Nazarite Organization" with Mr. Abell were also God-fearing and holy men, as has been shown—men of undoubted integrity and veracity, and whose general intelligence and credibility have never been even questioned to this day. The necrological records of the Methodist Episcopal Conference to which some of them belonged at the time of their death bear strong testimony to their sterling virtues as Christian men, and to their loyalty and usefulness as Christian ministers. In view of these facts we would ask, with Mr. Roberts:

> In making up a history of events in which such men bore a prominent part, is their testimony respecting these events to be set aside, without even assigning any cause? Is it to be assumed, without evidence, that they placed themselves on record as falsifiers of facts with which they were well acquainted? And is such assumption to pass into history unchallenged? Is partisan prejudice, or denominational pride to supersede the necessity of candidly weighing evidence, and honestly endeavoring to ascertain and state the truth? If no notice is to be taken of the testimony of such men as these, what is the use of human testimony? History may as well be written wholly from the imagination.

If these men are to be believed, then is Bishop Simpson's statement that the Free Methodist Church had its origin in an "association of ministers" who "privately adopted a platform, and in this organization were known as Nazarites," utterly false. *

It is at least exceedingly unfortunate that men of such standing and reputation as Bishop Simpson and Dr. Buckley should have helped to give general currency to statements so grossly misleading as those under consideration, by publishing them as though they were all attested facts of history, while there is not a word of historical truth in them. It would seem that they must have been betrayed into taking the aspersions cast upon the so-called "Nazarites" by their enemies as statements of historical truth, without investigation, and were thereby misled in their published statements. But the effect has been just as injurious as though the statements had been deliberately false.

---

*"Why Another Sect?"

CHAPTER IX

HISTORICAL MISREPRESENTATIONS—"NAZARITE DOCUMENTS" AND GENESEE CONFERENCE ACTION

It has been claimed, however, that there were "Documents of the Nazarite Union;" and the inquiry has been raised, "Does not the existence of such 'Documents' assume the existence of such an organization?" We reply, Not necessarily so. It is universally known that it is the very nature of fiction to represent events to which it relates as though they were actual occurrences. But no one on that account quotes them as authentic history. The only show of proof adduced of the existence of a "Nazarite Union" unto this day, so far as we have been able to discover, is based upon the writings of a single man—his personal letters, and his "Documents of the Nazarite Union of the Genesee Conference of the M. E. Church;" and on the action of the Genesee Conference based on said "Documents."

The "Documents" are comprised in a pamphlet* which the Rev. Joseph McCreery read before the Genesee Conference of the Methodist Episcopal Church at Olean, New York, in 1855. But McCreery was particular to state very definitely at the time that *he* constituted "the Nazarite Union," and that *he alone* was responsible for the whole affair. Others, supposed to belong to this "Union," corroborated his statement, all agreeing that the whole matter was a creation of McCreery's own fancy. Moreover the author of the "Documents" practically avers the same in the Preface to his pamphlet, when he says:

A certain pamphlet published in New York has represented the

*See Appendix C.

Nazarites as a secret society devoted to the propagation of doctrinal tenets. It is enough to say that its author has been imposed upon by his zealous correspondent, both as to the fact and purpose of the Nazarites. It is only as yet a mere proposal to return to the "old paths."

Thus the author of the pamphlet containing the "Documents" virtually declares that no such society existed, and that "It is as yet only *a mere proposal* to return to 'the old paths.'" Is there not a manifest difference between "a mere proposal" and an accomplished fact? Is not proof of the proposal having been put into effect necessary to justify the positive assertion of the existence of such a society? And has Bishop Simpson, or any one of the several who have written on this matter, furnished any such proof? No one can affirm that they have, because no such proof is in existence.

The fact is, the statement regarding Free Methodism having originated in a "Nazarite Union," or "Organization," partaking the character of a secret society, etc., was made originally without warrant, and with a view to casting odium and discredit upon the new movement; and those who have since given dignity to the fabrication by incorporating it in Cyclopedias or Histories have either done so through willingness to give the falsehood as wide a circulation as possible, or through allowing themselves to be misled in the matter by their failure to investigate the case as its merits deserved. It is not at all complimentary to such authors, whichever alternative they or their friends may choose to take; but the facts should be known, whatever the consequences may be.

Here it will be proper to furnish further evidence that the alleged "Nazarite Union" was a matter for which one member of the Genesee Conference was solely responsible, and that whatever may have been his intention, the matter was chiefly fictitious, and never became anything more than "a mere proposal." At the session of the Conference held in Perry, New York, in 1858, Joseph McCreery testified as follows:

I wrote everything relating to the Nazarite Band. I wrote the Documents. I did design an Association, and prepared the Documents in anticipation of such, but when we got to Conference we had enough to do of other business. We did not organize, and the question of organization has been an open question ever since. I never administered the vow to any one, and I never took it myself—not formally. The Association was never practically formed; I stated nearly so on the floor of the Olean Conference. I stated that the whole thing was provisional and prospective, and *I alone was responsible for the whole concern.* The Preface to the pamphlet is a mythical concern altogether.

Here we have the case plainly stated, and that by the very man whose fancy conceived the idea of the "Nazarite Union," but who himself had never formally taken the Nazarite vow nor administered it to another, and who declares "that the whole thing was provisional, and that he alone was responsible for the whole concern." Can anything plainer or more definite be desired?

"But did not the Genesee Conference, as a matter of fact, declare by its vote that such an organization or society existed? And did not the same Conference at a later time order and conduct a judicial investigation of the alleged 'Nazarite Organization?' And are not both of the foregoing actions matters of record on the Conference Journal?" To these questions an affirmative answer must be given. Having answered them affirmatively, we inquire, What of it? The record of a Conference action only shows that the Conference took such action; it can not show whether said action was right or wrong, based on fact or fiction.

In his "History of the Genesee Annual Conference of the Methodist Episcopal Church" the late Rev. F. W. Conable, quoting from Dr. F. G. Hibbard, says: "The first time the Genesee Conference came in formal contact with Nazaritism was at its session in Olean in 1855. The following action was taken at the first sitting: '*Resolved*, That all papers in hand relating to the Nazarite Society be now read to the Conference.'" We are then informed that "The reading of papers and discussions engrossed two days." The final action of the Conference at that time is given as follows:

"*Resolved,* That while we doubt not there is much room for improvement among us in spiritual religion, and in observance of our beloved institutions, we regret that, in view of such deficiencies as may exist, and with the ostensible purpose of returning to first principles, any of our members should have *associated together,* AS WE FIND THEY HAVE DONE, under the name of the 'Nazarite Band,' or other similar appellations, WITH SOME FORMS OF SECRECY, and with THE CLAIM TO BE PECULIAR IN THIS RESPECT; and we pass our disapprobation upon such associations, and hereby express our full expectation that it will be abandoned by all members of this Conference. We especially, but affectionately, condemn the calumnious expressions read in relation to the Methodist Church and her ministers within her bounds; and we do hereby submit these views to the special consideration of all who are concerned in this matter, and expect them, hereafter, to govern themselves accordingly."*

Later, at the Perry Conference, the existence of a "Nazarite Organization" having been disputed, the matter was judicially investigated. No effort was spared to prove the existence of such an organization. The only proof adduced, however, was the "Nazarite Documents," to which we have already referred. But if the "Documents" are admissible in evidence, so is their author's statement concerning them. Moreover, his testimony on this point should be entitled to equal weight with the "Documents" themselves. But his declaration is, that "The whole concern is a fiction—prepared and ready to become a fact, when we should see fit to make it such;" also that "the whole thing was provisional and prospective, and *I alone am responsible for the whole concern.*" The time never came for that which was wholly prospective and provi-

*Pages 638-640.

sional, and for which one man alone was responsible, to materialize, and so the alleged "Nazarite Organization" never came into existence.

"But is not the action of the Olean Conference, as above quoted, evidence that such an organization did then really exist?" Regarding this point we quote again from "Why Another Sect?"

We must confess our inability to understand this language. It looks absurd to charge that the "Nazarites" "claimed to be peculiar" in respect to having "some forms of secrecy." That men who had for years been opposing secret societies should be charged with making such a "claim," seems extremely marvelous. They knew that there were many societies which had "forms of secrecy."

It is by no means certain, supposing this to be a true copy of the record, that the record is correct. We have known instances where secretaries quite as competent as the one who made that record, have, without intending it, in copying documents upon the Journal, made such mistakes as seriously to affect the meaning.

But supposing the copy and the record to be correct, suppose the Conference voted as it is here said they did, their vote that a fact existed does not prove that it actually existed. Shall we concede infallibility to the Genesee Conference, blinded by partisan fury, when we deny it to the Pope and his General Council, acting in a dispassionate manner? The vote does not even prove that the Conference *believed* that what they voted was true. It simply proves that they had power to pass such a vote, and did pass it. This same Genesee Conference at its session at LeRoy in 1857, voted as a fact what every man voting KNEW *was not a fact.* They did so on my trial. With my printed article before them, they voted that I said in that article, *what they knew I did not say.* I called their attention to it, and made it so plain that the dullest could not fail to see it.

That the vote of a Conference that a fact exists is no proof of its existence, is shown by the records of a far more respectable body of the M. E. Church than the Genesee Conference.

The Journal of the General Conference held at Philadelphia, May, 1864, has the following record:

"The long contest on the subject of slavery seems drawing to a close, and no doubtful tokens indicate the will of God, and point unerringly to the destruction of a system so inhuman.

"We rejoice that we have, from the beginning, been foremost among American Churches, in the contest against slavery."

The men who voted this self-congratulation were elected from the various Conferences to represent the piety and the wisdom of the Church. They were men above the average of Methodist preachers.

These men must have known that there were upon the Journal of the General Conference, having the force of law, resolutions passed only twenty-eight years before, which plainly contradict the above claim to "have from the beginning been foremost among American Churches in the contest against slavery."

We doubt whether any respectable body ever gave a greater insult to a reading people.

We copy from the Journal of the General Conference of the M. E. Church for 1836:

"Resolved by the delegates of the Annual Conferences in General Conference assembled:

"1. That they disapprove, in the most unqualified sense, the conduct of two members of the General Conference who are reported to have lectured in this city recently upon, and in favor of, modern Abolitionism.

"Resolved, 2. That they are decidedly opposed to modern Abolitionism, and wholly disclaim any right, wish, or intention to interfere in the civil and political relation between master and slave as it exists in the slaveholding States of this Union.

"Resolved, 3. That the committee appointed to draft a pastoral letter to our preachers be, and they are hereby instructed to take notice of the subject of modern Abolition that has so seriously agitated the different parts of our country, and that they let our preachers, members, and friends know that the General Conference are opposed to the agitation of that subject, and will use all prudent means to put it down."

Can you, after reading the action of these two General Conferences of the M. E. Church, believe that the vote of a Methodist Episcopal Conference proves anything more than that they passed it?*

It now seems that, if human testimony is not to be altogether discredited, evidence enough has been produced to prove conclusively to every fair-minded reader that the alleged "Nazarite Organization" within the bounds of the Genesee Conference of the Methodist Episcopal Church

*Pages 39-43.

BISHOP BURTON R. JONES

[Plate Nine]

was non-existent during all the years of that agitation which finally disrupted the Conference and resulted in the organization of the Free Methodist Church; that the whole affair was entirely fictitious, the product of one man's fancy, and for which that one member of the Conference was alone responsible; that the organization of the Free Methodist Church was neither directly nor indirectly, neither proximately nor remotely, connected with any such organization or society, and could not have been, for the very best of reasons, namely, because no such organization or society ever existed; and that the attempts of certain writers to make it appear that the Free Methodist movement had its remote origin in a secret society known as the "Nazarite Band" must be accounted for otherwise than on the ground of their desire to have the history of the Genesee Conference difficulties of that period impartially written.

The first published declaration that a "Nazarite Association" had been formed within the Genesee Conference appeared in the editorial columns of the *Buffalo Advocate* issued June 19, 1855. The following is a copy:

We have learned from a reliable source, and have had sufficient evidence placed in our hands to prove that there exists, among the ministers of a certain Protestant sect of Western New York, a secret, religious organization, where one would be least suspected. The purpose of this Jesuitical order we will not at this time attempt to explain; but the consequences of it, unless its progress shall be arrested, and its existence blotted out, it takes no prophet's eye to foresee,—incurable, ministerial factions and ruined Churches must otherwise be the inevitable result. This order has been designated by various appellations; but the authorized cognomen is, "THE NAZARITE BAND." It is to be hoped that those who have assumed this solemn and suggestive title have weighed well what they are doing, and what the solemn imposition of the name upon themselves implies. To us it appears like impious mockery, and if "any good can come out of THIS NAZARETH," then can a clean thing come forth from an unclean. We know well the men who are the originators of this singular movement, and have been watching their down-sittings and uprisings for a long time. Our editorial, secret drawer contains the secret of many curious facts relating to the ministerial career of some of these eminent and most notable characters.

We learn that the society is constituted by three degrees or "divisions." Into the third or highest, are admitted only the leading spirits of the order, or those whom it is supposed will heartily favor the purpose of the order. The first degree, it would appear, is so indefinitely constituted, that one may get into it, and not be himself aware of the fact. It is only required of the candidate that he express his approbation of certain men and measures, and forsooth he straightway becomes a Nazarite, and that before he knows it. He is, after this, carefully approached, and his opinions drawn out with respect to certain other measures, and if he can be "trusted," is advanced! There are many considerations which give this new organization a novel, not to say ludicrous aspect. One is, that its originators have heretofore made themselves somewhat notorious, by their blazing hostility to secret societies. They have published and spoken great and hard things. They have for years been bent on giving both lay and clerical Odd-Fellows and Masons "particular jesse." Indeed, it is a main purpose of this Nazarite Band to oppose the influence which, it is alleged, secular secret societies are seeking to exert in religious affairs. Another beautiful feature of this new order is the peculiarly lovely, personal and religious characteristics of those by whom it was conceived and brought forth. Their character is a strange compound of sanctity and slander, of pompous humility and humble pride, of peccability and perfection. Their preaching of the Gospel of peace is always attended or followed by jealousies, heart-burnings, and fanatical dissensions. Peevish and fretful tyrants at home, they have a very ardent charity for the "dear sisters" abroad, some of whom "they lead about." Without any remarkable "sanctity of manners undefiled," their professions reach to heaven, and clothe them with the most spotless garment of assumed purity. As a specimen of this class, we would refer the reader to a certain individual living in Orleans County, called, according to the Nazarite nomenclature, BANI, who is, we are informed, the high priest of this new profession.

The accusation against all parties supposed to be concerned in the alleged "Nazarite Association" is very specific and strong in the foregoing editorial, while the spirit in which it was written does not appear to have been commendable. The promised proof that such an organization did then exist was never furnished, however, because the "sufficient evidence" failed the editor of the *Advocate* in his time of need. From the next number of the paper it appears that the accusation had received a prompt denial by the only person competent either to affirm or deny the charge. That was the man who alone was responsible for the letters written concerning a "Nazarite Union" and for the "Documents." In a straightforward, manly way he came forward and assumed the responsibility for all that he had written on the subject, and fully exonerated his misrepresented brethren.

The editor of the *Advocate* then found himself under the necessity of making some sort of apology or defense, and his manner of meeting this responsibility appears in the following extract from a succeeding number of his paper:

> We learn that "Bani" denies that the NAZARITES are an organized band, as we asserted them to be in our last week's issue. We would remind this very conscientious and notable individual of the importance of keeping truth on his side, as far as circumstances will permit; and not by gratuitous and voluntary denials of facts, place himself in a very embarrassing position, and one in which honest men seldom find themselves. Bani, it is not right, it is decidedly wrong to make statements which you know to be false, and you must not do so any more.

The foregoing extracts, which are fair samples of various articles appearing in the columns of the same periodical from time to time, speak for themselves as to the spirit by which they were dictated. Certainly it was not the Spirit of the Master. Their spirit is bitter, their language coarse, vulgar, and unbrotherly, and their declarations are false. Moreover, the last of the foregoing extracts shows a disposition on the part of its writer to be wittily and sarcastically evasive, where straightforwardness and love of truth would have led him to humble confession and apology for the wholesale misrepresentations contained in his former article.

The sum of the whole matter regarding the alleged "Nazarite Union" is thus given in "Why Another Sect?":

> Rev. Joseph McCreery wrote several letters to different preachers, proposing that they work in harmony in their efforts to persuade the people to return to the old paths of Methodism. There, in all probability, the matter would have rested; but some of these letters were shown to the editor of the *Buffalo Advocate*, who made the most of them, and stirred up some excitement. Anticipating that the subject would be brought up at Conference, the Rev. J. McCreery prepared a statement of the whole affair, including copies of the letters he had written. This he read to the Conference at Olean in 1855. This "Document" or "Roll," as it was called, was greatly misrepresented. To correct these misrepresentations it was published by Rev. Wm. C. Kendall. This is all there was to this affair as far as the preachers belonging to the Conference were concerned. After the FREE METHODIST CHURCH was organized, some who opposed its organization, held meetings by themselves, and called themselves "Nazarites." Some of these still retained their membership in the M. E. Church, and some did not; but all arrayed themselves against the FREE METHODIST CHURCH.
>
> They have always been its unrelenting opponents. They insist that a great mistake was made in leaving the M. E. Church, or in not, when thrust out, uniting with it again, and keeping up the agitation within its pale.*

We have now given a true account of the alleged "Nazarite" movement within the Genesee Conference of the Methodist Episcopal Church, from which movement various writers of that Church have positively and persistently affirmed that Free Methodism sprang. We have furnished the proofs for our statement of the case, while they do not make the slightest attempts to furnish proof or to cite authority for their statements, except in case of Mr. Conable, who cites the action of the Conference, as formulated by Dr. Hibbard, regarding the investigation of "Nazaritism." This, as has been shown, proves nothing except that the Conference took such action.

We believe we have shown to the satisfaction of unprejudiced readers that the versions of the Origin of the

*Pages 62, 63.

Free Methodist Church as given in Conable's "History of the Genesee Conference," Simpson's "Cyclopedia of Methodism," and Buckley's "History of Methodism in the United States," are clearly historical misrepresentations.

CHAPTER X

MINISTERIAL CONCLAVE IN GENESEE CONFERENCE

The secret society men of the Genesee Conference, although in the minority, were very adroit in their manner of securing control in Conference affairs. Their relation to the Secret Empire appears to have suggested the way, which no scruples of conscience restrained them from effectively pursuing.

"In any deliberate assembly, a minority composed of men of average intelligence, bound together by secret oaths, unknown to the rest, can generally carry their measures. Scattered about, their *concerted* action appears to be spontaneous; and they often secure a favorable decision before their opponents have time to rally. In this way the Jacobin Club gained control of the National Assembly, or Legislature of France. In this way the secret society men of the Genesee Conference obtained the controlling influence."*

For a number of years, unsuspected by their brethren outside the Lodge, these men had been doing the very thing they falsely accused the others of doing—combining *in secret* to carry out their own ends in the transaction of Conference business. The "Nazarite Union" has been shown to be wholly a fiction, and that the product of a single brain; but the secret conclave composed of the "Regency" preachers in the Genesee Conference was no fiction, but a most disastrous reality. Nor was it in any sense a one-man affair, as was the alleged "Nazarite Union," but a conclave of from thirty to sixty men, working under cover of darkness, and each pledged to the

*"Why Another Sect?" p. 64.

others to keep their doings secret. Nor would their course have been so reprehensible had it been directed merely toward the shaping of the general policy of the Conference; but it is the fact that their secret meetings were used as means for crushing those brethren of the Conference who would not tamely submit to their proposed policy, that exhibits the iniquitous character of their designs and operations. Having thus attempted to carry out iniquitous ends by crooked measures, they appear to have tried to divert attention from what they had done, and were still doing, by charging the innocent objects of their aversion and plotting with a similar offense. A glaring inconsistency, indeed, but one which is both natural and common among those who secretly plot against the welfare of good men.

"But if these things were done in secret, and under pledge to keep them secret, how can the public be assured of what was thus done?" This question is a most natural one, but also one that admits of being easily and satisfactorily answered. A friend of the Rev. B. T. Roberts furnished him with the *original minutes* of one of their meetings. Then, during his trial, Mr. Roberts called a number of preachers who had attended the secret meetings, as witnesses, and from their testimony we learn something of the doings of the secret conclave. The following is a copy of the minutes furnished Mr. Roberts by his friend:

LeRoy, Sept. 3, 1857.

Meeting convened according to adjournment; Brother Parsons in the chair. Prayer, by Brother Fuller. Brethren present pledged themselves by rising, to keep to themselves the proceedings of this meeting.

Resolved, That we will not allow the character of Rev. B. T. Roberts to pass until he has had a fair trial. Passed. *Moved,* That we will not pass the character of Rev. W. C. Kendall, until he has had a fair trial. Passed.

Moved, That Brother Carlton be added to the committee on Brother Kendall's case. Passed.

This document, though brief, is full of significance. The following points concerning it are deserving of particular notice:

1. It was read before the Conference, and was repeatedly published, yet its genuineness was never called in question; whereas, had it not been genuine beyond a possibility of dispute, no such silence would have been maintained with reference to so important a paper.

2. The document contains *prima facie* evidence of the holding of secret meetings, organized and officered in the regular way.

3. The foregoing paper also proves that the meeting of which it is the record was a secret meeting, and that every member was pledged to keep the doings of that meeting to himself.

4. The contents of the document also show conclusively that the object of the meeting was to secure secret and pledged agreement to embarrass, and if possible, destroy, the standing of certain members of the Conference, who were altogether unaware of these underhanded measures—an object and method more worthy of Jesuitical persecutors than of Protestant Christians of the Methodist persuasion.

5. The foregoing minutes also make evident the fact that those in attendance at that meeting, though a minority of the Conference as later evidence will show, proposed through their concerted action to assume prerogatives that belonged alone to the Conference as a whole; as, for instance, when they say, "*Resolved,* That we will not allow the character of So and So to pass until they have had a fair trial." The Conference alone was competent to determine whether any of its members should be placed under arrest of character, or whether their characters should be passed. The doings of that meeting remind one of the doings of the Jewish Sanhedrin the night before the crucifixion of Jesus.

The clue which the foregoing minutes gave Mr.

BISHOP WALTER A. SELLEW

[Plate Ten]

Roberts was carefully followed up; and, as a result, a number of the preachers who had attended these secret meetings were called as witnesses in his trial, and were questioned regarding the character and proceedings of said meetings. This placed them in an embarrassing position. Some were honest enough to give important information, though with more or less reluctance. Others resorted to such evasions as were difficult to reconcile with Christian simplicity and guilelessness.

From the testimony of those who reluctantly gave information it was learned that a secret organization of ministers had been maintained in the Conference since the session of 1856, at least, and how much longer could not be ascertained. This appears to have been a base prostitution of their secret society relationship, such as was not only a moral wrong to their brethren of the Conference, but an unenviable advertisement of the Lodges they represented as well.

The Rev. Sanford Hunt was one of the men whom Mr. Roberts called as a witness, and he testified as follows:

"I was present at meetings at the house of John Ryan. I think there was a chairman and a secretary at the meeting. We had about three meetings. There were generally twenty or thirty at the meeting" [clearly a minority of the Conference].

At a later session, held at LeRoy, the number was increased by others having been induced to join the conspiracy, until it was about twice as large as formerly; but still the number composing the conclave was a decided minority of the Conference.

The Rev. Thomas Carlton being called as witness testified:

"I attended three of the meetings held at the house of John Ryan during the session of the Medina Conference. I attended some of the secret meetings at LeRoy; not all. I should think there might have been sixty at one of the meetings, at another forty; they ranged from thirty to sixty."

The Rev. D. F. Parsons was also called, and gave the following testimony:

"I was chairman of these meetings held at LeRoy. There was a person who kept brief minutes of the meetings."

The foregoing testimonies clearly establish the fact that secret meetings were held at various Conferences, that they were organized in due form by the election or appointment of officers, and that regular minutes of the proceedings were kept.

Moreover, the operations of this association were so secret that its members had been stealthily doing their work and acquiring control in the Conference for at least two years before their brethren had even suspected the existence of such a secret combination. They had noted the unanimity with which some thirty or more preachers voted on all questions bearing with any directness upon the issues between Methodism of the primitive type and that of the modern kind, but this was accounted for on the ground of natural predilection and the influence of Lodge relationships. The representatives of John Wesley Methodism, though possessed of ordinary sagacity, and though on the alert for shrewd tactics from their opponents, had not even dreamed of such a *coup* as that which the Regency party had so successfully concealed and effectively operated during at least two sessions of the Conference. It is significant, too, that when the facts concerning this secret association within the Conference did at last come to light, through providential circumstances, it was certain members of the conclave who, with reluctance, yet with definiteness, furnished the information.

If Bishop Simpson, Dr. Buckley, and others who have assumed to trace the ultimate origin of Free Methodism to a "Nazarite Association" partaking the nature of a secret society, could not believe the testimony of those seventeen ministers of the Genesee Conference, accused of belonging to the said association, in their unanimous statement that there was not and never had been any such association or organization, did they credit or discredit the testimonies of Sanford Hunt, Thomas Carlton, and D. F. Parsons, as to the various secret, organized meetings which they and from thirty to sixty others had attended from time to time?

Seventeen men denied the existence of a "Nazarite Association," and one man declared that he alone was responsible for the fiction which gave occasion for the allegations regarding its existence; three men testified to the existence of an association of ministers which was regularly organized, which held its meetings secretly, and which pledged each member to keep secret the doings of those meetings, and also testified that they attended those meetings from time to time. Here, then, was the *only* secret society that ever existed within the bounds of the Genesee Conference of the Methodist Episcopal Church. This, too, was the only "association of ministers" in the aforesaid Conference that ever had anything to do *as* an association in bringing about the formation of the Free Methodist Church. It was in the secret meetings of this "association of ministers" that those persecutions were instigated and those proscriptions predetermined which made the organization of the Free Methodist Church seem necessary to those who were thereby deprived of their Church home.

It will now be proper to give some further attention to the work accomplished in these secret meetings, as also to the method of its accomplishment.

The first attempt appears to have been in the direction of securing certain changes in the Presiding Eldership. In this L. Stiles, Jr., and I. C. Kingsley were the victims. Mr. Stiles has been described as "one of the most devoted, eloquent, gifted, noble-hearted men in the ministry of his denomination." He was particularly acceptable on the district, and effective in conserving and building up both the temporal and the spiritual interests entrusted to his supervision. Mr. Kingsley was also popular on his district, and highly useful in the advancement of the work of God. Apparently the only thing against these two men was the fact that they were strong advocates of entire sanctification, and were not in sympathy with those secret society preachers who were plotting to secure the control of the Conference. Hence, in a secret meeting of the Regency* preachers it was decided that these men must be removed. A petition was prepared, signed by about thirty of the preachers, and presented to the Bishop, requesting their removal. The Bishop was also informed that unless they were removed, the thirty signers of the petition would decline to take work. Proof of this is furnished by the subsequent testimony of some of their own number at the LeRoy Conference.

The Rev. William Barrett, being called, testified:

"I saw at the Medina Conference a petition asking for the removal of Brothers Stiles and Kingsley from the office of Presiding Elder. I can not state the wording of the petition, but understood it to be this; that we would refuse to take work if Brother Stiles and Kingsley were continued in the Presiding Elder's office."

The Rev. J. M. Fuller was also called and gave the following testimony:

Ques. "Did you state at the Medina Conference that you would not take work under either Stiles or Kingsley?"

Ans. "I did."

Ques. "Did you hear any one else say the same?"

Ans. "I heard others say what would amount to about the same."

Who that reads the foregoing testimonies can enter-

*A name designating those preachers who had surreptitiously secured control of the Conference.

tain a doubt as to secret meetings having been held, and that for the purpose of securing control of the Conference by the minority, without respect to the fairness or righteousness of the measures employed?

In order to the accomplishment of the end sought, good men must be sacrificed and men of inferior qualifications and piety put in their places. In fact, these secret society preachers in their unauthorized secret ecclesiastical meetings were habitually doing exactly what they had charged upon their brethren as doing, and for the alleged doing of which they were now, in an underhanded manner, seeking their removal from office and expulsion from the Church. The so-called "Nazarites" were falsely accused of having formed a "Nazarite Organization" partaking the nature of a secret society for the purpose of securing control in the Conference; and this was the real ground of all the proceedings against Roberts, Stiles, McCreery, and others, as also the ground upon which it was sought to have Stiles and Kingsley removed from the Presiding Eldership.

Such action lacks the common fairness and honesty which respectable men who make no profession of Christianity are accustomed to exhibit. Any argument for the justification of such a course would be equally valid in justification of those who, living by the commission of crime, secure the punishment of honest and upright men by falsely accusing them of the commission of similar crimes.

CHAPTER XI

DOINGS OF THE MINISTERIAL CONCLAVE

The session of Conference held in Medina in 1856 was a time of severe testing to Methodists of Western New York who sympathized with the doctrine and work of holiness as promulgated by Wesley and his co-laborers in early Methodism. The Rev. L. Stiles, Jr., who, as Presiding Elder of the Genesee district, had taken strong ground in favor of the radical and thorough work of God already in progress on his district, was brought to trial on trumped-up charges; and, although he was acquitted of the charges, as a result of the petition presented to the Bishop, both he and Presiding Elder Kingsley were removed from the Cabinet, and also were transferred to the Cincinnati Conference. In fact, being satisfied that one or both of them would be removed, they both requested to be so transferred. Men were appointed in their places who were meekly subservient to the will of the Regency party. The man who succeeded Stiles as Presiding Elder on the Genesee district, at one of his early quarterly meetings distinguished himself and his accession to power by entertaining, putting to vote, and allowing to be passed and recorded as "Quarterly Conference Proceedings," a preamble and resolutions condemning certain persons of the opposite party in their absence, and who were in no sense amenable to that tribunal.

Not until near the close of the Conference, when the list of appointments for the ensuing year was read, did the friends of the holiness work realize the extent to which its enemies had triumphed. Ignorant up to this time of what had been going on, when the facts in the case dawned upon them, they experienced a feeling of great despondency, and, for a time, their hearts sank within them. That wonderful man of God, the Rev. William C. Kendall, was a notable exception, however. Nor was it because he failed to comprehend the situation, for he saw things as his desponding brethren saw them. In addition to the generally deplorable state of affairs, he had himself been removed from his circuit after a single year's pastorate, and placed in charge of a much less important work. But as the Conference business was concluded, and the Bishop called on some one to sing before the closing prayer, without announcing any particular hymn Kendall arose, and, with clear and steady voice, began,—

"Come on, my partners in distress,
My comrades through the wilderness
  Who still your bodies feel;
Awhile forget your griefs and fears,
And look beyond this vale of tears,
  To that celestial hill."

The Bishop was about to offer prayer, but Kendall, all absorbed in his singing, continued:

"Beyond the bounds of time and space,
Look forward to that heavenly place,
  The saints' secure abode:
On faith's strong eagle pinions rise,
And force your passage to the skies,
  And scale the mount of God."

Again the good Bishop would have led in prayer, but the clear voice of the singer continued the third stanza:

"Who suffer with our Master here,
We shall before His face appear,
  And by His side sit down.
To patient faith the prize is sure,
And all that to the end endure
  The cross, shall wear the crown."

By this time the desponding spirits of the persecuted "Pilgrims" were rallied, their heads were up, their hearts aglow, and, as they also joined in the song, faith revived, hope grew strong, and shouts of victory pealed forth from every quarter. In the meantime the voice of Kendall continued to fill the auditorium with heavenly melody as he led the song to the close of the last stanza:

"Thrice blessed, bliss-inspiring hope!
It lifts the fainting spirits up,
  It brings to life the dead.
Our conflicts here will soon be past,
And you and I ascend at last,
  Triumphant with our Head.

"That great mysterious Deity
We soon with open face shall see:
  The beatific sight
Shall fill the heavenly courts with praise,
And wide diffuse the golden blaze
  Of everlasting light."

Concluding prayer was then offered by the Bishop, the doxology was sung, the benediction pronounced, and the "Pilgrim" preachers went unmurmuringly to their appointments, feeling that they could joyfully go to the ends of the earth, if need should require, to proclaim the Gospel of a free and full salvation.

Another measure adopted by the Regency party was that of defeating the admission into Conference of devout young men who offered themselves as candidates, if it was supposed that they would hesitate to place themselves fully under their guidance and control. A number of promising young men, of good educational qualifications and of deep piety, who both professed and preached entire sanctification, were compelled to knock at the doors of other Conferences for admission. Concerning this action, and indicating it to be the settled purpose of the Regency party, the Buffalo *Advocate,* which was their organ, published the following:

Hot-heads and fanatics, from any quarter, will find it hereafter difficult soil on which to produce any of their mischief or scandal. Some attempted to gain admittance to the Conference at its last session, but were repulsed at the threshold, and passed away, disgusted with the forebodings of order and manliness, which [if] a kind Providence permits shall govern hereafter. These, with their sympathizers in and out of the body, are the agencies employed in writing scandal of those who now hold the reins, and who mean to live and govern for God and holiness—and respectable position.

Here is a published admission of what is charged in the preceding paragraph; and the tone of fancied superiority and of triumphant self-satisfaction in which it is expressed, as also what it suggests by way of inuendo and sarcastic flings, are clear indications of the bitter, persecuting spirit which prompted both it and the action to which it refers.

Strange as it may appear, the cause of holiness, which was supposed to have received a decided set-back because of the conditions and circumstances narrated in the foregoing paragraph, continued steadily to advance. In fact, it was more prosperous than during previous years. The camp-meetings on the Genesee and Niagara districts, though held without the coöperation of the Presiding Elders, were larger and more fruitful than any that had been held in later years. The districts were aflame with revival interest. Conversions were numerous, and large numbers sought and obtained the blessing of full salvation, or "perfect love." "So mightily grew the word of God and prevailed."

The year soon rolled its round, and at the next session of the Genesee Conference, upon the request of a large number of preachers and laymen, I. C. Kingsley and L. Stiles, Jr., were re-transferred to that body. This led a certain Regency Presiding Elder to remark, *"If these men come back, we are in for a seven years' war."* And, true enough, the war was begun at that very session, by the presentation, through the influence of the ministerial conclave, of one bill of charges against B. T. Roberts, and two bills of charges against William C. Kendall. That against Roberts was prosecuted and declared sustained. The proceedings will be presented and reviewed in a subsequent chapter. The charges against Kendall were deferred for lack of time to prosecute, but with the assurance that they would be prosecuted the following year.

In fact, the gravest wrongs ever done by the Genesee conclave of ministers were those of using their organization for the purpose of shielding the guilty and punishing the innocent. "Charges backed up by the most responsible parties, made against some of its members for dishonest transactions amounting almost to state's prison offenses, were summarily dismissed; while men of spotless lives, accused of being Nazarites, were turned out of the Church under pretexts so slight as to admit of no defense."*

William C. Kendall was one of their first victims. He came from an old and highly respected Methodist family of Wyoming County, New York. He and B. T. Roberts were classmates in the academy, in college, and in their Conference course, and their hearts were knit together like the hearts of David and Jonathan. Kendall sought and obtained the experience of holiness during his course in Wesleyan University, at Middletown, Connecticut. He exemplified the grace which he professed, and kept the flame of perfect love alive by diligently laboring to bring others into the same blessed experience. He was graduated in 1848, and within a short time thereafter he united with the Genesee Conference on probation. By natural endowment, educational equipment, and a rich experience in the grace of God, he was eminently qualified for successful labor in any department of the Lord's vineyard. He has been described as of "a fine, manly form of noble bearing; a frank, open countenance on which rested a sweet, heavenly smile; a pleasant voice of unusual compass and power, perfectly at his command; a mind carefully stored with divine truth as well as with classic lore —and above all a heart fully sanctified to God."

Mr. Kendall was acknowledged as one of the most godly, zealous, and successful Methodist ministers in

*"Why Another Sect?" p. 70.

Western New York. An intelligent layman who had long been intimately acquainted with him once said to the author, "I have known many good men, many spiritual men, many holy men, but I regarded William C. Kendall as the *divinest* man I ever met." This in substance seems to have been the general verdict of those who had been blessed with the benefits of his ministry. Yet great, and good, and holy as he was, he was one of the most persecuted men in Western New York Methodism. The ministerial conclave never stooped to more contemptible and disreputable work than when it instigated the charges against this noble man of God to which reference has been made. He was not tried, as we have noted, for lack of time, but was sent to a circuit with the charges still pending, and with the assurance that he would be tried on both bills of charges at the next session of the Conference.

Those who desired and anticipated his ecclesiastical decapitation were providentially disappointed, however, as he was removed from the impending evil by death before the close of the Conference year. In this respect he has been likened to the holy Rutherford, whom he so much resembled in spirit, and who, hearing on his deathbed that he had been summoned to answer at the next Parliament for high treason, calmly remarked that he had got another summons, to appear before a superior Judge and Judicatory, and returned the following message: "I behoove to answer my first summons; and ere your day arrives, I will be where few Kings and great folks come."

The only real offense Mr. Kendall had given was that he was in hearty sympathy with the holiness revival which was sweeping over Western New York and other sections of Methodism, and on this account was classed with the "Nazarites." From the beginning of his ministry he made a specialty of preaching full salvation, being led thereto, in part at least, by a remark of Bishop Hamline which deeply impressed his mind. Certain preachers had been accused of making "a hobby of holiness," whereupon the

Bishop remarked, "Woe to the Methodist preacher, that son of perdition, who does not make holiness his hobby!"

Mr. Kendall's first circuit was Cambria, Niagara County, New York. He went to his work fully determined, according to an intelligent interpretation of the Bishop's words, to "make holiness his hobby." During his two years' pastorate at Cambria his ministry was prosperous. Many were converted, and many believers were sanctified wholly. He also served successively at Royalton and Pike, on both of which fields successful revivals attended his labors. At Pike he received one hundred souls into the Church who had been converted in the revival which he held there. On all these fields he preached holiness, or entire sanctification, as the privilege and obligation of all believers, insisting upon inward purity and outward righteousness, and never lowering the standard of Scriptural justification in presenting sanctification as a second work of grace.

Of course such a ministry could not but be fruitful; and those converted under such labors were clear in experience, as well as vigorous and growing Christians, from the start. Many of them pressed on rapidly into the definite experience of sanctification, and exhibited a freedom and power in laboring for the salvation of others far beyond that of ordinary professors of religion. But this, instead of being generally hailed with joy on the part of many older members of the Church, was an occasion of jealous criticism and bitter opposition. At last a committee was appointed to wait on Mr. Kendall and request him to preach less on holiness, *"lest he should drive away men of influence needed by the Church."*

"Foremost among those who were afraid of holiness, lest it should divide the Church, was a leading member, who had long been prominent in the community. It was afterwards proved that for ten years, including this period, this man had been forging indorsements to bank-notes! These he paid on maturity; but at last being sick when a note became due, his crime was discovered, and he punished. Chiefly through the influence of this man, Brother Kendall was removed at the close of the year. On the Covington Circuit, to which he was sent, a large number were saved."*

*"Why Another Sect?" p. 73.

CHAPTER XII

FURTHER DOINGS OF THE MINISTERIAL CONCLAVE

In the autumn of 1854 Mr. Kendall was sent to the Albion charge. He went to his circuit strongly determined as ever to "know nothing among men save Jesus Christ, and Him crucified," and to preach through Christ salvation to the uttermost. He was warned, however, by his predecessors that it would never do to insist in his preaching here, as he had done in other places, on plainness of attire, since the people would not receive it. He did not swerve from his convictions of duty in the least because of these warnings, however, but firmly yet kindly declared what he believed to be "the whole counsel of God," regarding members of the Methodist Church as under peculiar obligations, because of their Church covenant, to accept and also to exemplify the truth as he was accustomed to preach it regarding dress.

His fidelity to conviction and to the distinctive principles of Methodism excited violent opposition from his Official Board, and involved him in a most unpleasant strife, but God was with him, and his labors resulted in one of the most extensive and thorough revivals Albion had ever known. "Hundreds were converted and sanctified, and over a hundred added to the Church." Several years later the author was pastor of the Free Methodist Church in Albion, where he ministered to many of those who had been saved in that revival, and where he found Mr. Kendall's name as "ointment poured forth." The fame of the Kendall revival in the Methodist Church of Albion was still alive on every hand.

At the close of one year he was removed from Albion

and sent to Brockport. Why we can only guess. At Brockport he was doomed to encounter fiercer opposition than he had known before. The opposition here was of a more organized character. He steadily pursued his course, however, and saw many graciously saved under his ministry. Instead of rejoicing at this, the dominating elements in the Church branded the converts as fanatics, and a former traveling preacher took it upon himself to write a pamphlet against the work, which was put into extensive circulation.

Some further insight into the trials which oppressed this minister of Jesus Christ is given in the following extract from a letter which he wrote about this time:

"In the afternoon we had our official meeting, at the close of which two hours were devoted to my case. The council, of course, were divided—we have *some* brethren who are firm on the side of religion. I did, myself, little more than deny untrue assertions. We adjourned without final action on my case. Next Monday evening is our regular meeting again. What will befall me then, I know not."*

Amid all these difficulties he was ever accustomed to say in his preaching: "I stand on the Bible and the Methodist Discipline; when I get outside of them, lay hands on me."

At the close of one year he was again removed, and this time was sent to Chili, a much less important charge. This was at the Medina Conference, referred to in the preceding chapter. We have already seen the composure with which he received this appointment, and how, when the hearts of the faithful were sinking in despondency over the triumphs of the Regency party, he rallied them with one of the inspiring songs of Zion. In this calm and triumphant optimism he proceeded to the charge assigned him, determined to do more thorough work for God than ever.

*"Why Another Sect?" p. 74.

The next session of the Conference was held at LeRoy. Here is where the two bills of charges were brought against him, which were not prosecuted for lack of time. From this Conference he was sent, with the two bills of charges still pending against him, to the West Falls circuit, generally considered one of the poorest in the Conference. It appeared as though, other measures of the Regency having failed, they intended to try starving him out. His Presiding Elder informed him that, "If he pleased the people pretty well, they might board him and his wife around, from house to house, but they would not be able to support him if he kept house." The people on the charge had also been told by their Presiding Elder, prior to the Conference, that he "doubted whether there was a man in the conference small enough for them."

Such was the reward this faithful man of God received from the Genesee Conference of the Methodist Episcopal Church for his years of earnest, self-sacrificing, and fruitful service on the various charges to which he had been sent. Here was a man eminent for piety, endowed with rare natural gifts, a graduate of the foremost University of American Methodism, thoroughly cultured, and in every way capable of filling the very best pulpits of the land, who had proved his efficiency by successful labors on seven different charges, now appointed to the most obscure, unpromising, and unremunerative circuit within the bounds of the Conference!

To this "starvation circuit" Mr. Kendall meekly but courageously went. Perhaps a few tears fell when it fully dawned upon him what the action of the Conference in his case meant, but he soon brushed away the tears, and, smilingly and triumphantly, he was heard to say: *"I will trust God to make them repent that they ever sent me to West Falls to cure or punish me."* On reaching his circuit he found things worse than they had been represented. Of vital godliness there was practically none, and even the form of true religion had well-nigh disappeared. He went to work, however, with much faith, courage and zeal, in hope of seeing a genuine revival; and his labors were soon abundantly blessed, and fruitful beyond all his expectation. One of the first who rallied to his support was an old Quaker friend, who, at the close of one of his most searching sermons, approached him, placed a sum of money in his hand, and said: "William, I perceive that God is with thee."

His biographer, writing of his labors on this charge, says:

> A revival broke out that swept with almost resistless power all through that region. With untiring zeal, he went from house to house and prayed with the people. Whole families were converted. Stout-hearted infidels fell prostrate under the power of God, and were glad to have those pray for them whom once they had hated. It was said that for eight miles along the main road there was not a house but that some of its inmates had been converted in this revival. In the village when he entered it there were but three houses that had family prayer—when he left it there were but three in which they did not have family prayer.

Some twenty years later West Falls was embraced in the Conference District over which the author was appointed to preside, and here again he found precious fruits of the Kendall revival, and learned that, though the man of God had fallen on sleep a score of years before, his memory was fresh and inspiring to all who had known him and who had attended upon his ministry.

His labors on the West Falls circuit, and his persecutions by the Regency, finally proved too much for his strength, however, and his naturally strong constitution was at length undermined and gave way. On Saturday, January 16, 1858, he manifested symptoms of typhoid fever. As there was no one available to fill his appointment the following day, he undertook to do it himself. He rode eight miles to reach it, preached twice with much unction and power, after which he returned home, and feeling ill, took to his bed, and that to rise no more. His condition gradually became more alarming, but he remained conscious and happy. At times he would sing some of his favorite hymns. At one time it would be:

> "How happy every child of grace,
> Who knows his sins forgiven;"

and again:

> "My soul's full of glory,
> Inspiring my tongue."

On waking one morning he exclaimed: "I have seen the King of Glory, and slept in His palace. I was so intimate with the angels!"

His sufferings at times were excruciating, but were borne without murmuring. On "Sabbath morning, the 31st of January, he was thought to be dying, and his room was filled with a weeping multitude. His voice failed, and he lay gazing into heaven, all entranced with its glories that were beaming down upon him. He was waving his hands in triumph. His wife bent her ear to his lips, and heard him whisper, 'Hail! hail! all hail!!'

"After a short silence, he suddenly roused and sang:

> " 'We'll praise Him again
> When we pass over Jordan.'

"His father asked: 'William, is all well?' With a look of unspeakable joy he answered three times, 'All is well.'

"Gradually the silver cord was unloosed, and on Monday morning, February 1, 1858, at half-past ten o'clock, this Christian warrior, who had ever been valiant for the truth, laid aside his armor to wear his crown. But he was victorious in death, as in life."*

No sooner was the good man gone than those who had been his most bitter persecutors were foremost in proclaiming his sterling and manly virtues, and in otherwise vying to do honor to his memory. Such has been the age-long custom with religious persecutors.

At its next session after Mr. Kendall's death the Genesee Conference, instead of prosecuting the two bills of

*"Why Another Sect?" pp. 78, 79.

Yours sincerely,
Wilson T. Hogue.

[Plate Eleven]

charges presented against him at the previous session and left over till another year for lack of time (upon which, in all probability, they would have expelled him from the Conference and the Church had he lived), adopted the following deserved and glowing tribute to his memory, which is recorded on the Conference Journal, has since been published in "Why Another Sect?" and, with some omissions, in Conable's "History of the Genesee Conference of the Methodist Episcopal Church:"

He fell at his post, in the midst of one of the most promising revivals that had ever attended his labors. It was remarked by his Presiding Elder, Rev. G. Fillmore, that notwithstanding all his previous ministerial success, he had never known a time when there was such a prospect before him of extensive usefulness as when he was taken sick; and he had never known an instance where a preacher had so interwoven himself into the affections of all the people.

It may be said of Brother Kendall, that he fell a martyr to his work. The day after he was taken sick, he went to an appointment, and preached with much earnestness and power; and when his wife endeavored to dissuade him from going to another, his Christian reply was, "I want to say something to the people at Potter's Corners, which they will always remember." He made the effort, but was soon obliged to stop. This was his last effort. He was taken home, and never after left his house till he was conveyed from it to his resting place in the grave.

His end was such as a life like his can not fail to insure. It was not only peaceful, but triumphant. A short time before he died, he said, "I have been swimming in the waters of death for two days, and they are like sweet incense all over me." Sometimes he would wave his hands in ecstasy, saying, "Why, heaven is coming down to earth! This is heaven! I see the angels! They are flying all through the house." He often sang his favorite hymns, suggestive of the bliss of heaven.

Just before his departing, his afflicted companion held her ear to catch the accents of what he seemed to be uttering in a whisper, and distinctly heard him breathe out, as from his inmost soul, "Hail! Hail! All hail! I see light, light!" *I see* was uttered with emphasis. One asked, "Is all well?" He sweetly replied, and repeated it three times, "All is well!" He suffered a brief conflict with the powers of darkness, but soon obtained the victory, and exclaimed, "Jesus the Conqueror reigns!" Thus lived and died our beloved brother, William C. Kendall, a man honored of God, and greatly beloved by all who knew him.

According to all human appearances William C. Kendall should have lived and labored for a score or more of years. He was descended from a family quite distinguished for their longevity, possessed of a strong and vigorous constitution, and for years had exhibited unusual capabilities for hard work and unusual powers of endurance. But the strongest constitution could not indefinitely bear the strain of such indignities and hardships as were forced upon him for years simply because of his loyalty to God and to the principles of Methodism.

If the foregoing suggestion seems to be uncharitable, let it be remembered that it expresses a view which was held at the time of Mr. Kendall's death by many of his friends, not merely among those who were in derision called "Nazarites," but as well among those who were never suspected of being schismatics, or in any wise disloyal to the Methodist Episcopal Church. The following extract from a letter written to the Rev. B. T. Roberts by the Rev. Seymour Coleman, a prominent member of the Troy Conference, a man who lived and died in the Methodist Church, illustrates the thought and feelings of many regarding the responsibility for Mr. Kendall's apparently untimely death:

> This morning I received your letter, giving the information of the death of our dear Brother Kendall. You say he died in triumph. Let us raise the shout of victory for him here, while he sings praise above. He will have no more hard appointments; thank God!
>
> The hours I have spent with him are very pleasant in their recollection. I think the Church and the world might have had him longer, if they had used him better.

The closing words of this extract, "*I think the Church and the world might have had him longer if they had used him better,*" are expressive of the general conviction of all who knew the circumstances save those who were his bitter enemies; and we doubt not that at heart they also regarded him as a martyr victim of the persecutions that had raged so long and fiercely against him.

CHAPTER XIII

RELIGION OF THE DOMINANT PARTY—"NEW SCHOOL METHODISM"

In his "History of the Genesee Conference of the Methodist Episcopal Church" the Rev. F. W. Conable says:

"Nazaritism assumed that the great body of the Conference and a large portion of the membership of the Church had backslidden from the essential spirit of Methodism; that upon the part of such within the territory described the Discipline of the Church had become a dead letter; that on the subject of 'Scriptural holiness,' understood in the Wesleyan sense, many had become heterodox, and many more were grievously derelict; and that general worldliness, extravagance, and vanity had spoiled and made desolate the once fair heritage of Zion." *

In his "Cyclopedia of Methodism" Bishop Simpson has expressed himself to the same effect, though in fewer words, as follows:

"In their writings and speeches they complained of the decline of spirituality in the Church, charging the Church with tolerating, for the sake of gain, the worldly practises of its members, and its departure both in doctrine and discipline from the teachings of the fathers."†

In both of the foregoing extracts it is clearly assumed that the claims made by those who were contending for genuine Methodism were unfounded. The issue at this point is a most vital one. If the claims of those men who were finally proscribed and expelled from the Church regarding the religion of the dominant party were unfounded, then the action of the Genesee Conference of the

*Page 629. †Art. on "Free Methodists."

Methodist Episcopal Church in their arraignment and expulsion was in some measure justifiable, and the Free Methodist Church has no justification for its existence. On the other hand, if the assumptions and allegations respecting Methodism's departure from her original standards of faith and practise can be established, then the aforesaid action of the Genesee Conference is wholly unjustifiable, and partakes the character of a persecution so malignant and persistent as fully to justify those whom it proscribed and excommunicated in their final organization of a separate branch of Methodism.

In this and the following chapter we shall endeavor to give the reader a correct idea of the two types of religion and of the two kinds of Methodism which existed in the Genesee Conference at the time referred to, and between which the conflict was hotly waged. It is believed that by comparison and contrast the unbiased reader will be led to render a verdict to the effect that Methodism had sadly deteriorated in Western New York, fully justifying the claims and allegations of the so-called "Nazarite" brethren, who earnestly contended for a return to Methodist simplicity and purity; and likewise that the religion of the proscribed brethren, instead of being, as the Regency affirmed, "fanaticism," "enthusiasm," "extravagance," "wildfire," et cetera, was simply what Dr. Chalmers declared the Methodism of his day to be—"Christianity in earnest."

In presenting the character of the dominant religion we shall first insert an article on "New School Methodism," published by the Rev. B. T. Roberts, then pastor at Albion, New York, as embodying the views of the reformers regarding the Church's departure from her original standards; and then we shall present certain published statements of those representing the dominant party in the Conference to show that conditions were decidedly worse than they were represented as being in "New School Methodism."

A few years previous, in the providence of God, Asa Abell, Eleazer Thomas, I. C. Kingsley, and C. D. Burlingham, men who believed in, taught, and personally enjoyed the experience of holiness or perfect love, were placed in the Presiding Eldership, and many others of like faith and experience were closely associated with them in the prosecution of their work. In their district work these Presiding Elders put the subject of holiness as taught by the fathers of Methodism to the front, and urged not only the necessity of regeneration upon the unsaved, but also the privilege and duty of being sanctified wholly upon believers. Nor was this done in a merely formal and perfunctory manner, but with heaven-born zeal, and "in demonstration of the Spirit and in power." Multitudes were converted, and scores of both preachers and laymen "received the word with joy," sought and obtained the sanctifying baptism with the Spirit, and "began to speak with other tongues [though in the same language], as the Spirit gave them utterance."

Around the standard of holiness as uplifted by these godly men quickly rallied such ministers as B. T. Roberts, William C. Kendall, Joseph McCreery, Loren Stiles, Jr., William Cooley, Amos Hard, and others "whose names are in the Book of Life," all of whom were men of marked ability and of unchallenged standing among their Conference brethren. Wherever these men went, revivals broke out, in which large numbers were converted, many were sanctified wholly, the Church was quickened and built up, and Methodism became characterized by the power of earlier days.

At the same time, under the ministry of those who represented the modernized type of Methodism, spirituality steadily declined, worldliness as steadily and rapidly increased, and the primitive glory of Methodism as constantly waned.

Under these conditions the "Nazarite preachers," as those who contended for "the old paths" of Methodism were contemptuously called by their opponents, began to be in demand in the Conference to an extent which alarmed the "progressives" lest it should eclipse their glory and interfere with their prospects for position and income. Hence a systematic effort was inaugurated for bringing the more aggressive preachers and their labors into disrepute. They were branded as "fanatics," "enthusiasts," "false prophets," "spurious reformers," and with even more offensive epithets than these. Their preaching was characterized as "cant," "rant," "clap-trap," "arrogant boasting," "haranguing the people," and such other terms as would tend to bring odium upon it. Against their work were raised the old-time cries of "irregularity," "extravagance," "fanaticism," "wildfire," and so forth. From pulpit and press they were assailed and misrepresented with great bitterness, and in language of which the foregoing is the least offensive.

In fact, strong language was employed on both sides; but the use of terms offensive to refinement and decency is chargeable exclusively to the "Regency" party, as the opponents of the reform movement were called, as will be seen in a subsequent chapter. But the movement had acquired too much momentum and secured too large a following to be suppressed by such measures; and "so mightily grew the word of the Lord and prevailed."

Then followed those secret meetings whereby the "Buffalo Regency" sought and obtained control of the Conference, with the consequences which have already been related.

The time had now come when to the leaders in the work of revival and reform it seemed wise to set themselves right before the general public, so far as practicable, with regard to the chief differences between them and their opponents. The official periodicals of the Church being closed against them, so far as these issues were concerned, they had recourse to the columns of the *Northern Independent*, a paper published at Auburn, New York, whose able and fearless editor, the Rev. William Hosmer, allowed them free scope in defense of their cause. Accordingly in 1857, Mr. Roberts wrote and published a paper entitled, "New School Methodism," which was a very able presentation of the case. In his clear and incisive style, he set forth the departures of the Methodist Episcopal Church from her primitive standards, fortifying himself in each principal allegation made by ample quotations from men high in the councils of the Church.

He also defined the position of the other party in terms which they never attempted to deny, and showed wherein the brethren whom he represented disagreed with them. This paper, as will be seen from the following reprint, was a dignified, straightforward and dispassionate presentation of the case, without one discourteous utterance or offensive epithet contained therein. Following is the text of Mr. Roberts's paper:

NEW SCHOOL METHODISM

The best seed, sown, from year to year, on poor soil, gradually degenerates. The acorn, from the stately oak, planted upon the arid plain, becomes a stunted shrub. Ever since the fall, the human heart has proved a soil unfavorable to the growth of truth.

Noxious weeds flourish everywhere spontaneously, while the useful grains require diligent cultivation.

Correct principles implanted in the mind need constant attention, or monstrous errors will overtop them and root them out. Every old nation tells the tale of her own degeneracy, and points to the golden age when truth and justice reigned among men.

Religious truth is not exempt from this liability to corruption. "God will take care of His own cause," is a maxim often quoted by the cowardly and the compromising, as an apology for their base defection. When His servants are faithful to the trusts reposed in them, it is gloriously true; when they waver, His cause suffers. The Churches planted by the Apostles, and watered by the blood of martyrs, now outvie heathenism itself in their corruptions. No other parts of the world are so inaccessible to Gospel truth as those countries where the Romish and Greek Churches hold dominion.

As a denomination, we are just as liable to fall by corrupting influences as any were that have flourished before us. We enjoy no immunity from danger. Already there is springing up among us a class of preachers whose teaching is very different from that of the fathers of Methodism. They may be found here and there throughout our Zion; but in the Genesee Conference they act as an associate body. They number about thirty. During the last session of this Conference, they held several secret meetings, in which they concerted a plan to carry their measures and spread their doctrines. They have openly made the issue in the Conference. It is divided. Two distinct parties exist. With one or the other every preacher is in sympathy. This difference is fundamental. It does not relate to things indifferent, but to those of the most vital importance. It involves nothing less than the nature itself of Christianity.

In showing the doctrines of the New School Methodists, we shall quote from *The Advocate* of the sect, published at Buffalo. This is the organ of the party. It is sustained by them. They act as its agents. Where their influence prevails, it is circulated to the exclusion of other religious papers. Its former title was "*The Buffalo Christian Advocate.*" But since its open avowal of the new doctrines, it has significantly dropped from its caption, the expressive word "*Christian.*" This omission is full of meaning. It is, however, highly proper, as we shall see when we examine its new theory of religion. We commend the editor for this instance of honesty. It is now simply "*The Advocate;*" that is, the *only* Advocate of the tenets it defends.

The New School Methodists affect as great a degree of liberalism as do Theodore Parker and Mr. Newman. They profess "charity" for everybody except their brethren of the Old School. In an article on "Creeds," published in *The Advocate* of April 16th, under the signature of W. the Rev. writer, a prominent New School minister, lays it on to "the sects whose watchword is a creed," in a manner not unworthy of Alexander Campbell himself. He says, "No matter how holy and blameless a man's life may be, if he has the temerity to question any tenet of 'orthodoxy,' he is at once, in due ecclesiastical form, consigned to the Devil—as a heretic and infidel. Thus are the fetters of a spiritual despotism thrown around the human reason. * * * * And so it has come to pass, that in the estimation of multitudes—the teachings of Paul are eclipsed by the theories of Calvin, and the writings of John Wesley are held in higher veneration than the inspired words of St. John." Is not this a modest charge?

But their theory of religion is more fully set forth in the leading editorial of *The Advocate* for May 14th, under the title —"*Christianity a Religion of Beneficence Rather than of Devotion.*"

Though it appears as editorial, we have good reason to believe that it was written by a leading New School member of the Genesee Conference. It has not been disavowed by that party. Though it has been before the public for months, no one has expressed a dissent from its positions. It is fair to suppose that it represents the views of the leaders of this new movement.

It says, "Christianity is not, characteristically, a system of devotion. *It has none of those features* which must distinguish a religion grounded on the idea that to adore the Divine character is the most imperative obligation resting upon human beings. It enjoins the observance of but very few sacred rites; nor does it prescribe any *particular mode* for paying homage to the Deity. It eschews all exterior forms, and teaches that they who worship God must worship Him in spirit and in truth."

The Old School Methodists hold, that "to adore the Divine character" is the most imperative obligation resting upon human beings—that Christianity has *all* of those features that must distinguish a religion grounded on this idea. That he who worships God rightly, will, as a necessary consequence, possess all social and moral virtues; that the Gospel does not leave its votaries to choose, if they please, the degrading rites of heathenism, or the superstitious abominations of Popery; but prescribes prayer and praise and the observance of the sacraments of baptism and the Lord's Supper, "as particular modes for paying homage to the Deity;" that there is no necessity for antagonism, as Infidels and Universalists are wont to affirm, between spiritual worship and the forms of worship instituted by Christ.

The following sneer is not unworthy of Thomas Paine himself. It falls below the dignity of Voltaire. "Christianity in nowise gives countenance to the supposition that the Great Jehovah is so affected with the infirmity of vanity, as to receive with *peculiarly* grateful emotions, the attention and offerings which poor, human creatures may pay directly to Him in worship."

The above may be sufficient to show what Christianity is not, in the opinion of these New School divines. Let us now see what it is. "The characteristic idea of this system is benevolence; and its practical realization is achieved in beneficence. It consecrates the principle of charity, and instructs its votaries to regard good works as the holiest sacrifice, and the most acceptable which they can bring to the Almighty. * * * *

"Whatever graces be necessary to constitute the inner Christian life, the chief and principal one of these is *love to man.* * * * The great condition upon which one becomes a participant of the Gospel salvation, is—some practical exhibition of self-abnegation, of self-sacrifice for the good of others. *Go sell all that thou hast, and give to the poor,* were the only terms of salvation which Christ proposed to the young man, who, otherwise, was not far from the kingdom of heaven."

The Old School Methodists hold that benevolence is only *one of the fruits* of true religion, but by no means the thing itself. In their view, "The principal grace of the inner Christian life" is LOVE TO GOD; and the most acceptable sacrifice we can render HIM, is a broken and contrite heart. They teach that the great condition upon which one becomes "a participant of the Gospel salvation" IS FAITH IN CHRIST—preceded by repentance. They read in the Gospel that the young man referred to was commanded by Christ to "*come, take up the cross and follow me.*" The giving of his goods to the poor was only preparatory to this.

The New School Methodists hold that justification and entire sanctification, or holiness, are the same—that when a sinner is pardoned, he is at the same time made holy—that all the spiritual change he may henceforth expect is simply a growth in grace. When they speak of "holiness," they mean by it the same as do evangelical ministers of those denominations which do not receive the doctrines taught by Wesley and Fletcher on this subject.

According to the Old School Methodists, merely justified persons, while they do not outwardly commit sin, are conscious of sin still remaining in the heart, such as pride, self-will, and unbelief. They continually feel a heart bent to backsliding; a natural tendency to evil; a proneness to depart from God, and cleave to the things of earth. Those that are sanctified wholly are saved from all inward sin—from evil thoughts, and evil tempers. No wrong temper, none contrary to love, remains in the soul. All the thoughts, words and actions are governed by pure love.

The New School ministers have the frankness to acknowledge that their doctrines are not the doctrines of the Church. They have undertaken to correct the teachings of her standard authors. In the same editorial of *The Advocate,* from which we have quoted so largely, we read: "So in the exercises and means of grace instituted by the Church, it is clearly apparent that respect is had, rather to the excitation of the religious sensibilities, and the culture of emotional piety, than the development of genial and humane dispositions, and the formation of habits of active, vigorous goodness."

Here the evils complained of are charged upon "*the exercises and means of grace, instituted by the Church.*" They do not result from a perversion of the means of grace, but are the effects *in-*

tended to be produced in their institution. It is THE CHURCH, then, that is wrong—and so far wrong that she does not even *aim* at the development of proper Christian character. "The means of grace," in the use of which an Asbury, an Olin, a Hedding, and a host of worthies departed and living, were nurtured to spiritual manhood, must be abolished; and others, adapted to the "development of genial and humane dispositions," established in their place. The Lodge must supersede the class-meeting and the love-feast; and the old-fashioned prayer-meeting must give way to the social party! Those who founded or adopted "the exercises and means of grace instituted by the Church"—Paul and Peter, the Martyrs and Reformers, Luther and Wesley, Calvin and Edwards—all have failed to comprehend the true idea of Christianity—for these all held that the sinner was justified by *faith in Christ*, and not by "some practical exhibition of self-abnegation." The honor of distinctly apprehending and clearly stating the true genius of Christianity was reserved for a few divines of the nineteenth century!

USAGES—RESULTS

Differing thus in their views of religion, the Old and New School Methodists necessarily differ in their measures for its promotion. The latter build stock Churches, and furnish them with pews to accommodate a select congregation; and with organs, melodeons, violins, and professional singers, to execute difficult pieces of music for a fashionable audience. The former favor free Churches, congregational singing, and spirituality, simplicity and fervency in worship. They endeavor to promote revivals, deep and thorough; such as were common under the labors of the Fathers; such as have made Methodism the leading denomination of the land. The leaders of the New Divinity movement are not remarkable for promoting revivals; and those which do, occasionally, occur among them, may generally be characterized as the editor of "*The Advocate*" designated, one which fell under his notice, as "*splendid revivals.*" Preachers of the old stamp urge upon all who would gain heaven the necessity of self-denial—nonconformity to the world, purity of heart and holiness of life; while the others ridicule singularity, encourage by their silence, and in some cases by their own example, and that of their wives and daughters, "the putting on of gold and costly apparel," and treat with distrust all professions of deep Christian experience. When these desire to raise money for the benefit of the Church, they have recourse to the selling of pews to the highest bidder; to parties of pleasure, oyster suppers, fairs, grab-bags, festivals and lotteries; the others for this purpose, appeal to the love the people bear to Christ. In short, the Old School Methodists rely for the spread of the Gospel upon the agency of the Holy Ghost, and the purity of the Church. The New School Methodists appear to depend upon the patronage of the worldly, the favor of the proud and aspiring; and the various artifices of worldly policy.

If this diversity of opinion and of practise among the ministers of our denomination was confined to one Conference, it would be comparatively unimportant. But unmistakable indications show that prosperity is producing upon us, as a denomination, the same intoxicating effect that it too often does upon individuals and societies. The change, by the General Conference of 1852, in the rule of Discipline, requiring that all our houses of worship should be built plain, and with free seats; and that of the last General Conference in the section respecting dress, show that there are already too many among us who would take down the barriers that have hitherto separated us from the world. The fact that the removal is gradual, so as not to excite too much attention and commotion, renders it none the less alarming.

Every lover of the Church must feel a deep anxiety to know what is to be the result of this new order of things. If we may judge by its effects in the Genesee Conference, since it has held sway there, it will prove disastrous to us as a denomination. It so happened, either by accident or by management, at the division of the Genesee Conference eight years ago, that most of the unmanageable veterans, who could neither be induced to depart from the Heaven-honored usages of Methodism, by the specious cry of "progress" nor to wink at such departures, by the mild expostulations of Eli, "Why do ye thus, my sons!" had their destination upon the east side of Genesee River. The first year after the division, the East Genesee Conference had twenty superannuated preachers; the Genesee Conference but five. "Men of progress" in the prime of life, went west of the river, and took possession of the Conference. For the most part, they have borne sway there ever since. Of late, the young men of the Conference, uniting with the fathers, and thus united, comprising a majority of the Conference, have endeavored to stop this "progress" away from the old paths of Methodism. But the "progressives" make up in management what they lack in numbers. Having free access at all times to the ears of the Episcopacy, they have succeeded, for the most part, in controlling the appointments to the districts and most important stations. If, by reason of his obvious fitness, any impracticable adherent of primitive Methodism has been appointed to a district or first-class station, he has usually been pursued, with untiring diligence, and hunted from his position before his constitutional term expired.

In the bounds of the Genesee Conference, the people generally are prepossessed in favor of Methodism. During the past eight years there have been no external causes operating there against our prosperity that do not operate at all times and in all places. Within this period, the nominal increase of the Church in that Conference has been but seven hundred and eighty. The East Genesee Conference has had an increase, within the same time, of about two thousand five hundred. In order to have simply kept pace with the population, there should have been within the bounds of the Genesee Conference, one thousand six hundred and forty-three more members than there are at present. That is, in eight years, under the reign of new divinity, the Church has suffered, within the bounds of this one Conference, a relative loss of fifteen per cent in members.

The Seminary at Lima, at the time of the division, second to none in the land, has, by the same kind of management, been brought to the brink of financial ruin.

We have thus endeavored to give a fair and impartial representation of New School Methodism. Its prevalence in one Conference has already, as we have seen, involved it in division and disaster. Let it generally prevail, and the glory will depart from Methodism. She has a special mission to accomplish. This is, not to gather into her fold the proud and fashionable, the devotees of pleasure and ambition, but, "to spread Scriptural holiness over these lands." Her doctrines, and her usages, her hymns, her history and her spirit, her noble achievements in the past, and her bright prospects for the future, all forbid that she should adopt an accommodating, compromising policy, pandering to the vices of the times. Let her go on, as she has done, insisting that the great, cardinal truths of the Gospel shall receive a living embodiment in the hearts and lives of her members, and Methodism will continue to be the favored of Heaven, and the joy of earth. But let her come down from her position, and receive to her communion all those lovers of pleasure, and lovers of the world, who are willing to pay for the privilege, and it needs no prophet's vision to foresee that Methodism will become a dead and corrupting body, endeavoring in vain to supply, by the erection of splendid Churches, and the imposing performance of powerless ceremonies, the manifested glory of the Divine presence, which once shone so brightly in all her sanctuaries.

"Thus saith the Lord, Stand ye in the ways, and see, and ask

for the old paths, where is the good way, and walk therein, and ye shall find rest for your souls."—Jer. 6:16.

The publication of this clear and comprehensive statement of the points at issue gave universal offense to the "Regency" party, and therefore furnished the pretext for the commencement of still more oppressive and unrighteous measures, even for that whole series of "proscriptions, prosecutions, and expulsions which led to the formation of the Free Methodist Church." Mr. Roberts was the first victim of expulsion. He was tried on a charge of "Immoral and Unchristian Conduct" for the writing and publication of the foregoing article. This being the case it is only fair to conclude that the article in question was considered as the most striking specimen of fanatical raving and of libelous speech or publication that could be produced. Otherwise Mr. Roberts would not have been the first and only victim tried on such a charge and with such specifications.

Referring to the writing and publication of the foregoing article some years later, in "Why Another Sect?" Mr. Roberts said:

We had previously been styled "New School Methodists," in an article published in the *Buffalo Advocate*, the organ of the dominant party. We showed that the appellation properly belonged to our opponents. Though differing with them, we wished to treat them fairly. So we took this course. For fear that we might misrepresent their views, we stated them as we found them expressed by one of their leading preachers in an editorial of the *Buffalo Advocate*, and copied into the *New York Christian Advocate and Journal.* It set forth, as we believed then, and as we believe still, the doctrinal views from which we differed. This article, from which we quoted fairly, was indorsed by leading men of the dominant party. We never heard of its being disapproved by any of that party. The fact that there was a great division in the Conference had become notorious. Our opponents had, from time to time, in the *Buffalo Advocate* and other papers, in neither truthful nor respectful language, set forth their version of matters. We thought the time had come for us to set ourselves right before the public. This we endeavored to do in the following [foregoing] article, which was published over our well-known signature in the *Northern Independent* of which I was at the time a corresponding editor.

The article on "New School Methodism" represented Mr. Roberts's views of the state of religion in the Genesee Conference at the time it was written. He stated the case plainly and strongly, but in courteous and dignified terms, and with no traces of bitterness, or of offensive personalities. Men must have been unduly sensitive who could have regarded anything said therein as personally offensive and libelous; and yet it was on this ground that the writer of that article was regarded as deserving of being arraigned and tried by his Conference.

Various persons in responsible positions in the Methodist Episcopal Church expressed themselves regarding the article at the time in decidedly favorable language, as the following letters and extracts from letters will show.

Dr. F. G. Hibbard, who, at that time, was editor of the *Northern Christian Advocate,* and to whom Mr. Roberts at first sent the article for publication, though declining for prudential reasons to publish it, wrote its author as follows:

DEAR BROTHER ROBERTS:

I return your communication as you requested, not feeling it prudent to publish. I presume you can not see things as I do from my standpoint. Your communication would involve me in hopeless controversy, which would make me much trouble and perplexity, with no hope, as I view it, of doing substantial good to the Church, or cause of Christ. I do not speak this against your article considered by itself, but of the controversy which your article would occasion. *Your article appears to me to be written in as mild and candid a tone as such facts can be stated in.* Be assured, my dear brother, that in the doctrine of holiness, in the life and power of religion, in the integrity and spirit of Methodism, I have a deep and lively interest. I labor to promote these. But I could not feel justified in taking sides in the question that now unhappily divides the Genesee Conference. May the Lord bless you and all His ministers, and give peace and purity to the Churches.

Ever yours in Christ,

AUBURN, Aug. 10, 1857. F. G. HIBBARD.

Later, when it had become clear that Mr. Roberts was in the minority, Dr. Hibbard wrote against him, though with much more zeal than fairness. But in the foregoing letter he certainly writes favorably regarding the merits of the article in question. How otherwise can we interpret the words: "I do not speak this against your article considered by itself, but of the controversy which your article would occasion. *Your article appears to me to be written in as mild and candid a tone as such facts can be stated in.*"

On September 1, 1857, a Presiding Elder of the Oneida Conference, referring to the article on "New School Methodism," in a personal letter to Mr. Roberts, said:

"I am gratified with your exposure of the 'New Divinity' that is cursing the Church. It is creeping into our Conference and doing immense mischief. Keep the Monster in the light."

Another minister of prominence in the same Conference also wrote him, saying:

"If you had belonged to our Conference, we would have given you a vote of thanks for writing that article."

Thus Mr. Roberts's article on "New School Methodism" received the indorsement of distinguished and fair-minded men, who were every way capable of judging as to whether its statements were true to facts or otherwise, and whose loyalty to Methodism would have prevented them from indorsing it, had they considered it as in anywise misrepresenting the type of religion the dominant party was endeavoring to promote. The fact is, that the article, which proved to be so offensive to a majority in the Genesee Conference as to sustain a charge of "Immoral and Unchristian Conduct" based upon its statements, was a much more mild and sober statement of the situation than might have been made without the least sacrifice of truth or indulgence of extravagance.

CHAPTER XIV

RELIGION OF THE DOMINANT PARTY—TESTIMONY OF ITS OWN REPRESENTATIVES

That the dominant religion had departed as far from the original standards of Methodism as Mr. Roberts's paper on "New School Methodism" represented, is fully corroborated by representatives of the dominant party, whose candor and moral courage led them to express their convictions from time to time, as certain extracts from the public press, which will presently be subjoined, most clearly show. A careful comparison of these reprints with Mr. Roberts's article will, in the author's opinion, lead to a general verdict that they afford a stronger arraignment of the religion of the dominant party in the Genesee Conference at the time of the agitation in question than that for which the author of "New School Methodism" was cited to trial and expelled by his Conference.

The following appeared as an editorial in the *Buffalo Advocate*, organ of the "Regency Party," and was reprinted in the *Christian Advocate and Journal*, now known as the New York *Christian Advocate:*

RELIGIOUS INTEREST IN BUFFALO

We have none; we have no more than is usual through the year. We do not intend to convey the idea by the above that there is any special movement among us, or that there is any marked effort toward getting souls converted, or keeping those converted who are already in the Church. The great movement among us is, we judge, to determine how far the Church can go back to the world, and save its semblance to piety, devotion, and truth. Hence, many, many Church members have become the most frivolous and pleasure-loving, and folly-taking part of our town's people. They love, give and sustain the most popular, worldly amusements, such as dancing-parties, card-parties, drinking-parties, masquerade—and surprise—parties, and have no disposition to come out from the world and be separate from it. All this may be seen, read and known in more or less of the Buffalo Churches.

The city of Buffalo was the headquarters of the "Regency" party, and the state of religion there was in all probability a fair example of the religion of the dominant party generally. And we submit to the candid reader this question: Is there anything in Mr. Roberts's article to compare with the foregoing editorial in the way of depreciating the state of religion in the Genesee Conference? To the person who calmly surveys the situation at this distance from the occurrences referred to, it at least appears gravely inconsistent to persecute the so-called "Nazarites," even to the extent of excommunication from the Church, for statements regarding the decline of Methodism as moderate as that contained in "New School Methodism," and then send forth in the official publications of the Church such an indictment of the Church for its backslidden condition as that contained in the foregoing editorial.

Following the appearance of the foregoing editorial in the periodicals referred to, the Rev. William Hart published in the *Northern Independent* an article in which he commented on it as follows:

Now the question is, are these charges true or false? If false, is the *Advocate* aware what it costs to slander the Church in these days? It saw a couple of men beheaded for an offense which dwindles into superlative insignificance, when compared with these wholesale charges. Let us look at them.

1st. "No effort towards getting souls converted."

2nd. "No effort to keep souls converted."

3rd. "The great movement," "the marked effort is to gain a position where they can just balance between God and the devil."

4th. "The Church members are frivolous, folly-loving, and pleasure-taking, *even more so* than those who are openly in the way to hell."

5th. "They love, give and sustain dancing parties, card-parties and drinking-parties, etc., and have no disposition to do otherwise."

These are the charges; now for the testimony. Brother Robie [Editor of *The Advocate*] called: Are the above charges true respecting the Churches in Buffalo? Ans. "All this may be seen, read and known in more or less of the Buffalo Churches."

Dr. Stevens [then editor of the *Christian Advocate and Journal*] sends out these awful charges to his thousands of readers, on the simple assertion of *The Advocate*, without waiting to know the facts. How he has anathematized the *Northern Independent*, as vilifying and slandering the Church; but since its commencement, to the present day, where will we find anything to equal the above from Bros. Robie and Stevens? Now if the above charges cannot be sustained, should not Brother Robie be prosecuted for slandering the Buffalo Churches, and Dr. Stevens for "publishing and circulating" "slanderous reports?" If they belonged to the Genesee Conference, and were charged with abusing and slandering the Church, they would, ecclesiastically, be sent higher than Haman. In the Genesee Conference, the above extract from *The Advocate* would be considered as slanderous, whether true or false. So, Messrs. Editors, you had better take care. What was Brother Roberts's and McCreery's fault, compared with yours? Where or when have these brethren ever said anything half so severe as this from *The Advocate?* But, if what Brother Robie writes be true, why all this hue and cry against the so-called Nazarites? The same ungodly influences, and the same proneness to comply with them exist in other places as well as Buffalo. And would it be strange, if like causes produce results like those now being experienced by the Churches in Buffalo? The same state of things narrated by *The Advocate*, has [existed] and does exist in other places. The temptations of the devil have been listened to, and the prayer-meeting has given way to the social party; entire consecration has died out, and the spirit of compromise between the Church and the world obtains; formality and indifference respecting the salvation of souls have taken the place of spirituality, and the love which constrains "to seek the wandering souls of men." To counteract these effects, a few faithful souls stood up for Jesus and, like the Hebrew children, declared they would not fall down and worship the worldly gods which those "frivolous, folly-loving and pleasure-taking members" and ministers are setting up. This, as everybody knows, that knows anything about it, was the origin of Nazaritism. The natural antagonism between sin and holiness has caused all the trouble. While the current flows along, as Brother Robie says it does in Buffalo, and nobody stands up for Jesus and proclaims the whole truth, they will have peace and prosperity; but it will be the peace of death, and the prosperity of those "whose eyes stand out with fatness." If Brother Robie would stand out as an uncompromising exponent of the whole truth, and in the might of the Spirit bear a decided and open testimony against all worldly connections and associations that are cursing the Churches in Buffalo, he would see such a commotion and storm of opposition as has been seen and felt in other places. But, glory to God! souls would be awakened and saved. Then would commence the work of persecution; for, as he that was born after the flesh, persecuted him that was born after the Spirit, "*even so is it now.*" If Brother Robie would take this position with an eye single to the glory of God, and seek to root out dead formality, by a living, earnest Christianity, and make "*special efforts*" for the conversion of sinners, he would be to all intents and purposes a Nazarite. Will Brother Robie take this stand, and see and feel the salvation of God, or will he let the Buffalo Churches drift down to everlasting woe, unwarned, he following in their wake?"

The editorial in question and its republication in Methodism's leading journal certainly go to show that Mr. Roberts's article on "New School Methodism," although plainly showing that the dominant religion in the Genesee Conference at that time had lost well-nigh all semblance to original Methodism, was fully justified by facts, even his enemies themselves being judges.

That the reader may get, if possible, a still clearer view of spiritual conditions then prevailing, however, a few pages will now be devoted to the *means* by which representatives of the dominant party sought to promote the type of religion not inaptly characterized as "New School Methodism."

The following extracts from a long article, which was published in the Buffalo *Courier* in the way of friendly mention of a "clam bake and chowder festival" held for the benefit of the Niagara Street Methodist Episcopal Church, will throw much light on this point:

CLAM BAKE AND CHOWDER

The spot selected for the clam bake was Clinton Forest, situated about a half a mile from the road. This place, containing about twenty acres, was surrounded by a neat board fence, and ten cents was demanded from each visitor for admission within the enclosure. Within we found thousands of people, some ventilating their garments on swings, some playing games of different descriptions, hundreds eating ice-cream, coffee, ham, fowls, and other substantials, while the great mass opened, swallowed or gorged themselves with clams. Clams was the cry—from every corner came the echo, clams! clams! and the odor of clams went up and down, odorous as exquisite ottars, and fragrant as a back-kitchen about dinner-time.

At other points on the ground were many tables, spread with delicacies of all sorts, behind which handsome women added their voices to urge on appetite; flower tables were many, where young and pretty damsels waylaid pecunious young men with their eyes, and persuaded them into floral purchases; ice-cream booths, where shillings were exchanged for the frigid luxury, accompanied with parallelogrammatic sections of sponge cake; there were other places where money could be laid out to advantage in many ways, but of them we remember none. At the rope-walk, a building which appeared to us to be a mile long, a large crowd had collected, and to the music of two bands were jumping about and perspiring to their heart's content, which privilege cost each dancer ten cents. The air in this place was so intensely hot and high-flavored, that we positively failed to get the program of the dances.

The festival altogether was a success, and has initiated a new order of excursions, which we hope will be followed up. The receipts at the gate were over four hundred dollars, we understand, and at the different booths, etc., several hundred dollars more. The proceeds are for the benefit of the Niagara Street Methodist Church, and will prove a great assistance to them in paying off the debt of the Church. The ladies, particularly, deserve the highest encomiums for their efforts and attempts to make the festival a model one, and carrying it on to triumph.

It has been said, and published, and, so far as we know, has never been contradicted, that "The person who stood at the door of the rope-walk and collected 'ten cents' from each one who attended the dance, was a member of one of the M. E. Churches in the city; and that the proceeds, after 'paying for the music,' went to the benefit of the Church." By such means did the dominant party seek to promote the work it professed to be doing in the interest of the kingdom of God!

The subsequent history of the Niagara Street Church is of peculiar interest. In "Why Another Sect?" Mr. Roberts writes of it as follows:

> The Niagara Street Church, for the benefit of which this festival was held, was the oldest M. E. Church in the city. It was once highly prosperous. Here Eleazer Thomas preached holiness, after the pattern of Asbury, in the power of the Holy Ghost. At this Church we were stationed the fifth year of our ministry. It was the only appointment made for us with which we ever tried to interfere. We felt deeply our lack of ability, experience and grace, to fill so important a position. We entreated the Bishop not to send us there. But when we were sent, we resolved to do our duty faithfully. God kept us from compromising, and gave us a good revival of religion. The members generally were quickened and many sinners were converted. A few—less than half a dozen—composed of secret society men, and one or two proud women, encouraged by a former secret society pastor, held out and opposed the work.
>
> Ever since the Church edifice had been built, there had been on it a mortgage of a few thousand dollars. This we agreed to see paid if they would make the seats free. We had a good proportion of the amount necessary to do it pledged, when at the end of the first year, through the influence above referred to, we were removed, and a man of the other party was sent in our place. The people were finally persuaded that what they needed was a more imposing Church edifice. So the Church—a very substantial stone building—was remodeled, a new front built, a large organ placed in the gallery, and tall gothic chairs in the pulpit. All the money was raised that could be raised by selling the pews, by taxing the members to the utmost of their ability, and by making one of the largest liquor dealers in the city Trustee and Treasurer. So great was the zeal excited among the members to "save the Church," that one of the most godly women we had known up to this time, was induced to preside at one of the tables at the clam-bake and chowder entertainment!
>
> But all was of no avail—the Church edifice was sold to pay the indebtedness upon it, and the members were scattered. This Church has, for many years, been a Jewish synagogue.*

Still later, while the author was pastor of the Virginia Street Free Methodist Church in Buffalo, the property again changed hands, the stone Church building

*Pages 105, 106.

was torn down, and a Masonic Temple was erected on the site!

One might naturally suppose that, with the Conference freed from the troublesome "Nazarites," who had been pronounced "disturbers of its peace," and excommunicated therefor, "New School Methodism" would have made rapid advancement. Such does not appear to have been the case, however, according to the published testimony of its chief promoters. Declension in interest and in numbers followed for many years. In 1865, just a decade after the persecution of the so-called "Nazarite" preachers began, and five years after the organization of the Free Methodist Church, the Genesee Conference of the Methodist Episcopal Church published a report on "The State of the Work," which bewailed the declining condition of religious affairs, and on which the Editor of the *Northern Independent* ably and courageously commented as follows:

GENESEE CONFERENCE OF THE M. E. CHURCH

A copy of the Minutes of the last session of this Conference lies upon our table. Its mechanical execution is excellent, and reflects credit upon all concerned. With the matter in general, we are equally pleased. Each page, if we except the account of the "Conference Camp-meeting," bears marks of diligence and candor. But what strikes us most, is the report on the "State of the Work." It is able, pungent, truthful, humiliating. Yet it would have been more so had all the facts in the case come out. Their language of confession wants translating, and then it would read much like the following:

"They said one to another, we are verily guilty concerning our brother, in that we saw the anguish of his soul, when he besought us, and we would not hear: therefore is this distress come upon us." And Reuben answered them, saying, "Spake I not unto you, saying, Do not sin against the child, and ye would not hear? Wherefore behold also his blood is required."—Gen. 42:21, 22.

But let us have their own statement of the sad condition of affairs in a Conference from which all traces of Nazaritism and "Contumacy" have been carefully excluded. As this purgation has been eminently expensive to common sense, moral principle, and

Methodist Discipline, one would suppose that it might have been prolific of mere numbers and of a certain kind of self-respect. Yet, even in these poor results it fails, and hence they say:

"1. Our revivals have not been, either in number or extent, what we desired, or had reason to expect. Are we God's ministers, commissioned and sent forth by the great Head of the Church, to win souls to Christ, and must we, in so many instances, pass on, year after year, with no marked results? Are we doing our whole duty, as preachers of the everlasting Gospel, while the years go by, and that Gospel seems essentially powerless in our ministrations? While we are the appointed guardians of the Churches, must we, of necessity, see them moving on to inevitable extinction? This is not God's will. The fault lies, in part, at least, at our own doors. There is, on the part of many of us, cause for profound humiliation before God, and for the most serious inquiry whether we are not essentially failing of the great ends of our ministry.

"2. Another unfavorable feature in our condition is the fact, that in many, perhaps in most of our Churches, the membership is made up, almost wholly, of persons far advanced in life. We see among them very few of the young. In a large portion of our Churches, we rarely find a young man in the Official Board. This indicates a lamentable want of extensive revivals among us, for the PAST TEN YEARS. These aged persons in our Churches are true and faithful, and worthy of all honor. But they will soon pass to the Church triumphant. There are, perhaps, scores of Churches in our Conference, the very existence of which seems to depend on the lives of one, two or three men now far advanced in years. These men are rapidly passing away. It is obvious that, in many places, nothing can save our cause but powerful and far reaching revivals of religion.

"3. Another very great evil among us, and one fraught with most damaging results to God's cause and all our interests as a Conference, is the engaging in secular pursuits by so many of our ministers. This evil, during the past two years, has been largely on the increase. It is needless to spend time to show the error of a practise so obviously contrary to both the spirit and letter of our commission, and of our ministerial vows. We claim to have obeyed the voice of the Master, 'Go ye into all the world and preach the Gospel to every creature,' at the altars of the Church. In the presence of God and man we have solemnly pledged to be men of one work, and how can we, conscientiously, engage in occupations that must divide our interest, energies, time and affections. This practise is alarmingly shaking the confidence of the people in us, as ministers of the Lord Jesus. They say we are as greedy of gain, as covetous of large possessions, as easily swept into wild speculations as any other class of men. This loss of confidence in the ministry is not confined to those alone who engage in secular pursuits, but extends measurably to the whole body. Thus the innocent suffer with the guilty, and our hold upon the people is lost."

The chronology of the above is worthy of note, and we have marked it by putting the words in capitals. It is now almost ten years since that Conference arrested the character of one of its ablest and most useful ministers, and finally expelled him for slander—which slander consisted in writing an article for this paper, on "New School Methodism." The article reflected pretty severely on some usages current in that and other Conferences, but was not one whit more scathing than this report on the "State of the Church." Its allegations indeed were not as broad, nor were its developments as alarming. A keen observer, however, at that time saw the evil in its incipiency—saw a ministry shorn of its strength, secularized, unsuccessful, and the Church dying out—saw exactly what this official document declares began to exist ten years ago. The brave man whose eyes, anointed of God, saw this deplorable condition of the Genesee Conference, should have been rewarded by something better than expulsion, for he meant well, spoke well, and is now fully indorsed by the Conference itself. We saw the injustice done, saw it at the time it was done, and gave notice of the fact; but our words were then, as they probably will be now, unheeded, and the Conference went on its way trying men for "Contumacy" and expelling such large numbers of their very best ministers and laymen, that absolute ecclesiastical annihilation stares them in the face. This result will surprise none. It is but the inevitable consequence of a wrong course. Had the leaders of that once prosperous section of the Church listened to good counsel, they would not be uttering their *De profundis*, but their *Nunc dimittis*, and each valiant soldier of the cross, looking back over a well contested field, could say, "I have fought a good fight."

Ten years of spiritual barrenness, the secularization of the ministry to such an extent that the people have lost confidence in them, and many other evidences of decline should satisfy the Conference that it has done wrong—that its administration has cast down those whom God has not cast down. By way of helping them out of their trouble, we suggest that the Conference at once reconsider its action in the case of all who have been expelled on mere technical grounds, and thus restore those on whose account God has sent leanness into all their borders.

The Conference as a body continued its struggle to promote "New School Methodism" for a number of years, but with continually declining numbers and influence. "Many of the leading preachers had lost the confidence of the people to that degree that they took transfers to other Conferences. New men were introduced to supply the work. But all was of no avail. They could not get up even a show of prosperity. They were united with other Conferences for a time—their name changed—and after a general change of preachers, were again restored as a Conference, with the old name."

At the celebration of the centennial anniversary of the Genesee Conference of the Methodist Episcopal Church, in the fall of 1910, its secretary, the Rev. Ray Allen, read a historical sketch of the Conference; and, in referring to the events of the period we are now considering, he paid the following tribute to the brethren whom the Conference expelled at that time, and also gave the added showing as to the decline of the Conference subsequent to those expulsions:

> This heroic treatment might have seemed necessary at the time, but looked at half a century later, it seems unjust, and therefore exceedingly unwise. Those expelled brethren were among the best men the Conference contained, and scarce any one thought otherwise even then.
>
> The troubles of the Genesee Conference were not cured by a surgical operation. Following 1859 came the darkest years of her life, and her membership steadily fell year by year until in 1865 it was at the lowest level ever reached. She then had only 7,593 —a sadly wasted figure! In 1866 she began to amend, but the territory which in 1859 held 10,999 members never got back to that number again for nineteen years. Truly she came up out of great tribulation, and it is to be hoped she washed her robes white.

When it is remembered that the Conference had over one hundred preachers at the beginning of this period, and that the territory it embraced was of a very promising character, and predisposed in favor of Methodism, the foregoing statement makes a still more unfavorable showing.

The brethren who were contemptuously called "Nazarites" had the spiritual vision to perceive that widespread declension had begun, and diligently strove to awaken others to a like vision, and to unite as many as possible in an earnest effort to check the downward tendency and turn the tide the other way. In this they were misunderstood, misrepresented, bitterly opposed, cruelly persecuted, accused of disloyalty, ridiculed as "fanatics," and, finally charged with "Unchristian and Immoral Conduct," tried, and expelled from the Conference and the Church. Thus to some extent they shared the fate of those earlier prophets of God who stood in the breach in times of great spiritual declension and sought to turn the trend of affairs in favor of true godliness.

The matters to which we have been referring were to a considerable extent local; but that a like declension in Methodism was also general is evidenced, as will be seen later, by events occurring at about the same time in Illinois and other parts of the country, and with similar results. Then, too, the testimony of some of Methodism's most prominent men is in evidence on the same point. Regarding the state of religion generally, the Rev. Jesse T. Peck, later elected Bishop, wrote as follows:

"What a mass of backsliders there are now in the Church, for the very reason that they have been satisfied without going on unto perfection!"

Concerning the special reception of the Holy Ghost as "a baptism of light," he says:

It discovers dangers that were never before realized. It shows the perilous track of a wandering Church within the unhallowed precincts of sin. It compels the soul to shrink and abhor the very things which before it has earnestly coveted. It trembles to see

BISHOP WILLIAM PEARCE

[Plate Twelve]

that the outward splendors of the Church, once deemed reliable evidences of success, are but the attire of a harlot, both revealing and inviting illicit commerce with a godless world.

The Rev. E. Bowen, D. D., in preaching a semi-centennial sermon before the Oneida Conference of the Methodist Episcopal Church, in 1864, was constrained to preach on the general subject of "The Church's Defection from God," and, in his peroration, said:

Our task has been one of painful interest; not only because of the pain we have felt in being called upon, in the order of Providence, to present to the Church the ugly portrait of her own character; but more especially for the reason that she was not in a condition to sit for a better picture. We mourn over her defection from God, and from Methodism, which we still love, as ever, with an almost idolatrous devotion. We still love the Methodist Episcopal Church, and mean no disrespect towards her in anything we have said in this discourse. And if we have felt it incumbent on us to sound the note of alarm, and to admonish her, in this way, of her impending overthrow, it is not because we desire such a catastrophe, but because we fear it.

Since the foregoing paragraphs were prepared the author has come into possession of an autograph letter from Dr. Bowen, written at the time referred to, of which the following is a copy:

CORTLAND [N. Y.], JULY 13TH, 1864.

DEAR BROTHER ROBERTS:

I thank you for the kind interest you have taken in the circulation of my Semi-centennial. I have grieved much for a few years past over the rapid decline of experimental and practical piety in our Church; and dared not refrain, at our late Annual Conference, from an exposé of my honest convictions upon the subject, as indicated by the clear openings of Providence. If in giving a correct likeness of the Church, I have made a bad picture, she must remember that her own ugly features, and not the hand of the operator, is responsible for it. I felt that "a life and death remedy" was called for: and having administered it in the name of the Lord, I must leave the result with Him. * * *

Respectfully yours,

ELIAS BOWEN.

The following extracts from an editorial in the Buffalo *Christian Advocate* of November 19, 1856, also goes to show that, in that day, especially in the city Churches throughout our country, the state of religion was that of bankrupt faith, false and hypocritical pretension, sham performance, and destitution of spiritual power:

RELIGION OF CITY CHURCHES

Many of our city Churches are abominably corrupt, and there is no disguising of the fact. Corrupt men and women belong to them. They have money, fashion, and position, but with all these they have a bankrupt faith and hearts as depraved as Satan's.

* * * *

Our cities are full of sham religion, of false and hypocritical pretensions, of forms and ceremonies without power, and of graceless and shapeless appearance which passes for the real and saving in the economy of the gospel.

In the writing of this chapter it has been our aim to show, from Mr. Roberts's article on "New School Methodism," from the hearty indorsement of that article by prominent Methodists in other Conferences, from confessions made by representatives of the dominant party, and from uncontradicted reports of the secular press, those religious conditions within the Genesee Conference of the Methodist Episcopal Church which demanded reform, if genuine Methodism was to be rescued from its danger of utter apostasy; and also to show from the testimony of men prominent in the councils of the Church that the conditions prevailing in the Genesee Conference were by no means merely local conditions, but were prevalent throughout the country. The reader will be able to decide for himself whether we have accomplished our undertaking or not. Have we not, at least, made it appear to unbiased minds that Mr. Roberts's statement of the case in "New School Methodism" was moderate, and, in the fullest sense of the word, justifiable?

CHAPTER XV

RELIGION OF THE SO-CALLED NAZARITES

The so-called "Nazarites" were generally characterized by their opponents as a set of "fanatics," "spurious reformers," "false prophets," and by other equally offensive epithets, all designed to make it appear that they were made up of a class of irrational and irresponsible weaklings, to be regarded with mingled pity and contempt. It will only be fair and right, therefore, to give the reader such a view of their religion in its practical workings as the times then current variously reflected, that he may judge for himself as to whether their opponents were right or wrong in so characterizing them.

As we learn much about the true character of early Christianity by what its enemies said and wrote about the Christians of those days, so we may learn much as to the character of the proscribed religion in the Genesee Conference of the Methodist Episcopal Church in the decade between 1850 and 1860, by what its enemies said about those who were active in its promotion.

For the articles which the proscribed brethren of that time published the writers assumed full responsibility by publishing such articles over their own names. This is probable evidence that they wrote the truth, and were neither ashamed of it, nor afraid to assume the responsibility for what they had written. Many of those who wrote against them, however, did so over fictitious names, thereby concealing their identity, and declining to be generally known as responsible for what they wrote. For what appeared in the editorial columns of the *Buffalo Advocate* and the *Northern Christian Advocate*, the editors naturally assumed responsibility. Numerous articles were written which were both false and basely vindictive in character by parties whose identity was not disclosed. Such writers were wholesale assassins of reputation, attacking their victims and striking their murderous blows under the cover of darkness.

One of the basest and most reprehensible things a man can be guilty of, in the way of personally wronging others, is to try to blacken character and conceal his identity while doing so. Yet this course was repeatedly pursued with reference to those who labored to bring about religious reform in the Genesee Conference of those days. The following selections from an article, which was published in the Medina *Tribune,* a secular periodical of considerable local influence, September 11, 1856, about one year before the publication of "New School Methodism," is one of the most respectable of its kind. Internal evidence shows it to have been written by some member of the Genesee conference:

NAZARITE REFORMERS AND REFORMATION

Spurious reformers are as plenty as blackberries, and as contemptible as plenty. Incapable of comprehending the moral condition and wants of society around them, and also of understanding the modes or processes by which reformation is to be effected, they believe, or affect to believe, that they are the chosen instruments of some greatly needed social regeneration—whose necessity or possibility, none, besides themselves, are able to discover. Mistaking a desire to do something grand, for a call to a great undertaking, and the wish to be known to fame, for a prophetic intimation of some splendid achievement—they go forth before the world, putting on strange and uncouth airs, which they expect everybody will regard as proof of the "divine fury" with which they are possessed; and repeating nonsensical and claptrap phrases, which they have mistakingly selected as the watchwords of a reformatory movement. The ridiculous figure they cut excites the laughter and jeers of all—save those who are as addled and silly as themselves. By such, however, they are frequently mistaken for real prophets; and the gaining of a few proselytes always confirms both in their lunacy.

RELIGION OF THE SO-CALLED NAZARITES

We, of the Genesee Conference, have such a batch of false prophets—such pseudo reformers among us. And such a group of regenerators as the Nazarites compose we can not believe was ever before brought together by the force of a common belief in a divine call to a great work. Whence, or why the idea ever struck them that *they* were the chosen ministers of a new reformation, will probably never be rescued from the dimness and uncertainty of speculation. They probably felt the motion of something within them—it may have been wind in the stomach—and mistook it for the intimations of a heaven-derived commission, summoning them to the rescue of expiring Methodism, and the inauguration of a new era of spiritual life in the history of the Wesleyan movement.

To them, religion still appears to be a system of outward forms and symbols, of material ceremonies, and corporal manifestations, of animal influence and nervous sensations. With them, a long face and sanctimonious airs answer for inward purity and goodness of heart. In their creed, a high-sounding profession takes precedence of a holy life, and getting happy in a religious meeting is laid down as an indubitable proof of the divine favor. With them, a broad-brimmed, bell-crowned hat is equivalent to "the helmet of salvation," and a shad-bellied coat to the robe of righteousness.

But what *means* do these reformers employ to accomplish their ends? Do they go forth to the people with words of truth and soberness, striving to make men better by pressing, with fervent eloquence and earnest, rational appeals, the declaration of God's Word upon the heart and conscience of the hearers? No; their harangues to the people consist of factious addresses, cant phrases, and rant; of protestations of their own spotlessness, and both open and concealed imputations upon the Christian and ministerial character of their brethren. JUNIUS.

Compare the offensive style, the bitter spirit, and the coarse language of these utterances with the dispassionate, dignified, and manly tone of the paper on "New School Methodism," and then decide which is more in keeping with the spirit, precept, and example of Jesus Christ.

"Arguments could not, however, be framed that could answer the spirit of this libel and caricature, so 'offensive in style, bitter in spirit and false in statement.' You can not argue against a sneer. The calm tone in which the facts so distasteful and discreditable to the Regency were stated in New School Methodism only awakened a spirit of bitter hatred against, and a determination to crush, its author."*

Among the older members of the Genesee Conference generally understood to belong to the class against whom the foregoing diatribe was penned were such men as Asa Abell, Benajah Williams, John P. Kent, Samuel C. Church, and Amos Hard—men whose years of loyal devotion to the cause of Methodism merited kinder treatment from the dominant party in the Conference. Then there were such men as William C. Kendall, Loren Stiles, Jr., Benjamin T. Roberts, and I. C. Kingsley, among the younger preachers,—men who, in natural ability, educational acquirements, and general information, were equal if not superior to any of those who opposed them, and in spirituality and general fruitfulness very far exceeded them. What a disgrace to the name of Methodism that such men as these should have had to bear such contempt and vilification from their own conference brethren as is contained in the foregoing article!

As the reader compares the anonymous article on "Nazarite Reformers and Reformation" with Mr. Roberts's article on "New School Methodism," he should bear in mind that the former is quite respectable compared with others of its class, which have been deemed too indecent and scurrilous for general publication.

The following, which appeared as an editorial in the *Buffalo Advocate* of September 15, 1859, though briefer, is quite in keeping with the extract which precedes it, and indicates how its author, as the representative of a large constituency, had so far departed from the spirit and practise of early Methodism that he could write contemptuously of the very type of worship Methodism was originally raised up to perpetuate in the earth:

The approaching session of the Genesee Conference will un-

*"Benjamin Titus Roberts, A Biography," by his son, Benson Howard Roberts, A. M., p. 125.

doubtedly congregate multitudes of people at Brockport, both friends and opposers of the Church. The Nazarite faction, we understand, are to be there in force. Exhorter Purdy [the Rev. Fay H. Purdy, of evangelistic fame in those days] will pitch a large tent, and a thousand or less smaller ones will be smuggled into surrounding lots. We expect to see and hear *a bellowing crowd*,* and anticipate an exciting week. The Conference, of course, will do its business in its own way, irrespective of the outside pressure and attendance, for which it will be no more responsible than it would be for a circus or a menagerie."

Comment is scarcely necessary on an article of such a character. In endeavoring to create a wide-spread prejudice against the earnest and zealous evangelistic efforts of a true son of the Methodist Episcopal Church and those devout and godly men and women who were coöperating with him in seeking a revival of spiritual religion, the writer of the foregoing betrayed unmistakable signs of religious declension, and at the same time unintentionally gave witness that the so-called "Nazarite faction" was composed of men and women alive to God, and filled with the spirit of "aggressive evangelism," regarding which the Methodist Church has been trying in recent years to awaken general interest.

It must be remembered that, according to the nomenclature of the "Regency" faction, "Nazaritism" was a term used in contemptuous designation of old-fashioned Methodism, or "Christianity in earnest." With this recollection borne in mind the reader is asked to consider the following, from the same author as the foregoing extract:

THE TRUE TYPE OF GENERAL NAZARITISM

"An illegitimate offspring often carries with it through life the marks of the sin which gave it being! Excitement governs more people than reason, which accounts for much of the evil, physical and moral, in the world. This quality is a very characteristic element of Nazaritism, leading its followers to improprieties and excesses in religious worship, which give offense to dignity, common sense, and even common decency. Sober, thinking men, whose minds have a balance wheel, are not Nazarites. It is

*Italics are the author's.

the shallow one, of quick impulses, who goes off on short notice, like a brand of fire thrust into a powder magazine; these are the individuals who embrace this modern interpretation of ancient religious notions. Excitement is their life; and if they can *live* by embracing Nazaritism, and be religious in the same connection, nothing is to them more acceptable.*

Once more from the same editor of the "Regency" organ the reader is treated to the following:

NOT OPPOSED TO THE CHURCH

What a fit! Do these men who are constantly raving at the Church, creating divisions, and passing contempt on order and authority, suppose that anybody will believe them when they say that they are friendly to it, and mean to remain in it? Not a word of truth in the assertion. They now only remain in the Church to make a little more capital, for use, not a twelve-month ahead. No element so repulsive and disorganizing can be permitted much longer existence in a Church which seeks peace and good-will among its membership. It is noteworthy that forbearance has not long since ceased, and that these enemies of the Church and haters of its order have not been summarily disposed of and sent adrift.†

The columns of the *Buffalo Advocate* from 1855 to 1860 abound in articles of such a character as those from which these extracts were taken. While meant to do harm to the so-called "Nazarites," unintentionally they reflect the fact that it was opposition to their zeal, intensity, spirituality and uncompromising devotion to the principles of early Methodism that called forth such coarseness and bitterness as they clearly manifest.

But what was the true character of the religion denounced in such intemperate spirit and language? Was it of that irrational, unseemly, fanatical, and dangerous character as to its manifestations which its opponents in the Genesee Conference represented? Was it revolting to men of intelligence generally, and of such a type as would appeal only to the weak-minded, the uneducated, the un-

*Editorial in "Buffalo Advocate" of June 23, 1859. †Do., June 2, 1856.

balanced, the visionary, and the erratic classes in the community? Fortunately we are not dependent alone on the representations regarding this matter which the "Regency" men of the Genesee Conference have left on record for our information. Other men, ministers from other Conferences of the Methodist Episcopal Church, some of them of high standing, who had opportunity to see and learn for themselves, have also left on record their testimony, and that in favor and appreciation of the proscribed religion, as simple, old-fashioned Methodism. A few of these testimonies will now be given.

The first is a report of the Bergen camp-meeting, written by the Rev. William Reddy, a devoted man of God, and for many years Presiding Elder in the Oneida Conference, and published in the *Northern Christian Advocate.* This camp-meeting was regarded by the Regency as one of the worst exhibitions of the religion they so vehemently denounced. It was declared by some among them to be "a hot-bed of fanaticism." The particular meeting here referred to was held in the spring or early summer of 1858, a few months prior to Mr. Roberts's expulsion.

THE BERGEN CAMP-MEETING

There were one hundred and four tents on the ground, in a delightful woods owned by the Association, and which may be very much improved with a little outlay. God was there. I believed, I felt, He was there; and many were the living witnesses of His power to save, not only to forgive, but also to cleanse from all unrighteousness. I heard old Methodists from Boston and from Connecticut say, with streaming eyes and bounding hearts, "This is as it used to be forty years ago." I confess that I felt my heart strongly united with these "fellow citizens of the saints, and of the household of God." The doctrine of sanctification after the John Wesley standard, the definite way of seeking the blessing, the spontaneous confessions of having obtained it, on the part of intelligent and mature persons, the duty of exemplifying it by self-denial and universal obedience, the keeping the rules of the Discipline, "not for wrath, but conscience' sake," the patient and loving endurance of opposition and persecution for Christ's sake, if need be, were all earnestly taught and enforced, and many were the witnesses. And some of "the priests [ministers] were obedient to the faith," i. e., they were wonderfully blest and baptized.

I learned that quite a large number were converted. I left Brother Ives preaching, while Brother Gorham, of the Wyoming Conference, was to exhort after him.

AUBURN, June 25, 1858. WM. REDDY.

The Rev. B. I. Ives, D. D., also reported this meeting, and much more at length. He was a man whose high and unchallenged standing in New York State Methodism guaranteed his ability to know and to judge as to whether the religious devotions of this meeting were the senseless vaporings and insane ravings of irresponsible men and women, or the simple, earnest, fervent, and intelligent worship of men and women who, like the Methodists of an earlier time, were laudable examples of "Christianity in earnest." Hence we herewith present his report in full:

BERGEN CAMP-MEETING

The meeting was by far the largest that I have ever attended, and is said to have been the largest and best that has ever been held in Western New York. There were a *hundred and four* cloth tents, and many of them were very large, and *all* of them appeared to be well filled. The congregations were large and very attentive all through the meeting. On the Sabbath there must have been at least five thousand people present, and yet, so far as I could discover or learn, the best of order prevailed, and all appeared anxious to hear the "words of salvation."

There were two things connected with this camp-meeting with which I was particularly impressed. The first was the number of intelligent business and influential men that were there with their families, tented upon the ground, and who stayed all through the meeting, laboring for God and the salvation of souls. This is as it should be.

The second thing that I noticed particularly, was the spirit of prayer and labor for the conversion of sinners, and the sanctification of believers, that was manifested from the very commencement to the close of the meeting. I saw nothing like mere visiting or idling away precious time, which I am sorry to say we sometimes see at camp-meetings. But here all appeared to feel as though they had come for one object—the glory of God and the salvation of souls. So much was this the case that when strangers came upon the ground, they were led to say, as several brethren in the ministry and others did to me, "God is here. There is power here; there appears to be a stream of holy fire and power encircling this camp-ground." And so it was. There appeared to rest upon *all*, as they came within the circle of tents, a holy impression that God was there in awful power, to awaken, convert, purify, and save souls. This was realized and felt, not only in the public congregation, and under the preaching of the Word, but in the class- and prayer-meetings that were held in the different tents. Such was the power of conviction that rested upon many of the uncoverted, that in several instances they came unasked into prayer-meetings, and, weeping, requested the people of God to pray for them. And I can but believe that this would be the case all over our land, if the Church of God were baptized with holiness and power. Who does not feel like singing,—

"Oh, that it now from heaven might fall!"

There were over thirty different ministers present, to say nothing of the large band of local preachers who were on hand, "full of faith and the Holy Ghost," and who had a "mind to work." There were several preachers at the camp-meeting from other Conferences, such as Bros. Parker, Gulick, Wood, Wheeler, Brown, Tinkham, of East Genesee, Wm. Reddy, of Oneida, and B. W. Gorham, of Wyoming.

Rev. S. C. Church and Asa Abell (both ex-presiding elders, I believe) had charge of the meeting, and they both appeared very much at home in that kind of business. The preachers all appeared to vie with each other in trying the most effectually to preach Christ to the people, and of course the blessing and power of God attended their efforts. And not in a single instance were sinners invited to come to the altar and seek the Lord, but what there were more or less that came, and generally a large number.

I left the ground the night before the meeting closed, so that I do not know the probable number that were converted or reclaimed, but there must have been a large number; and no doubt *hundreds* will praise God in eternity that they attended the Bergen camp-meeting.

I must not stop until I speak of the Love-Feast that was held at eight o'clock on Wednesday morning, which was indeed a "feast of fat things," and a time of salvation, power, and glory. I was particularly interested in hearing some of the veterans of the cross relate their experience, some of which were the richest I have ever heard; and to see their countenances beam with joy, and lighted with glory, as they would say, "This makes me think of my conversion. This reminds me of the early days of Methodism in this country. This is such a camp-meeting as we used to have thirty, or forty, or fifty years ago."

I saw nothing that appeared "like wild-fire," or mere "animal excitement," during the entire meeting. The motto was: "Order and power." And all the people of God seemed to be baptized with the real, old-fashioned "Jerusalem fire." And I pray God that we may have more of this in all our Churches. Praise God for camp-meetings, and let all the people say, Amen.

AUBURN, June 28, 1858. B. I. IVES.

The following year, but a few months after the first expulsions, another meeting was held on the same ground. The report of this meeting was also written and published by a minister from the Oneida Conference. We also reproduce it in part, that in the mouth of two or three witnesses every word may be established regarding the Bergen camp-meetings, which were so decidedly offensive to the Regency party.

BERGEN CAMP-MEETING

We arrived on the ground on Friday morning (the second day of the meeting) and it seemed that the meeting was farther advanced, in interest and power, than some meetings we have attended were during their last days. It is evident that these persons live nearer to God at home and bring the *real fire* with them.

Saturday morning, June 23.

B. T. Roberts preached at ten o'clock. What was remarkable in this sermon, the speaker did not as much as refer to his troubles, but the sweetest and most heavenly spirit seemed to reign through the whole discourse. If he continues to maintain the spirit he now possesses, his foes must all fall powerless at his feet. Dr. Redfield preached at two p. m. from Matt. 5:16.

At four o'clock the Laymen's Convention met.

We did not see anything in their proceedings, but what we could indorse. These laymen are men of intelligence, power and prudence. May God give the Church more such all over this land. In the evening A. L. Backus preached from Rom. 5:1, subject, Justification by Faith. Sunday morning the writer talked a little from Matt. 21:22. Subject, Prevailing Prayer. The Lord helped. At ten o'clock Dr. Redfield preached from Jer. 9:3. "They are not valiant for the truth." After this, there were prayer circles formed all over the ground, and the *power of God* was greatly manifested among the people. Perfect order reigned, though there were probably 12,000 people on the ground. God's order evidently obtained.

This meeting was one of the strongest we ever attended. We had heard so much about this people, that when we went on the ground, for a little while we were on the *come-and-see bench*, but we soon found that these persons had nothing but what a *few* of our people have in the Oneida Conference. They are a people full of faith, and when they pray, they look for immediate results. They are as intelligent a class of people as you will find in any congregation in the State of New York. They are clear in their views of holiness, according to our standard authors, and according to Scripture. We want to be identified with the principles and doctrines held by this much persecuted people. If there is any shame connected with them as long as they stand where they *now do*, we want to bear our part. J. F. CRAWFORD.

MARATHON, July 15.

CHAPTER XVI

RELIGION OF THE SO-CALLED NAZARITES—CONTINUED

The same year a camp-meeting was held at Black Creek, near Belfast, New York, and not far from the author's early home, which was historic in its character. For more than half a century we have heard people refer to "the Black Creek camp-meeting" as the beginning of their experience either in conversion or in entire sanctification. The author's own father was one of the latter class. He little knew, however, that his attendance at that meeting would cost him his ecclesiastical home; yet such was the case. The next Sabbath he attended the Methodist Church as usual at Cadiz, New York, and there heard his own name "read out" with fourteen others as having withdrawn from the Church, which he had never thought of doing, and all because of attendance upon the so-called "Nazarite camp-meeting."

Two reports of that meeting are worthy of insertion here, the first written by a member of another denomination, and the second by a local preacher from New York City.

LAYMEN'S CAMP MEETING

I have lately attended a Laymen's camp-meeting, which was held near Belfast, Allegany County, New York, ably conducted by Rev. C. D. Burlingham. I sat under the preaching of Rev. B. T. Roberts and Rev. J. McCreery, who are charged with fanaticism and enthusiasm. They are in earnest to have the Church gain heaven, and seek full salvation from all sin. These men are blessed of God. I arrived on the camp-ground Sunday evening. The stars shone brightly on the smiling earth; the voice of prayer rang with music from the leafy temple; a flood of celestial light came down from heaven; the spirit of praise inspired each Christian with the fulness of divine melody; a solemn awe pervaded the hearts of the people; a voice from heaven spake to the impenitent, and rent the veil of sin. Scores were reclaimed and converted to God. Great and powerful manifestations were made. These men of God were conformed in their instructions to the wisdom of God, which flowed down upon them like a golden stream of light from heaven. "Shall they prevail in the combat of evil elements?" In spite of all opposition, and the secret combinations of men, "*They shall prevail.*" Jesus says, "Fear not, I am with you."

PHILLIPSVILLE, July 25, 1859. IRA A. WEAVER,
A Wesleyan.

The following report of the same meeting, and also of the Bergen meeting, was written by a New York local preacher:

OLD-FASHIONED METHODISM

The above is the most proper name I know of to give to the preaching and exhortations and exercises I heard and saw at a camp-meeting which commenced on the sixth and closed on the thirteenth of this month, near Black Creek, in Western New York, and also at a meeting in Bergen, N. Y., which commenced on the twenty-third of last month. I attended both meetings, and heard the blessing of entire sanctification preached and enforced as it used to be by Wilbur Fisk, B. C. Eastman, A. D. Merrill, Asa Kent and others of the old time. Perfect order was observed, and the wicked, as they came on the ground with their large cudgels, seemed to be awed into reverence by the power of the Spirit which prevailed. Many found the Savior, some of whom told us they came to make fun, but God answered prayer, and convicted and converted them; and many heeded the warm invitations of God's servants, and sought and found full redemption in the blood of the Lamb. Oh! that the religion of Western New York may spread over these lands. J. PALMER.

Another laymen's camp-meeting was held in the autumn of 1858, this time within the bounds of the Niagara district. A preacher, said to have been from the Philadelphia Conference, published the following report of it:

MAMMOTH CAMP-MEETING

September 2, 1858. We arrived at Gasport about one o'clock, and took private conveyance to the great, mammoth camp-meeting, about two miles from the depot. This meeting had commenced the day previous, and was in Niagara County, about twenty-five miles from Niagara Falls. Some sixty or seventy tents were pitched on the ground, which has a fine elevation, and is finely shaded with beautiful sugar maple and highland oak.

I had the pleasure of introductions to numerous brethren, and spent some profitable moments with Brothers Roberts, McCreery and Jenkins, and also Brother Johnson of the Wesleyan Connection.

The preaching of the brethren was eminently experimental and practical. Prayer, praise and shoutings were heard from every part of the ground. On Sabbath it was supposed that ten thousand persons were on the ground. I saw no rowdyism during the meeting. I was surprised to learn that camp-meetings were a new thing in that immediate neighborhood. On Sabbath morning, after Brother Roberts had concluded his sermon, Miss Hardy, a member of our Church, and a graduate of Genesee College, arose and delivered an affecting exhortation before the vast auditory. I am glad to see this feature of Methodism revived among us. When Methodism was young and vigorous, we had female class-leaders and exhorters. Brother Ives preached in the afternoon, and notwithstanding the strong wind, his splendid, camp-meeting voice arrested the attention of thousands. On Monday morning we left for Niagara Falls, and the meeting was to continue till Wednesday. I have not heard the final result; but no doubt it was glorious. J. D. Long.

The following is a detailed account of the dedication of the Congregational Free Methodist Church at Albion, New York, which was published in the Buffalo *Morning Express:*

We rejoice in every provision that is made for preaching the Gospel to the masses. The tendency of the exclusive system upon which most of the Churches in the cities and large towns in Western New York are conducted, is to alienate the masses from religious worship. In a Church where a few have their pews which they occupy, as a right, the many will not feel like intruding, nor will they consent to advertise their poverty, from Sabbath to Sabbath, by occupying seats reserved for the poor. Hence, we are glad to chronicle the success which has crowned the efforts to build a Free Church in Albion. The Rev. L. Stiles, who, with others, was expelled by the Genesee Conference, at its last session, for doing his duty as a Christian minister, was invited by the great majority of the Church at Albion, which he had served with great acceptability for the two previous years, to continue his labors among them, as a minister of Jesus Christ, and he accepted the invitation. Rather than have any disturbance, they gave up the Church property, to which they were legally entitled, and proceeded at once to purchase a lot, and erect a house of worship. This house was yesterday dedicated to the worship of God by the Rev. E. Bowen, D. D., of the Oneida Conference of the M. E. Church. His sermon, on holiness, founded upon 1 Cor. 6:20: "For ye are bought with a price," etc., was most able, and impressive, and made a profound impression upon the vast congregation in attendance. In the evening, the Rev. B. I. Ives delivered one of his powerful appeals from the words: "We will go with you: for we have heard that God is with you." The thrilling shouts of the people showed that the truth fell upon ears capable of appreciating it. The house was crowded to its utmost, some 1,300 being present, and many left, unable to get in. The house thus dedicated is a substantial structure, 101 feet by 55. The audience room—the largest in the place—pleasant and commodious, will seat about one thousand persons. A basement, the whole size of the building, entirely above ground, affords pleasant and convenient rooms for class and prayer-meetings, and Sabbath-school. The lecture room in the basement will hold six hundred persons. The house is plainly and neatly furnished, and lighted with gas. The cost of the whole has been in round numbers about $10,000. The whole has been paid or provided for. About $4,500 was raised yesterday and last evening. For this result, credit is due to Rev. B. I. Ives, through whose indefatigable exertion, the whole amount called for was secured. Mr. Stiles has collected a large and intelligent congregation, a devoted, pious, working Church, and with their present facilities for doing good, the best results may be anticipated. The meeting was continued over the Sabbath, the Rev. B. I. Ives preaching with more than his usual power. The sacrament was administered to some four hundred or more communicants, and the season was one long to be remembered. In the evening, the altar was filled with penitents.

With reference to the general charge of fanaticism made against those engaged in the work of revival and reform within the Genesee Conference the Rev. Asa Abell published the following in the *Northern Independent:*

I have been a member of the M. E. Church for over forty-three years, and an unworthy preacher of the Gospel for nearly or quite forty years, and whether I do or not, I am sure I ought to know what is that form of Christianity called Methodism; and although the pressure which some have felt upon them from the strange and unhappy circumstances existing among us for several years past, has, as I have thought, unfavorably modified, in a few instances, (but so far as I recollect, in a comparatively slight degree,) the spirit manifested by some, yet am I constrained to declare that to my apprehension, there is nothing among us where I am acquainted, which justifies the charge of a new type of Methodism. I regard the charge as false and unkind, unless beyond the limit of my acquaintance sentiments are held and acted on, very different from any I know of. I desire, while God lends me breath, to do what—with my feeble powers I can do—to preserve undegenerate and in full force and virtue the true Wesleyan views of *Christian doctrine, experience and practise*, and help propagate the same as extensively as may be among mankind.

I know of no *ecclesiastical political* designs. If any persons have such designs they have not seen fit to entrust them to me. I have often been associated with those who I suppose are meant in the charges, to have such designs, and I cannot call to mind any expression looking in that direction. I think the one grand design of these earnest people, preachers and others, is to spread vital religion among mankind—that is, a real, not a diluted and powerless Christianity."

The Rev. B. T. Roberts in "Why Another Sect?" says:

Men of God from a distance, seeing so much published in the papers against us, came to suspect that the cry of "fanaticism" was only a new form of the old opposition to vital godliness, and many came among us to see and hear for themselves. Thus the venerable Dr. Elliott, author of "Elliott on Romanism," though an entire stranger, came on purpose to see us and attend our meetings. He spent several days with us, in our family, and gave the work his most hearty, public indorsement; and helped it on by preaching and exhorting in the demonstration of the Spirit.

The representations of the religious services of the so-called Nazarites, given in this and the preceding chapters, were written by those who were not of their number; who were not, unless in a single instance, members of the Conference to which they belonged; and some of whom were decidedly bitter against them. Excepting the first four, which are manifestly gross caricatures and contemptuous flings, they bear on their very face the marks of truthfulness. No effort appears to exaggerate or to conceal anything. Moreover, these meetings were the most offensive to the "Regency" power of any they ever complained of; and, if they were merely scenes of senseless ranting, of wild fanaticism, and of such generally indecent performances as has been charged upon them, is it not strange that none of the writers from various Conferences and different denominations who reported them for the religious periodicals thought it worth while to mention such excesses and excrescences?

Take even the article from the Medina *Tribune,* which was written by a Regency Doctor of Divinity, and is not the sneering, bitter, and contemptuous tone of the article, as also its scurrilous and indecent language, and the fact that its author concealed his identity by a fictitious name, at least presumptive proof that it was a case of Cain persecuting Abel, of Ishmael persecuting Isaac, of him that was born after the flesh persecuting him that was born after the Spirit, which is to be the invariable order until the Millennial dispensation dawns? The article reads much like the many coarse and base assaults that were made through the public press against the Methodists of John Wesley's time, and which were provoked by that fearless faithfulness which made the early Methodists such a mighty band in the exposure of formalism and false religion, and for the rebuke of sin both without and within the nominal Church. Such faithfulness spares no man's idols; and when the vanity, falsity, and diabolical character of a man's idolatry is exposed, whether it be the idolatry that worships gods of wood, stone, brass, or other material, or the idolatry of wealth, fame, fashion, pleasure, society, or fraternity relations, that man is either going to break with his idolatry, or, "joined to his idols," become a malicious persecutor of those who have exposed his idolatrous wickedness.

Consider also that many of these persecuted brethren lived for years after these slanderous things were published. During those years they held such prominent positions as brought them into general recognition. Moreover, some of them are still living and filling such positions; and during all this time, neither those who are now dead nor those who are still alive betrayed any tendencies to ranting fanaticism or wild enthusiasm. Their work was ever constructive and permanent, of which the Free Methodist Church is in evidence in our own and other lands. These things, we contend, have proven the false and slanderous character of all such allegations and publications as that of the article quoted from the Medina *Tribune* and others similar.

CHAPTER XVII

ECCLESIASTICAL PROSCRIPTION BEGUN—CASES OF JOSEPH M'CREERY AND LOREN STILES, JR.

Forms of persecution sometimes change, but the persecuting spirit never. In St. Paul's day Christians sometimes lost their heads because of their devotion to Jesus Christ. The Apostle himself was awaiting the executioner's ax when he wrote to Timothy, "I am now ready to be offered, and the time of my departure is at hand. I have fought a good fight, I have finished my course, I have kept the faith: henceforth there is laid up for me a crown of righteousness, which the Lord, the righteous Judge, shall give me at that day." 2 Tim. 4:6-8. Nor did he have long to wait before the fatal blow was given, and his body was sent headless to the tomb. But for him the death of the body meant the liberation of the soul, and its translation to the Paradise of God.

Satan's power is greatly restrained in these later days, and in civilized lands, and he is able no longer to instigate those brutal persecutions in which the heads of unoffending Christians are literally sacrificed. The spirit of persecution remains the same, however; and, though its methods are more polite and refined, its animus is as dark and damnable as ever. Though the heads of Christians are not chopped off in our day in the literal sense, yet legions of unoffending followers of the Christ have lost their heads in the ecclesiastical sense, even in this boasted age of Gospel light and freedom, because of their uncompromising devotion to the Master and the principles He represents. Moreover, it has generally been carnally-minded and compromising professors of Christianity who have been the tools of Satan for the accomplishment of this reprehensible work.

Those agitations within the Genesee Conference of the Methodist Episcopal Church which we have been considering in the foregoing chapters finally issued in the ecclesiastical decapitation of many faithful men of God. When all other methods of endeavoring to suppress the revival that had been kindled failed, the "Regency" resorted to the extremity of bringing disciplinary action against prominent leaders in the work. They were charged with "immoral and unchristian conduct," and subjected to partisan trials on trumped-up specifications.

The first victim of this extreme method was the Rev. Joseph McCreery. He was a deeply devoted man, of striking originality, remarkable talents, and with the courage of his convictions. He is said to have been quiet rather than demonstrative in his pulpit ministrations, and yet to have wielded a power under which large audiences were not only deeply moved, but "raised to the highest pitch of excitement." His way of putting things, which was peculiarly his own, had much to do with the effect of his preaching. He spoke to be understood and remembered. He also preached with the unction of the Spirit, and as a result he saw extensive and thorough revivals under his ministry.

Mr. McCreery was of Methodist lineage, and took a just pride in that fact. He was a nephew of the eminent Dr. Samuel Luckey, whose name and fame were familiar throughout American Methodism toward the middle of the last century, and was a most devoted adherent and representative of the Methodist Episcopal Church.

The Rev. B. T. Roberts says of him:

His course reminds us of an Irish girl, whom her Catholic mother had driven from home, because she had been among the Methodists, and become converted.

The girl had found a place as servant in a pious family by which we were entertained, during a session of Conference. The

JOHN S. MacGEARY
Missionary Bishop

[Plate Thirteen]

mother came to the house one morning, and poured upon the poor girl such a torrent of abusive eloquence as we never heard equaled. Becoming intolerable, the gentleman of the house gently put her out. She then went to the gate, and hurled back anathemas and execrations, until, overcome by her rage, she fell in a swoon. The daughter rushed out, bathed her temples, wept over her, and became almost frantic with grief. As we endeavored to console her, she said, with a depth of feeling seldom witnessed, "She is my mother, let her do what she will."

So Joseph McCreery said of the M. E. Church. When turned out on the most trivial accusation, he joined again on probation. When he was dropped, because of the clamor raised by his enemies, and the Free Methodist Church was organized by those with whom he had labored to promote Methodism, he refused for five years to join, and when at last he did unite, such were his yearnings for the Old Church, that he left the Conference in about two years, and went away to the frontier.*

When Mr. McCreery was stationed at Lyndonville, in 1854, he found the work on that charge in a sadly run-down condition. Instead of being content either to let things go on as they had been going, or giving up in discouragement and quit the field, he at once went to work with a view to creating revival interest, restoring the faith of the people which had declined, and building up the work of God in general. He earnestly called upon the people to return to "the old paths" of Methodism and of primitive Christianity. In accordance with the much neglected requirement of the Methodist Episcopal Discipline, he read and explained the General Rules, and in connection therewith reminded the members of the obligations they took upon themselves in joining the Methodist Church. He also informed them that they would be expected to fulfil those obligations, but that if any did not wish to be governed by those rules, such persons would be permitted quietly to withdraw. Such a beginning may seem somewhat extreme to people of this lax age, but Methodists of an earlier time were more accustomed to it, having been educated to strictness in the enforcement of

*"Why Another Sect?" p. 139.

Church discipline. None of the members left, but all newly pledged themselves to conform their conduct to the General Rules, and united in looking for a general outpouring of the Spirit and revival of God's work.

Mr. McCreery also abolished choir singing; or, to use his own words, "Drove out the doves who were billing and cooing in the gallery, and introduced congregational singing, exhorting all and not one in ten only to join in this part of the service." He preached the Word with great fervor, and in demonstration of the Spirit. Nor was his preaching in vain, for great interest was soon awakened, and people were attracted from miles away in all directions, though the snow-drifts were higher than the fence-tops, and a glorious revival followed.

But on this charge lived the Rev. Dr. Chamberlayne, a superannuated preacher, who owned a farm within the bounds of the circuit, on which he resided. "He was a strong man, of a metaphysical turn of mind, cold temperament, and undemonstrative in his manners. He was an advocate of the 'gradual' theory of holiness. Encouraged by large appropriations from the superannuate fund, he suffered himself to be made prominent by the dominant party in Genesee Conference, in their open attacks upon those they called 'Nazarites.' His zeal was also quickened by the fact that his wife, a noble woman, of strong mind, and deep, uniform piety, identified herself with those who were proscribed as 'Nazarites,' and afterward expelled."*

Having allowed himself to be made the tool of the Regency party in the Conference, Dr. Chamberlayne appears to have set about his work of entrapping "Nazarites" like one accustomed to the trapping business. During the year of Mr. McCreery's pastorate over the circuit within which he resided Doctor Chamberlayne kept a memorandum, in which he wrote down a lengthy list of McCreery's odd, characteristic sayings, as they were uttered from the pulpit, but detached from their original connection with

*"Why Another Sect?" pp. 140, 141.

the general trend of his pulpit utterances. This was evidently for the same purpose that moved the scribes and Pharisees of old to send "certain of the Pharisees and Herodians" unto Jesus—"to catch Him in His words."

The following are samples of Mr. McCreery's objectionable sayings: Describing a Church festival of those days, he said: "A whiskered and blanketed blackleg will come along, and pay his quarter for the privilege of fishing a rag-baby from a grab-bag." Referring to the opposition raised against him because of his efforts to bring Methodism back to her former simplicity and purity, he spoke as follows: "Some of the younger boys have taken my mother, the Methodist Church, in her old age, painted her face, curled her hair, hooped her, and flounced her, and jeweled her, and fixed her up, until we could hardly tell her from a woman of the world. Now when I have taken the old lady, and washed her face, and straightened out her hair, and dressed her up in modest apparel, so that she looks like herself again, they make a great hue and cry, and call it abusing mother."

In more recent times many a Methodist minister has been very active in securing the services of the Rev. Sam Jones, a Southern Methodist evangelist, to lecture or conduct revival services in his Church or community, and in providing largely for his remuneration, and that knowing that the chief part of his discourses would be made up of burlesque, sarcasm, and ridicule, directed against the very Church which had secured his services, compared with which the foregoing utterances of Mr. McCreery are certainly venial. But McCreery was a "Nazarite," and McCreery was *in earnest* in his dealings with Methodism; and these were the things that made his utterances so offensive and intolerable to the dominant party in the Genesee Conference.

At the next session of the Annual Conference, held at Olean, Dr. Chamberlayne read before that body the list of sayings he had culled from the Rev. Mr. McCreery's pulpit utterances, and which he considered objectionable and offensive, and, on the strength of those statements, arrested the passage of his character. At this Conference Mr. McCreery also publicly read the "Nazarite Documents," after which his character was passed, subject to an examination before his Presiding Elder, of any charges which might be brought against him. He was removed to another circuit. The Rev. Loren Stiles, Jr., was his Presiding Elder; and, when at last the charges were preferred, he ordered that the trial should be held in Lyndonville, where the alleged offenses were committed, and where the witnesses resided, though it was outside of his district. At the opening of the trial, the counsel for the prosecution made objection to the ruling of the Chairman, refused to proceed with the case, and so the trial was brought abruptly to a close.

The next session of the Conference was held at Medina. Charges were now brought against Mr. Stiles for his administration in Mr. McCreery's case. The Rev. Thomas Carlton and the Rev. James M. Fuller prosecuted the case. At the request of the defendant, the Rev. B. T. Roberts acted as his counsel, and a verdict was secured in favor of the defendant.

This turn of affairs was naturally very exasperating to the "Regency" party. Hitherto they had been in control of only two of the five Presiding Elderships, and were able to muster only about thirty in their secret meetings. Hence they had been unable to control votes enough to secure Mr. Stiles's conviction. Therefore something desperate had to be done, and the necessity of the case suggested the method of procedure. By a threat made to the presiding Bishop that they would all refuse to take work unless Stiles and Kingsley were removed from the Presiding Eldership, and men of their liking appointed in their stead, which has been noted in a previous chapter, these men accomplished their purpose. Apprised of the situation, Stiles and Kingsley were transferred to the Cincinnati Conference at their own request. The design of the Regency party was thereby accomplished.

Then followed an act of administration which can only call forth the disapproval and condemnation of intelligent and unbiased minds. The charges against the Rev. Mr. McCreery were withdrawn, and a series of resolutions reflecting seriously upon him were adopted, in place of a conviction by due process of law. Then, under the reflections thus cast upon him by his Conference, he was again sent forth to shepherd "the flock of God," and to labor for the salvation of lost men. The final action in his case is detailed in a subsequent chapter.

Of course, the men who could be guilty of such unrighteousness in their administration of discipline, could be equally blind to ethical demands when members of their own party were involved in dishonest and scandalous transactions, as the sequel will clearly show.

Complaints of a serious character were lodged against three members of the "Regency" faction at this same Conference. Regarding the character of those complaints and the way they were dealt with by the Conference, we quote from "Why Another Sect?" as follows:

> Enoch Pease, an old Methodist of Niagara County, had lent these preachers about one thousand dollars. They gave him for security what they said was a first mortgage, duly recorded, upon a piece of real estate which they claimed to own, at Lima, N. Y. He let the mortgage run till it was due. The parties meanwhile had failed. On the suit for foreclosure, it was shown that they had bought this property of Dr. T. They paid down only a nominal sum, and gave back a mortgage for the purchase money. At the time of the purchase, Mrs. T. was away from home. The deed and mortgage were both left with the lawyer who drew them up, until Mrs. T. could sign the deed, and then both deed and mortgage were to be recorded together. While these papers thus lay *in escrow*, this mortgage was executed to Enoch Pease. *He never got his money.* These men might not have known which mortgage would hold—but they did know that they had given to one or the other of the parties with whom they were dealing, a worthless security. As soon as the complaints were brought be-

fore the Conference, one of the leading men of their party, I think it was T. Carlton, moved to lay the whole matter on the table. It was seconded and carried, and there it still lies.

With the guilt of the parties we have nothing to do; but we do hold that the Conference which refused to investigate such complaints, made by such a man as Enoch Pease,—in such a manner—for we took his affidavit of the facts in the case, WAS GUILTY OF COVERING UP FRAUD!

Another case is as follows: The same firm, consisting of these three prominent preachers, again wished to borrow money. One of them took a note which the three had signed to Geneseo to borrow five hundred dollars of a Brother White, a Methodist man, who kept a private bank there. Being strangers to him, he took the note to his pastor, the Rev. Jonathan Watts, of the East Genesee Conference, and asked his advice. Mr. Watts told him that he supposed the men whose names were on the note were honest, they were Methodist preachers in good standing, and ought to be, but he knew nothing of their financial responsibility. "But," said he, "the father-in-law of one of them, Dr. B., I know to be a man of means; if he indorses their note, it will be safe." Mr. White took the note back to this preacher, and told him if he would get Dr. B. to indorse it, he would himself indorse it and go to another bank and get the money for them, as he had no money on hand, and would like to accommodate them. The preacher returned the next day with the note indorsed with the name of the Doctor. Mr. White indorsed it, and got them the money on it. The note when due was protested, and Brother White looked to his indorser, Dr. B., for the pay; but instead of him, the Doctor's son, who was financially irresponsible, at their request had signed the note! The note and costs amounted to six hundred dollars, and not a cent was ever paid to Brother White. Soon after, he failed in business, and was reduced to want. He requested Mr. Watts to see one of these preachers, and ask him, as he was getting a good salary as pastor of one of the leading Churches, to pay his proportion or a part of it, to relieve his pressing necessities. *This*, he utterly refused to do. Rev. Mr. Watts sent Brother White money at the time, to keep him and his family from starvation.

We made complaint of this fraudulent transaction to the Conference, backed up by the statement of Rev. J. Watts, in substance as here given. The complaint *was promptly laid upon the table*.

Why did not the victims of such dishonesty prosecute these preachers in a criminal court? Enoch Pease was an old man, wealthy, and did not want the trouble of a prosecution, as he knew he could not get back his money. He was a devoted Methodist, and did not want the Church disgraced.

Mr. White got the preacher who negotiated the note with him indicted, and the preacher fled the state. He joined a conference West, and was, the last we knew of him, a regular preacher in good standing, in the M. E. Church.

At this same session, the Rev. L. Stiles stated to the Conference that he had letters, written by men of good standing in the community, two of them members of the Methodist Episcopal Church, calling in question the business integrity and honesty of a member of the Conference. He asked that a committee might be appointed, to whom these letters might be referred for such action as the committee might deem proper. *But the Conference refused to appoint the committee, or even to hear the letters!**

Do not these things show the animus of the "Regency" faction in its persecution of the so-called "Nazarites," and in its professed zeal to stamp out fanaticism from Western New York Methodism?

---

*Pages 143-147.

CHAPTER XVIII

ECCLESIASTICAL PROSCRIPTION CONTINUED—PROCEEDINGS AGAINST B. T. ROBERTS

The battle over the issue of "Scriptural holiness" was now becoming more and more closely drawn. The "Regency" faction was desperate in the extreme. Matters were well-nigh equally intense on the part of the reform party. Both were coming to feel that the case was one of life or death, and so girded themselves for intenser warfare. What had already occurred was only light skirmishing; what was to follow was warfare that tried men's souls.

When it was found, at the next session of the Conference, that, in accordance with a petition signed by fifteen hundred members of the Church within the Conference bounds, the Rev. L. Stiles, Jr., and the Rev. I. C. Kingsley had been re-transferred to the Genesee Conference, the desperation of the "Regency" element was kindled to the utmost intensity. They saw clearly that heroic measures must be inaugurated, lest they should be brought to account for their misdoings. Accordingly they hired a hall, without even being suspected by the so-called "Nazarites," and held secret meetings at night to plan their method for the continuation of the warfare.

The method adopted was characteristic of the men who planned it, and suited to the end they sought to accomplish. As we have already seen, they now had a majority of the Presiding Elders subject to their control. The next step was to let the young preachers, and those who were unacceptable, understand that the character of their appointments depended upon which of the two parties in the

Conference—the "Regency" party or the so-called "Nazarites" they henceforth identified themselves with. By so doing they were soon enabled to draw enough men from these classes into their secret meetings to make a majority of the Conference. THEN THIS MINISTERIAL CONCLAVE, COMPOSED OF MEN WHO WERE TO CONSTITUTE THE JURY, AND WHOSE PREVIOUS SECRET VOTES COULD BE COUNTED ON IN ADVANCE TO SECURE A CONVICTION, VOTED TO PRESENT A BILL OF CHARGES AGAINST B. T. ROBERTS AND W. C. KENDALL!

Mr. Roberts had just published his article on "New School Methodism," and the charges formulated against him were based upon the contents of that article. The general charge preferred was that of "Unchristian and immoral conduct." The entire bill of charges will be given presently. But first it is proper to state what Mr. Roberts offered to do in order to obviate the necessity of a trial in his case. On presentation of the bill before the Conference, he arose and said:

> I have no intention to misrepresent any one. I do not think I have. I honestly think that the men referred to hold just the opinions I say they do. But if they do not, I shall be glad to be corrected. If they will say they do not, I will take their word for it, make my humble confession, and, as far as possible, repair the wrong that I have done. I will publish in the *Northern Independent*, and in all the Church papers they desire me to, from Maine to California, that I have misrepresented them.

What fairer proposition could he have made? What more could he have been expected to do? What but a predetermination that the man must be sacrificed on the altar of expediency could have induced the majority in an Annual Conference to have rejected so fair and noble a proposition? Not one among them was willing to say that he had been misrepresented in anything Mr. Roberts had written; and yet, as we shall soon see, he was tried and convicted of "unchristian and immoral conduct" for alleged misrepresentations of these brethren in what he had published in "New School Methodism." Why this strange inconsistency? The only solution of the question would seem to be that the "Regency" had been at such great pains to secure their majority for the crushing out of "Nazaritism," that the leaders felt they must now use it, both as a matter of self-justification, and as a damaging blow, if not a death-blow, to the alleged fanaticism of the "Nazarites." One of their number had boastfully declared, and now they must try to make good the boast, "*Nazaritism must be crushed out, and we have got the tools to do it with.*"

The Conference proceeded with the trial. The following account of the proceedings was published by Mr. Roberts in 1879, in "Why Another Sect?" and during all the intervening years has remained unchallenged, which is conclusive evidence of its correctness:

There was little to do, as I admitted that I wrote the article. In my defense I showed:

1. That it is an undisputed principle of common law, that in all actions for libel, the precise language complained of as libelous, must be set forth in the indictment.

"An indictment for libel must set forth the very words; it is not sufficient to aver that the defendant published a certain libel, the substance of which is as follows."—*Brightley's Digest, Vol. II, page* 1631.

"In an action for libel, the law requires the very words of the libel to be set out, in order that the Court may judge whether they constitute a good ground of action."—*Sergent & Rowlin's Reports, Vol. X, page* 174.

2. That if you make a man responsible for the construction which his enemies put upon his words, you might condemn any man that ever wrote. Nay, you could on that principle condemn the Savior Himself. He said: "All that came before me were thieves and robbers." Noah, Job and Daniel came before Him. Therefore He slandered Noah, Job and Daniel, by calling them *thieves and robbers.* In fact our Savior was condemned for the construction which His enemies put upon His words.

3. I showed that in all the important specifications they not only had not given my words; but they had perverted my meaning. I claim the ability to say what I mean. That the contrast between their charges and my words may be the more easily seen, we give both in parallel columns:

"CHARGES AGAINST REV. B. T. ROBERTS.

"I hereby charge Rev. B. T. Roberts with unchristian and immoral conduct.

"1st. In publishing in the 'Northern Independent' that there exists in the Genesee Conference an associate body numbering about thirty, whose teaching is very different from that of the fathers of Methodism.

"2d. In publishing as above that said members of Genesee Conference are opposed to what is fundamental in Christianity—to the nature itself of Christianity.

"3d. In classing them in the above-mentioned publication with Theodore Parker and Mr. Newman as regards laxness of religious sentiment.

"4th. In charging them, as above, with sneering at Christianity in a manner not unworthy of Thomas Paine, and that falls below that of Voltaire.

"5th. In charging them, as above, with being heterodox on the subject of holiness.

"6th. In asserting that they acknowledge that their doctrines are not the doctrines of the Church; and that they have undertaken to correct the teachings of her standard authors.

"WHAT HE DID SAY.

"1st. Already there is springing up among us a class of preachers whose teaching is very different from that of the fathers of Methodism. They may be found here and there throughout our Zion; but in the Genesee Conference they act as an associate body. They number about thirty.

"2d. This difference is fundamental. It does not relate to things indifferent, but to those of the most vital importance. It involves nothing less than the nature of Christianity itself.

"3d. The New School Methodists affect as great a degree of liberalism as do Theodore Parker and Mr. Newman.

"4th. The following sneer is not unworthy of Thomas Paine himself. It falls below the dignity of Voltaire.

"5th. The New School Methodists hold that justification and entire sanctification, or 'holiness,' are the same—that when a sinner is pardoned, he is at the same time made holy—that all the spiritual change he may henceforth expect is simply a growth in grace. When they speak of 'holiness,' they mean by it the same as do evangelical ministers of those denominations which do not receive the doctrines taught by Wesley and Fletcher on this subject.

"6th. The New School ministers have the frankness to acknowledge that their doctrines are not the doctrines of the Church. They have undertaken to correct the teachings of her standard authors. In the same editorial of *The Advocate*, from which we have quoted so largely, we read: 'So in the exercises and means of grace instituted by the Church, it is clearly apparent that respect is had, rather to the excitation of religious sensibilities and the culture of emotional piety, than the development of genial and humane dispositions, and the formation of habits of active, vigorous goodness.'

"7th. In charging them as above, with attempting to abolish the means of grace—substituting the Lodge for the class-meeting and love-feast, and the social party for the prayer-meeting.

"7th. The means of grace in the use of which an Asbury, an Olin, a Hedding and a host of worthies departed and living, were nurtured to spiritual manhood, must be abolished; and others adapted to the 'development of genial and humane dispositions,' established in their places. The Lodge must supersede the class and the love-feast, and the old-fashioned prayer-meeting must give way to the social party.

"8th. In representing as above, the revivals among them as superficial, and characterizing them as 'splendid revivals.'

"8th. The leaders of the new Divinity movement are not remarkable for promoting revivals; and those which do occasionally occur among them may generally be characterized as the editor of *The Advocate* designated one which fell under his notice, as 'splendid revivals.' Preachers of the old stamp urge upon all who would gain heaven, the necessity of self-d e n i a l—non-conformity to the world; purity of heart, and holiness of life; while the others ridicule singularity, encourage by their silence, and in some cases by their own example, and that of their wives and daughters, 'the putting on of gold and costly apparel,' and

"9th. In saying, as above, that they treat with distrust all professions of deep religious experience.

"REUBEN C. FOOTE.

"LeRoy, Sept. 1st, 1857."

"9th. Treat with distrust all professions of deep religious experience."

I explained to them so clearly that the dullest could not fail to see,

1. That men may "*act* as an associate body," who do not "exist as an associate body." It was true that they had a regularly organized "associate body," but I did not know it, or even suspect it, and so I did not say it.

2. That men might have a difference about what is "fundamental,"—about "the nature itself of Christianity," without any of them being "opposed to what is fundamental," or to the nature of Christianity. In point of fact, the Calvinists and the Arminians —the Unitarians and Trinitarians do so differ.

3. That there is a wide difference between "liberalism," "possessing charity," and "looseness of religious sentiment."

4. That saying "the following sneer is not unworthy of Thomas Paine," is by no means equivalent to saying, "They sneer at Christianity in a manner not unworthy of Thomas Paine."

5. That in saying they mean by "holiness" the same as "evangelical ministers" of the other Protestant Churches generally do,

is by no means charging them with being "heterodox on the subject of holiness."

6. That the article from which I quote fully sustains all I say upon the point involved in the sixth specification.

7. That in showing that if certain views of religion prevailed, "the Lodge must supersede the class and the love-feasts," I did not charge them with attempting to do it, but that this would be the logical result of the teachings that I was reviewing.

8. That in calling their revivals "splendid revivals," I simply quoted from an editorial of their own organ.

9. That in saying they "treat with distrust all professions of deep, religious experience," I simply told what was notoriously true. I heard one of these preachers say, "When I hear a man profess holiness, I feel for my pocketbook." Another said, "If I should find Jesse T. Peck's book on "The Central Idea of Christianity," in my house, I would take it with the tongs and throw it into the fire."

Yet with the matter thus plainly before them, a majority of the Conference voted these specifications, (except the 4th, which was withdrawn) sustained. In doing that, every man of them voted as true what *he knew to be false.* We can not come to any other possible conclusion. They were not ignorant men who did not know what they were about. They were not acting hastily over a matter they did not understand. The case was fairly laid before them. *They deliberately voted that I wrote what they knew I did not write.*

I was sentenced to be reproved by the chair. I received the reproof and appealed to the General Conference.

When the appointments were read, near the end of the session, Mr. Roberts was read off for Pekin, Niagara County, New York. This was about the only part of the Conference territory in which he was a total stranger. So far as he knew he had never seen any one belonging to the Pekin circuit. With faith and courage he proceeded to his new field, but before he reached it a prominent preacher of the "Regency" faction had preceded him, and had informed the members that the preacher sent them had been convicted at the Conference of "unchristian and immoral conduct." This report was also published in the Buffalo *Advocate,* and that *without a word of explanation,* thus leaving people to imagine the grounds upon which his conviction had been secured. They had no means of knowing whether he had been convicted of fraud, drunkenness, licentiousness, or some other crime; and this course was evidently pursued with the intention of embarrassing him on his new field of labor as much as possible, if not with a view to blocking his way to being received on the circuit.

What circuit would willingly receive a preacher whom none of its members had ever seen, and whose coming was preceded by the unqualified statement from a prominent minister of the Conference to the effect that the new appointee had just been convicted of "unchristian and immoral conduct"? It is not to be wondered at, that, in recording the event, Mr. Roberts should have said, "We doubt if any itinerant ever had a colder reception. Even Father Chesbrough, one of the noblest of men, and one of the most loyal of Methodists, at first thought he would not go to hear me preach. 'What have we done,' he exclaimed, 'that a man convicted of immoral conduct should be sent as our preacher?' "

Nevertheless, when the first Sabbath morning of Mr. Roberts's pastorate came round, Mr. Chesbrough concluded not to deviate from his uniform and life-long custom of attending Church service, saying, "It can do no harm to hear him once, anyway." So with his family he attended the service. His son often related afterward how, on their way home, the venerable man rode in silence over a mile, and then said: "Well, Sam, I know nothing about the man, but I do know that what we have heard to-day is Methodism as I used to hear it in the old Baltimore Conference, and as I have not heard it in Western New York."

Mr. Roberts gave himself to the work of the circuit with his characteristic ability and energy, not allowing himself to be cast down or in any wise discouraged by the evil that had befallen him at and following the Conference session. Notwithstanding the indifference of the Presiding Elder, and the open opposition of a few members of the Official

CONGREGATIONAL FREE METHODIST CHURCH
Erected by L. Stiles, Jr., at Albion, N. Y., in 1858

[Plate Fourteen]

FREE METHODIST CHURCH AT ALBION, N. Y.
Remodeled from that erected by L. Stiles, Jr.

[Plate Fifteen]

Board, a mighty revival soon broke out, which continued with increasing power and fruitfulness throughout the year. The work reached the young people, especially, and went so thorough among them that many of them, in their earnest seeking after God, forsook the world, gave up their jewelry and finery, and gladly took the narrow way. Dissatisfied because of this, one of the stewards started prayer-meetings in his house across the street, probably as a counter-attraction. Mr. Roberts paid no attention to this, however, and they soon came to naught, while the work of God went on unhindered.

At the district camp-meeting of that year Mr. Roberts had one of the largest tents on the ground, and many of those who had been saved in his meetings were also present with him and his devoted wife. The meeting was held but three miles from the home of the Presiding Elder, and yet, for some reason, he had never mentioned the subject to Mr. Roberts. During the first three days of the meeting no opportunity was given for public testimony, evidently lest some of those who had been saved in the Pekin revival should tell what God had done for their souls under the labors of Mr. Roberts. Finally one woman, who was free in Christ, broke through the conventionality, and testified with the blessing of God upon her, from which time the tide of salvation began to rise. During the intervals between the meetings at the stand they were kept going in the Pekin tent, where many were converted and many were fully sanctified.

The following report of the work on the Pekin circuit that year was published in the *Northern Independent:*

It can not be denied that we received to our Church as our pastor, a man whom *The Advocate* informed us was tried and found guilty of "immorality;" and judging from the articles which have appeared from time to time in that paper, it would seem that his opposers think "if we let him alone, all men will believe on him;" and the only way to destroy his usefulness is to pursue him with "slanders" and "persecutions."

A recent article in *The Advocate*, which descends to language unbecoming one Christian speaking of another, is hardly worth noticing, as the shafts hurled at Brother Roberts fall far below him. The statement, however, that he was not returned to Niagara Street Church on account of his unfitness, will do well enough among those who have never heard from Brother Thomas [Eleazer Thomas, D. D.] all the facts in the case, which, thank God, there are many who understand as fully as the editor of *The Advocate*, and who dare to tell the whole truth when called upon.

In view, then, of all these things, the grand question to be answered is this: Has the Church prospered under his labors, and has God honored his labors by bestowing His blessing upon them? We feel glad to say that the Church has prospered through the blessing of God, during the year. And all the honor and glory we lay at the feet of Jesus, for without Him His children can do nothing.

Though we have not been favored during the year with the "able, impressive and appropriate prayers," that some of the other Churches have been, we feel thankful that we have had "the effectual, fervent prayer[s] of the righteous man, which avail much." Notwithstanding the many reports which have circulated to the contrary, God has been at work among the people. Between fifty and sixty have professed conversion, about forty of whom have joined on probation. The preaching has been plain, simple and pointed, and in accordance with the doctrines and Discipline of the Church. The consequence has been, very many of the members of the Church have been seen at the altar of prayer, some for justification, some for sanctification. Quite a number have publicly professed to have received the blessing of sanctification. Without an exception, every aged member in our Church has rejoiced to see the return of the days of Wesleyan Methodism, with its uncompromising and earnest spirit.

When Brother R. came among us, our Sunday noon class numbered about fifteen; now the average attendance is, and has been for some time, from seventy-five to eighty. Our prayer-meetings and week evening class-meetings, and they occur every night in the week at various points on the charge, have been better sustained through "haying and harvesting," and have been more interesting than for years past. The Sunday-school has also reached a point in attendance and interest never before attained in its history. There are scores in the Church to-day, who feel to thank God for having sent him among us.

S. K. J. Chesbrough.

South Pekin, Sept. 24, 1858.

The writer of the foregoing was a son of "Father Chesbrough," referred to in a previous paragraph. Later, with his excellent wife, he became a member of the Free Methodist Church, which he served with great efficiency in the ministry for a number of years, and, still later, as Agent of the Free Methodist Publishing House for nearly twenty years. As editor of the *Free Methodist* the author was in close touch with him for nearly nine years of his twenty in the Publishing House, and often heard him relate in substance the events which are narrated in this chapter. They were fully corroborated by his testimony.

CHAPTER XIX

THE CONFLICT DEEPENING—MR. ROBERTS AGAIN ON TRIAL

The determination to crush out "Nazaritism," which was but another name for "the holiness movement," had now become the fixed and settled policy of the Regency power in the Genesee Conference; and the purpose to be true to God and to the work of "spreading Scriptural holiness over the land," for which Methodism originally claimed to have been raised up, was equally settled on the part of the persecuted preachers and their friends. Each party was fully committed to the conflict, which was constantly deepening, and had ventured too far into it to entertain any idea of retreating or surrendering now. The conspirators for the crushing of "Nazaritism" were sharpening their tools and laying their plans for doing desperate execution at the next session of the Conference. We shall see presently how they proceeded.

In his "Cyclopedia of Methodism," Article on "The Free Methodists," Bishop Simpson says: "In 1858, two of the leaders were expelled from the Conference." This is partly incorrect. Two preachers were expelled at that time, but one of them, Joseph McCreery, though prominently identified with the holiness movement and the work of revival and reform in the Conference, not only was never a leader in the Free Methodist Church, but was opposed to its organization in 1860, and did not connect himself with it until five years after it was organized.

With regard to the penalties the Bishop's statement is also equally misleading. The statement would lead one who did not know otherwise to suppose expulsion *from the Conference* was the full extent of the penalty inflicted in these cases. Such, however, is not the case. They were both "expelled from the Conference, and *from the Church.*" Why the whole truth is not stated must be largely a matter of conjecture. It has been suggested that possibly the Bishop was "unwilling to have it appear that the laws of the M. E. Church, *as then administered,* were like the laws of Draco, and punished the slightest offense, or even no offense, with death; or, worse still, like the edicts of Nero, which tortured men for being Christians."

Of course, one would naturally suppose that the offenses committed by these preachers must have been of an exceedingly aggravated character, to merit the infliction of the highest penalty known to ecclesiastical law. Whether or not such was the case will fully appear as we consider the trial proceedings.

The reader will remember what was said in the preceding chapter regarding the report sent out, after Mr. Roberts's first trial, that he had been convicted by his Conference of "immoral conduct." That report was evidently shaped and circulated with a view to producing the impression that he had been guilty of gross iniquity. And what a shame! It is not to be wondered at that many among his close personal friends were deeply wounded at this indignity, added to what he had already borne. Nor is it at all strange that such treatment of a God-fearing minister of Jesus Christ should have been strongly resented and reprobated by some. The attempt on the part of one of his friends to free his own soul regarding what he considered a most unrighteous verdict in the case was finally seized upon and charged to Mr. Roberts himself, by the Regency, as the basis of the second bill of charges, on which he was tried, and expelled from the Conference and from the Church.

That friend was a layman, named George W. Estes, who resided on the Clarkson circuit. He was a man of intelligence, as the sequel to the story will show. He was also a man of influence in his community. He was decidedly alive in religious experience, and had labored effectively with Mr. Roberts in the revival meetings he conducted in Brockport while pastor there.

Entirely on his own initiative, and with Mr. Roberts wholly uninformed as to what he purposed to do, Mr. Estes during the year republished the article on "New School Methodism," together with a short account of the trial, in pamphlet form, defraying all the expenses from his own purse. The following is the complete text of the Estes article, except the bill of charges, which we have already given in the preceding chapter:

TO WHOM IT MAY CONCERN

The foregoing *article in the *Northern Independent* was made the subject of general consultations in private caucuses of the Buffalo Regency, held in a room over Bryant & Clark's book store, at LeRoy, on Thursday, Friday and Saturday evenings of the first week of the Conference, the result of which was the Bill of Charges given below. The manner of committing the feebler of the preachers to the condemnation of Brother Roberts in advance, was on this wise, as related by one present. One of the chiefs of the Regency, acting as chairman, asked: "What shall be done in the case of Brother Roberts? All in favor of his prosecution raise your hands?" The "immortal thirty" raised their hands, and a few presiding elderlings. The chairman then delivered a flaming exhortation to unanimity—that they must be united enough *to carry the matter through*, or it would not do to undertake it. After sundry exhortations, the vote was taken again, and a few more voted. After another season of fervent exhortation, a third vote was taken, in which all, save one, concurred; and the trial and condemnation were determined upon. Beautiful work this for godly, Methodist preachers, deriving their support from honest, religious societies among us! We put their Bill of Charges, with all its ingenious distortion of facts, on record here before the people as follows: (See pages 148, 151).

For several years past there has been the annual sacrifice of a human victim at the Conference. It has been a custom. The religious rites and ceremonies attending this annual lustration assume a legal complexion. The victim is immolated according to law. E. Thomas, J. McCreery, I. C. Kingsley, L. Stiles and B. T. Roberts constitute the "noble band of martyrs" thus far. Who is

*"New School Methodism."

selected for the next annual victim is not yet known. The midnight conclave of the "immortal thirty" has not yet made its selection. No man is safe who dares even whisper a word against this secret Inquisition in our midst. Common crime can command its indulgences—bankruptcies and adulteries are venal offenses—but opposition to its schemes and policies is a "mortal sin"—a crime "without benefit of clergy." The same fifty men who voted Brother Roberts guilty of "unchristian and immoral conduct" for writing the above [named] article, voted to readmit a brother from the regions round about Buffalo, for the service performed of kissing a young lady in the vestibule of the Conference room during the progress of Brother Roberts's trial. "Nero fiddled while the martyrs burned."

Brother Roberts's trial—if it deserves the name of trial—was marked by gross iniquity of proceedings. There are no regular Church canons in the M. E. Church to govern the specific manner of conducting trials. All is indefinite. A glorious incertitude and independence of all legal regulations prevail. The presidential discretion must of necessity have large latitude and range, either high or low, as prejudice or policy may incline. Thus, when a witness was asked if he knew of a private meeting of about thirty preachers at Medina during Conference, he answered, "Yes." When asked for what purpose they met, he answered for "consultation." Here the prosecution perceiving that all this secret caucusing at the Medina Conference to lock out the prayer-meetings, arrange the appointments, oust Presiding Elders, etc., etc., were likely to be brought out, objected to all the questions in the case which were not exactly covered by the verbal terms of the specifications which *they themselves* had artfully framed. And their objections were sustained by the Bishop. Every question as to the meetings of the "immortal thirty"—their doings and teachings —was objected to and ruled out as irrelevant to the specifications.

Having been charged with affirming the existence of an associate body of about thirty preachers in the Conference for purposes indicated in his article, he was denied [the right] to elicit the facts in justification, which he could have proved by thirty witnesses. This right, which any civil or military Court would have allowed him, was denied. Of course, where witnesses refuse to testify, and the judge refuses to compel them to do so, there was no use wasting time in defense. Brother Roberts refused to continue the defense.

Also a commission to take testimony was sent to Buffalo. But when they arrived they found an emissary from the Conference had been sent on before them to take charge of the *Advocate* office, who refused to sell or lend, or suffer to be transcribed, any of the copy of the papers or articles bearing on the case, and who put everybody "on the square" to refuse testimony. Having no power to compel witnesses to testify, the Committee returned with such testimony only as honest men voluntarily offered, which will be hereafter published.

A venerable Doctor of Divinity read the "*auto da fe*" sermon, (prepared for the victim of the previous year) wherein he consigned, in true inquisitorial style, Brother Roberts, body and soul, to hell. This was done in his most masterly manner, evincing no embarrassing amount of idiosyncrasy or other mental cause for superannuation. This venerable D. D., though nominally superannuated, and an annual claimant of high rate upon the Conference funds, is nevertheless quite efficient in embarrassing effective preachers in their work, by concocting "bills of information" and "bills of charges;" and pleading them to hell for the crime of preaching and writing the truth. Whether his plea will enhance the amount of the superannuated collections for the coming year remains to be seen.

It was moved that the vote in Brother Roberts's case should be taken by yeas and nays; but the same spirit of concealment and dread of light, fostered by secret society associations, prevailed here also. Like some in the olden time, they "feared the people," and voted down the motion. The vote to sustain the charge of "unchristian and immoral conduct," for writing and publishing these strictures on New School Methodism, was *fifty-two* to *forty-three*, being a majority of nine. Several members of Conference were absent, and several dodged through fear of the Presiding-Elder influence upon their appointments.

The following preachers, as near as can be ascertained, voted to sustain the charge: I. Chamberlayne, G. Lanning, E. C. Sanborn, H. May, D. Nichols, M. Seager, R. C. Foote, G. Fillmore, A. D. Wilbor, P. Woodworth, R. L. Waite, H. Butlin, S. M. Hopkins, E. E. Chambers, G. W. Terry, J. Latham, H. W. Annis, Z. Hurd, T. Carlton, J. M. Fuller, W. H. Depuy, D. F. Parsons, S. Hunt, J. B. Lanckton, J. McEwen, H. R. Smith, S. C. Smith, G. Smith, L. Packard, C. S. Baker, W. S. Tuttle, J. McClelland, J. G. Miller, J. N. Simpkin, S. Y. Hammond, A. P. Ripley, H. M. Ripley, M. W. Ripley, E. L. Newman, A. Plumley, B. F. McNeal, R. S. Moran, E. M. Buck, J. J. Roberts, S. Parker, F. W. Conable, J. B. Wentworth, S. H. Baker, J. Timmerman, K. D. Nettleton, G. Delamater, W. C. Willing.

Another significant fact was apparent in the case: the power of the Presiding Eldership. Quite a number of preachers would not vote at all. Too honest to aid the conspiracy, and too cowardly to face the "loaves-and-fishes" argument presented by the Presiding-

Elder influence, they sat still and saw the condemnation of the innocent, when they might have prevented it.

The influence of the Book Concern had its effect upon the case. It has become a maxim in politics "that the debtor votes the creditor's ticket." So some indebted to the Concern discreetly refrained from voting at all; while two preachers, having refused to attend the private caucuses of the conspirators, and to pledge themselves in advance to vote for the condemnation of Brother Roberts, were scandalized with a public report of delinquency, in open Conference, by the Book Agent.

But it was the influence of the slavery question which was paramount in the case. The Episcopacy is understood to be conservative on that subject, and "to refer to it judiciously in all the chief appointments." Hence the Buffalo Regency in these days (notwithstanding high professions lately to the contrary, on the eve of election of delegates to the late General Conference) is also eminently conservative on that subject; and must needs commend itself to the central Episcopal sympathy by great zeal against the *Northern Independent.* Its associate editor in this Conference must be *black-washed* in revenge for the temerity of the people in subscribing for the paper. They could not wreak their vengeance on the people, except by proscribing one acknowledged, above all others in the Conference, to be the PEOPLE'S MAN.

The infamous Brockport Resolutions* against the Nazarites, were tacitly indorsed by the Conference in its refusal to entertain the question of official administration involved in their passage. This is their reward for their spaniel loyalty to the *Northern Advocate,* and every other thing that wears the label of "law and order," affixed by a pro-slavery administration. It is stated that two or three Nazarites voted with the Regency against the publication of the slavery report in the *Independent.* Surely it must be true of them, as reported, that they court persecutions and rejoice in being killed off at every Conference. Their strong hold upon the popular mind can not long survive their further blinking the slavery issue. We shall see.

So, brethren in the membership of the Genesee Conference, you see we have a clique among us called the Buffalo Regency—conspiring and acting in secret conclave to kidnap or drive away, or proscribe and destroy, by sham trials, and starvation appointments, every one who has boldness to question their supremacy in the Conference. By threats of insubordination, and farcical outcries of strife and division, they frighten the Episcopacy to give them the Presiding-Eldership power, with its patronage of appointments, and

*See page 223.

having that, of course they command the Conference vote, so far as they dare for fear of the people. We are fast losing our best men. The fearless champions of true Methodism are being cloven down, one after another, in our sight; and we sit loyally still, and weep and pray, and pay our money, yet another and another year, hoping the thing will come to an end.

A thousand of us asked the Bishop to rid us of this incubus, which is crushing us into the earth.

"We will do the best we can," was the stereotyped reply to our loyal entreaties. How many more victims must be immolated, how many societies must be desolated, while the Episcopacy is making up its mind to grapple with this monster power, which is writhing its slimy folds around the Church of God, and crushing out its life? The Episcopacy, which alone has the power, having failed to redress our grievances and rid us of this unmethodistic and foreign dynasty, there is no remedy but an appeal to personal rights. The remedy of every member is within his own reach. For one, I shall apply that remedy. For me, while looking on those preachers standing to be counted (no wonder they objected to the yeas and nays) in the vote to condemn Brother Roberts, at LeRoy, I made up my mind that not one of them—preacher, Presiding Elder or superannuate—should ever receive a cent of my money, on any pretense or by any combination whatsoever. I shall punctually attend Church at my own meeting house—prayer-meetings, class-meetings, love-feasts, and all the means of grace; but if one of those men come there to preach—I can't help that—that is not my business. But I shall neither run a step, nor pay a cent. And if, as has been told, all the domestic missionary appropriations in this Conference are varied from year to year—made and withheld to suit the pockets of Regency men appointed to them—this, as long as it continues, will absolve me from obligations to that cause. The same of the superannuate fund, so long as it is controlled by that dynasty. I agreed to support the M. E. Church as a Church of the living God; not as the mere adjunct of a secular or political clique. GEORGE W. ESTES.

With regard to the foregoing Mr. Roberts says:

I never saw this article until some time after it was published, and was in no wise responsible for its publication. But Mr. Estes —a man of means, an exhorter in the M. E. Church, was responsible, and like a man, he assumed the responsibility. At the last Quarterly Conference in the year, the question of the renewal of his license came up. The Presiding Elder asked George W. Estes if he was the author of that pamphlet? He replied that he was.

Without a word of objection, the Presiding Elder renewed his license as an Exhorter, and soon after went to Conference, and *voted to expel me from the Conference and the Church*, on the charge of publishing *this very pamphlet.**

This is clearly another instance of sacrificing consistency and fairness on the altar of expediency. The Presiding Elder in question was a tool of the Regency faction, one of those men so wanting in the element of moral stamina that when Simon said, "Thumbs down," he was servilely obedient, without any consideration of the inconsistency or unrighteousness of his action. In secret caucus the Regency power had predetermined that Mr. Roberts's ecclesiastical head must go; and, when the test came, the Presiding Elder, though fully informed that George W. Estes, and not B. T. Roberts, was the author of the pamphlet, gave his vote to expel Mr. Roberts from the Conference and the Church on the ground of having republished and circulated "New School Methodism," or having assisted in doing so.

The following is the second bill of charges preferred against Mr. Roberts:

CHARGES.—I hereby charge Benjamin T. Roberts with unchristian and immoral conduct.

SPECIFICATIONS

First, Contumacy: In disregarding the admonition of this Conference, in its decision upon his case at its last session.

Second, In republishing, or assisting in the republishing and circulating of a document, entitled "New School Methodism," the original publication of which had been pronounced by this Conference "unchristian and immoral conduct."

Third, In publishing, or assisting in the publication and circulation of a document, printed in Brockport, and signed, "George W. Estes," and appended to the one entitled "New School Methodism," and containing among other libels upon this Conference generally, and upon some of its members particularly, the following, to wit:

1. "For several years past there has been the annual sacrifice of a human victim at the Conference."

*"Why Another Sect?" pp. 160-168.

2. "No man is safe who dare even whisper a word against this secret inquisition in our midst."

3. "Common crime can command its indulgences; bankruptcies and adulteries are venal offenses; but opposition to its schemes and policies is a mortal sin—a crime without benefit of clergy."

4. That "the same fifty men who voted Brother Roberts guilty of unchristian and immoral conduct voted to readmit a brother for the service performed of kissing a young lady."

5. That "Brother Roberts's trial was marked by gross iniquity of proceedings."

6. That "on the trial, a right which any civil or military Court would have allowed him, was denied."

7. That "a venerable Doctor of Divinity read the 'auto da fé' sermon, wherein he consigned in true inquistorial style Brother Roberts's body and soul to hell."

8. That "this venerable 'D. D.' is quite efficient in embarrassing effective preachers in their work and pleading them to hell for the crime of preaching and writing the truth."

9. That "there is a clique among us called the Buffalo Regency, conspiring and acting in secret conclave, to kidnap, or drive away, or proscribe and destroy, by sham trials and starvation appointments, every one who has the boldness to question their supremacy in the Conference."

10. That "the fearless champions of Methodism are being cloven down one after another in our sight."

11. That "the aforesaid members of this Conference are a 'monster power,' which is writhing its slimy folds around the Church of God and crushing out its life."

Signed, DAVID NICHOLS.

PERRY, October 11, 1858.

The Rev. Thomas Carlton and the Rev. James M. Fuller acted as counsel for the prosecution.

Mr. Roberts was not altogether without premonition of the coming storm. He had been credibly informed of threats made against him. The following is given as an instance:

The Rev. S. C. Church, an old Presiding Elder, and a Freemason as well, but one of those noble-minded members of the fraternity who are better than the principles of their order, and who was indignant that Masonry should be scandalized by being pressed into service by ministers of Jesus Christ for the control of Conference affairs, gave him intimation of what he might have to reckon with in the following communication:

> During the last session of our Conference, at LeRoy, I was conversing with Rev. H. Ryan Smith, about the remark made by Rev. B. T. Roberts on the floor of the Conference, to the effect that the Committee on Education was packed.
>
> Smith said, "One more such statement will blot Roberts out."
>
> In the same conversation, he said, "You had better take yourself out of the way, or you will be crushed."
>
> CARYVILLE, October 20, 1857. SAMUEL C. CHURCH.

Anticipating the arrest of his character, Mr. Roberts had engaged the Rev. B. I. Ives, of the Oneida Conference, to act as counsel in his defense, and Mr. Ives was present for that purpose. But the Bishop ruled that counsel from another Conference was not allowable, and firmly adhered to that ruling.

Then, as a majority of the Conference claimed to have been slandered, in their individual character, by what Mr. Roberts had written, and also as he was now informed that they had already virtually voted, in their secret caucus, to condemn him, he called for a change of venue, quoting the wise provision of the civil law, as follows:

"The venue may be changed to another County when the defendant conceives that he can not have a fair and impartial trial in the County where the venue is laid."

He also pleaded that "not one man of the majority would be permitted, under similar circumstances, to sit on a jury in a Civil Court, if twenty-five cents only were at issue." He also quoted the following as authority for the granting of his request:

"If the law says a man shall be judge in his own cause, such being contrary to natural equity, shall be void, for *jura naturae sunt immutabilia;* they are *leges legum.* Natural rights are immutable. They are the laws of laws."—*Hobart's Report, page* 87, *Day vs. Savage.*

It will be plain to every unbiased mind that, in a case

like this, where ministerial reputation was at stake, a thing which the true minister of Jesus holds as dear as his own life, the defendant should have been entitled to everything that could defeat injustice and contribute to a fair trial. But ecclesiastical Inquisitions are usually deaf to all pleadings from the oppressed and persecuted for anything like fairness and justice. *The request was persistently refused.*

Having failed in both the foregoing efforts to obtain anything like fairness in the trial of his case, Mr. Roberts as a last resort, urged that he might be tried by a committee, according to the provision of the Discipline. He expressed his preference for a committee small enough so that each member would feel a sense of personal responsibility for his action, even though the committee should be composed of those who were most strongly committed against him, rather than to have it go before the entire Conference, where members could hide behind each other. To one who reads the story more than half a century later, when all the heat of controversy and all the personal animosities that entered into the case at the time have passed away, the foregoing appears as an altogether fair and reasonable request. *But again his request was refused!*

It has been said by an eminent writer that "Law is not law if it violates the principles of eternal justice." And certainly "the principles of eternal justice" were so involved in this case that, from the present point of view, it is difficult to see how, with any regard for those principles, all the foregoing requests could have been denied. We are not surprised that Mr. Roberts, writing of these decisions nearly twenty years afterward, should have said:

> All this, we know, sounds more like the proceedings of the English "High Commission" in the days of James the Second, and Charles the First, than like the doings of a Conference of Christian ministers, presided over by a godly Bishop, in the nineteenth century. Macaulay says of those Commissioners, who covered themselves with infamy, and sent many a godly minister to beg-

gary or to prison: "They were themselves at once prosecutors and judges."

But the facts that we here relate have never been called in question.

These are the conditions and circumstances under which Mr. Roberts was finally subjected to trial. Any one who carefully considers them can not fail to see that his enemies had done all they could do, and still have the semblance of formal ecclesiastical proceedings, to block the wheels of justice. "Nazaritism" must be stamped out at any cost; Roberts was a leader among the alleged "Nazarites;" therefore it had been predetermined to strike at the head of the offensive system, and when the blow was about to be given it was very necessary to preclude the possibility of effective self-defense on the part of the man chosen for sacrifice. How otherwise can such wanton disregard for personal rights and for "the principle of eternal justice" be accounted for?

CHAPTER XX

CRISIS OF THE CONFLICT—ROBERTS AND M'CREERY EXPELLED

Mr. Roberts finally chose his personal friend, the Rev. L. Stiles, Jr., to assist him in his defense, and so the trial proceeded. *No effort whatever was made by the prosecution to prove that the contents of the Estes pamphlet were slanderous, or that they were in any degree untruthful.* This was an undertaking for which they had not the courage. They chose rather to take this point, so vital to the case, for granted. "So at the outset it was assumed that the pamphlet, *the avowed author of which was still an official member* of the M. E. Church, was so wicked in its character, that to aid in its circulation was a mortal offense."

For an offense of so grave a character as that named in the bill of charges one would naturally suppose that a Conference of ministers, in proceeding to try a brother minister, would have such an abundance of reliable evidence as to carry conviction to honest minds generally. Was such the case? Let us see.

The only testimony furnished by the prosecution to sustain the general charge and the three principal specifications, was that given by the Rev. John Bowman—and his testimony was impeached! It was particularly in the essential point of assisting in the publication of the Estes pamphlet, a matter which was stoutly contradicted by Mr. Estes, that Mr. Bowman gave the following testimony:

> I have seen this document entitled, "New School Methodism," and "To whom it may concern," signed "George W. Estes," before. I first saw it on the cars between Medina and Lockport. Brother Roberts presented it to me; several were presented in a package;

there were, I think, three dozen. Brother Roberts desired me to leave a portion of them at Medina, conditionally. He requested me to circulate them; he desired me to leave a portion of them with Brother Codd, or Brother Williams of Medina, provided I fell in company with them. I put a question to him whether they were to be distributed gratuituously or sold. He said he would like to get enough to defray the expense of printing, but circulate them anyhow; he desired me not to make it known that he had any agency in the matter of circulating the document, if I could consistently keep it to myself. I do not know where Brother Roberts got on the cars. My impression is, we were traveling east. I do not know as anything more was said about the payment of printing them; my recollection is not very distinct; he mentioned he had been at some considerable expense."

The prosecution had hoped to put another witness on the stand, namely, the printer of the Estes pamphlet. They had imported him to the seat of the Conference, from thirty-five miles across the country, on the supposition that he would give testimony damaging to the case of the defendant. But when they found that he would tell the truth if put on the witness stand, they had no further use for him. And yet the Rev. F. W. Conable, in his "History of the Genesee Conference," has the effrontery to say: "The printer refused to testify as to the authorship, and we have no law to oblige attendance at an Ecclesiastical Court."*

In a brief review of Mr. Conable's book,† in "Why Another Sect?" Mr. Roberts says:

"Mr. Conable, and all his indorsers who were at the Perry Conference, *know that this is not true.* The most unscrupulous, unless rendered desperate, seldom venture upon a falsehood so glaring. The printer of the Estes pamphlet *was* present at the trial! One of the preachers opposed to me took him there and back, about seventy miles across the country, in a carriage. *They did not* call upon him to testify."

Mr. H. N. Beach, editor of the *Brockport Republican,* was the printer of the pamphlet; and in a personal note to Mr. Roberts, he said:

*Page 646. †See Appendix B, for full text of this Review.

The Rev. E. M. Buck got me to Perry in the case, at the time of the Conference; but I was not called to testify, because, I suppose, my evidence was not what was wanted.

It will be seen from the foregoing that Mr. Conable thus became responsible for the publication of two unmitigated falsehoods—first, in saying the printer of the pamphlet did not attend Court, and second, in saying that the printer refused to testify. Moreover, these statements were voted into the archives of the Genesee Conference of the Methodist Episcopal Church by men who were fully apprised of their utter falsity! "If the light that is in thee be darkness, how great is that darkness!"

In his defense Mr. Roberts proved, from George W. Estes, that he had nothing whatever to do with the publication of the pamphlet. On the direct examination Mr. Estes gave the following testimony:

Brother Roberts had nothing to do with publishing, or assisting in publishing the document under consideration, to my knowledge, and I presume to know. He had nothing to do with the writing of the part that bears my name; I do not know that he had any knowledge that its publication was intended; he never gave his consent that the part entitled, "New School Methodism" should be republished by me, or any one else, to my knowledge; he was never responsible for the publication, either in whole or in part; he never contributed anything to the payment of its publication, to my knowledge; I intended that so far as sold, it should go to defray the expenses of publication; I never sold him any.

On cross-examination he said:

"I never forwarded, or caused to be forwarded, any of them to Brother Roberts; I never gave him any personally; I do not know of any one giving or forwarding him any. I never gave orders to any one to forward Brother Roberts any, to my knowledge."

In regard to the alleged circulation of the pamphlet Mr. Roberts offered the following testimony:

Rev. Russell Wilcox called:

"I am a local Deacon of the M. E. Church in Pekin. I am intimately acquainted with Brother Roberts, the pastor of the Church in Pekin. I do not know that he has ever circulated this pamphlet anywhere; I first saw it after I left home, on my way to this Conference."

Rev. J. P. Kent called:

"I did ask the defendant for one of these pamphlets; I wished to see one of them, and I asked Brother Roberts if he could let me have one; he said he did not circulate them, but he had no objection to my seeing the one he had. This was a few weeks ago, at the Holley or Albion grove meeting; perhaps it was about the first of August."

The only testimony the prosecution brought forward to prove the specifications, and in support of the general charge, was that of the Rev. John Bowman, and even he confessed, *"My recollection is not very distinct,"* and was not sure as to the direction in which they were traveling when, as he alleges, Mr. Roberts gave him a copy of the pamphlet and desired him to assist in its circulation, but says, *"My impression is, we were traveling east!"* Moreover, his testimony was impeached by several members of the Conference.

On the other hand there was nothing hesitant or hazy about the recollection of George W. Estes, whose every statement was direct, positive, and very distinct, like that of a man who means to tell the truth, and is conscious that he is doing so. He asserts that he, and he alone, was responsible for the republication of "New School Methodism," and that Mr. Roberts "never gave his consent" to its republication; that "He [Roberts] had nothing to do with the part that bears my name;" and, also, "I do not know that he had any knowledge that its publication was intended;" that "he never contributed anything to the payment of its publication;" and, finally he says, "I never sold him any."

Mr. Roberts himself says: "The fact is, I had nothing to do with the publishing of the pamphlet, and took but little interest in it. I was busy with other work."

Yet in face of all these contradictions of Mr. Bowman's testimony, and without even circumstantial evidence of any kind to corroborate it, that one man's testimony appears to have outweighed all other testimony given in the case, in the minds of a majority of the Conference—a fact for which there is no other explanation than that of their having predetermined Mr. Roberts's fate in the secret meeting held before any steps toward a trial had been taken. Could any man or party of men sustain a case before an honorable Court of Justice anywhere in the United States on such limited and doubtful evidence? Do not divine and human laws alike provide that "in the mouth of two or three witnesses shall every word be established"? But here is a case in which, by the mouth of one witness, and he hesitant and nebulous in his recollection, the testimony of several witnesses, of distinct recollection and of direct and positive statements, is set aside as valueless! With those who had condemned Jesus Christ before an unlawful secret meeting of the Sanhedrin, no evidence of his innocence could possibly have any weight. It is ever thus when enmity, jealousy, and persecuting hatred usurp the place of calmness, deliberation, and love of righteousness.

It should be remembered that Mr. Roberts, desirous of throwing light on various points raised in the Estes pamphlet, examined many witnesses on those points. In doing so he proved, by witnesses favorable to the prosecution, that secret meetings had been held, and what was done in those meetings, as well as other things not to the credit of the prosecution, some of which have already been considered.

The prosecution and the defense had both rested their cases, and the pleadings were concluded, at an early hour in the evening. The impression made was such that, had the case gone to vote that evening, it can scarcely be doubted that a verdict would have been rendered in favor of the defendant. That is when the case should have been voted on, to say the least, as the chances were then much more favorable for an honest verdict than they could be at a later time. Fearing that a vote that night would insure an acquittal, the leaders of the "Regency" party secured an adjournment, *held another secret meeting,* and so strengthened the nerve of those considered weak and doubtful in the case, that the majority came into the sitting the next morning and voted a verdict of guilty, and then voted the defendant's expulsion from the Conference and from the Church!

Later it was alleged, as an attempted justification of the proceedings in Mr. Roberts's case, that he was expelled because he undertook to prove the Estes statements true. There are two things wrong, however, with that theory: First, Mr. Roberts made no kind of attempt to prove the truth of the statements contained in the Estes pamphlet. With their truth or falsity he had nothing to do in the whole course of his trial. He did, however, state in open Conference, to his accusers, that if shown that he had misrepresented any of his brethren in what he had written, he would, with suitable apology, publish corrections of the same in the various Church periodicals. No one claimed to have been misrepresented, and so no corrections were made.

Not only was the foregoing allegation a baseless fabrication, but it shows the animus of the proceedings by which Mr. Roberts was expelled from the Conference and from the Church in a still stronger light. Think of it! In thus trying to excuse a palpably unrighteous action, at least tacit admission is made of having condemned the object of their persecution, and inflicted upon him the most extreme penalty known in ecclesiastical jurisprudence, *for an offense of which he had not been accused.* He was arraigned and tried on a charge of "Contumacy," but was condemned and ecclesiastically executed for being a "fanatic" and a "Nazarite."

It is not strange, therefore, that the Rev. C. D. Burlingham, commenting on the trials of Mr. Roberts in 1857 and 1858, should have expressed himself in the following pertinent and forceful language:

> It is a notorious fact that those verdicts are not based on *testimony proving criminal acts or words.* Several who voted with,

and others who sympathize with the "majority," have said, "Well, if the charges were not sustained by sufficient proof, the Conference served them right, for they are great agitators and promoters of disorder and fanaticism."

There you have it. Men tried for one thing and condemned for another! What iniquitous jurisprudence will not such a principle cover?

Why not try them for promoting disorder and fanaticism? Because the failure of such an effort to convict would have been the certain result.*

As an evidence that his persecutors did not seriously regard Mr. Roberts as "unchristian" or "immoral" during the period in which proceedings were pending against him, attention is now called to the following facts:

1. His appointments during this somewhat protracted period were all that he could have asked, and were of such a responsible character as they would not likely have been had the "majority" really believed him "unchristian and immoral."

2. Twice during his last trial his brethren in the Conference paid him such tokens of respect as would have been self-stultifying on their part had they believed him guilty of any criminal offense, and such as perhaps no one ever heard of being paid by a Court to a man under trial for a crime of any character. Once they adjourned the trial for a day to attend a funeral in honor of the Rev. W. C. Kendall, who had died during the year; and, perceiving the eminent fitness of the selection, by unanimous vote they appointed Mr. Roberts to preach the funeral sermon before the Conference. He responded to the appointment, and preached on the occasion, with two of the Bishops sitting in the pulpit. On another occasion pending the progress of the trial, the anniversary of the American Bible Society was celebrated, and Mr. Roberts was appointed to preside over these public exercises!

Referring to these events in "Why Another Sect?" Mr. Roberts asks: "Was this in imitation of the old idolaters

*"Outline History," p. 40, Sec. 21.

who first crowned with garlands the victims they were about to sacrifice; or, was it rather the natural homage which men often instinctively pay to those whom they know to be right, even while they persecute them?"

We now briefly present the account of the trial of the Rev. Mr. McCreery on a twofold charge of "Contumacy" embodying substantially and almost identically the same specifications as those accompanying the like charge in the case of the Rev. Mr. Roberts. The proceedings were published in 1860, in pamphlet form, entitled, "Trial of Rev. J. McCreery, Jr., Before the Genesee Conference of the Methodist Episcopal Church, at Perry, N. Y., October 22, 1858," and were reported by S. K. J. Chesbrough, and J. McCreery. The account we now submit was probably written chiefly by Mr. McCreery himself, but is in substantial accord with the officially reported proceedings, a copy of which is before the author as he pens these pages. Some allowances must be made by the reader for the occasional sarcasm indulged, but he may rest assured that the substantial facts in the case are correctly given, while Mr. McCreery's version of it, by its racy style, enlivens the account, and also serves to show, with characteristic conciseness and pungency, the farcical character of his so-called trial before the Conference. The following is his way of putting the matter:

THE TRIAL OF REV. J. MC CREERY, JR.

"Died Abner as a fool dieth."—2 Sam. 3:33.

Rev. J. G. Miller was appointed to assist in conducting the prosecution.

The defendant declined any counsel. He had not been summoned to his *real* trial which had been going on in secret for several nights past in the Odd Fellows Hall, in Perry, and did not think it worth while to trouble any one to act as counsel in a judicial farce.

The prosecutor said they had concluded not to traverse the

items of the Bill of Charges, which had occupied so much time in the preceding trial. "We will limit the case to the two main points of the *Publication* and the *Circulation.*"

The defendant replied they might omit the whole, if they chose —or any part they pleased. He was not at all particular about the matter. It would save time to forego the trial and vote the verdict at once. I appeal to the General Conference. The Bishop remarked that the notice of appeal was premature.

Revs. C. P. Clark and W. Scism testified that defendant had circulated the Estes pamphlet. The prosecution here introduced as testimony, a card about three inches by two, of rather dingy appearance, and seriously nibbled at one corner, and marked on one side with certain ominous and cabalistic letters and figures. * *

The card was grabbed up by S. M. Hopkins, as stated in his testimony, and carefully kept unto the day of doom. The defendant had traveled the Parma circuit, one of the best and most Methodistic in the Conference, for the two years previous, and Hopkins had been sent on by the Buffalo Regency, to watch Brother Abell, and pick up something that might be used in this conspiracy against the defendant. For this service, his masters voted him *sixty dollars* out of the Conference funds, under the pretense that this faithful discharge of duty had lessened his receipts to that amount. On canvassing the Conference, it was found impossible to get a majority committed against Brother Abell; and there was also lack of adequate "help in the gate" to warrant the undertaking. Carlton, who was at the bottom of all this trickery (all the while as sober and solemn as a saint), did not think it policy to attack him seriously. The character of Brother A., was merely arrested, slurred a little, and allowed to pass. So this card was the only available crumb of Hopkins' scratching and picking. After being duly testified to, as herein followeth, it was marked "R" with commendable gravity, and solemnly filed among the documents of this persecution.

Rev. J. B. Wentworth called.—Are you acquainted with defendant's handwriting? Ans.—I am. I have received letters from him. It is my opinion that this card is in his handwriting. I am quite sure it is.

Rev. J. M. Fuller called.—Are you acquainted with defendant's handwriting? Ans.—I am, sir. I have no doubt this card is in his handwriting. I can't say when or where I first saw this card; it was a few weeks since.

Rev. S. M. Hopkins called.—Did you ever see this card before? Ans.—Yes. I saw it first in the pulpit of the M. E. Church, in Parma Center, about the middle of last November. There was a four days' meeting there, called by some a general quarterly meeting. Defendant was there. I saw the Estes pamphlet at that meeting; there was an abundance of them. I saw, as near as I could judge, a hundred or a hundred and fifty copies. I bought some from a carriage in which Sister McCreery rode, and also Sister Fuller, who had been living with them. I did not see the defendant come to the meeting; but, on inquiry, I judged it to be his carriage.

Cross-questioned.—I first saw the card lying on the kneeling stool in the pulpit. I considered it an important document. I thought it might shed light on the fountain whence these fly-sheets came. I am not positive whose buggy the fly-sheets were in. I bought eight copies from the arm-full that was brought from the buggy by Sister Fuller, to whom I paid the money. I do not recollect the exact price I paid. Brother Estes was at the meeting. I do not know whether they were sold on his account or not. Sister Fuller seemed to do the business; whether the money went to Brother Estes or somebody else, I cannot say. I bought a dollar's worth. Part of them I found in the house of Brother Dunn. I paid all the money to Sister Fuller. I do not know that she was living at Brother Duel's at the time; she was at the defendant's house during Conference. I soon found these pamphlets in almost every Methodist family on the circuit.

Ques.—Did you send a copy to any Methodist by mail?

This question was objected to by the prosecutor, who remarked that Brother Hopkins was not on trial for circulating the document. Though a hundred were engaged in a crime, it would not excuse any individual participant.

The defendant wished to show that everybody had circulated the pamphlet. No one ever dreamed of crime or contumacy in doing so. Both Regency and Nazarite preachers, men, women and children, did it with all the freedom they would an almanac or Foxe's Book of Martyrs. The charge of contumacy for doing what everybody else did was a ridiculous farce. Seven hours ago, at the bidding of his masters, this witness stood up and voted Brother Roberts expelled from the Church, on a charge of circulating this pamphlet; and has pledged himself in secret conclave to do me the same service a few hours hence. Now, I wish to say by implication, that the criminality in the case is an after thought; a fiction fabricated for the occasion. Other witnesses have volunteered to tell what they did with their packages. I wish to know what the witness did with his dollar's worth.

The witness stated that he had had a bill of charges served on him, exactly like that against the defendant; in fact it was the identical bill with defendant's name erased, and his own inserted in its place.

The Bishop decided that the witness could not be required to answer so as to criminate himself.

Ans.—I think I did the Church no harm in what I did with the copies I bought; I had the best interests of the Church in view.

The testimony of Brother Estes was substantially the same that he gave in Brother Roberts's trial, to wit: That he alone was the responsible author and publisher of the pamphlet bearing his name. He did not forward a copy to defendant for proof-reading. He had no recollection of ordering the printer to do so. He presumed he ordered it to be sent somewhere, to some body. As the Conference had seen fit to assume that the publication was a crime, he should not put them on the track of any more victims by saying to whom he ordered it sent. Several laymen saw it before it was published. Some advised the publication, and some dissuaded from it. He had been threatened with a civil prosecution for the publication. He was ready for it any day. He alone was responsible; and he was ready and able to prove all he had published, in a civil Court, whenever he should be called upon. Everybody had circulated it.

Testimony for the defense:

Rev. S. Hunt called.—Have you seen in the *Buffalo Christian Advocate*, a notice of the proceedings of the last Conference in the case of Brother Roberts?

Ans.—I think I read a reference to it. (Here Bishop Baker hastily left the chair, and Bishop Janes took it). Ques.—Did that paper give the charge and specifications of the trial? This question was objected to as irrelevant, by the prosecutor, who said, "We are not trying newspapers here."

Defendant: "But we are doing the next thing to it—we are trying a pamphlet. Now I wish to show that newspaper falsehood is justification for pamphlet truth as an antidote. The trial of Brother Roberts had become a notorious newspaper fact. The *Buffalo Advocate* had published *ex parte* reports, whitewashing one side, and blackballing the other. And when it was asked, as it was concerning one guilty of something like the same crime, eighteen hundred years ago, "Why, what harm hath he done?" the only response of this organ of the Genesee Conference Sadducees was: *Unchristian and immoral conduct!* On this text, furnished by a judicial trickery of the lowest grade, the changes were rung; while *the thing he did* was carefully kept out of sight. Truth demanded the republication of "New School Methodism," that people might know what sort of writing it was that was so criminal. And a justifiable curiosity demanded a faithful exposé of the several Carltonian modes of reasoning employed by the masters of this judicial ceremony, to bring the Conference to this strange verdict of "*Immorality*," in the case. The defendant claims it his right to show this in justification of the facts charged in the indictment.

The objection was sustained by the Bishop. Whereupon all further defense was silently declined.

Thus the defensive testimony amounts in all, to two questions and one answer.

The prosecutor made a grandiloquent plea.

The defendant answered not a word.

The defendant was voted guilty of the specifications, and of the charge.

And he was expelled from the Conference and from the Church, by the usual number of votes—50.

SYNOPSIS OF THE VOTE

Regular Regency men	33
Presiding elderlings	15
Serious ninnies, affrighted with the bugbear of Nazaritism	2
Total for expulsion	50
Members who voted against expulsion	17
Members of Conference who did not vote at all	53
Total who did not vote for expulsion	70
Total number of members	120

It will be noticed that a remarkably large number of the preachers did not vote. Carlton had managed to have it carefully whispered around, so loud that all could hear it, that the Bishop was going to make the appointments of the preachers according to their *standing up for the Church, i. e.*, the regency faction,—in this eventful crisis. All the Presiding Elders were *fast friends of the Church, i. e.*, the tools of Carlton, Robie & Co.,—except one; and he was removed at this Conference, and expelled at the next. The skilful rattling of the loaves and fishes in the market baskets labelled P. E. did the thing. It worked both ways; gaining both votes, and blanks, or *no votes.*

This accounts for a large number who would not vote wickedly, and dare not vote righteously. The appointing power is omnipotent;—and he who has the faculty of fawning, or bullying, or deceiving it into his service, can do or be anything he pleases.

Both Mr. Roberts and Mr. McCreery gave notice of appeal to the General Conference, having full confidence that if their cases could come before that body their vindication would be complete, and their restoration to the Church and to the Conference would follow. Their appeals were never permitted to come before that body, however, greatly to their own disappointment and to the disappointment of thousands throughout the borders of American Methodism. The reason will appear as we proceed with our story.

CHAPTER XXI

FURTHER PERSECUTIONS—"A REIGN OF TERROR"

Following the trials of Roberts and McCreery, and pending their appeals to the General Conference—a period of about two years—the spirit of persecution, which had wrought like madness hitherto, was kindled to a vastly higher pitch, even as the fiery furnace of Nebuchadnezzar was heated "one seven times hotter" than its customary temperature for the reception of the Hebrew children. In his "History of the Origin of the Free Methodist Church" the Rev. Elias Bowen, D. D., referring to this period, says:

> The spirit of persecution, already inflamed against the so-called Nazarites, became rampant, and burst forth with a violence which threatened their universal and speedy extirpation. The madness of Saul of Tarsus in persecuting the saints of his time, even unto strange cities, scarcely exceeded the rage with which the living portion of the Church were hunted down by the secret society, worldly-minded, apostate majority of the Conference during this period. The truly faithful, without respect to age, sex, or condition, were brought before inquisitorial committees; and large numbers, lay and clerical, were hustled out of the Church in some way, or forced into the leading-strings of the dominant party. It was, indeed, a Reign of Terror. Ridicule, disfranchisement, sham trial, and various other contrivances, well known to the order of Jesuits, were put under contribution for the crushing out of the life and power of religion; and wide-spread desolation, as the result of these outrageous persecutions, was seen to pervade the Conference throughout all its borders.

The author was old enough at the time to remember quite vividly some of the stormy scenes which were then common, and the general and intense agitation which they produced. His early religious training and impressions were received amid those exciting scenes, in which he was taught, both by precept and example, the nobility of sacrificing everything else for the sake of righteousness and for fidelity to God.

In those days loyal Methodists were not infrequently shut out of the church edifices their money had helped to build; and, when they took to preaching in the schoolhouses, all usually went well until some disaffected preacher or layman would incite the atheists, infidels, Roman Catholics and Spiritualists of the community, and occasionally the members of other Churches as well, to oppose the using of the schoolhouse for religious services. Then these places would be closed against them, whereupon they would betake themselves to private houses, the streets, the woods, rented shops, farmers' barns, occasionally to the Court-houses and theater buildings, and the author recalls one instance of a large and excellent service being held under a Church horse-shed, because of the Church building being closed and locked against their admission. The people were seated in wagons and carriages, and clinging to the timbers of the shed, while the rain was falling copiously without.

But even in these places they were not immune from the spirit of persecution that raged against them. Attempts would often be made to break up their services; under false complaints the officers of the law would be induced to interfere, and arrests and imprisonments would occur; and at other times the worshipers would be made the victims of malicious mischief, their harnesses being cut to pieces, or other property destroyed, while they were engaged in the worship of God. They were also caricatured and basely misrepresented by some of the secular papers, and occasionally were maligned from evangelical pulpits. Even their children were in some cases the victims of this spirit of persecution at the public schools, and instances could be related of this character from the author's personal knowledge which would seem utterly incredible.

FURTHER PERSECUTIONS

Of course some of the grosser forms of this opposition and persecution emanated from the rowdy elements in the various neighborhoods, and so are not to be charged directly to Church members; but the spirit of religious opposition to the "Nazarites" was intense, and the spirit of persecution against them ran high, on the part of the "Regency" element and those who were its tools, and it was chiefly this that "stirred up certain lewd fellows of the baser sort" to heap upon them some of the grosser indignities in the foregoing count.

The following account of outrages perpetrated upon unoffending members of the Methodist Episcopal Church in Niagara County, New York, by the instigation of one of the Genesee Conference preachers, was published in the Niagara City *Herald* of October 8, 1859; and so aptly illustrates the spirit by which it was sought in those days to exterminate the "Nazarites," that it has seemed proper to insert it here:

RELIGIOUS PERSECUTION

Outrages at Cayuga Creek—Methodists Hand-Cuffed and sent to Jail on the Sabbath

The days of persecutions have returned. The spirit of the old inquisition is among us. Our informants, who are some of the most respectable citizens at Cayuga Creek, and wealthy gentlemen, witnessed the strange spectacle of peaceable, devoted Christians, while quietly listening to the preaching of an aged and honored local preacher of the M. E. Church, being arrested, *hand-cuffed as felons, and hurried away to jail,* on charges manufactured for the purpose. We could hardly persuade ourselves we were residents of a free and enlightened country, in the 19th century. It would seem as if the wheel of time had rolled us back to the Dark Ages.

The history of this outrage is briefly as follows: The Cayuga Creek Church forms a part of the Niagara Falls charge. The same preacher officiates at the Falls in the morning, and at the Creek in the afternoon of each Sabbath. Soon after Conference, the pastor went covertly to work to carry out the anti-Methodist doctrine of the "Pastoral Address,"* adopted by the stronger or "Regency"

*An address delivered by the Rev. I. Chamberlayne, of the Genesee Conference of the Methodist Episcopal Church, at its session held at Perry, New York, party of the Genesee Conference. The faithful and efficient Sabbath-school Superintendent, and the Class Leaders were changed, and persons whom the pastor could use, were appointed.

The key of the Church, up to February 15th, had been in possession of A. M. Chesbrough, a trustee, also, hitherto a warm personal friend of the preacher. Mr. C. always had the house open for meetings, furnished lights, and had paid more for building and supporting the Church than any other man. Mr. Simpkins, the preacher, obtained the key and gave it to another trustee, who is not a member of any Church, and who had been the chief agent of "the Regency" in these operations at Cayuga Creek. On the evening of the 16th of February, the Rev. John Cannon, who had been for over thirty years a local preacher, and for some twenty-three years a member of the M. E. Church at Niagara Falls, had an appointment to preach at Cayuga Creek. When the time arrived for opening the meeting, the house was well filled, and to the astonishment of all Mr. Simpkins, *who knew of the appointment*, stepped in and took the control of the meeting, without saying one word to Mr. Cannon. This created quite an excitement, for Mr. C. had preached there often, and is highly beloved.

On the evening of the 23rd of March, when the people met for prayer-meeting, the Church was locked. For the first time since the Church was built, the windows were fastened down. Mr. Chesbrough pried open a window, the door was unbolted, and a meeting was held. The Sabbath morning prayer-meeting, which had for some months been held at an unoccupied house in another neighborhood, had been removed to the Church.

Mr. Simpkins called a meeting of the trustees, two of whom were under his influence. The question of opening the house for Sunday morning prayer-meeting came up. One of the trustees, and not a professor of religion, objected, that the "meetings were too noisy." The newly elected trustee said "the people could pray at home in their closets, or in their fields, that they did not need to come to Church to pray."

Mr. Chesbrough urged that the house should be opened for

---

in the autumn of 1858, and adopted by the "Regency" majority of that body. While assuming to be a plea for union, it was rather a general rebuke of the so-called "Nazarites" for their alleged insubordination, fanaticism, disregard for reputation and the ordinary proprieties of life, and for the introduction of schism into the Churches. To this Pastoral Address a most respectable minority of the Conference presented and later published a very dignified and strong Protest, which, to one reading the history of both sides of those proceedings nearly sixty years later, and with his mental vision unobscured by prejudices, appears to have been a very justifiable denial of the doings with which they were charged. The Protest was signed by L. Stiles, Secretary of the Protest Committee. A Review of the Pastoral Address was also published by "Jonadab," presumably Joseph McCreery, in which with his usual vigor he declared the Address to be "partisan," "slanderous" and "false;" and marshaled a strong array of evidence to sustain his propositions.

prayer-meeting. From this time till the 17th of April, the meetings were held as usual. On that day, Sabbath morning, the people met together at the Church for their customary prayer-meeting. *One of the Regency trustees was posted outside the door with three or four hired men and dogs, to prevent the people from going into the Church.* Mr. Chesbrough asked him by what authority he closed the door. He said "by the authority of the preacher in charge, and a majority of the [two] trustees." He also said, "he was sent to protect the door, and *was going to do it at all hazards.*" The people becoming disgusted, returned home. For four weeks no prayer-meeting was held on Sabbath morning. Mr. Chesbrough visited the preacher twice to get his consent to have the house opened, which was refused each time, and the preacher said that the trustee who guarded the door "knew his wishes."

In the meanwhile the members became uneasy at having no meetings during the long Sabbath mornings. No religious services were held in the place save in the Methodist Church, and it was too far to go anywhere else. An appointment was given out for Father Cannon to preach on Sabbath morning, June 19th. Mr. Chesbrough having obtained a key, opened the door. While he and two others were sitting in the Church waiting for the congregation, the new trustee came up with another man and locked them in, and said, "Mr. Cannon shall not speak here; Mr. Simpkins told me to protect the door at all hazards." His comrade said, "If there is any fighting to be done I want a hand in it." Mr. Cannon quietly held his meeting under a tree, and appointed another in two weeks. When the time came the Regency trustee was at the door with six or seven hired men, and said if they went into the Church that day, before the regular time, they would walk over his dead body. Again the meeting was held under the trees, and another appointment left for two weeks.

When that Sabbath morning came the Regency trustee, Samuel Tompkins, was posted at the door with eleven men—not one of them, save his brother, ever paid one cent towards the erection of the Church,—most of them hired men and boys, with five dogs. Seats placed beside the Church were torn down, and a line was marked out, over which the people were told they must not pass at their peril.

On the evening of the 28th of July, there was an appointment for a prayer-meeting. Mr. Chesbrough had in the meantime put a new lock upon the door, and by his authority the Church was opened. Before the people had assembled, a hired man of the Regency trustee, stepped into the Church and fastened the door by putting a brace against it. The members assembled, but being told by the guard that they could not enter the Church, they quietly dispersed. When they had gone some fifty rods or more, some boys threw in a handful of firecrackers through a broken pane of glass at the man who was holding the door. On Saturday night as the Regency guard were watching the Church, that they might have possession Sunday morning, they said two persons came up to the window and whispered, "There they lie near the door," and then broke some eight or ten panes of glass.

The probability is that it was done by some of the Regency party, in order to make out as bad a story as would best suit their side, *for in fact, they did not even go to the door to see who was there breaking the windows.*

The Regency trustee obtained warrants of a Justice, a special friend, and business partner of his. They were kept through the week, and on Sabbath morning, August 7th, as Rev. John Cannon was preaching in a grove, some four or five constables armed with revolvers, clubs, and shackles, led on by the Regency trustee, came to the congregation, and arrested one of the members of the M. E. Church, and a respectable citizen. They then went to the house of another member, tore him from the bedside of a sick wife, took him near the meeting, and *hand-cuffed* him with the other. They were left *in irons* near the meeting until a part of the constables could go to the village and arrest some five or six more. They were *put in shackles* and then driven in the hot sun, through the dust about a mile. They were crowded into an old lumber wagon used for hauling brick, and hurried to jail. While they were kept near the meeting, some of the most responsible men in Niagara County offered to give any amount of security required; but nothing would answer—to jail they must go.

The form of an examination was gone through with, and though no evidence of guilt was adduced, yet the Justice, to screen his friend, as is supposed, bound them over for trial.

Thus have our free institutions been disgraced by an act of religious persecution that would be better befitting Italy or Rome. The Christians arrested are as quiet and inoffensive men as can be found. Their *real* offense consists in their unwillingness to put their conscience in the keeping of their pastor, and in their earnest endeavors to gain heaven. In short, they are old-fashioned Methodists, designated by their opposers in the Genesee Conference by the persecuted name of Nazarites.

Another and a favorite species of persecution in those days consisted in subjecting those who would not tamely submit to the Regency power to the ecclesiastical guillotine. It was perilous then for a man or woman to have a quickened conscience and the courage to obey its dictates. Such a person might about as well have lived under Roman Catholic rule in the days of the Spanish Inquisition, as to have been a member of the Methodist Episcopal Church in the Genesee Conference. The machinery of the Church would be made quickly effective for his ecclesiastical decapitation. As a specimen of the way in which this was done, even in the case of laymen who had ever been devoted to God and loyal to the Church, we herewith reproduce excerpts from an article which originally appeared in the *Olean (N. Y.) Advertiser*, of April 26, 1860, and with no other apology for the length of the quotation than its pertinency to the subject under consideration:

METHODIST CHURCH DIFFICULTIES

Solemn Mockery of a Trial—Ecclesiastical Guillotine on the neck of Seymour J. Noble!

Mr. Editor: After your very appropriate remarks and suggestions upon this trial, it might perhaps, by some, be thought advisable to allow this matter to rest without further comment. But there are some features of the case that demand the attention of the public, and which concern every man who has a reputation that he would preserve, and place beyond the reach of injury, from such assaults and with such means as were employed in this case.

On Friday, April 6th, at nine A. M., the component parts of an Inquisitorial Court were assembled in due order, in the basement of the church edifice. The judge appeared, solemnly grave. The minister in charge seemed complacently satisfied as he viewed the arrangements, and the jury expressed a "*certain conviction*" in their countenances, as they eyed the accused, standing before them, conscious of his own rectitude, and surrounded by his many friends and sympathizers.

A hymn was read in slow and measured terms. Then all kneeled in prayer, while the Rev. Mr. Hammond, of Portville, who was to preside as Judge, supplicated the throne of grace for wisdom from on high, to direct aright the duties imposed upon him; and as the words—"let no act stand in the way of the salvation of souls," broke in upon the silence, one long, loud, earnest Amen was the response, bursting involuntarily, as it were, from the lips of the kneeling victim of their displeasure.

The religious exercises being closed, the inquisitorial character of the Court began to develop itself by the Presiding Elder rising in his place, and going through the transparent farce of formally deposing W. C. Willing, from his official position as Pastor of the First Methodist Episcopal Church of Olean. No reason was given for this summary proceeding, but it was easy to conjecture why it was done. He had made out the charge, selected the judge, empannelled the jury, and summoned the witness, but there was as yet no prosecutor! The arrangement would not be complete, unless he performed the part of that functionary! The whole Court was the creature of his making, carefully selected and brought together for the arraignment, trial, and *certain* expulsion of one of the members of the M. E. Church. He had done all he could in his *official* position without infringement upon the "Discipline," and hence this "deposition" to enable him to do, what no lay member of the whole society was willing to perform—prosecute SEYMOUR J. NOBLE, on the charge of "IMMORAL AND UNCHRISTIAN CONDUCT!!!"

Mr. Noble plead a general denial and requested the Court to allow him the assistance of Wm. Culver and Doctor Bigelow as counsel.

The *Court* decided the latter gentleman would not be permitted to take part in the trial, as he was not a member of the society.

Dr. Bigelow arose from his seat in a retired part of the room, and said it was unnecessary to make any ruling so far as he was concerned, for before *such* a Court he should be like a "sheep dumb before its shearers."

Mr. Noble objected to W. C. Willing acting as prosecutor, on the ground of his not belonging to the society.

The *Court*, with a distinction so delicate as to make the difference not discernible to ordinary minds, ruled precisely the reverse of its last decision, and W. C. Willing was allowed to act.

Mr. Noble objected to Hiram Webster sitting as one of the jurors, for having said "he would not believe a Nazarite any quicker than he would the devil." He called one witness who testified to Webster's assertion, and offered to bring more, telling the Court, that in his defense he would have to rely upon the testimony of those stigmatized as Nazarites, and if men were to sit upon the jury, who would not believe them quicker than they would the "father of all lies," it looked to him as if the case was already prejudged.

The *Court*, with a coolness challenging precedent, very blandly decided Mr. Webster competent.

Upon the declaration of this decision, the accused, acting under the impression very naturally made upon him, held the Court for half an hour, with an earnest, heart-felt speech; telling them that he could hope for no justice at their hands—that this trial was decided upon long before the alleged consummation of the act for which he stood arraigned—that it was a foregone conclusion, he must be expelled from the Church, and these forms and ceremonies were only designed as an outside show of justice. The flushed countenances, bowed heads, and averted faces of all connected with the Court, told how pungently these scathing truths were realized.

When the accused had stepped from the threshold, his friends followed him, leaving the inquisition comparatively alone. It began its work, and with indecent haste, hurriedly consummated it. A few witnesses were hurriedly examined—the prosecutor hurriedly summed up the case—and the jury rendered a hurried verdict.

The verdict was precisely what it was intended it should be, and what every one conversant with the proceedings had very clearly foreseen, and SEYMOUR J. NOBLE,—a man whose heart and purse, for the last eighteen years, have been open to the requirements and necessities of the Church—whose hard-earned substance during all that time has constantly flowed into her treasury, and whose prayers have been regularly offered up at her sacred altars, is pronounced by a foreign emissary, * * * * * * * as no longer deserving of association. Though his heart yearns for the Church as that of a tender child for its mother, he is not allowed to bend the knee there, but is sent forth into the world with a stigma upon his name, and a reproach upon his Christian character.

In view of all this, may we not reasonably ask, of what value is human reputation in a community where such high-handed efforts to blast and destroy it can be successfully indulged? If *such* attacks upon private character can possibly injure the object aimed at, it shows the necessity of some legal enactment to protect honest men from the operations of such machinery, and from the influence of a spirit that, in other countries and in other ages of the world, has sent men to the rack and to the scaffold, for alleged or suspected heresies.

But in this particular instance, and in this immediate community, the malice that originated these proceedings, and set them in motion, is comparatively impotent and harmless. Mr. Noble has lived here too long, is too well known, and his position as a sincere, earnest Christian, too well established to suffer any permanent injury from such persecutors. It may have some effect abroad, where the parties are unknown; but here, it is looked upon as a farce, and only injures those who have been engaged in the transaction. The charges do not in any way refer to any act of his, as a citizen, a man, or a Christian. In order to have a semblance of a charge against him, his accusers were compelled to fasten upon what has ever been regarded in all civilized communities, as a privileged proceeding. He was engaged as counsel for JAMES H. BROOKS, when arraigned before a similar tribunal, and defended him with a zeal and ability that before any other body of men, would not have been without a saving influence. In the excitement of debate, and the earnestness of his argument, he undoubtedly used strong expressions, and characterized the proceedings as they deserved. It is for language used under such circumstances, that he has now been accused, arraigned and expelled from his Church.

The ruling powers in the Methodist denomination, have by this act proclaimed that no man can remain in their midst who has the courage to assert his manhood and independence; and that no brother in the Church shall defend another accused of heresies, without subjecting himself to the risk of being also expelled, if he employs language that is offensive to the Inquisition before which he appears. In all other tribunals, where men are charged with offenses, the counsel who appears on behalf of the accused is permitted to express his honest convictions of the case, in such terms as his judgment shall dictate; and he is nowhere, and under no circumstances, liable to be called to account, or even censured for a choice of adjectives that the case or the evidence may suggest. When a man joins the M. E. Church, is it to be understood that he surrenders all his rights and privileges in this respect, and if accused of offenses, is the method of his trial, the character of the evidence he offers, and the language he employs in his vindication—all to be dictated and prescribed by those who may be constituted his judges? If this be so, it is well to let the community know it, that they may govern themselves accordingly.

Instances of maladministration like the foregoing were then the order of the day; and not only did they pass unrebuked by those who held the reins of authority, but were gloried in, even as Romanism once gloried in the blood of the martyrs, and would still glory therein over most of the world, did not the civil powers restrain its persecuting spirit.

Churchism had largely taken the place of primitive Christianity, and denominationalism had lamentably supplanted the fervid simplicity and spirituality of the earlier

Methodism. Loyalty to the Methodist Church, as represented by a denominational platform, interpreted and enforced "by 'Conference resolutions,' Episcopal decisions, the precedents of sham trials, and the like, arbitrarily administered," practically constituted the only authoritative system of ecclesiastical jurisprudence in the Methodism of that day. Under this régime, law could be pleaded—either constitutional, statutory, or constructive—for almost any course of administration one might be inclined to pursue, no matter how repugnant to common sense and common justice such course might be. Comparatively little attention was paid to the Constitution, or to the statute laws of Methodism; they were practically obsolete. Special legislation had largely taken the place of that equal legislation for all, which should be the glory of any ecclesiastical body, so far as it engages in legislative functions.

The administration now had for its general objects the securing of personal interests, partisan ends and ecclesiastical popularity, rather than the conservation and promotion of "righteousness and true holiness." Measures were adopted which conscientious brethren could not subscribe to, and then for their refusal to support them, the machinery of the Church was put in motion, by corrupt administration, for their punishment by defamation and expulsion from the Church.

Dr. Bowen has given us an excellent illustration of the working of this principle in the following paragraphs:

> The clergy, who constitute both the legislative and executive departments of the Church, aware of their gross departure from God and Methodism, and the hopelessness of obtaining their support, on the voluntary principle, from a people who had lost all confidence in them as Christian ministers, resolved upon coercive measures; and to insure a support they could not otherwise receive, made it a condition of membership. This new law, introduced into the Discipline in so clandestine a manner as to leave the people unconscious, at least for a while, if not of its existence even, yet of its true import and bearing, was thenceforth to be regarded as a test of loyalty; its one great object being to compel the people to

support the preachers sent to them by the Conference, whatever their character might be; or, in case of failure, to authorize the expulsion of all non-paying members.

Many have already been expelled from the Church—ostensibly for something else, but really for their neglect or refusal to support a Christless, persecuting ministry. Of late, however, the guise has been thrown off, and members have been expelled for the avowed reason that they declined to support the preacher who had been placed over them by the Conference.

The events narrated in this chapter show the spirit that prevailed in the Genesee Conference of the Methodist Episcopal Church prior to that rupture in the Methodist communion which led to the formation of the Free Methodist Church. This spirit led to and instigated the trials of Roberts and McCreery, and was chiefly responsible for the final split in the Church and for the organization of another Methodist communion. The spirit of persecution continued against the representatives of vital godliness until hundreds were driven from their Church home, and hundreds more were so cruelly oppressed within that body which they supposed to be a Church home, that they chose to separate from it, and "go forth without the camp bearing His reproach," rather than to make those compromises of principle that were demanded of them in order that they might have the fellowship of their brethren.

Those were times that tried men's souls and tested their spiritual mettle. In the midst of all these unpleasant and cruel things, however, the persecuted ones generally possessed their souls in patience, and even rejoiced that they were accounted worthy to suffer reproach for their Master's name. The word of the Lord mightily prevailed, the work of the Lord greatly prospered, and the persecuted people of God were filled with peace, and love, and holy joy, and were enabled to say, in the words so often on the tongue of John Wesley, while wicked persecution raged about the heads of the early Methodists, "The best of all is, God is with us."

CHAPTER XXII

LAYMEN'S CONVENTION—A DIGNIFIED PROTEST

The violent course pursued in the trial and expulsion of Roberts and McCreery, and in the general persecution of the so-called "Nazarites" which followed, naturally created wide-spread excitement, not only throughout the Conference, but as well in the "regions beyond." Both the religious and secular papers took the matters under discussion, and nearly all save those which were conducted or utilized in the interest of the "Buffalo Regency," unqualifiedly condemned the action of the Genesee Conference for its oppressive and unrighteous course. Various official bodies throughout the Conference also passed resolutions strongly expressing their disapproval of the outrages the Conference had perpetrated against innocent and holy men.

At length the laymen within the Conference bounds became thoroughly aroused, and felt that something must be done on their part to check, if possible, such oppressive and cruel measures. Isaac M. Chesbrough, of Pekin, Niagara County, N. Y., was the first to suggest the definite line of action to be pursued, namely, the holding of a Convention of representative laymen from all those societies within the bounds of the Conference who were opposed to the oppressive measures adopted and pursued in dealing with the men who had been expelled.

Mr. Chesbrough had been a Methodist for half a century or more. He was a man of much intelligence, sound judgment, unswerving integrity, large experience in practical affairs, and who was generally held in esteem and veneration by all who knew him. "He was always ready to succor the distressed, to encourage the desponding, and to stand by the oppressed. He saw quickly through mere pretensions, abhorred shams, and was not afraid to act up to his convictions." He was one of God's true noblemen, a man such as would be an honor to any community, to any Church, to any nation, in any generation, or in any age.

Mr. Chesbrough's proposal met with general approval. Accordingly a call for such a Convention as he suggested was issued, bearing the signatures of more than one hundred of the leading laymen of the Conference, representing twenty-two circuits and stations. In response to this call one hundred and ninety-five representative laymen, from forty-seven circuits and stations, met in Albion, N. Y., December 1, 1858, to hold a Convention for the purpose of deliberating as to the course to be recommended and pursued in view of existing conditions.

The Convention was preceded by a Laymen's Love-feast, which was held in the Methodist Episcopal Church the first evening. This was a meeting novel in its character, but attended with much of the Holy Spirit's presence, and hence was a service of much interest.

The Convention proper was held in Kingsland's Hall, the first sitting following the Love-feast, at 8:30 p. m. After appropriate devotional exercises the organization was effected, by the election of the following officers: Hon. Abner I. Wood, president; Isaac M. Chesbrough, George W. Holmes, S. C. Springer, G. C. Sheldon, J. H. Brooks, George Bascom, and C. Sanford, vice-presidents; S. K. J. Chesbrough, W. H. Doyle, and J. A. Latta, secretaries.

A committee on resolutions was appointed, consisting of S. K. J. Chesbrough, W. H. Doyle, G. W. Estes, S. S. Rice, John Billings, A. Ames and J. Handly; also a committee on finance, consisting of Nelson Coe, Claudius Brainerd, S. P. Briggs, S. S. Bryant and George W. Holmes. Addresses were made by several, after which the Convention adjourned until 9:00 a. m. the following day.

HON. ABNER I. WOOD
Chairman of all the Laymen's Conventions

ALANSON K. BACON
Member of the Pekin Convention which organized the Free Methodist Church

REV. J. B. FREELAND

MRS. M. H. FREELAND

[Plate Sixteen]

At the second sitting, after devotional exercises and the reading of the minutes, the following Call was read, as setting forth the object of the Convention:

GENESEE CONFERENCE LAYMEN'S CONVENTION

There has been manifested, for several years past, a disposition among certain members of the Genesee Conference, to put down, under the name of fanaticism, and other opprobrious epithets, what we consider the life and power of our holy Christianity. In pursuance of this design, by reason of a combination entered into against them by certain preachers, the Rev. Isaac C. Kingsley, and the Rev. Loren Stiles, Jr., were removed from the Cabinet at the Medina Conference; and the last Conference at Perry, after a trial marked by unfairness and injustice, expelled from the Conference and the Church two of our beloved brethren, Benjamin T. Roberts, and Joseph McCreery, for no other reason, as we conceive, than that they were active and zealous ministers of our Lord Jesus Christ, and were in favor with the people, contending earnestly for those peculiarities of Methodism which have hitherto been essential for our success as a denomination; and have also dropped from the Conference two worthy, pious and devoted young men, viz., Frank M. Warner and Isaac Foster, who, during their Conference probation, approved themselves as more than ordinarily acceptable and useful among the people; and also, at the last session of the Conference, removed from the Cabinet Rev. C. D. Burlingham, the only remaining Presiding Elder who opposed their sway. For several years past they have also, by consummate "clerical diplomacy," removed many of our worthy members from official relation to the Church, for no other reason than that they approved of the principles advocated by these brethren.

Therefore, in view of these facts, and others of a similar nature, we, the undersigned, hereby invite all our brethren who, with us, are opposed to this proscriptive policy, to meet with us in Convention at Albion, on Wednesday and Thursday, December 1st and 2nd, to take such action and adopt such a course as the exigencies of the case may demand. Brethren, the time has come when we are to act with decision in this matter. The Convention will commence Wednesday evening, at 7 o'clock, by holding a laymen's love-feast. We hope our brethren who are with us in this matter will attend.

Following the reading of the Call the matter of enrolment was taken up, and the names of one hundred and ninety-five laymen were given in as being in full sympathy with the purposes of the Convention.

The committee on Resolutions then reported as follows:

As members of the Church of Jesus Christ, we have the deepest interest in the purity of her ministers. To them we look for instruction in those things that affect our everlasting welfare.

Their ministrations, and their example, influence us to a far greater extent than we are perhaps aware of. As Methodists, we have no voice in deciding who shall be our respective pastors. Any one of a hundred, whom those holding the reins of power may select, may be sent to us, and we are expected to receive and sustain him. We may, then, properly feel and express a solicitude for the purity of the ministry at large, and especially for that portion of it comprising the Genesee Conference, within the bounds of which we reside.

In the New Testament, we learn that the Apostles—enjoying, as they did, the inspiration of the Holy Ghost—were accustomed, on important occasions, to consult the brethren at large, and to proceed according to their expressed decisions. We claim that reason and revelation both, give us the right to form and express our opinions of the public actions of the ministers who occupy our pulpits, and are sustained by our contributions. In theory, at least, we, as Protestants, deny the doctrine of Infallibility. It is possible for a majority of a Conference to be mistaken; it is also possible that they may take action which is unjust and wicked. We believe that Conferences, as well as other public bodies, may err, and that their acts are proper subjects of criticism, to approve or condemn, as the case may demand; and that individual members, for an honest expression of their convictions, ought not to be rewarded with proscription or excommunication: otherwise, concealment and corruption would be the order of the day.

We look upon the expulsion of Bros. Roberts and McCreery as an act of wicked persecution, calling for the strongest condemnation. It was also a palpable violation of that freedom of speech and of the press, which is guaranteed to all by our free institutions.

The facts, as we understand them, are these: For years past, among the preachers, there has prevailed a division, growing out of the connection of some with secret societies—a diversity of views upon the doctrine of holiness, and the holding of different views of the standard of justification.

Writers of the Regency party published, in the *Advocate* and other papers, articles doing great injustice to those who were trying to keep up the old landmarks of Methodism. Their partisan representations were producing their designed effects. Many felt that the time had come when a representation of the other side ought to be made.

Accordingly, Rev. B. T. Roberts wrote an article under the title of "New School Methodism," setting forth his views of the questions at issue. The candor and good spirit of his article is apparent. We have ourselves heard different preachers, in sympathy with the "Regency party," set forth views similar to those ascribed to them in "New School Methodism."

For writing this article, a charge of *immorality* was preferred against Rev. B. T. Roberts. He stated in open Conference, to the parties who accused him, that if he had misrepresented them, he would correct and publish his mistake. No correction was made: no one claimed to have been misrepresented.

The charges were sustained by a majority vote, though in the specifications he was accused of having written what no honest construction of his words would bear. It was eagerly published, far and wide, that this useful preacher had been convicted of "immoral and unchristian conduct." To satisfy the general anxiety and desire to know in what the "immorality" consisted, one of our number published a second edition of "New School Methodism," the charges, specifications, and a short account of the trial. For circulating this document, these two brethren were tried at the last Conference, for "immoral and unchristian conduct," and expelled. One witness, and one only, Rev. J. Bowman, testified that Brother R. handed him a package of these pamphlets for circulation, but which he never circulated.

Had the specifications been proved ever so clearly, they would not have constituted an offense *deserving of censure.* Upon such grounds were these men of God, Brothers Roberts and McCreery, expelled from the Conference and the Church. It would have been reasonable to have supposed, that common malignity would have been satisfied with deposing them from the ministry. But such was the malevolence of those controlling a majority of the votes of Conference, that they could not stop short of the utmost limit of their power. Had they not been restrained by the civil law, the fires of martyrdom might have been kindled in the nineteenth century, in Western New York.

So trifling was the accusation against these brethren, that in all the efforts that have been made to vindicate those voting for their condemnation, no one has attempted to show that the testimony justified the decision. Their only defense is, "If these men did not deserve to be expelled for circulating the pamphlet, they did for promoting enthusiasm and fanaticism." If so, why were they not tried for it? Where is the justice of trying men for one thing, and condemning them for another?

In reference to this charge of "fanaticism and enthusiasm," we feel prepared to speak. Our means of information are far more reliable than that of those preachers who bring the accusation. We have attended the "Camp-meetings and General Quarterly Meetings," against which a special outcry has been made as the "hot-beds of enthusiasm." We have sat under the preaching of these brethren who are charged with promoting these disorders—have heard some of them by the year. *We know what Methodism is;* some of us were converted, and joined the Church, under the labors of her honored pioneers. We speak advisedly, then, when we say that the charge brought against Brothers Roberts and McCreery, and the class of preachers denominated "Nazarites," of promoting fanaticism, is *utterly false and groundless.* They are simply trying to have us in earnest to gain heaven. Instead of attacking the Church, they are its defenders. They preach the doctrines of the Methodist Church, as we used to hear them preached years ago; and through their instrumentality many have been made to rejoice in the enjoyment of a PRESENT AND FULL SALVATION. We cannot say this of their opposers. The Regency affirm that they preach the doctrines of holiness. We have yet to hear the first person who has, of late years, experienced this blessing through their instrumentality. On the contrary, we believe some of them have put down the standard of justification, far below what Methodism and the Scriptures will warrant. Whether, therefore, we consider the ostensible, or the real cause of the expulsion of Brothers Roberts and McCreery, the act calls for and receives our hearty and earnest condemnation.

Nor can we pass by, as undeserving of notice, the course pursued by the "Regency party," whenever complaints of a serious character have been brought against any of their number.

Reports that some of them have been guilty of "crimes expressly forbidden in the Word of God," and involving a high degree of moral turpitude, have been current. Complaints have been made, and though the proof of their guilt was deemed ample, yet they have been summarily dismissed, and in such a way as to discourage all efforts to bring to justice, before the Conference, any of the Regency preachers, no matter how wicked and immoral he may be.

Whether in their secret meetings (the existence of which they at first so stoutly denied, but afterwards attempted to defend, when they were fully exposed), any combination, expressed or implied, was entered into to screen their guilty partisans, and persecute their innocent opposers, we have no means of knowing; but it appears to us such has been the result. That we can have confidence in the Christian character of those whose votes are given to condemn the innocent, and to screen the guilty, is impossible. We also strongly disapprove and condemn the course taken by the dominant party in keeping out of Conference young men of approved piety, talent, and promise simply because they have too much Christian manliness and conscience to become the tools of designing and ambitious men. We are true, loyal, God-fearing Methodists. We have not the slightest intention of leaving the Church of our choice. We believe the evils complained of may be cured, and for this purpose we will leave no proper means untried.

One patent remedy is within our reach—the power to withhold our supplies. We are satisfied that no matter how strongly we may condemn the course of the Regency faction, they will not amend, so long as they are sustained. Besides, we cannot in conscience give our money to put down the work of the Lord. Therefore, we wish it distinctly understood, that we cannot pay one farthing to preacher or Presiding Elder, who voted for the expulsion of Brothers Roberts and McCreery, only upon "contrition, confession, and satisfactory reformation."

It may be thought, by some, that such action on our part is revolutionary. But from the following extracts, it will appear that we are only exercising our undisputed rights in a constitutional way.

We are giving unquestionable proofs of our loyalty to the Church, by thus endeavoring to correct one of the most oppressive and tyrannical abuses of power that was ever heard of.

We trust that none will think of leaving the Church; but let us all stand by and apply the proper legitimate remedy for the shameless outrages that have been perpetrated under the forms of justice.

We quote from an Essay on Church Polity, by Rev. Abel Stevens, LL. D. This book has been adopted by the General Conference as a text-book in the course of study for young preachers. Hence it is of the highest authority.

Dr. Stevens says, "Church Polity," page 162: "What check have the *people* on this machinery? It is clear that as the preachers appoint the Bishops, and the Bishops distribute the preachers, the people should check the whole plan by a counterbalance upon the whole ministerial body. This is provided in the most decisive form that it could possibly assume, namely, the power of pecuniary supplies. No *stipulated contract* for support exists in the Methodist economy. The Discipline *allows* a certain support, but does not enforce it; and no Methodist preacher *can prosecute* a civil suit for his salary. The General Conference disclaims all right to tax the property of our members.

"A Methodist Church has no necessity, in order to control or remove the preacher, to prosecute him by a tedious and expensive process at law, but simply to signify that after a given date HIS SUPPLIES CEASE. He cannot live on air; he must submit or depart.

"This would be a sufficient guarantee, certainly; and this check applies not merely to a specific prerogative of the ministry, but to the *whole* ministerial system. The lamented Dr. Emory thus states it:

" 'We have said that the Methodist Episcopal Church possesses effective and substantial security against any encroachments of tyranny on the part of her pastors. For the sober truth is, that there is not a body of ministers in the whole world more perfectly dependent on those whom they serve than the Methodist itinerant ministry. Our system places us, in fact, not only from year to year, or from quarter to quarter, but from week to week, within the reach of such a controlling check, on the part of the people, as is possessed, we verily believe, by no other denomination whatever.' "

Dr. Bond, in his "Economy of Methodism," page 35, says: "The General Conference have never considered themselves authorized to levy taxes upon the laity, or to make any pecuniary contribution a condition of membership in the Church. Our preachers are totally dependent upon the voluntary contributions of the laity; and we thereby have over them a positive and absolute control; for whenever their flocks shall withdraw their support, the preachers will be under the necessity of abandoning their present pastoral relations, and of betaking themselves to some secular occupation. The traveling preacher who depends for bread, both for himself and family, upon the good-will of the lay brethren, can have no temptation to any unwarrantable or odious exercise of authority over them."

In "Ecclesiastical Polity, by Rev. A. N. Fillmore," page 166, we have the following: "Methodist preachers have no means of enforcing the payment of a cent for their support, for although the Discipline provides for a certain allowance, it furnishes no means to obtain it; and there is no article even to *expose a member to censure* for neglecting or refusing to contribute for the support of the Gospel."

Thus the right to withhold supplies, upon good and sufficient reasons, is conceded and urged by standard authors of our Church.

That such a reason now exists, must be apparent to every one that is not entirely blinded to the claims of justice and humanity.

Nor can we approve of the action of the Bishop, in appointing to the office of Presiding Elders, men who participated in the proscriptive measures of the Regency party. We think that station ought to be filled with men who are in sympathy with the life and power of godliness, and who are laboring to promote it. We look upon the Church as an organization established to aid in securing the salvation of souls, and not mainly to raise money.

This Convention originated among ourselves. The first suggestion was made by one of our number. Neither the brethren expelled, nor any of the members of the Conference, had anything to do whatever with calling this Convention. We mention this fact, because the insinuation is frequently made, that the people can do nothing except at the instigation of the preachers. We are not papists—requiring to be instructed by the priesthood at every turn, what action we shall take, or what papers and books we shall read.

We assure our ministerial brethren—both those who have been thrust out of the Conference, and those who remain, who are devoted to the work of spreading Scriptural holiness—that they have our ardent sympathy; and as long as they employ their time and talents in endeavoring to promote the life and power of godliness, we pledge ourselves cordially to sustain them, by our influence and our means, whether they are in the Conference or not. Therefore,—

Resolved, That we have the utmost confidence in Brothers B. T. Roberts and Joseph McCreery, notwithstanding their expulsion from the Conference—ranking them as we do among the most pure and able ministers of the New Testament.

Resolved, That we adhere to the doctrines and usages of the fathers of Methodism. Our attachment to the M. E. Church is earnest and hearty; but we do not acknowledge the oppressive policy of the secret fraternity in the Conference, known as the Buffalo Regency, as the action of the Church, and we cannot and will not submit to the same. We hold it as a gross maladministration under the assumed sanction of judicial forms.

Resolved, That the laity are of some use to the Church, and that their views and opinions ought to command some little respect, rather than that cool contempt with which their wishes have been treated by some of the officials of the Conference, for several years past.

Resolved, That the farcical cry of disunion and secession is the artful production of designing men, to frighten the feeble and timid into their plans of operation and proscription. We wish to have it distinctly understood that we have not, and never had, the slightest intention of leaving the Church of our choice, and that we heartily approve of the course of Brothers Roberts and McCreery in rejoining the Church at their first opportunity; and we hope that the oppressive and un-Methodistic administration indicated in the Pastoral Address as the current policy of the majority of the Conference, will not drive any of our brethren from the Church. Methodists have a better right in the Methodist Episcopal Church than anybody else, and by *God's* grace, in it we intend to remain.

Resolved, That it is a matter of no small grievance and of detriment to the Church of *God,* that these preachers, in their local pastoral administration have deliberately set themselves to exclude from official position in the Church, leaders, stewards, and trustees, members of deep and undoubted Christian experience, because of their adhesion to spiritual religious Methodism, and to supply their places with persons of slight and superficial religious experience, because of their adhesion to a worldly-policy Methodism.

Resolved, That we will not aid in the support of any member of the Genesee Conference who assisted, either by his vote or his influence, in the expulsion of Brothers Roberts and McCreery from the Conference and the Church, until they are fully reinstated to their former position; and that we do recommend all those who believe that these brethren have been *unjustly* expelled from the Conference and the Church, to take the same course.

Resolved, That we recommend Rev. B. T. Roberts and Rev. J. McCreery to travel at large, and labor, as opportunity presents, for the promoting of the work of God and the salvation of souls.

Resolved, That we recommend Brother Roberts to locate his family in the city of Buffalo.

Resolved, That in our opinion, Brother Roberts should receive $1,000 for his support during the ensuing year, and Brother McCreery should receive $600.

Resolved, That we recommend the appointment of a committee of fifteen to carry out the above resolutions, each of whom shall be authorized to appoint collectors as they may deem necessary; and we also recommend the appointment of a treasurer, to whom all moneys received for the purpose shall be paid, and who shall pay out the same, pro rata, to Brothers Roberts and McCreery, and receive their receipts for the same.

Resolved, That a copy of the foregoing preamble and resolu-

S. K. J. CHESBROUGH
In 1865

MR. AND MRS. ISAAC M. CHESBROUGH

[Plate Seventeen]

tions be forwarded to the *Northern Independent*, with a request that the same be published.

S. K. J. Chesbrough, Pekin,
William Doyle, Youngstown,
George W. Estes, Brockport,
S. S. Rice, Clarkson,
John Billings, Wilson,
Jonathan Handly, Perry,
Anthony Ames, Ridgeville,
Committee on Resolutions.

Considerable discussion followed the reading of the report, particularly regarding the exact purport of certain of the resolutions; but the nature of the discussion was such as to bring about a general understanding and agreement, after which the report as a whole was adopted.

The earnest and dignified utterances of the foregoing report, adopted by such a respectable body of God-fearing men, produced a deep impression upon the community. Besides giving an account of the officers elected and of the business done by the convention, the *Orleans American*, by way of editorial comment, expressed itself regarding the doings of the occasion as follows:

On Thursday morning the Convention proceeded to business. The discussions were carried on with animation, in a good spirit, and with marked ability. The action of the Convention was harmonious to a degree that we had not anticipated. It was composed of able men who had set themselves to work in earnest to correct what they believed to be a great evil in the administration of Church affairs. Whether the course adopted will produce the desired result remains to be seen. The number in attendance was much larger than anticipated, all portions of the Conference being represented. W. G. Colegrove came from Smethport, McKean Co., Pa.; G. C. Sheldon from Allegany, and James Brooks from Olean. There was a large sprinkling of gray heads in the Convention. Prominent among the old men was I. M. Chesbrough, of Pekin, who first suggested the holding of a convention, a noble looking old gentleman, formerly from Baltimore. Mr. Jeffres, of Covington, also won golden opinions by the pertinency and ability of his remarks.

In accordance with the recommendation of the Convention, Messrs. Roberts and McCreery gave themselves to laboring throughout the Conference in the name of Christ and for the furtherance of His kingdom, conducting religious meetings as laymen, and laboring as best they could for the salvation of their fellow men. They were careful, however, to state that they claimed no authority from the Methodist Episcopal Church to hold such services, but that they did so because feeling called of God to such labors for the salvation of souls, and on their own responsibility as men and as Christians.

Since their expulsion these brethren had again united with the Church on probation (believing, for reasons to be shown later, that it was right and proper for them so to do), and had received licenses to exhort; but the presiding officer at a subsequent Church trial had decided that they were not members of the Methodist Episcopal Church, even on probation. Besides announcing that they were proceeding in their work as men feeling called of God thereto, and on their own responsibility as men and as Christians, Mr. Roberts published the following in the *Northern Independent:*

> It seems to be a question among the doctors whether I belong to the Church or not. I did the best I could to stay in; and when I was thrust out without my fault, I tried to get back, and really thought I had accomplished it, but the president of a recent Church trial, which trials, by the by, are becoming quite numerous in Genesee Conference, decided that I was not a member, even "on probation." As this was a "judicial decision," an "act of administration," of course it settles the question. But in or out, I trust I may still be permitted to entertain "a desire to flee from the wrath to come." Our excellent Discipline specifies as among the fruits of this desire, "instructing, reproving, and exhorting all we have any intercourse with." This, then, is what I am doing. The Lord has opened a wide door, into which I have entered. I disclaim all authority from man, but simply "instruct, reprove and exhort," because I believe He has called me to it, and He blesses me in it. Everywhere we go, large and attentive congregations listen to the Word with apparently deep interest.

It is speaking within the bounds of moderation to say

that, following developments at the Laymen's Convention, and the entrance of Roberts and McCreery upon their work as advised by the Convention, the "Regency" men became greatly excited. Their excitement found expression at first through the columns of the *Buffalo Advocate* and the *Northern Christian Advocate,* which seemed to vie with each other in pouring upon these excommunicated men, and upon the detested "Nazarites" in general, the vials of their wrath and abuse. The editor of the former journal had appeared inclined to treat them kindly for a season, but now a decided change had come over him. Writing regarding his course Mr. Roberts says:

> Dr. Hibbard treated us with great consideration until a clear majority was obtained against us. Then he went to every length to vindicate every act of the majority, and to create public sentiment against those whom they had proscribed.
>
> The statements which he published in his paper about the proscribed party of the Genesee Conference were so incorrect, that Rev. W. Hosmer, who aimed to tell the truth, wherever it might hit, and who could not bear duplicity, gave him, in an editorial of January 29, 1859, this reminder: "We hope he will remember that even an official Editor is under some obligations to speak the truth."*

Thus, by the means of these publications, assisted by such others as secret society influence enabled them to control in their interest, the opposing majority continued to send forth an incessant stream of exaggeration, misrepresentation, and barefaced falsehood for the defamation of these objects of their scorn and hatred. So glaring and shameless were these periodicals in the foregoing respects that a prominent member of the East Genesee Conference felt constrained to say, somewhat sarcastically, perhaps, of one of them, through the *Northern Independent:*

> If the *Advocate* and the clique whose servile and mercenary organ it is, will only keep from praising us, we shall consider ourselves most fortunate. Their abuse is the highest eulogy.

*"Why Another Sect?" pp. 202, 203.

Their commendation would be insufferable. With any marks of their approbation upon us, we should, as Cain did when he was branded, go out from the presence of the Lord, crying, "My punishment is greater than I can bear."

Moreover, the Editor of the *Northern Independent*, a man of convictions and equal courage to avow them, and whom Church authorities could not awe into silence when he believed he ought to speak, wrote of "The Advocate's Course" as follows in one of his editorials:

The Editor of the *N. C. Advocate* is driving furiously at the "Nazarites." As if the unfortunate brethren designated by this slang term had not been sufficiently persecuted, he pitches into them with characteristic bravery and acumen.

He affects to believe that such a thing as a Nazarite society once existed; other people, however, know better, and his historical developments pass for nothing. By the way, the Editor writes on this subject with little discrimination. He seems to forget that among the most unbearable of things is the triumph of official arrogance over fallen virtue. He should know that the man at whom his shafts are principally aimed, is his equal, in every way, and his superior in learning, in talents, and in all the higher elements of ministerial character. We say these things the more freely, because we have never been a defender of the Nazarites. We have deemed it our duty to let them defend themselves—a work which they are well able to do. Our columns shall always be open to the persecuted. Two papers—the *N. C. Advocate*, and the *Buffalo Advocate*, are fully occupied in the noble work of extirpating these brethren, and to shut our columns against them in this extremity, would be a depth of meanness to which we care not to descend. We have not attacked the Regency, as the dominant party of the Conference is termed. One act of the Genesee Conference we have condemned, because it seemed to us both unwise, and unjust, in a very high degree. Others may approve of the expulsion of Brothers Roberts and McCreery if they please, as this is a free country; but we shall have our own opinion of that matter, together with its cognate difficulties. In dissenting from a majority of the Conference, we occupy no partisan relation —it is an independent judgment of a particular occurrence. All oppression, whether at the North or the South, whether of black men, or white men, is alike wicked, and deserves our cordial detestation. We claim that men should have a fair trial, and that an arbitrary, high-handed way of disposing of them, is only a fresh display of the same rampant spirit of oppression that has kept the African trodden down for ages. But the most singular thing in all this is the remarkable prowess of Brother Hibbard. Whenever the ecclesiastical guillotine cuts off a man's head, he immediately squares himself, like a knight errant, and assaults the dead carcass. He is terrible—against such a foe, Luther and Knox could not equal him.

Other men of prominence in the Church did not hesitate to speak out in unequivocal terms regarding the reputation of the afore-mentioned periodicals for exaggeration and misrepresentation in their utterances regarding the "Nazarites" and "Nazaritism." The Rev. Hiram Matteson, D. D., wrote: "Who does not remember that just before the last General Conference Brother Hibbard had several long articles in the *Christian Advocate,* in advocacy of the very doctrines that he now calls "Nazaritism"? And the Rev. C. D. Burlingham expressed himself as follows: "The *Advocate* is doing its best to maintain its current reputation. For misrepresentation and abuse the *Northern Christian Advocate* is fully entitled to the palm. *Zeal, intense zeal* is usually a prominent trait in the character of a young convert."

CHAPTER XXIII

WAR AGAINST THE LAYMEN

Matters were now approaching a crisis. The dominant party seemed seized by a sort of universal impulse to carry their opposition to the work of God to a degree seldom known in all the history of Protestantism, and which appeared to have in it all the essential elements of ancient Jesuitical persecution.

"Conscious of their strength and flushed with their victory, the preachers used every means to bring the members who opposed the oppressive acts of the Conference into subjection. We have never read, in any period of the Church's history, of the employment by the preachers, of more arbitrary and tyrannical measures than those adopted by the dominant party in Genesee Conference to subjugate those members who would not bow implicitly to their authority. Had such tyranny been exercised by the priests of the Roman Catholic Church, there would have been an outcry raised which would have been heard all over the land and across the Atlantic."*

Professedly they directed their energies to the suppression of extravagance, enthusiasm, and fanaticism; while in reality they were pursuing every one who dared to affiliate or show sympathy with those they believed to have been unjustly expelled from the Conference with attacks more bitter and relentless, if possible, than those by which Roberts and McCreery had been cast out. War was now inaugurated against all who would not bow to the "Regency" faction, *but especially against the laymen.* The most summary proceedings were instituted against

*"Why Another Sect?" p. 206.

them, in which the preacher in charge would frequently appear as prosecutor, witness, judge, and practically as jury, the jury being a servile body of his own selection. Where it was found impracticable to secure enough such pliant tools to serve his purpose, he had no hesitancy in importing them from some distant charge. Disciplinary provisions for safeguarding the rights of members were ruthlessly overridden, the Jesuitical theory that "The end justifies the means" being the rule of almost universal application. The "Nazarites" must be exterminated, and any measure adapted to the accomplishment of that end appeared legitimate, irrespective of its ethical character.

"I will not do your dirty work for you," was the indignant reply of a local preacher on one of the circuits, when asked by the pastor to sit on a jury to expel Claudius Brainerd, an ordained local preacher of piety, ability and irreproachable character. Upon his refusal to accept the position, a man was imported from Buffalo, seventy miles distant, to fill the place.

The special objects of persecuting wrath were those laymen who had attended and participated in the Albion Convention. To have taken this liberty was to have been guilty of a crime meriting the extreme penalty of the Church. Twenty-five or even fifty years of faithful membership in the Church; the most invaluable services rendered in both material and spiritual things; the most ardent piety and the most unsullied reputation for purity of character and holy living, counted for nothing against the flaming wrath of the incensed "majority" in case of any member who had dared to befriend those whom the Conference had excommunicated and anathematized. The more loyal and helpful such a one had been, and the more influential the position he occupied, the more likely he was summarily to be sent to the ecclesiastical guillotine.

It is a matter of historic record that one of the preachers, the Rev. Rufus Cooley, had his character arrested for praying with Mr. Roberts after his expulsion. Mr. and Mrs. Cooley and Mr. and Mrs. Roberts met at the home of Mrs. Cooley's mother. After their adjournment from the tea table, they had a season of prayer, in which both Mr. Cooley and Mr. Roberts prayed. For this offense Mr. Cooley was called upon to answer to a complaint lodged against him at the next session of the Genesee Conference.

One of the first among the laymen on whom the "Regency" sword of vengeance fell was Claudius Brainerd, of North Chili, N. Y. For a number of years he had been a faithful, acceptable, and useful traveling preacher. But his health failed, and he found it necessary because of this to locate. He continued to preach, however, as his state of health would permit, and his services were both acceptable and needed. He was a man of extensive acquaintance, and wherever known was respected as a man of deep spirituality, unbending integrity, and genuine piety—a Christian man of the New Testament pattern. But he had been active in the Albion Convention, and so his head must go. "To make the matter sure, the Rev. J. B. Lankton, preacher in charge, summoned a committee of local preachers from a distance—men who could be depended upon to execute the will of the 'Regency;'" and before that committee he was tried and expelled, on February 14, 1859, for attending the Laymen's Convention at Albion. The bill of charges contained three charges and nineteen specifications, all based upon his relation to that Convention.

Referring to his expulsion in the *Northern Independent* of February 15th, 1859, Mr. Brainerd said:

> Yesterday, I was expelled from the M. E. Church, for attending the Laymen's Convention. No other charge was preferred. For all harsh words or unchristian expressions, just retraction was made. My expulsion was for the expression of my honest sentiments. Had I given up my judgment to an Annual Conference, I could have retained my standing in the Church. But then I should not have been a minister of the Lord Jesus Christ, nor even a Christian. I would die a martyr's death for my own judg-

ment, rather than yield my judgment to an Annual Conference. My soul sweetly rests in Christ. A consciousness of right, and the approval of my Judge, sustain me. I shall unite on trial, the first opportunity, with the M. E. Church. It is time the laity were awake to their own rights in the Church.

Mr. Brainerd appealed his case to the Annual Conference. But that body, contrary to an express provision of the Methodist Episcopal Discipline, refused to entertain the appeal. The provisions of the Discipline were set aside as of no force whatever, except in so far as they could be used for the punishment of "Nazarites."

After his expulsion Mr. Brainerd united with the Methodist Episcopal Church again as he said he would. The Rev. S. McGerald, a converted Roman Catholic, as pastor at Henrietta in the East Genesee Conference, received him. When it was known that Mr. McGerald had received Mr. Brainerd into the Church, the former was waited upon by a committee and threatened with a bill of charges at the forthcoming Conference. He assured Mr. Brainerd, however, that he would stand by him. But Mr. Brainerd said, "No; I would not have the trouble get into the East Genesee Conference;" and then authorized Mr. McGerald to drop his name from the Record. In this way Mr. McGerald was preserved from an attempt to expel him from the Church.

Some years later, and after he had become a Free Methodist, Mr. Brainerd was invited to fill the appointment of the Methodist Episcopal pastor at Churchville, New York. It was nearly the last time he preached. His family were afraid that going without his dinner after preaching would be too much for him. But the very man who preferred charges against him was present, and invited him to dine with him. He told of this on getting home; and his daughter, with some surprise, asked, "Did you go to Mr. Grunendike's?" and he replied, "If he could ask me, I certainly could go; and we had a good time."

He was truly a good man. A Roman Catholic neighbor

once said of him, "He is such a good man that I want to get him into the Catholic Church." His face was so radiant, even in death, that Daniel Steele, a relative, said of him, "As he entered heaven, the glory shone through the gates and rested on his face."

The Rev. William D. Buck was a personal friend of Mr. Brainerd, and yet voted against him. When asked why he did so, he answered, "*Because Bishop Simpson told me to.*" "Happy for the world if this were the only time when Bishops and clerics had forgotten justice and truth," says Prof. B. H. Roberts, in commenting on the event in the biography of his father.

Efforts were made to conceal the fact that Mr. Brainerd was really expelled for his part in the Albion Convention, because of there having been three charges against him. William Hosmer, faithful and fearless Editor of the *Northern Independent,* and the one man among the editors concerned with Genesee Conference matters who was fully awake to the enormity of the wrongs that were being perpetrated by that body, and who had the honesty and courage to expose them to public reprobation, editorially wrote concerning this case as follows:

> Three charges were, to all intents and purposes, one charge, and but one, unless the specifications relied on to support them had their origin in circumstances apart from the Albion Convention.
>
> The crime of attending that Convention might have been prosecuted under forty different heads, and by a thousand different specifications, and yet all would have been substantially one and the same charge. In order to show that there was in reality more charges than one, it should have been made to appear that crimes unconnected with said Convention, and of a wholly different character, were alleged against the party accused. For prudential reasons, it is not uncommon in criminal prosecutions of this kind to disguise the real offense under formidable allegations which no one expects to prove or ever supposed to be true. In such a case, though the charges are not proved, they help blacken the character and cover the nakedness of the attempt. If sham charges are made, some will believe them, and in the meantime the ac-

cused can be convicted with better grace on the less flagrant points in the indictment. What the facts in this case are can only be known from the specifications themselves, and the entire history connected with the trial. The matter is in itself of very great moment, because it clearly involves the right of the laity to assemble for the redress of grievances. If attendance on such meetings is to be construed into a crime; or, if words spoken there are to be prosecuted under the grave head of "contumacy," "slander," "sowing discord," etc., then whatever may happen, our laymen must be silent on pain of expulsion. Such a condition of things would be nothing better than now falls to the lot of the deluded votaries of the Catholic Church. Can the brethren concerned in this apparently unfortunate piece of administration show that Brother Brainerd was not expelled for words spoken, or deeds done, at the Albion Convention? Had this case stood alone, we should not have noticed it, as occasional errors are to be met with in the best administrations; but there is good reason to suppose that it connects with a principle which is to have a wide application.

When ecclesiastical persecution assumes a judicial form, it is one of the most tremendous scourges ever let loose upon society. The fires of Smithfield were kindled by misguided Church judicatories, and every Romish *auto-da-fé* has the same origin. Believing not only that these ecclesiastical decapitations are the worst kind of murder, but that slavery will demand in other Conferences a repetition of the scenes enacted in the Genesee Conference, we shall both apprise the public of what is going on and strip the proceedings of their assumed sanctity.

Two other laymen on the same circuit, Thomas Hannah and Alexander Patten, were next among the victims, both being expelled on charges similar to those brought against Mr. Brainerd. They were prosperous farmers, and both men of sound judgment and sterling piety. There was nothing against them, except that they took part in the Laymen's Convention. Mr. Hannah had recently given $300.00 for a Church on the circuit, and had given his note for $300.00 more. This latter amount was collected, although he had been most unjustly excluded from worshiping in the house for which the amount was subscribed. Consistency, whither wert thou fled?

Following these expulsions a more summary method

of dealing with such cases was adopted, namely, that of simply reading the undesirable parties out of the Church as having "withdrawn." Mr. John Prue, Mrs. Sarah Prue, Mrs. Elizabeth Porter, Mrs. H. Loder, Fanny Smith and Mrs. N. S. Brainerd were thus disposed of at a single stroke, and without their consent. This method, though in direct contravention of the Methodist Discipline, was afterward worked effectively on many charges as an easy wholesale method of disposing of embarrassing cases.

At Churchville, N. Y., Mr. Hart Smith, a conscientious and devoted Christian, was expelled by the Rev. Sumner Smith, aided by a committee from Chili, an adjoining circuit, the members at Churchville refusing to act in the case.

On April 13th, 1859, Mr. Thomas B. Catton, a stanch, God-fearing Englishman, possessed of more than ordinary intelligence, was brought to trial by the Rev. W. S. Tuttle, pastor of the Perry society. The indictment against him contained four charges, and twenty-three specifications. The pastor assumed from the start that he was to be expelled, and so cited him to appear at the time and place specified, "to answer to the charges and specifications, *and show cause why you should not be expelled from the M. E. Church.*" (Italics are the author's.)

Can the reader imagine such a thing in civil Court as a citizen under arrest cited to appear and show cause why he should not be punished? Is it not common law in all civilized lands that "the prosecution must show cause why the accused should be punished"? And does not the foregoing citation on the face of it show such a reversal of this law as to make it appear that one accused of being a "Nazarite," or of being a sympathizer with "Nazarites," deserves the extreme of Church penalties, and must show cause why such penalty should not be inflicted? Moreover, to aggravate this case still more, the Rev. Mr. Tuttle, like the Rev. Mr. Lankton, claimed to be one of those against whom the Laymen's Convention directed its action—that is, he virtually claimed to be a party in the case—and yet "he acted as judge, selected the jury, and in reality conducted his own case."*

Writing to the Rev. B. T. Roberts an account of his trial soon after it occurred, Mr. Catton said:

> You can get only a very faint idea of the proceedings, from the minutes. Brother Hibbard said in speaking of your trial, that "all the forms of law were exhausted;" we think in my case that all the forms of law were outraged. When a Methodist minister can take such a stand as the Rev. W. S. Tuttle took in this trial, and can find devotees to carry out his desires, it is high time for the laity to be aroused. There can be no safety when a man claiming to be slandered, can, on the trial of the one accused of slandering him, sit as judge, and appoint the jury, and repudiate the laws of evidence, which have been established for ages. Who ever heard, outside of the Genesee Conference, of a member of the M. E. Church being tried and receiving a penalty because he could not in conscience pay the minister appointed? Yet Mr. Tuttle stated that he had written to Bishop Baker, and had his sanction for commencing an action under this new rule. I am now satisfied that the worst construction that can be put upon the language used by the Albion Convention—if it was not true then, is certainly true now.

During the progress of this trial certain developments occurred which threw some light upon the trial of Mr. Roberts by his annual Conference. Several witnesses of good repute testified that they personally knew of so-called "Regency" preachers being absent from the Conference sittings a day at a time while the Roberts trial was in progress. Also "E. Sears, Thomas Jeffres and J. Grisewood testified that, at different times, they heard different preachers who voted for the expulsion of B. T. Roberts say that they did not vote for his expulsion *because* of the evidence adduced. The only reason any of them assigned was, because he undertook the defense of the Estes pamphlet. They heard seven different preachers at various times make this statement."†

Mr. Catton put up such a vigorous defense in his trial,

*"Why Another Sect?" p. 212. †"Why Another Sect?" pp. 213, 214.

and public sympathy on his behalf was so strong, that for the time being the prosecution was unable to accomplish its purpose to expel him. This was a notable event, and seemed like the scoring of such a point in his favor as might put in check the spirit of persecution which had instigated his trial. It was not as it seemed, however. Though not expelled, he was censured; and later he was again brought to trial for "contumacy," a charge which was the stock-in-trade with the "Regency" faction, even as "inflexible obstinacy" was the stock-in-trade accusation against those who yielded up their lives to martyrdom in olden time under Roman Catholic persecution. His case was finally disposed of in connection with the cases of seventeen others who were "read out" of membership in the Methodist Episcopal Church, without their consent, and contrary to the canons of the Church.

This short and easy method was also pursued in the case of Mr. George W. Holmes, a man of remarkable intelligence, refinement, candor and piety on the Kendall charge. In his quarterly report to the society, at a lovefeast, the pastor announced, "George Holmes, withdrawn." "Not so," replied Mr. Holmes with clear and manly voice from his place in the congregation. "I never withdrew." He was out, however, though by illegal process, and, like others who were similarly deprived of their Church membership, he knew it would be in vain to invoke the higher authorities of the Church for redress, inasmuch as this method of disposing of members who would not servilely bow to the will of the "Regency" was known to be operated with the approval of those higher authorities.

Mr. Jonathan Handly, of Perry, N. Y., a quiet and unobtrusive character, but a man of deep piety and of genuine worth, who had been a Methodist for over thirty years, was likewise a victim of the prevailing persecution, and was expelled for attending the Laymen's Convention.

The case of James H. Brooks, Esq., of Olean, N. Y., who was expelled on the same grounds, excited so much interest that the Olean *Advertiser* commented on it as follows:

> James H. Brooks, Esq., a resident of Olean these thirty odd years, a man of unblemished private character, a member of the Methodist Episcopal Church ever since he was fifteen years old, a Christian of acknowledged worth and usefulness, and a citizen against whom the breath of calumny has never breathed until now, has been expelled from the Church. This fact being announced, the inquiry is natural and pertinent—"Why?" This is just what we would like to know.
>
> James H. Brooks has grown up in our midst from boyhood; his private worth is as familiar to our citizens as a "thrice told tale." Generosity, integrity, honesty, and living piety, are eminent characteristics of the man. For the last twenty-eight years he has been a member of the Methodist Episcopal Church, and has contributed liberally for the advancement of Methodism, and the promulgation of the Gospel. The ministers and brethren of the Church have ever found a place at his board, and a welcome at his fireside. It was indeed a truthful exclamation of the accused after his conviction, and was not contradicted by his accusers, "My old mother sitting there, has given more meals to Methodists, than all the rest of this Church together."
>
> The trial and expulsion of such a man naturally produces in the public mind a supposition that he has been guilty of some heinous offense, either against good morals or the peace of society, and that the proceedings were necessary to purify the Church, and to warn the world against an unchristian example.
>
> We, however, learn, and are gratified in being able to say that such is not the case, that he has neither adopted a spurious faith, nor has been guilty of any heresies condemned by the doctrines of his Church, nor has he indulged in any impropriety of conduct, that would warrant under any ordinary circumstances, his expulsion from the Church.
>
> In every human mind there is an innate sense of justice which is offended and aroused at acts of oppression and palpable wrongs. We confess we partake of the general feeling pervading this community, that a grievous wrong has been done Mr. Brooks.

So cruel and relentless were the measures resorted to by the Church for the purpose of either subjugating the "Nazarites," particularly the laymen, or exterminating their so-called fanaticism, that the oppression became unbearable, and finally resulted in the calling of another

Laymen's Convention. This is the Convention to which the Rev. Mr. Crawford refers in his published account of the Bergen camp-meeting.* The call was issued by Hon. Abner I. Wood, president, and the Rev. S. K. J. Chesbrough and Mr. W. H. Doyle, secretaries, and was particularly addressed to the members of the Laymen's Convention held at Albion, N. Y. The following is a copy:

DEAR BRETHREN: At our session at Albion we were authorized to call a meeting again in June. We feel that the difficulties among us demand such a meeting. Ever since our action at Albion, we have been misrepresented, and our characters slandered. No stone has been left unturned, either by flattery or threatenings, to intimidate many from the positions then taken. How many have been led thus to withdraw from us, we know not; nor is it our concern. If any one feels duty thus calls him to retract, let him thus decide, and walk no more with us. We feel satisfied that not only a vast majority of those that attended still adhere to those resolutions, but many more who did not adhere, are now convinced that we have the right on our side, and *to-day are in sympathy with us. Important* interests are at stake; we feel the iron heel of oppression heavily laid upon us as laymen. We feel unwilling to become the slaves of any power. Many of our beloved brethren, who acted with us there, have been tried for attending that Convention—some have been expelled. Let us meet together, and show to them that the cause is one, and when they suffer, we suffer with them. If our action there is to be the "war-note," and the moving cause of our decapitation or removal from office, wherever possible, the time has come, yea, fully come, for us to stand firm and reiterate that our sentiments and our resolutions are still unchanged, and that we intend to maintain the position then taken, let the cost be what it may to us; the fear of expulsion or removal from office should never drive a Methodist from doing his duty.

We need also to reaffirm our undiminished confidence in our beloved Brothers Roberts and McCreery, and our condemnation of the unjust expulsion of these brethren from the Conference. Let us, to a man, stand by them; they are worthy of our sympathy and our "material aid."

We cordially and earnestly invite all our brethren who are in sympathy with us, and who are willing to act, to meet us in Convention at North Bergen, on the Genesee Camp Ground, Thursday,

*See pages 128, 129.

June 20, 1859, at 4 p. m., to take such action as may there be deemed advisable.

This Convention, being held in connection with the camp-meeting, appears to have done but little, except to deliberate and determine on the holding of a second Annual Convention, which was called to meet at Albion, November 1 and 2, 1859.

Reference has been made several times in the foregoing part of this chapter to the practise of reading members out of the Church without even the form of a trial. The answers of one of the Bishops to certain questions submitted to him are supposed to have been responsible for the adoption of this summary and undisciplinary method of dealing with the so-called "Nazarites."

At any rate a paper was left among the effects of the late Rev. Henry Hornsby, inscribed over his signature on the reverse side, as follows: "Questions answered by Bishop Morris, S. Parker preacher in charge at Lockport, Gen. Conf. The reading out of members in the M. E. Church was based on these answers. This paper given me by Schuyler Parker." That paper is before the author as he writes, and its contents are as follows:

QUESTIONS

proposed to Bishop Morris by S. Parker and answered by him—Date of letter, "May 21, 1859."

Ques. 1.—Can members of our Church go by themselves in any number and organize for the purpose of holding public religious services, independent of our Church and its authorities? Ans.—No.

Ques. 2.—Does not such an act without anything further upon their part, constitute a separation from our Church? Ans.—Yes, virtually so.

Ques. 3.—Does it make any difference what name or obligations they have taken, so long as they are unknown in our Discipline and the object is to hold religious meetings independent of the preacher in charge of the Church where their names are recorded? Ans.—No.

Ques. 4.—Has a preacher on one charge a right to receive members who have been expelled on another charge, when he knows such to be the fact, without their making confession, etc.? Ans.—No.

A true copy.

The Bishop said I could report them withdrawn, if the official brethren so advised, in preference to bringing them to trial and expelling them.

The last item in this paper appears to have been the authority under which the "Regency" men acted in pursuing the "reading-out" method. But no Bishop could ever have so advised without having been guilty of maladministration.

CHAPTER XXIV

MORE PREACHERS ECCLESIASTICALLY BEHEADED

Before the time arrived for the second Laymen's Convention at Albion the Genesee Conference had sent a number more of its preachers to the ecclesiastical block. Two of them, J. W. Reddy and H. H. Farnsworth, were disposed of by locating them. Four others, namely, Loren Stiles, Jr., John A. Wells, William Cooley and C. D. Burlingham, were "expelled on trivial, trumped-up charges, after the mockery of a trial, at the Conference held at Brockport, in 1859."

This session of the Conference was held in October, less than a month before the time fixed for the holding of the second annual Laymen's Convention. During the year no stone had been left unturned, no opportunity had been unimproved, by the "Regency" faction to destroy the influence of the men expelled at the preceding session. All these efforts, however, had ended in signal failure. Notwithstanding the fact that those men went forth to labor for God under the ban of Conference expulsion, and stigmatized as both "unchristian and immoral," they were never more cordially received by the Christian public, nor did they ever have a wider and more effective hearing, than during this year. The blessing of God followed them wherever they went, and "the word of the Lord grew mightily and prevailed."

The determination to crush out "Nazaritism" had never been more manifest, or more iniquitous in its methods and measures, than during this year. The *Buffalo Advocate* and the *Northern Christian Advocate* more than maintained their usual reputation for the vilification of all such as would not bow with servile deference to the will of the dominant faction. Their columns teemed with articles of the most inflammatory character appealing to their constituencies to make an utter end of the "Nazaritism" still remaining in the Conference. Hence, when the session met, the majority had come together ready to execute any measures proposed by their leaders, in order that the work of extermination might be consummated.

This spirit of bitter hostility was kindled to a consuming flame by the demonstration which they witnessed on convening. The Rev. Fay H. Purdy, a well-known evangelist of the Methodist Episcopal Church, had pitched a large tabernacle in the outskirts of the town, yet within sight and almost within hearing of the Church where the Conference was to be held, and was engaged in a series of evangelistic services which were to continue throughout the Conference session. The tabernacle would accommodate about 3,000 people. About it were several rows of family and society tents, occupied by "a large number of intelligent, devoted, earnest Christians, who were stigmatized by the dominant party as 'Nazarites.'" This clearly showed that "Nazaritism" was not so nearly extinct as its enemies had hoped and supposed. It was not even weakened, much less destroyed.

The defenders of vital godliness in the Conference were aware from the beginning that extreme measures would be adopted at this session, and were ready to face whatever might be their fate. However, for unblushing audacity, for Jesuitical diplomacy, and for Pharisaic madness, in trampling upon the rights of members and dishonoring both human and divine law, the action of the majority far exceeded their anticipations. The capacity of the "Regency" for injustice in the name of righteousness had been underestimated. It was supposed that they would at least feel under some obligation to honor the Constitution of the Methodist Episcopal Church, yet even this was ruthlessly overridden. That Constitution allows to the

Annual Conferences no legislative powers. The General Conference is the only properly constituted law-making body in Methodism. The Annual Conferences may execute such of its laws as, by constitutional provision, fall within their province; but they can neither legislate, give to their own enactments the force of law, nor affix penalties for their violation. To attempt any of these things is to usurp the prerogatives belonging to the General Conference alone.

The Genesee Conference at this session, however, usurped the authority of a law-making body, and, on the second day of the session, passed the following "resolutions," the first four of which were intended to force the preachers who sympathized with their expelled brethren to cease from public manifestations of such sympathy, and the fifth of which was designed to make any who should violate the enactments of the first four answerable to the Conference therefor, and subject to expulsion:

Resolved, 1st. That the safety and prosperity of a Church can only be maintained by a solemn deference to its councils and Discipline, as legitimately determined and executed.

2nd. That we consider the admission of expelled ministers, whether traveling or local, to our pulpits, and associating with them and assisting them as ministers, until they have, by due process, as described in the Discipline, been restored to the fellowship of the Church, as subversive of the integrity and government of the Church, directly tending to the production of discord and division and every evil work.

3rd. That we disapprove and condemn the practise of certain members of this Conference, in holding in an irregular way, or in countenancing by taking part in the services, of camp-meetings, or other meetings thus irregularly held.

4th. That in the judgment of this Conference, it is highly improper for one preacher to go into another preacher's charge and appoint meetings, or attend those that may be appointed by others in opposition to the wishes of the preacher in charge, or the Presiding Elder.

5th. That if any member of this Conference be found guilty of disregarding the opinions and principles expressed in the above resolutions, he shall be held to answer to this Conference for the same.

Having passed the foregoing resolutions, the Conference proceeded to make them a test in examining the characters of the preachers. The characters of such as would promise to be governed by the resolutions were passed, while those who would not so promise were put on trial and expelled, unless they chose to locate. Bishop Simpson presided over the Conference session, and was reported as having given the test resolutions his emphatic approval. Having passed these enactments, and that with the Bishop's approval, the Conference was now prepared for desperate measures in dealing with "Nazarites" and "Nazaritism." As to what those measures were to be, the sequel will unfold.

Acting in harmony with the spirit of the test resolutions the Bishop ordered a number of preachers who had come from other Conferences to assist Mr. Purdy in his meetings to refrain from taking further part in them. Some of them did as ordered; but the Rev. D. W. Thurston, a Presiding Elder from the Cortland district of the Oneida Conference, still continued to labor with Mr. Purdy as before. The Bishop called him before a committee and admonished him, but the admonition was unheeded.

It was evident that the test resolutions had been adopted as a convenient measure for bringing "Nazarite" preachers and their sympathizers to punishment. Accordingly, under their operations, J. W. Reddy and H. H. Farnsworth were located, while Loren Stiles, Jr., John A. Wells, William Cooley and Charles D. Burlingham, refusing to submit to such tyrannical rule as the Genesee Conference had assumed, were placed on trial and expelled from the Conference and from the Church.

The following is a copy of the bill of charges prosecuted against the Rev. Loren Stiles, Jr.:

I hereby charge Rev. L. Stiles, Jr.,

I. With falsehood.

In testifying in the case of B. T. Roberts, at the session of our Conference held at Perry, October 6, 1858, that he did not receive or read the proof sheet of a document printed at Brockport, signed George W. Estes, and entitled "New School Methodism," and "To Whom it May Concern;" and, in the case of J. McCreery, Jr., occurring at the same Conference, testifying that he did receive a paper purporting to be the proof sheet of such document—with an accompanying note explanatory of its nature, and *did* read it, or a portion of it.

II. With contumacy.

1. In receiving into his pulpit, and treating as a minister, an expelled member from this Conference.

2. In going into the bounds of F. W. Conable's charge, and there holding meetings and organizing a class, contrary to the admonition of his Presiding Elder. J. B. Wentworth.

The first of these charges was evidently made as an attempt to smirch his reputation and "blacken his character." For lack of evidence, however, it could not be sustained, and the majority were constrained to vote him acquitted of that charge. Thus was he providentially preserved from having the stain of falsehood put upon him by his enemies.

Regarding the prosecution of the second charge and its specifications General Superintendent B. T. Roberts has left on record the following, the truth of which has never been called in question so far as we can ascertain:

Of the first specification under the second charge there was no proof whatever. It was shown that once during the year Rev. B. T. Roberts was at a General Quarterly Meeting at the M. E. Church at Albion, of which Brother Stiles was pastor. One evening, after Rev. B. I. Ives preached, B. T. Roberts, by his invitation, exhorted. But in defense of this, it was shown that he had at that time drawn up in due form, a regular exhorter's license! Mr. Roberts was treated simply as an exhorter and nothing more! He was not called upon to perform and did not perform one of the functions of "a minister!"

This second specification was admitted to be *nominally* true. Holley, N. Y., is a large village between Brockport and Albion. There had been no Methodist society and no Methodist preaching there for a number of years. When I was stationed at Brockport, I occasionally preached by invitation at Holley. I went to Albion from Brockport, and still now and then preached in Holley—sometimes in the Academy, and sometimes in the Presbyterian Church. After Mr. Stiles went to Albion he kept up these occasional appointments at Holley. The interest increasing, and souls getting converted, Mr. Stiles formed a class, which, we may add—has grown into a prosperous Church, which has built one of the finest edifices in the place. No objection was made, until after the work of expulsion was begun, and "occasion" was sought against Mr. Stiles. Mr. Conable had no appointment at Holley, and never had. His nearest appointment was about three miles away. Mr. Stiles' appointment to preach was generally on a different day and hour from his. Mr. Conable had a smaller number of members—two or three—living at Holley. But they did not have him make an appointment at their place.

It was not claimed that these members at Holley did not contribute, as usual, to Mr. Conable's support. So that Mr. Stiles, in going to Holley to preach, interfered in no way, either with his appointments or his salary.

It was not attempted to be shown that Mr. Stiles had violated any provision of the Discipline. On the contrary, he read from the Discipline—from the *rules* for a preacher's conduct: "You have nothing to do but to save souls: therefore spend and be spent in this work; and *go always not only to those that want you, but to those that want you most.*" This was precisely what he had done—nothing more—and nothing less.

On such a charge, thus sustained, the majority voted to expel from *the Genesee Conference* AND THE M. E. CHURCH, Loren Stiles, Jr., one of the most devoted, eloquent, gifted, noble-hearted men then in the ministry of that denomination.

Of all the Methodist papers, official or independent, there was but one that spoke out in condemnation of this violent, illegal action. Yet a few years later, when Rev. S. Tyng, Jr., was mildly censured by the authorities of the Protestant Episcopal Church, for preaching in the parish of another clergyman without his consent, the Methodist papers, with much warmth and zeal, condemned such an encroachment upon personal liberty! Yet there was this difference: Mr. Tyng's Church had a plain law, forbidding the act: the Methodist Church had no law forbidding its ministers to do as Mr. Stiles had done. Mr. Tyng preached in the immediate neighborhood of an Episcopal Church. There was not a Methodist Church or preaching place within three miles of the place where Mr. Stiles preached! Mr. Tyng preached at the regular hours for service. Mr. Stiles preached generally on a week-day evening, when it did not interfere with any preacher—anywhere.

Will the Methodist editors explain *why* it was wrong for the Episcopal Church to censure Mr. Tyng—and right for the Methodist Episcopal Church to expel Mr. Stiles from the ministry and the Church, for the same act—when all the points of difference were in favor of Mr. Stiles?*

The Rev. Charles D. Burlingham was another who was required to answer before this session of the Genesee Conference to a charge of "Contumacy," under which were three specifications, intended to sustain the charge. The charges were preferred by the Rev. D. F. Parsons. Mr. Burlingham prepared a paper and presented the same to the Conference as his defense against his accusers. It was entitled, "A Statement by C. D. Burlingham to the Genesee Conference, responding to a charge and specifications, preferred against him by Rev. D. F. Parsons." The following extracts from it are submitted as giving the best available light on the case:

BROCKPORT, October 15, 1859.

Charge, "*Contumacy.*"

1st specification: "*In receiving an expelled member of the Genesee Conference, into the Church on trial without confession or satisfactory reformation.*"

I received Benjamin T. Roberts on trial, in Pekin, November 7, 1858, in a general society meeting, pursuant to a *unanimous* vote, without his confessing the alleged crime, for which he had been expelled.

My *reasons* for so doing are:

1. I believe that there are exceptional cases, in the application of the rule of Discipline referred to, because if the strict letter of the rule must always control in the cases of applicants for admission on trial, then it follows that an *innocent* person, who has been wrongfully expelled, can never be re-admitted into the Church.

I understand Bishop Baker to confirm this view: (See Guide Book, page 159, paragraph 9). "When a member or preacher has been expelled, according to our form of Discipline, he can not

*"Why Another Sect?" pp. 222-225.

afterward enjoy the privileges of society and of the sacraments in our Church, without contrition and satisfactory reformation; but if, however, the society becomes convinced of the *innocence* of the expelled member, he may again be received on trial without confession;" the *principle* in the *conclusion*, covering of course both cases, "*member or preacher*," in the premises.

2. I believe that such admission into the Church could not remove the ground of his appeal to the General Conference, because that body, I judged, could act in the case, only on those points submitted in the appeal; he being responsible for his subsequent acts to his Conference, should the General Conference reverse the *decision* by which he was expelled.

3. The next day after the expulsion, the appeal having been notified, the question of his admission into the Church was discussed informally, by Bishops Janes and Baker, and the Presiding Elders. The point was not, can he be received by confessing the alleged crime, for of *course that* would remove the ground of his appeal; but the question was, can he be received on trial, and not injuriously affect his appeal. Those *aged and experienced* Presiding Elders—for some of them were such,—with the two Bishops, were in doubt on the question, showing at least, that such a question had not, then, been definitely settled, in the administrative rules of the Church, as intimated by our president a few days since.

Subsequently, Bishop Janes, as Brother Roberts informed me, when I first met him in Pekin, said to him, that he had not lost confidence in him, and that he could join the Church again, or words to that import, leaving that distinct impression on his mind.

I put *this* and *that* together, and connecting both with advice from some eminent ministers, within and without our Conference bounds, and after receiving all the light *then* accessible to me, I received him on trial. I confess that I was in doubt on the question, a year ago; and, having occasion to act in this case, with such light as dawned upon me, I did what I thought was right and proper.

4. A fourth point in this argument is a case, perfectly analogous, in reference to the principle of receiving a person on trial "without confession," etc., of more than ordinary notoriety, that transpired within our Conference bounds. A prominent member was expelled. He appealed. The quarterly conference, for some informality, sent the case back for a new trial. He was expelled the second time. Under the *instruction and advice* of the deeply experienced Presiding Elder of the district—a man of profound erudition—this expelled person was received on trial, without confession, in a charge a few miles distant; and then

JAMES M. CUSICK
Member of Convention that organized the Church

LEWIS E. CHASE, Local Elder

MRS. CORNELIA CASTLE

Living Members of the first Free Methodist class organized

[Plate Eighteen]

took a letter and joined a new charge, nearer his home, without either changing his residence, or confessing the crime for which he had been expelled. This administration may have been correct —I do not know, because I do not know the whole case; but, if correct, it is so on the ground of my first reason herewith presented; and if correct, then it covers in a moral point of view my act of receiving "without confession," etc. Of course, a wrong administration in that case will not justify a wrong one in another case. But when wiser men than I am are allowed thus to practise, without being treated as contumacious, surely I ought to have the benefit of such clemency.

5. After I had learned from an authentic source—Bishop Baker—what was the Episcopal decision that would apply to this case, and might remove the ground of his appeal; after consultation with Brother Roberts, who has expressed from time to time a desire and purpose to prosecute his appeal, and with some eminent ministers who have the confidence of the Church, and who may act as his counsel in the case, I have obeyed the implied advice of the Bishop, and granted the request of Brother Roberts, by discontinuing his probationary membership in the same manner he had been received. The conclusion then, from these five points, each and all, is summed up in few words: There is not—can not be—a *shadow of contumacy*, either in principle, motive, or act. The fifth point, in connection with all the others, furnishes *evidence* of not a *perverse*, but a *teachable* spirit,—not *resistance* to and *contempt* of, but *submission* and obedience to the rules, and decisions, and authorities of the Church.

Second Specification.—"On giving said expelled member license to exhort, at the time of such reception on trial."

On the recommendation, nearly unanimous, by the same general society meeting that voted for his reception on trial, and on the same occasion, I gave him a license to exhort.

As the Discipline recognizes exhorters as members of Quarterly Conferences; and probationers can not be members of a Quarterly Conference; I stated in the certificate I gave him, that he was a probationary member; assuming thereby that a person, suitable in other respects to officiate in the capacity of an exhorter, might do so, before he, as a *member* of the Church, could perform official acts, as a member of Quarterly Conference.

My reasons, then, for giving him such a license, are:

1. That he might, in a regular and orderly way, exhort the people religiously.

2. I believed that he was *really* a probationary member in good standing, legally; and the Bishop's opinion, given five or six

days ago, confirms this view; and, therefore, in that respect, there was no impediment in the way.

3. And though the Discipline makes no provision for investing probationers with official powers, except it be an implied one, perhaps, indicated by the words, "member of *society*," as required in the Church relations of a local preacher, (Discipline, page 42): and the words, "member of the *class*," in that of an exhorter, (Discipline, page 66); a distinction in words, in the two cases, implying, perhaps, we say, that full membership is *required* in the *former case*, but not in the latter. Yet the law of usage,—possibly founded on this distinction that I have noted—allows and sanctions, in some cases, such administration as mine in the case before us: Rev. Bishop H. B. Bascom, D. D., was authorized to exhort, while on trial.

On these grounds, and not contumaciously, I gave B. T. Roberts license to exhort, in the form and manner I have stated. The idea of setting up my own private judgment in this case, and my personal convictions in opposition and resistance to the solemn decisions of the Conference, when sitting as a Court, has never found its way into my thoughts or heart, to be cherished for a moment.

If my administration was incorrect under the first or second specification, or both, it is certainly not an error of the heart; and surely, I ought not to be regarded as *contumacious* because I am not wiser: I know I intended to do, and I thought I did, for the reasons stated, just what ought to be done, in view of all my responsibilities.

Third Specification.—"In attending and assisting in a so-called 'General Quarterly Meeting,' held in Ransomville, some time in February last, within the bounds of the East Porter charge, and at the same time of the regular Quarterly Meeting of said charge."

On this specification, I say I attended such a meeting at Ransomville, and the following facts will show that I did not do it *contumaciously* against the Conference, nor contemptuously against the presiding officer of the district as implied in the specification:

1. In the light of the statement presented, I regarded Brother Roberts as authorized, at that time, to hold religious meetings where there was an opening, with the consent of the people and authorities of the locality; and, therefore, *under such circumstances*, I did not regard it as improper to be associated with him and others in religious worship.

2. The Wesleyans had invited this meeting to their Church; our people, as I understand, having neither Church nor preaching appointment in the locality.

3. I never knew or dreamed, until this bill was presented me,

that Ransomville was in East Porter charge, having understood that it was in vacant territory, between Wilson and Porter, and about the same distance from Pekin, my charge, as from either of those places.

4. The small-pox was prevailing, to some extent, in our place, and our meetings were suspended; and, under such circumstances our brethren deemed it proper to meet with other brethren in some locality where they would violate no Church order, and be likely to do some good in the name of the Lord; and I was with them a part of the time to do a little work and to see what such people were doing, as then and now, I can say, I know but little about such meetings from personal observation.

5. This meeting happened to occur on the day of the Quarterly Meeting of the Porter charge. I had nothing to do in getting up the meeting or fixing the time, but I have good reason to believe the appointment was made in ignorance that the other meeting was to be at the same time. When it became known that the Porter meeting would be at that time, it was too late to change the time of the other; but, as I understood from brethren with whom I conversed, knowing nothing of the localities myself then, that the circuit meeting would probably be held in connection with Youngstown, or at some point six or eight miles from Ransomville, I judged the one would not interfere with the other; and, therefore, I attended said meeting. It was a source of regret to me that the two meetings were to occur at the same time, for the reason that, possibly, the Porter meeting might be in the eastern part of the circuit, in the more immediate vicinity of Ransomville, and it might be thought that *this* meeting was designed to interfere with that, which was not the case. Brethren, I have endeavored to notice and meet every point in the Bill; and though I admit some little partiality for my client, I must say, in all candor, there is not, there cannot be, in your convictions in the case, the shadow of any evidence to sustain the charge; that though all the specifications are nearly literally true, there is not in the case the slightest degree of *contumacy*.

Does not the foregoing commend itself to the reader as an admirable and complete defense? Does it not breathe the spirit of candor and genuine piety, as well as of loyalty to the Church? Would not such a statement have cleared him before any unprejudiced deliberative body, secular or religious? And yet such was the state of things in the Genesee Conference that his defense was listened to as an idle tale; and, having predetermined him for judgment, and also having the votes with which to execute their purpose, the majority voted him guilty, and then inflicted upon him the severest punishment within their power—*expulsion from the Conference and from the Methodist Episcopal Church!* How much further they might have gone had the law permitted, can only be conjectured.

CHAPTER XXV

MORE PREACHERS ECCLESIASTICALLY BEHEADED—CONTINUED

The Rev. William Cooley's case also requires attention, since he was one of the preachers whose ecclesiastical head was sacrificed at this session of the Conference. The following complaint was lodged against him:

> I hereby charge Rev. William Cooley with contumacy.
>
> *First specification.*—In receiving into his pulpit and treating as a minister an expelled member of this Conference.
>
> *Second specification.*—In violating the wishes and requests of his brethren, as expressed by resolutions passed by them at this session of our Conference against affiliating with expelled members from the Conference. J. B. WENTWORTH.
>
> Brockport, Oct. 14, 1859.

Regarding the first specification the defense admitted that B. T. Roberts had once addressed the people at Kendall village, and that Joseph McCreery once addressed them at West Kendall, in both instances from the pulpit; that they had a four-days' meeting at Kendall, which Mr. Roberts attended, though not by his (Cooley's) request, and that at this meeting "I invited him to take part in the exercises, and to exhort;" also that Mr. McCreery came to a two-days' meeting at West Kendall, uninvited, and while there "went into the pulpit and addressed the people, as he said, on his own authority."

The Rev. A. D. Wilbor, his Presiding Elder, was called, and testified to having had conversation with Mr. Cooley about permitting expelled ministers to speak from his pulpit, and said Cooley had admitted to him in substance what he had just admitted on the witness stand. Mr. Wilbor also testified that he admonished him, but admitted, before his testimony was concluded, that this admonitory conversation had occurred since the commencement of the present Conference session. Strange that he had not seen fit to take up disciplinary labor with the defendant before!

Under the "second specification" the defendant admitted having preached at Mr. Purdy's camp-meeting, but declared he had not taken part in any irregular meeting that he was aware of. He also testified that his preaching at Purdy's meeting was *before* the "Resolutions" were passed by the Conference.

The following extract from the printed report of the trial gives the sequel to the proceedings under this specification:

Rev. R. E. Thomas called.—Were you present at the *Nazarite camp-meeting down here? I was. Did Brother Cooley take part in it? He sat on the platform; he knelt and prayed.

Rev. C. Strong called.—I was present at Purdy's camp-meeting a few times, as a spectator. Saw the defendant there two or three times. He appeared to be taking part in the exercises during the time of prayer-meeting or when a great deal of noise was being made, in what I should call the general hallooing and clapping concert.

I did not see B. T. Roberts there at the time of the sacrament, but at other times. I saw J. McCreery on the stand. I saw him come forward to the communion. A man I have heard called Purdy seemed to supervise this meeting.

Rev. K. D. Nettleton called.—I was present a part of the time during the sacrament and tent-meeting.

I was a spectator. Saw McCreery partake of the sacrament with the ministers. A man administered the sacrament, at the first invitation, whom Mr. Purdy called a Presiding Elder of the Oneida Conference by the name of Thurston. Saw defendant and McCreery go forward to the sacrament. Saw defendant take part in the exercises, and also expelled ministers.

Rev. B. F. McNeal called.—I was present at the sacrament on Tuesday evening of this week, as a spectator. Defendant and J. McCreery were there; I saw defendant, and McCreery, and a large number of ministers go forward to the sacrament, and immediate-

*Referring to Fay H. Purdy's Tent Meeting.

ly took my departure. A man they called Thurston presided at the sacrament.

Cross-examined.—There were from twenty to thirty ministers present at the sacrament.

Rev. A. D. Wilbor called.—The tent-meeting was not held by my consent, but against my wishes.

Cross-examined.—I have given no public expression to that effect. I did express my disapprobation at the Preachers' Meeting at LeRoy. The defendant was not there. I think the notice of the tent-meeting was published in the *Northern Christian Advocate.* I supposed the meeting to be held within the bounds of the Brockport charge.

Rev. E. M. Buck called.—Was Purdy's meeting in the bounds of your charge? Yes. I objected to this meeting to Purdy. I saw the notice of it.

Cross-examined.—I have no personal knowledge that defendant knew of my objections to Purdy's meetings.

Rebutting Testimony.

Rev. A. D. Wilbor called.—I did not inform defendant previous to the commencement of this session of the Conference, that his course was objectionable.

Cross-examined.—I admonished him the second or third day of Conference; it was before his character was arrested.

Rev. A. L. Backus called.—I received Joseph McCreery into the Church on probation, the second Sabbath after the adjournment of the last Conference. I dropped him the first Sabbath after the Bergen camp-meeting.

Cross-examined.—I did not license him to exhort or preach, or anything of that kind.

Direct testimony resumed: I did not give public notice that I had dropped him. I did report him dropped by name.

Rev. C. D. Burlingham's testimony, taken in Brother Stiles' trial and admitted in this trial: "I gave B. T. Roberts license to exhort, having first received him into the Church as a probationer, which was the second Sabbath after the last Conference."

Soon after his trial and expulsion, Mr. Cooley wrote the following comments and explanations concerning it, which are inserted here because of the additional light they throw upon the case:

1. The second specification was added after the trial was commenced, and altered twice; and at the suggestion of Bishop Simp-

son was most of it withdrawn, to prevent Brother Purdy's testimony, which would have made his meeting a regular one, because he had Rev. E. M. Buck's consent to hold the meeting when he did.

2. Brother Roberts exhorted at Kendall in the forepart of the Conference year, and the Presiding Elder, Rev. A. D. Wilbor, was four times on my circuit to hold quarterly meetings during the year, and had opportunities to admonish me of my great error in allowing Brother Roberts to exhort the people to serve God, and never passed a word with me as to this being an irregularity or wrong until the second or third day of this session of Conference. It certainly looks as though the design was not to check irregularities, but to find some occasion against me.

3. When my trial was nearly through, leading Regency ministers came to me, and said if I would locate, I might go out with clean papers, as a local preacher, to preach the Gospel. But I felt I had lived in all good conscience, and had done nothing to forfeit my Conference relations, and could not take any such responsibilities on myself.

4. Great efforts were made by the dominant party in the Conference to get me to subscribe to the "Five Puseyite resolutions," passed by the Conference, with the understanding that if I could do this, my character should pass; but I could not ignore my manhood and obligations to God to obey Him rather than man, so much as to bow down to that idol, set up by men. So I was expelled, first from Conference, and then from the Church; but God has been with me every hour since, saving and keeping my soul in glorious freedom, and I am enabled to say, "But none of these things move me, neither count I my life dear unto myself, so that I might finish my course with joy, and the ministry which I have received of the Lord Jesus to testify the Gospel of the grace of God."

Who that reads the account of Mr. Cooley's trial, and his subsequent statement concerning it, which has never been denied, can regard the action of the Conference in the case in any other light than that of Star Chamber proceedings? Was not the trial the barest mockery of justice, and the penalty an indication of persecuting wrath such as was a burning disgrace to the nineteenth century?

The last case of expulsion we are to consider as having occurred at this session is that of the Rev. John A. Wells. He was a man against whom nothing reproachful could justly be found, or was ever sought, until it became manifest that his sympathies were with those whom the majority of his Conference sneeringly and contemptuously called, "Nazarites." Then occasion was both sought and found against him sufficient, in the minds of the "Regency" faction, to warrant declaring him contumacious, and dealing with him accordingly. Following his trial and expulsion, he published an appeal to the general public which set forth the main facts in his case so clearly that we can do no better than to transcribe the most of it here:

APPEAL OF REV. JOHN A. WELLS.

To the members of the M. E. Church and all persons who respect the rights of humanity and religion.

Dear Brethren:—Allow me to present to you a candid statement of the facts in reference to my expulsion from the M. E. Church.

The Journal of the Genesee Conference for October 13, 1859, contains the following record:

"Resolved, That John A. Wells be expelled from the Genesee Conference and from the M. E. Church."

The charges which furnished the occasion for the above action are as follows:

"I hereby charge Rev. J. A. Wells with—

"1st. Contumacy—in recognizing as a minister, by admitting to his pulpit, and holding religious meetings in connection with B. T. Roberts, an expelled member from this Conference.

"2nd. Disobedience to the order of the Church, in going into the bounds of other brethren's charges, and holding religious meetings. (Signed,) "S. M. HOPKINS.

"Dated, Brockport, October 1, 1859."

It would be tame, indeed, for me to say that I am dissatisfied with the above action of Conference. A blow has been struck at the vitals of Christian liberty. I do not feel that I am guilty of contumacy, or disobedience to the order of the Church; neither if I were guilty to the extent of the specifications could I believe that the severest penalty known in ecclesiastical discipline ought to be inflicted on me. I now make my appeal to you, and hope to be received and treated in accordance with the verdict which your candor and religion shall render.

I admitted on my trial that I had permitted B. T. Roberts to speak in my pulpit; and that I had attended and took part in religious meetings conducted by him. Also, that I had preached in a few instances within the bounds of other brethren's charges. There was nothing material proved in addition to this.

I showed in my defense,—

1st. That B. T. Roberts, since his expulsion had been admitted to the M. E. Church on trial, and licensed to exhort, and as such I had received him. Bishop Simpson had decided that an error or irregularity on the part of an administrator of Discipline does not invalidate the title to membership of a person received into the Church. So that Brother Roberts was legally and properly a member of the M. E. Church on trial. Whether his license to exhort given him by Rev. C. D. Burlingham, he being recommended to do so by the unanimous vote of the society at Pekin, was valid or not, according to the letter of the law, it was at least a good reason in favor of my allowing him to speak. I could not forbid a man to speak in my pulpit who came with such recommendations. If there is contumacy in this, it must consist in a refusal of absolute subjection to the will of the Buffalo Regency, and not in resistance to the reasonable authority of the Church.

I showed in my defense,—

2. That not one of the preachers on whose charges I had preached had ever, by word or by letter, intimated to me that they were displeased with my preaching within the bounds of their charges; and also, that my Presiding Elder had never admonished me never to do so. If I was expelled for that, it certainly was a crime that none of the men who claim to be injured thought enough of to speak to me about it, though months elapsed between its commission and the Conference.

I contend that I am expelled from the Church for no crime whatever; either against the word of God, or the Methodist Discipline. In these things for which I was expelled, I have not violated my obligations to God, nor transcended my rights as a Methodist preacher.

I am not blamable in receiving Brother Roberts as I did. I received him and treated him as an exhorter. It was not proved that I did more than this. His relation to the Church, and the license which he held, fully entitled him, according to the Discipline and the usages of Methodism, to all the respect which I paid him. But I had higher reasons than these for doing as I did. I had for many years regarded Brother Roberts as a devoted servant of God, eminent for his usefulness. I really believed that his expulsion from the Church was only the result of hatred aroused by his faithful denunciation of sin, and that he was, in the sight of heaven, as much a servant of God and a minister of the Gospel after his expulsion as before it. I could not do less than receive him. To have forbidden him to speak in my pulpit, would have been a sin against God that I would not bear in the judgment, for all worlds.

3. I have not sinned in preaching within the territories claimed by other preachers. Simply preaching the Gospel is all that I did. I was not charged with doing more. So that the solution of the question, Has one preacher any right to preach on another's territory? will make me guilty or innocent. The commission which God gave me is, "Go into all the world." * * *

I have forborne to speak for others who are my companions in the same tribulation, partly because I left the seat of the Conference before the adjournment, and do not know how far the work of decapitation had proceeded, and partly because I prefer that they should speak for themselves. The charges against eight preachers were nearly the same as those on which I was condemned, viz.: contumacy and disobedience to the order of the Church.

The Conference, on the second day of its session, adopted a series of resolutions which amounted to an *ex post facto law* according to which every preacher's character was to pass. Every preacher who was supposed during the year past to have violated the code contained in the resolutions had his character arrested. No man could pass until he had testified his penitence for having violated them, (before they existed) and promised to observe them in future.

To what extent this persecution will be carried, the future alone can reveal. The majority of the Conference are evidently determined, by raising the mad dog cry of "Nazaritism," to drive out of the Church all who have religion enough not to indorse their measures. What others may do I cannot tell, but as for myself, I am yet firmly attached in heart to the M. E. Church. I believe her doctrines and love her Discipline. I have appealed to the General Conference. I shall get back into the Church again if I can.

J. A. WELLS.

BELFAST, Oct. 20, 1859.

The reader now has all the essential facts connected with the trial and expulsion of these four devoted, able and effective preachers of the gospel from the Genesee Annual Conference and the Methodist Episcopal Church, and therefrom can form his own opinion as to the spirit which instigated the trials and pushed them to their final conclusion. Was it hatred of sin? Was it love of righteousness? Was it zeal for the purity of the Church? Or, was it that same spirit of intolerance which, in earlier and ruder times, persecuted even unto martyrdom those who would not consent to be enslaved to their fellow men in matters of opinion and of conscience? What does the world not owe to those who, through the ages, have lived, labored and suffered as the pioneers of freedom to think, speak, act and worship in accordance with the dictates of conscience?

The editor of the *Northern Independent,* in reviewing the expulsions from the Genesee Conference, wrote with his accustomed vigor and fearlessness a critique which, we are persuaded, has met the approval of candid readers generally. In the issue of October 20, 1859, he said:

THE GENESEE CONFERENCE

Last week we referred to the trials going on in this Conference, and expressed an opinion that they were pernicious. It is now our painful duty to record the result of these most infatuated proceedings. Up to the time of this writing, four of the best members of the Conference have been expelled, both from the Conference and the Church. We have known ecclesiastical blunders before, but never one so great as this. We do not care to repeat what we have already said of these trials, nor do we wish to enter into the controversy further than to note what we think to be a very dangerous perversion of Conference authority.

Every man of common sense knows that contumacy is not necessarily a crime; and hence if the defendant had been guilty of all that was charged upon him, there was no occasion for his expulsion. Contumacy is often a virtue. It may be a minister's duty to comply with the rules imposed by a majority, or it may not; all will depend on the character of the rules—if right, he may keep them; if not right, he is bound to disregard them, or peril his soul. When Conference action is just and wise, it becomes obligatory; but when it is unjust and foolish, the obligation ceases. Else an Annual Conference, becoming perverse, might decree that all its members should abstain from praying, and the decree would be binding. As such a conclusion is absurd, we are obliged to reject the premises on which it rests, and hold that Conferences have power only so far as they keep to the right. So much for the merits of the case, even if contumacy had been among the things forbidden by the Church. But the fact is, we have not, and never had any rule making contumacy a sin. It is not an offense, either named or contemplated by our Discipline. It is a crime unheard of in the annals of Methodism—a miserable aping of the most questionable and dangerous prerogatives ever exercised by secular authority.

That a preacher may be expelled for "improper tempers, words, or actions," is true, and if the charge had been for either or all of these things, it would at least have been right in form, and might have been tried on its merits. But a trial for contumacy is quite another thing, and altogether beyond the record. In making these trials rest upon this basis, the Conference has, in fact, established a new law, and given sovereign power to every straggling resolution that may chance to be passed. Not to obey a perverse resolution, would be very far from evincing "improper tempers, words or actions," but it would certainly be "contumacy." Hence the unpardonable liberty taken in departing from the words of the Discipline, and manufacturing this new test of character.

This style of administration assumes an importance far beyond the individual instances of decapitation which have already occurred. Acting on the same principle, the Genesee Conference, or any other Conference, has only to pass a resolution that no member shall take the *Northern Independent*, or act as agent for it, and the work is done—thenceforth, whoever gets a subscriber or receives the paper into his house, is guilty of contumacy, and destined to be expelled. Thus this unfounded assumption seizes upon the press, sweeps away every vestige of personal liberty, and makes the minority of the Conference the veriest slaves. It is true, the Conference has not yet given the principle on which it is acting this particular application, but how soon it may, no one can tell. At this session the members have been forbidden to attend all meetings not regularly appointed, as will be seen from the third and fifth resolutions:

[The resolutions are omitted here, as they have already appeared on page 221, to which the reader is referred].

These resolutions are well enough, considered as merely declarative or advisory, but regarded as the ultimate law of the Church, they are a grievous outrage on the rights of every member of an Annual Conference. Annual Conferences may advise, and may execute laws already made, but they are not law-making bodies, and consequently cannot pass a resolution having the force of law. But if a man be expelled for non-conformity to a rule made by an Annual Conference, then is an Annual Conference, in the very highest sense, a law-making body. An Annual Conference may expel a preacher for violating the Discipline but not for violating one of its own rules. Were it not for this necessary restriction, each Annual Conference could make laws *ad libitum*, and the law-making power of the General Conference would be a nullity. Surely, in view of the above resolutions, every Methodist preacher may ask, Have we an organic law? Or, are we at the mercy of a bare majority, however obtained and however disposed? If a simple Conference resolution is law, we are without a Constitution, and in that respect worse off than a temperance society, or any other voluntary association whatever. It will be conceded by all, that an Annual Conference has no more right to make laws than a Quarterly Conference, and what would be thought if a Quarterly Conference should pass a series of resolutions, to be kept by all its members, under pain of expulsion? Such a thing is unprecedented, and yet would be quite as legal as the penalties threatened in the foregoing resolutions.

Are we then, says an objector, to endure the evils complained of in the foregoing resolutions? Not necessarily. There are other and milder remedies than expulsion. But even if the General Conference itself should make a rule prohibiting the things forbidden by these Genesee Conference resolutions, we should doubt the utility of the measure. Some things are better for being let alone. Not many ages since, the civil law undertook to regulate religious opinion; but after much blood had been shed to no purpose, it was found that toleration was better than legislation. So also in the operations of Methodism, it may perhaps be found that forbearance is a better cure than law.

It may be a sin, and a sufficient cause for expulsion, to treat an expelled minister as though he were yet a minister, but our Church has nowhere affirmed the fact. All the Discipline says on the subject is, that *after* an appeal has been had—mark that—a "person so expelled shall have no privilege of society or sacrament in our Church, without confession, contrition, and satisfactory reformation." Here is the sum total of the penalty to be inflicted, but none of it is fairly due until the appeal has been heard, for until then the trial is not ended—the case has not yet reached the highest Court. In civil law, the execution of the sentence awaits the action of the Appellate Court. We do not hang a man because the jury finds him guilty, but wait till the final hearing of the case before the highest tribunal. Following this analogy, a minister expelled by an Annual Conference, is at most barely suspended, and though not eligible to an appointment, may, nevertheless, not be wholly excluded from the courtesies due to ministerial character. It was this view of the case, joined with a full conviction of the injustice of the sentence, and modified also by the fact of the actual readmission of the expelled persons into the Church, which induced treatment of which complaint is here made. What relates to invading other charges is too trivial for notice.

These cases of expulsion will, no doubt, go up to the ensuing General Conference, where they are quite certain to be reversed, if they can be fairly heard. Some have intimated that the expelled brethren must be very cautious, and do all honor to the act of their expulsion, by remaining silent until their appeal is acted upon. We are glad that even in this respect there will be no little breadth to the question. If, after their expulsion, they labor on—not as Methodists, but as men—and do what good they can, it ought not to be imputed to them as a crime, nor in anywise prejudice their appeal. They still have what God and nature gave them—the right to speak and to act as men and as Christians; Methodism takes away only what it gave. The gift of life, the divine commission, and the assurance of pardon, are all from a higher source—a source over which Conferences have no control.

We are convinced that a principle is involved in the administration of that Conference which, if unchecked, must be fatal to Methodism. Our Annual Conferences would be converted into so many petty tyrannies, alike injurious to men and offensive to God. Majorities would become simply machines for the extirpation of progressive sentiment.

Since the above was written, we have received the following from Brother Roberts: "A resolution was passed on Saturday against any of the members of Conference acting as agent for the *Northern Independent*." Now, we all know what such a resolution means in the Genesee Conference. Every preacher who dare act as agent for us will be expelled for contumacy. Thus the war has commenced openly. It will now be known whether Methodists are slaves or freemen.

The following is the resolution regarding the *Northern Independent*, together with the comments of one of the corresponding editors:

"*Resolved*, That we disapprove of any member of this Conference acting as agent for the *Northern Independent*, or of writing for its columns, or in any way giving it encouragement and support."

The above is of "striking significance," from the fact that the

"Regency" has recently put on General Conference authority, and has become a law-making body. Every man who disobeys this resolution, does so at the peril of his ministerial office, and his membership in the M. E. Church. It would be as clear a case of "contumacy," as any for which the brethren were expelled, to whom we have referred. The "Regency," be it remembered, are legislators, jurors, judges and executioners, and woe to any member of the Genesee Conference who shall be found in any way giving it (the *Independent*) encouragement and support.

Dr. Hibbard is in raptures over the "extraordinary proceedings of Genesee Conference," and especially over the passage of the resolution against the *Independent*. "That was manfully said," he exclaims, "it ought to inspire all its sister Conferences," etc. It will inspire with supreme disgust all sister Conferences who are not steeped to the lips in pro-slaveryism and popery.

Three of the expelled brethren at once gave notice of appeal to the General Conference; but Mr. Stiles, who appears to have had a more correct idea of what the action of the General Conference would be than the others, said it was no use to take an appeal, and therefore he should waste none of his time, and incur none of the strain necessary, in the prosecution of an appeal, as he had no hope whatever that the General Conference would do justice in the case. He saw an opening before him to carry on the work of God independent of the Genesee Conference, which had so unjustly treated him and his brethren, and he chose to accept his expulsion and enter the open door to a new field of opportunity.

At the urgent request of the Albion people he returned to that village, whereupon the members of the Church and congregation who were in sympathy with him, and who "loved righteousness and hated iniquity," at once rallied about him, still believing him to be an earnest and holy man of God. They were overwhelmingly in the majority, and, according to equity, were entitled to the Church property. But when trouble arose over the question, instead of pressing their claim in Court they chose rather to avoid giving offense and cause for complaint, and "took joyfully the spoiling of their goods."

The friends of Mr. Stiles relinquished their claim to the Church property, and then proceeded, with much expedition, to erect for him a Church building, with a main audience room about 55 x 101 feet, a lecture room half as large, and four large and commodious class rooms, besides a spacious vestibule, hall-ways, etc., the largest Church edifice in the town. Here he continued to live and labor, in a community that loved him dearly, until, in the midst of his days, he was summoned from labor to reward. His memory was deeply enshrined in the hearts of his people, some of whom still survive, and all of whom ever mention his name in a spirit of reverent and deep affection.

The Church which he organized after his return to Albion took the name of the Congregational Free Methodist Church. Later Mr. Stiles attended the Convention at which the Free Methodist denomination was organized, assisted in the forming of its Discipline, and heartily cooperated in the election of B. T. Roberts as its first General Superintendent. After the formation of the new denomination the local Church he had organized in Albion joined it in a body.

Mr. Stiles was not permitted to give many years of service to the Free Methodist Church, however. The strain to which his sensitive nature had been subjected through the indignities he suffered at the hands of the Genesee Conference was too much for him. He was taken down with typhoid fever, which assumed a malignant type from the start, and never recovered. "He was greatly blessed in his soul when he was taken sick, and to this he often referred, even during spells of delirium," writes Mr. Roberts. "One evening, as we were watching with him, he thought he was in the hands of a secret society committee, and cried out, 'Brother Roberts, I want you should go out and tell the committee that I am ready to die in two hours, or one hour, or even this minute. The Lord has greatly blessed me, and I shall go straight to glory.' The day before he died he said to his physician, 'ALL IS

RIGHT.' He grew gradually weaker, and, without a struggle on the 7th of May, 1863, his pure spirit passed away to the realms of bliss."

The funeral of this noble man of God was attended by an immense congregation, the main audience room of the Church, which had a capacity of over 1,000 persons, was filled, and hundreds were outside, unable to gain admission. The Rev. William Hosmer, who had long been his fellow soldier in the warfare against all sin, preached on the occasion, an eloquent and impressive sermon, from Hebrews 11:27—"He endured as seeing Him who is invisible."

The Rev. Charles D. Burlingham, at the time of his expulsion, had been a member of the Genesee Conference nineteen years, and had proved himself an earnest and effective preacher, and an acceptable pastor as well, on the various charges he had served. He had also filled the position of Presiding Elder with general acceptability for four years. He is said to have been "a preacher of more than ordinary ability, original in his style, clear in his reasonings, and happy in the use of illustrations." His labors, however, had been excessive, and he was now "left broken in constitution, with a large, dependent family, and no means for their support."

Later Mr. Burlingham was restored to the Conference, though in a way which many considered as evidencing the injustice of the Genesee Conference almost as clearly as did his expulsion from the Conference and Church. He was called to his reward in 1874.

The Rev. Mr. Cooley had for seventeen years proved himself a diligent, useful and acceptable itinerant preacher when called to share the fate of others who had been expelled for their earnest advocacy of the principles of primitive Methodism. He has been described as "a quiet, peaceable, unoffending, upright man;" "a clear, Scriptural, searching preacher," who "generally had good revivals on the charges on which he labored." But these qualities were not allowed to stand in the way of sending any man to the ecclesiastical guillotine by the Genesee Conference of the Methodist Church in those days, if the crime of "Nazaritism" could be proved against him.

The Rev. John A. Wells had been a member of the Conference but seven years when called to meet his fate in expulsion on the charge of "contumacy." He had been successful as a minister, however, and had shown himself an able and practical preacher, a man of studious turn, wholly devoted to the work of God, without guile, and of unbending integrity. He finally united with the Presbyterian Church.

CHAPTER XXVI

THE SECOND LAYMEN'S CONVENTION

The second Annual Laymen's Convention was held, pursuant to call, in the Baptist Church at Albion, N. Y., November 1 and 2, 1859. At the permanent organization the Hon. Abner I. Wood was reëlected president; George W. Holmes, John Billings, Jonathan Handly, Edward P. Cox and S. C. Springer were chosen as vice-presidents; and S. K. J. Chesbrough, Stephen S. Rice, William Hart and Thomas Sully were chosen secretaries.

The following was adopted as the Declaration in part of the Convention:

When we met last year in Convention, we trusted that the preachers, whose course was the cause of our assembling, would be led to repentance and reformation. But our hopes have been blasted. The Scripture is still true, which saith that "evil men and seducers shall wax worse and worse, deceiving and being deceived."

That we have the right to take into consideration the public acts of a public body to which we are intimately related, cannot be denied. That such consideration has become our duty we are well satisfied. Our Lord has given us the test, "By their fruits ye shall know them." What have been the fruits for the past year of the party in Conference, known as the "Buffalo Regency"? Have they been such as we should expect from men of God? We are pained to be obliged to bear testimony to the fact that some occupying the place of Methodist ministers have used their influence, and bent their energies to put down, under the name of "fanaticism," what we feel confident is the work of the Holy Spirit.

The course pursued by some of our preachers, in expelling from the Church members in good standing and high repute for their Christian character, because they attended our Convention in December last, we look upon as cruel and oppressive, and it calls for our most decided disapproval. What does the right of private judgment amount to, if we can not exercise it without bringing down on our heads these ecclesiastical anathemas? To our brethren who have been so used, we extend our cordial sympathy, and we assure them that our confidence in them has not diminished on account of their names being cast out as evil for the Son of man's sake. The action of the majority, in expelling from the Conference and the Church, four able and devoted ministers, and locating two others, upon the most frivolous pretexts, is so at variance with the principles of justice and our holy Christianity as to cause minor offenses to be aggravated, when they would otherwise be overlooked. The charge against each was the convenient one of "contumacy." The specifications were in substance, the receiving as ministers those who were expelled at the previous session of the Conference, and for preaching in the bounds of other men's charges. Where in the Bible, or in the Discipline, is "contumacy," spoken of as a crime? It is a charge generally resorted to for the purpose of oppression. Let whatever the dominant power in the Church may be pleased to call "contumacy" be treated as a crime, religious liberty is at an end. There is not an honest man in the Conference but may be expelled for "contumacy," whenever, by any means, a majority can be obtained against him. There is not a member of the M. E. Church, who acts from his own convictions of right, but may be excommunicated for "contumacy," whenever his preacher is disposed to do so. Let some mandate be issued that cannot in conscience be obeyed, and the guilt of contumacy is incurred. The Regency party not only expelled devoted servants of God for contumacy, but did it under the most aggravated circumstances. An Annual Conference possesses no power to make laws. A resolution with a penalty affixed for its violation, is to all intents and purposes a law. The Regency passed resolutions at the last session of the Conference, and then tried and expelled men for violating them months before they had an existence! That any honest man can entertain any respect for such judicial action is utterly impossible. The specifications were in keeping with the charge. The first was for recognizing as ministers the expelled members of the Conference. The charge was not for recognizing them as Methodist ministers; for the expelled brethren did not claim to have authority from the Church. They acted simply by virtue of their commission from God. If a man believes he is called of God to preach, and God owns and blesses his labors, has he not the right thus to warn sinners to flee the wrath to come? At the second Conference held by Wesley, it was asked, "Is not the will of our governors a law?" The answer was emphatically: "No—not of any governors, temporal or spiritual. Therefore if any Bishop wills that I should not preach the Gospel, his will is no law to me. But what if he produced a law against your preaching? I am to obey God rather than man." This is the language of the founder of Methodism. How it rebukes the arrogant, popish assumptions of some of the pretended followers of Wesley.

The second specification was for preaching in other men's charges without their consent.

Where is there anything wrong in this? What precept of the Bible, what rule of the Discipline is violated? Does it not evidence the faithful minister of Jesus, burning with love for souls, rather than the criminal deserving the highest censure of the Church? Methodist ministers are bound by their obligations to serve the charges to which they are appointed by the Conference: *but they do not promise that they will not preach anywhere else.* On the contrary, the commission from Christ reads, "Go ye into all the world and preach the Gospel to every creature." The Discipline says, "You have nothing to do but to save souls; therefore, spend and be spent in this work; *and go always, not only to those who want you, but to those who want you most. Observe, it is not your business only to preach so many times, and to take care of this or that society, but to save as many as you can;* to bring as many sinners as you can to repentance, and with all your power to build them up in that holiness, without which they cannot see the Lord." On this ground, were these men of God, as we esteem them, Revs. Loren Stiles, Jr., John A. Wells, Wm. Cooley, and Charles D. Burlingham, excommunicated by the Regency party of the Genesee Conference at its last session. Fidelity to God will not allow us quietly to acquiesce in such decisions. It is urged that we must respect the action of the Church. But what is the Church? Our XIIIth Article of Religion says, "The visible Church of God is a congregation of faithful men, in which the pure word of God is preached, and the sacraments duly administered." *The ministers then are not "the Church."* If ministers wish to have their acts respected, they must, like other men, perform *respectable* actions.

These repeated acts of expulsion, wrong as they are in themselves, deserve the stronger condemnation from the fact, scarcely attempted to be disguised, that THE OBJECT *is to prevent the work of holiness from spreading among us—to put down the life and power of godliness in our Churches, and to inaugurate in its stead the peaceable reign of a cold and heartless formalism,*—in short, to do away with what has always been a distinctive feature of

Methodism. If the work which the men who were expelled both this year and last, have labored, and not without success, to promote, be "fanaticism," then has Methodism from the beginning been "fanaticism." Our attachment to Methodism was never stronger than it is at present, and our sympathy and our means shall be given to the men who toil and suffer to promote it. We can not abandon, at the bidding of a majority, the doctrines of Methodism, and the men who defend them.

The course of the Regency in shielding members of their faction, creates the suspicion that a stronger motive than any referred to lies at the foundation of their remarkable action,—*the principle of self-preservation.* It may be that the guilty, to prevent exposure, deem it necessary to expel the innocent. Their refusal to entertain charges; and their prompt acquittal of one of their leaders, though clearly proved guilty of a crime sufficient to exclude him from heaven, look strongly in that direction. The recent public exposure in another Conference of one of the founders of the Regency party, who took a transfer to escape from well founded suspicion shows how a minister may pursue, unconvicted, a career of guilt for years, when "*shielded*" by secret society influences, and willing to be the servile tool of the majority.

For the evils complained of we see no other remedy within our reach than the one we adopted last year:—WITHHOLD SUPPLIES. To show that such a remedy is "constitutional" and "loyal," we have only to refer to the "proceedings" of the Convention of last year and to authorities therein quoted.

In connection with the foregoing, and as a part of its Declaration, the Convention adopted eleven resolutions. The first of these, which was adopted unanimously, expressed the utmost confidence in the expelled preachers, commending them to the confidence and sympathy of the children of God wherever they might go.

The second affirmed their adherence to the doctrines and usages of Methodism, but also declared their unwillingness to recognize the oppressive policy of the "Regency" faction in the Genesee Conference as the action of the Church, and their refusal to submit to the same.

Resolution 3 recommended that all the preachers who had been expelled, and also the two who were located under the test resolutions at the Brockport Conference, "continue to labor for the promotion of the work of God and the salvation of souls, by preaching, exhorting, visiting and praying as they have opportunity," and assuring them that, "while they shall thus devote themselves to the work of the ministry, we will cheerfully use our means and influence for their support."

Resolutions 4, 5, and 6 provided for the districting of the work, gathering those who had been unjustly deprived of their Church home into Bands, in order to keep them from being scattered and so lost to the Church, and for regular collections from the various Bands as a means of securing adequate support for the brethren in the ministry.

The seventh resolution set forth the determination of the lay brethren to refuse their support to any member of Genesee Conference who assisted, either by his vote or influence, in the expulsion of the preachers charged with "contumacy," except upon "contrition, confession and satisfactory reformation."

The eighth had to do with repudiating the course of certain preachers whose action out of the pulpit was regarded as inconsistent with their utterances from the pulpit; while Resolution 9 declared against the five test resolutions of the Brockport Conference as "anti-Methodistic and Popish, the merest ecclesiastical tyranny," and recommended "that the preachers remaining in the Conference, who have the work of God at heart, repudiate in theory and practise the aforesaid resolutions."

Resolutions 10 and 11 provided for memorializing the General Conference to the effect that that body should set aside the action of the Genesee Conference in the alleged cases of "contumacy," and restore the six expelled preachers to their former Conference and Church relation.

CHAPTER XXVII

THE CRUSHING-OUT PROCESS CONTINUED

Following the second Laymen's Convention at Albion the war against "Nazaritism" was waged more fiercely than ever. Within a few weeks after its adjournment a letter was in circulation among the "Regency" preachers strongly encouraging them in their policy. Though without any signature, it was generally understood as being the production of a certain Bishop. Either it was or it was not of Episcopal authorship. If it was, it certainly speaks badly for the Bishop. If it was not, it certainly was a worse reflection upon the men who were responsible for its circulation. It reads like the production of one who regarded himself as qualified to speak with authority. We reproduce it here, from "Why Another Sect?":

January 3, 1860.

DEAR BROTHER:

A happy New Year to you. * * My advice is *decided* that you should remove every leader who takes part in the Albion Convention, or any of a similar character. *Do not be deterred* by threats of difficulty, or of leaving the Church. Better have no members than disorderly ones. The world is wide. Sinners are numerous. We will go with the Gospel to them, and God will give us fruit. I repeat then, by all means, stand firmly by the action of the Church. *Remove* every leader who arrays himself against it, no matter what may be his *influence*, or how great his usefulness, or how it may affect your congregation, or how it will result in the end.

As to private members, I would do nothing while they do not engage in opposition meetings. But if they get up and sustain meetings for expelled preachers, or resist Church action, I would cite them to trial, after proper admonition.

Let me again assure you, that the safety of the Church is in straightforward action. Yours truly,

It now looked very much as though any measure that seemed likely to crush out "Nazaritism" would be regarded with favor by the dominant party, and that without question as to its ethical character. "Nazarites" were regarded as ecclesiastical outlaws, more to be shunned than any other class of people. "These Nazarites," exclaimed the Rev. Thomas Carlton at the Brockport Conference, "are like Canada thistles, you cut down one and ten will spring up in its place." The remark strikingly reminds us of how, amid the persecutions of the early Christians, for every one who was sent to martyrdom dozens seemed to arise in his stead, until it resulted in the proverbial saying, "The ashes of the martyrs are the seed of the Church."

The foregoing remark of Mr. Carlton, though instigated by a spirit of contempt and hatred, was not in itself so very offensive. Other remarks connected with the same speech, however, betrayed a deep-seated malignity such as it is difficult to reconcile in any way with a Christ-like spirit. The Rev. C. D. Burlingham has thus described his speech:

> One of their leading champions, whose efficiency in originating and perpetuating the Conference difficulties is unsurpassed, and from whose official position decency if not dignity might be expected, while making a speech, in the "height of his argument," exclaimed with a perfect yell, that he "had rather meet a thousand devils than three Nazarites"—that is to say, in the estimation of this minister of Jesus, and General Conference official, one Nazarite is worse than three hundred and thirty-three and one third devils! But this was said in defense of the Church! Will not such zeal in her behalf be duly appreciated, and coveted honors be conferred accordingly? All such eloquence was met by the minority, as it should have been, by silent contempt.
>
> The chair very seldom saw proper to rebuke this kind of declamation."*

The effect of such a tirade at this particular juncture was highly inflammatory upon the "Regency" preachers.

*"Outline History," p. 52.

This, together with the persecuting example of the Conference, and the influence of the official but unsigned letter which has been quoted, instigated them to go to their respective appointments fully determined to rid the Methodist societies of all who uncompromisingly adhered to the doctrines and usages of original Methodism. In other words, they went forth with "Death to Nazaritism" as their slogan for the year. A few samples of their mode of procedure will now be given, but only a very imperfect idea of their spirit and manner can be conveyed thereby.

One of the first developments occurred on the Kendall circuit. There were a number of Methodist families here of more than ordinary intelligence, and who had well-defined and correct ideas respecting the doctrines and usages of Methodism. The doctrine of holiness, or Christian perfection, had been clearly and faithfully preached and enforced among them. As a result many professed to have entered into the experience, who honored their profession by uniform consistency of life. The late Conference at Brockport had sent a preacher of opposite and opposing tendencies to bring these people into subjection to the oppressive régime which it had inaugurated. It was a more difficult task than he had imagined, but he persisted, like a loyal son of the "Regency" faction. Most of the officials and leading members were stoutly opposed to "Regency" rule, and were plainly in sympathy with the proscribed preachers and laymen, and disposed to give the work of holiness their unqualified indorsement. How should he proceed? The following extract from "Why Another Sect?" will tell:

His first move was to get control of the Quarterly Conference. This is easily done in the M. E. Church in which the Quarterly Conference is substantially the creation of the preacher, who appoints all the leaders, nominates the stewards, and licenses the exhorters, by whom it is mainly composed. He put in new leaders, and, in order to get more leaders than there were other members of the Quarterly Conference, he appointed two leaders to one class. When the Quarterly Conference came together, he moved that the board of stewards be declared vacant. By the aid of his leaders he easily carried it. He then put in his own followers as stewards.

Then the preacher moved that several leading members who were known to stand opposed to the crushing-out policy of the Conference be declared withdrawn. This was also carried. In vain did these members protest that they did not withdraw, and did not intend to. The preacher read them out "withdrawn." Henceforth they were denied the privileges of members in the Methodist Episcopal Church! This was an improvement on the farce of going through the form of a trial. What need of witnesses when the verdict is made up beforehand without the slightest regard to testimony? Why call a jury for the sole purpose of pronouncing guilty whoever the judge arraigns? So, even the forms of justice were dispensed with, and by the most barefaced despotism many were turned out of Churches of which they had been the pioneers; and from houses of worship which their own money had built.

The Rev. A. L. Chapin, preacher in charge of the East Otto circuit, was one of the most bitter and violent tools of the "Regency party." He proceeded with a high hand in ridding the Church at East Otto of "Nazarites" and of those in sympathy with "Nazaritism." His admission to the Conference had been strongly opposed by the preachers of the reform party, on the ground that, though he was a man of good abilities, he was lacking in true religion. Revenge inflamed his zeal to the utmost bounds. Adopting the new, short and easy method, he expelled Dewey Tefft, Niles Tefft, E. S. Woodruff and Otis O. Bacon from the Church. He proceeded in the following manner:

First, he called the official members of the circuit together, and in fiery address informed them that the Methodist Discipline recognized no members who would not contribute to the support of the ministry. Then, with the aid of his official members, he made out an assessment of the amount each member should pay, with the understanding that they must either pay or be excluded from the Church. He wished the doings of that meeting to be kept strictly secret, and emphatically declared that if any one betrayed the secret, such conduct would be considered just ground for expulsion.

Next he appointed a time when he purposed to meet the class in the Tefft neighborhood, a country appointment some two or three miles from town. They met at the time appointed, and had a plain talk regarding the support of the Church, as a result of which the entire class plainly informed the pastor that they would contribute nothing toward his support, except upon his "contrition, confession and proper amendment." It was a daring deed for all. The Teffts, however, were men of means, highly intelligent, and with the full courage of their convictions. They had immigrated to that part of Western New York when it was a wilderness, "had been familiar with wild beasts, and were not to be frightened by the ravings of a preacher into acting contrary to their convictions." Their heroism inspired the others to take their stand with equal courage. Hence the fury of the preacher was unavailing.

As a third measure Mr. Chapin called another official meeting, at which he became more violent than at the former one. First, he demanded to know who had *published* the proceedings of their former meeting. Mr. Bacon replied to the effect that he did not know who had *published* its proceedings, but that he himself had informed one man of what was therein done. Mr. Chapin flew into a rage, shook his fist in Mr. Bacon's face, and vehemently and repeatedly said, "Who ever heard the like?" Mr. Bacon courageously replied, "I did not know that an official meeting was a secret association, but if it is, the sooner you remove me from it the better it will be for you." In this meeting it was finally decided that the refractory members should be brought to trial.

Charges were soon formulated and preferred against them. They were charged with "contumacy," the customary charge against so-called "Nazarites," and, in addition, with "taking and circulating the *Northern Independent*." Mr. Bacon was also charged, in one of the specifications, with objectionable words used in debate at the official meeting, and in another, with preaching in a remote neighborhood when forbidden to do so by his pastor. There appears to have been an effort on Mr. Chapin's part to cut the people of that neighborhood off from preaching services as a punishment for their contumacy. But Mr. Bacon refused to be a party to this work of proscription, greatly to the chagrin of his pastor.

The following exciting episode in connection with one of the trials is thus described:

> During the trial of Dewey Tefft, Mr. Chapin was so arrogant and overbearing that the manhood of one who came to the trial as one of his adherents revolted. Rising to his feet greatly excited, in thundering tones, Mr. Scott demanded, addressing Mr. Chapin:
>
> "Who are you?"
>
> "The grandson of Ethan Allen," replied Chapin, rising to his feet.
>
> "How mightily the race has degenerated," replied Scott. "You may be a smart man, but you are not smart enough to be judge, jury, prosecutor, and all, in one case. Now take your proper place and keep it. I want to see fair play."
>
> For a time the wildest excitement prevailed.

Like all the other cases we have considered, and which were very clearly predetermined, these trials resulted in the expulsion of all the accused persons from the Church. In pronouncing sentence, however, the preacher in charge took special care to state that they were not expelled for any breach of the rules of morality and religion, but for "a violation of our rules."

The action of the Brockport Conference thus began to bear fruit in the extermination of so-called "Nazarites" and "Nazaritism" from the Methodist Episcopal Church in Western New York. But the end was not yet.

Similar work of expulsion was vigorously prosecuted at Asbury Church, near LeRoy, by the Rev. S. M. Hopkins. Cyrus Sperry, Martin Seekins, Hiram Husted, and Sylvester Near—all reliable laymen and noble Christians, were expelled as a result of the most farcical trials. Mr.

Sperry, stanch, dependable, and of unbending rectitude, was tried on a bill of charges, said to cover two pages of foolscap, based on the proceedings of the Laymen's Convention. Similar charges were brought against the others. "Mr. Seekins was at work in his harvest field when summoned before the Church tribunal to answer charges which were then first presented to him. He asked for a delay of one hour. This was refused." Such summary proceedings could not be justified, save in case of most flagrant crimes.

At the expiration of the Conference year Mr. Hopkins was sent elsewhere, and the Rev. J. B. Lankton took charge of this work, and proceeded to finish what his predecessor had so vigorously begun, namely, the crushing out of "Nazaritism" from the circuit. First he summoned Mrs. Olive Sperry to answer to "Contempt and disobedience to the order and Discipline of the M. E. Church, by attending, and being interested in favor of a seditious meeting, on the 9th of August last at the meeting-house, and voting for some or all the resolutions there passed, which were violently rebellious against the Discipline and government of the M. E. Church."

The "resolutions" referred to in the foregoing charge were to the effect that those who voted for them would stand upon their rights, as members of the M. E. Church, to withhold support from such preachers as they believed had proved themselves unworthy of the same. We have failed to ascertain anything connected with the circumstances more "violently rebellious against the Discipline and government of the M. E. Church" than voting for those resolutions. Yet Mr. Lankton expelled fourteen or fifteen members on charges similar to those preferred against Mrs. Sperry.

This kind of work was now spreading like a contagion. The Rev. B. F. McNeal adopted the same policy on the Tonawanda and Ridgeville circuit. John Corliss and Anthony Ames had been efficient class-leaders for years, but he removed them from their office without due cause. Then the Presiding Elder, Rev. P. Woodworth, at the next Quarterly Conference, ruled that Tristram Corliss, superintendent of the Sabbath-school at Pendleton, on the Tonawanda and Ridgeville circuit, was not a member of the official board, because of Tonawanda being the first named society of the circuit. A board of stewards was then created composed of members of the circuit who would vote according to the wishes of the preacher in charge. The following Sabbath, the Rev. McNeal, without their consent, or even their knowledge of what he was going to do, "read out" as "withdrawn" from the Church, Anthony Ames and John Corliss, class-leaders; Tristram Corliss, Sabbath-school superintendent; W. R. Wilcox, J. Hunt, and Henry Kayner, stewards, and their wives; M. Folger and wife, and Mrs. Henry Pickard.

The rage for expulsions reached the Belfast circuit. The Rev. J. W. Reddy, one of the preachers who was located under the test resolutions at the Brockport Conference, was the first victim. A charge was brought against him for "evil speaking," in asserting that the Genesee Conference had expelled four of its holiest members for nothing, and also a charge of "disobedience to the order and Discipline of the Church," in holding separate religious meetings at the time of the regular services at the Church. When labored with for these things, Mr. Reddy explained that if he said those ministers were expelled for nothing, he did not mean to be understood in a literal sense; but that what he meant to express was that they were expelled for no crime meriting such action, but simply because of the uncompromising stand they took for earnest Christianity.

On the 12th of March, the charges were stated to Brother Reddy, with the specifications, verbally; and he was cited to trial in the same way, at the Quarterly Conference to be held the ensuing Saturday. He then asked for a written copy of the charges and specifications, that he might be able to prepare his defense. This was denied him by the preacher in charge, who said that he could and would bring him to trial, without any written charges. After the religious services of the Quarterly Meeting on Saturday, a copy of the charges was handed to Brother Reddy, and the Conference immediately met (not in the Church, as usual, but in the parlor of the parsonage, which was barely sufficient to admit the official members, to the exclusion of the private members, with one exception), and within half an hour proceeded to the trial. Before this, however, that the proceedings might be harmonious, four class-leaders, and one steward, who were supposed to have some sympathy with the accused, were removed.

Brother Reddy was arraigned, and pleading not guilty, asked for an adjournment of the case, in order that he might have time to secure counsel, and prepare his defense. This request was refused. The form of trial was then gone through with, the accused found guilty, condemned, and expelled.

Not all who were known to be opposed to the test resolutions passed at the Brockport Conference suffered arrest of character. A few were left without being pressed for a decision, supposedly in hope that witnessing the fate of others, who were more aggressive in withstanding the oppressive measures of the Conference, would cause them to weaken and finally submit to the "Regency" power. This was the effect with some, but not with all. After the refusal of the General Conference to entertain the appeals, which is yet to be considered, Asa Abell, C. D. Brooks and A. F. Curry withdrew from the Genesee Conference and from the Methodist Episcopal Church, and soon identified themselves with the Free Methodist Church, which had been founded in the meantime.

The case of the Rev. Henry Hornsby should also be noted here. He was a doughty Englishman, well-read, especially familiar with the history and traditions of Methodism, and with ecclesiastical jurisprudence. He was also a preacher of ability, who adhered to the principles of primitive Methodism, and was in full sympathy with the work of revival that had been going on in the Conference for some years. He was one of the most genial of men, but a hater of hypocrisy and of shams of all kinds.

He was also devout and pious—a man against whom nothing could be found, except it should be respecting his sympathy for "Nazaritism."

The Genesee Conference of 1861 was held at Albion. At this session the character of the Rev. Amos Hard was put under arrest, because of his having affiliated with those who had been expelled and those who had withdrawn. He was in feeble health, and hence could not assume the responsibilities of circuit work, though able to preach once a Sabbath. He was in love with the work of God, and delighted to labor as his health would allow for the salvation of men. Mr. Hard's preaching was too straight-edged, however, to be popular in the Conference, and so he had been invited to preach but three times during the year. Being invited to preach to others, he followed the disciplinary rule for preachers, "Go not only to those who want you, but to those who want you most," and accepted the invitation.

When he was arraigned before the Conference, Mr. Hornsby, as his personal friend, ventured to speak briefly in his behalf. The case of Mr. Hard was left with a committee, to be investigated during the year; and attention was then directed to Mr. Hornsby, who had been so injudicious(?) and "contumacious"(?) as to interpose in his defense.

"You are in the same boat with this man!" exclaimed the Rev. J. B. Wentworth, one of the most relentless persecutors of the so-called "Nazarites," "and we will attend to you; and though your character has been passed, it shall be reconsidered."

Then, on his motion, a committee was appointed, consisting of A. P. Ripley, J. B. Wentworth and A. L. Backus, to investigate the case of the Rev. H. Hornsby. The following is the sequel to the case:

The committee in his case reported that at different times during the year he had attended irregular meetings, and officiated

REV. JOSEPH TRAVIS
Editor of the "Free Methodist," 1882-1886

REV. JOSEPH G. TERRILL
Missionary Secretary, 1893-1895

REV. THOMAS SCOTT LaDUE
Pioneer of Free Methodism in several Conferences

REV. LEWIS BAILEY
Proprietor and Editor of the "Free Methodist," 1871-1873

[Plate Nineteen]

with expelled members of the M. E. Church, and closed with the following resolution, viz.:

"That he make open and frank confession of his faults in the matters above enumerated, and that he promise to conform in his conduct and administration in the future to the resolutions adopted at the Brockport Conference."

The Conference accepted the report and adopted the resolution. This report was presented in the forenoon, and he was called upon to answer to the resolutions. He told the Conference that he opposed the passage of the resolutions at Brockport, and refused to submit to them at that time, and was of the same mind now. Conference adjourned at noon, and in the afternoon session his case had the floor. C. D. Burlingham and S. C. Church tried to get the matter dismissed, but no! Dr. Chamberlayne, T. Carlton and J. B. Wentworth said no! It was submission, abject submission, such as no *man* would give, much less a Christian minister. He told them from the beginning he should not promise to be governed by the resolutions, as he would not bend. A. D. Wilbor came to him and said, "Now, Bro. H., you seem determined to make the Conference come to your terms, why not say *yes*, and it will be all right."

It was after five in the afternoon when his case was sent to the committee for trial. At seven P. M. that evening, T. Carlton was appointed prosecutor. Mr. Hornsby asked for the charges, if he was to be tried. Thomas Carlton replied, "They will be furnished in time." Mr. Hornsby went at the appointed time. Carlton came at 7:20, and gave him the Bill of Charges. "Contumacy. In violating a series of resolutions." Fourth specification was "refusing to confess to his sin in contemning the advice of the Conference in his case." He asked to locate. "No," says K. D. Nettleton, "if Mr. Hornsby should locate, he would be loose, and cause us more trouble than he has already. I think we had better go on with the case." He asked to be permitted to withdraw. The request was granted. The Conference did not know what the charges were upon which he was to be tried. It might infer what they would be, but they were never read in Conference. Neither did he have any time to prepare for trial. Common decency was trampled upon. Some of them seemed in a hurry to get him out. Some said, "He is a Nazarite all over, and may as well go now as any time."*

Matters went on in this way throughout the Conference generally until, and even for some time after, the

*Reprint in "Why Another Sect?"

General Conference of May, 1860. In the meantime a third Laymen's Convention was held at Olean, N. Y., February 1 and 2, 1860.

Just previous to the Olean Convention Mr. Roberts started a monthly magazine, called the *Earnest Christian,* of which he was editor and proprietor. The first number appeared in January, 1860. Its object was stated as that of furnishing the increasing number of sincere and earnest persons throughout the land anxiously inquiring for "the old paths," dissatisfied with being outer-court worshipers, desirous of "dwelling in the secret place of the Most High," and "anxious to know the conditions upon which eternal happiness can be secured," with a religious journal that should meet their needs. Mr. Roberts continued to edit and publish the *Earnest Christian* until his death, in the early part of 1893.

CHAPTER XXVIII

EARLY DEVELOPMENTS IN NORTHERN ILLINOIS

Methodism in Northern Illinois during the closing decade of the first half of the nineteenth century was in much the same condition of decline as we have seen characterizing it in Western New York. There were many who perceived this, and who grieved over the desolations of Zion, sought to withstand the general defection from God and from the principles and practises of original Methodism, and who were crying mightily, "O Lord, revive Thy work." Though regarded by the majority as fanatical troublers of Israel, whose groans and tears were not justified by the conditions of the Church, God finally heard their cries, and sent the revival for which they had so long and earnestly prayed.

In June, 1856, Dr. J. W. Redfield, on the invitation of the Rev. David Sherman, pastor of the Methodist Episcopal Church at St. Charles, Illinois, conducted a revival meeting in that town. Mr. Redfield was a Medical Doctor, and also a Local Preacher in the Methodist Church. He had a remarkable experience of conversion in early life, and subsequently an equally clear experience in the sanctifying grace of God. He began to exercise his gifts for Christian work immediately after his conversion by visiting the people in the community where he lived, and inviting them to the schoolhouse to prayer-meeting, where he exhorted them to seek the Lord with extraordinary ability for one of his years.

He seems at first to have engaged in these labors with no idea of preaching, but simply prompted by his love for the Savior and for the souls of men and women. The people, however, perceived the call of God upon him for the work of the ministry. Nor was it very long before his duty in this direction was made known to himself by the Holy Spirit. It was when he thought to desist from the labors in which he had been engaged under the impulse of his first love, that he felt restrained by the Spirit, and finally felt a powerful conviction that he was divinely called to preach the Gospel.

Happy would it have been for him had he always remained true to this conviction. But, as is the case with far too many, he debated the matter, and drew back from following his conviction from time to time. Finally he resolved to obey God, entered the work of the ministry, and was remarkably used of God in the salvation of men. Yet, after all this, he ran away from duty, and for a considerable time acted the part of the Prophet Jonah. This time he went farther from God than he had ever been. He turned infidel, gave himself to the study of anatomy, and to the investigation of natural, mental and moral science, and barely escaped landing in Materialism and Atheism. While thus fleeing from duty he also contracted a presumptuous marriage engagement, from which for many years he reaped, according as he had sowed, a harvest of bitter consequences.

After having been chastened, and all but killed, for his rebellion against the call of God, at the solicitation of a Methodist preacher in Lockport, New York, he yielded to God and consented to take the way the Lord had shown him. He finally allowed the Methodist preacher to present his name to the Church as a candidate for a license to preach. The time came for the meeting at which his case was to be considered. After a brief examination he was about to retire, that the case might be considered in his absence; whereupon one of those present asked how he stood on the question of Abolition. He answered, "I am an Abolitionist of the strongest type." "Then I shall oppose the recommendation," said the brother who had raised the question and who was a sympathizer with pro-slavery sentiment.

Dr. Redfield secretly wished that his recommendation would be rejected, as he seemed to think that would relieve him of responsibility in the matter. So to make them doubly sure that he meant it, when he said he was an Abolitionist of the strongest type, he now said, before retiring, "I wish it distinctly understood that if I am granted a license to preach, and that shall add anything to the influence I now possess, I shall certainly use it for God and the slave. So now your eyes are open, and you know what I am and what to expect." Again it was said, "We will contest the matter."

He retired; the vote was taken immediately, and he was licensed to preach. Before he had finally settled it to obey God and preach the Gospel he had a premonition, or conviction, that unless he did thus yield, he would be struck by lightning. Strangely, the people had scarcely reached home from the Church where he was licensed before a thunderbolt descended upon it. He was greatly impressed by this circumstance.

When, some time after this, he finally received his Pentecost and gave himself to his God-given calling, he was marvelously used of God in the conversion of sinners, in the sanctification of believers, in the quickening of the Church, and in the general promotion of the work of God. He held only a Local Preacher's license, and the Methodist Episcopal Church at that time had no provision for evangelists; but he gave himself to evangelistic labors, for which he was specially fitted, both by natural endowments and by his remarkable Christian experience. Neither time nor space admits of even a sketch of his evangelistic labors here, but if any one doubts that he was among the greatest evangelists of the nineteenth century, let him read "The Life of Rev. John Wesley Redfield, M. D.," by the Rev. Joseph Goodwin Terrill, and be convinced.

He labored on, much of the time against great opposition for years, as a member of the Methodist Episcopal Church; but finally found his place among those who had been proscribed as "Nazarites" in Western New York, and as "Redfieldites" in Northern Illinois, and at the Pekin Convention at which the Free Methodist Church was founded was a delegate from Illinois, and thus became one of the honored founders of the new denomination. Previous to this he had received a stroke of paralysis, from which he was considerably disabled; and subsequently he was the victim of two more strokes, which terminated his earthly career. But his end was triumphant. His body rests at Marengo, Illinois, and a small marble shaft above his grave bears this fitting inscription: "HE WAS TRUE TO HIS MOTTO—FIDELITY TO GOD."

Mr. Sherman, who had invited Mr. Redfield to St. Charles, had known him in New England, and, having been transferred to the Rock River Conference, and being deeply desirous of seeing the work of holiness promoted on his charge, had given him a pressing call to come to St. Charles and assist him in a series of revival services. Many of the more devout members gave their hearty indorsement to the Doctor's labors, and a remarkable revival followed, in which, notwithstanding the unfavorable season of the year, many were converted, and many also claimed to receive the experience of entire sanctification.

The successful character of this meeting, evidenced not only by the numbers saved, but also by the remarkable spirit of prayer and of labor for souls poured out upon the St. Charles society, led to Mr. Redfield being pressed with invitations to labor in various towns in Northern Illinois and Wisconsin. In consequence he remained in the West some two or three years, laboring effectively in those places where open doors invited. Elgin, Marengo, Woodstock, Aurora, Quincy, Galva and other communities in Illinois were greatly blessed through the faithful labors of this man of God. He also conducted revival services at a number of important centers in Wisconsin.

"The revivals at Marengo and Woodstock were wonders of grace," says the Rev. J. G. Terrill. "At the latter place, lawyers, doctors, the sheriff and other citizens were brought to Christ. Some of them became ministers of the gospel."*

Under the Doctor's labors in Illinois a number of men and women were raised up who were afterward to become influential in molding the character of the Free Methodist Church. Foremost among these we mention Edward Payson Hart. He had professed conversion before Doctor Redfield's advent to Illinois, but after hearing him for some time, perceived that his own religious experience did not conform to the New Testament type. He finally committed himself wholly to God, sought and found not only the witness of a renewed heart, but also the sanctifying baptism with the Holy Ghost. He soon recognized that God was calling him to preach the Gospel, withdrew from the Masonic Lodge, entered the ministry of the Methodist Episcopal Church, and finally united with the Free Methodist Church in 1860, labored successfully as pastor and as District Chairman until 1874, when the General Conference held at Albion, New York, elected him as General Superintendent, which name was changed to Bishop at the General Conference of 1907. He served continuously and with great acceptability in this office from the time of his first election until October, 1907, when, because of a nervous trouble seriously impairing his voice, he asked to be relieved from its duties. He and his most estimable wife are now living in comfort and amid pleasant surroundings at Alameda, California, which has been their home for many years. Mrs. Hart was wholly sanctified while but a girl, under Dr. Redfield's labors in Illinois. Both have for many years been a mighty inspiration to the Free Methodist Church.

Joseph Goodwin Terrill, who, as a boy, had been converted in a series of revival meetings held by his mother

*"History of St. Charles Camp-meeting," pp. 5, 6.

in her kitchen, at Aurora, Illinois, also received under Dr. Redfield's ministry a baptism with the Spirit, under the permanent inspiration of which he developed into a mighty man of God. As a "boy preacher" he was sent for to become the minister of a band of persecuted saints, who had rented and fitted up the dining room of an old hotel at St. Charles, as a place of worship. He went, and they began a series of meetings in which a hundred souls were saved. This meeting also resulted in the forming of a Free Methodist society, and in the erection of a new Church edifice. The "boy preacher" developed rapidly, and at length became one of the most able and eloquent preachers of the Free Methodist Church, a vigorous and entertaining writer of books and contributor to religious periodicals, a wise Church legislator, a musical author of fair ability, an enthusiastic leader in Sunday-school Convention work, a man who filled nearly all the important offices within the gift of the Church, and who at the time of his death, in 1895, was its Missionary Secretary. In all his manifold relations to the Church he was powerful in molding its character for good.

Another product of the Redfield revival was C. E. Harroun, Sr., who was brought out into the light of full salvation in the first meeting Doctor Redfield held in St. Charles. Feeling divinely called to preach the Gospel, like St. Paul he "conferred not with flesh and blood," but gave himself at once and fully to the work of preaching Jesus Christ; and, as Bishop E. P. Hart has aptly said, "In all his after life never could do anything else so well." For some years he preached at different points in Illinois and Wisconsin. Later he labored in Iowa, Kansas and Missouri. He was a number of times delegate to the General Conference, where he displayed much wisdom in counsel and legislation. His last labors were in Oklahoma, where for several years he assisted his son, the Rev. C. E. Harroun, Jr., in the work of the Oklahoma Conference, and where he also continued to live after age compelled him to superannuate, and finally passed peacefully to be with God. Bishop Hart has said of him: "In his ministrations he has, to a greater extent than any of his fellow laborers, both in pulpit and in altar work, retained the peculiar style and methods of Dr. Redfield. A fine singer, a powerful preacher, at times, as the Spirit moves him, congregations are aroused to a pitch of intense excitement."*

I. H. Fairchilds, a local preacher, who was led into the light of full salvation at the Marengo revival, also developed into an itinerant preacher of much usefulness, and later became quite prominent in starting and building up the Free Methodist Church in that part of Illinois.

Then there were also a goodly number of lay members who courageously rallied to the support of the work of holiness in the Doctor's meetings at various places in Illinois, and who bravely withstood the opposition and persecution that soon developed, remained uncompromisingly faithful, and finally figured prominently in making the early history of the Free Methodist Church. Among them should be mentioned Father M. L. Hart and his wife, parents of the Rev. E. P. Hart, General Superintendent (Bishop) of the Free Methodist Church since 1874. It was Father Hart who bore the invitation from the official board to Doctor Redfield to come from Elgin, twenty-five miles distant, where he was then laboring, and conduct a series of meetings at Marengo. This noble couple for their fidelity to God were finally made to feel the opposition and tyranny of the Church, in common with others of like spirit, to a degree that cost them the forfeiture of their Church home, and were among those who in the beginning identified themselves with Free Methodism, and gave their most earnest service to its work during the remainder of their days. "Mother Hart" had

*"Reminiscences of Early Free Methodism," p. 9.

been led into the experience of holiness years before under the labors of the celebrated James Caughey.

There was also the family of Bishops, who were prominently identified with Doctor Redfield's work, and later with the formation and subsequent history of the Free Methodist Church. W. D. Bishop, one of the sons, is now a superannuate member of its ministry in the California Conference; another son, M. F. Bishop, is an honored layman of the Church; and Martha, a daughter, familiarly called "Mattie," is the faithful and devoted wife of Bishop Hart.

Nor should we fail to mention J. M. Laughlin and his godly wife. Mr. Laughlin owned the magnificent grove near the village of St. Charles, which became historic as the location for many years of the famous "St. Charles Camp-meeting," and also as the place of holding the first Western Laymen's Convention. This Convention resulted in the formation of the Free Methodist Church in the West, and finally in the organization of the Illinois Annual Conference. Mrs. Laughlin is said to have been a woman of quick discernment, intense spirituality, and who was deeply experienced in the things of God. They both toiled and sacrificed for the welfare of Free Methodism until the good Lord bade them cease from labor and enter into rest.

We would also mention "Mother Cobb," "who for many years was the only living witness to the experience of perfect love in all those parts;" who had then "walked in the steady light of it for more than forty years;" and who "lived for nearly twenty more in the light of that experience, when God took her home." Though she never became a Free Methodist, she did much to foster the movement. "Mother Coombs" was likewise one of the "elect ladies" of that region and of those days—"a woman of deep piety, clear understanding, and consistent life," who feared not to stand by the truth and those who preached it, whatever might be the consequences.

The Church of this later period owes more than it can properly appreciate to the faithfulness of these men and women of God, and the many others associated with them, "of whom the world was not worthy," and "whose names are in the book of life."

One of the most prominent and influential laymen of Northern Illinois was the Honorable Benjamin Hackney. He was born in Canajoharie, Montgomery County, New York, May 15, 1805. Very early in life he was thrown upon his own exertions for a livelihood. The first money he ever earned was earned by working on the Erie Canal, and though he did not then make any profession of religion, he gave what he had earned toward the erection of a Methodist Church in the neighborhood where he lived.

He soon mastered the carpenter's trade, also the details of business life, and finally undertook several contracts for the building of canals in his native State. He was prominently connected with the Chemung Canal from its first inception, and after its completion acted as its Superintendent for a number of years. This was considered a very honorable position, inasmuch as it was a State appointment, conferred upon him by the Legislature. On resigning this position he accepted a contract on the Delaware and Hudson Canal, and eventually occupied a similar position on the Erie Canal.

On November 24, 1831, he was married to Miss Helen Bradley, of Chemung County, New York, with whom he lived happily until her death in August, 1852. Her sickness and death became the means of his awakening to feel his need of Christ, and of his thorough conversion to God. He erected a family altar, and for nearly two years led a praying life before experiencing a change of heart. Finally, in the spring of 1854, while walking in meditation, he paused for a moment beneath a mountain ash in a corner of his yard, and lifting his eyes toward heaven, called upon the Lord Jesus to help him. In a moment the long-sought peace and blessing came into his heart—the assurance of sins forgiven and of acceptance with God.

In September of the same year he was married to Mrs. Lydia T. Evans, who made him a most agreeable helpmeet in things temporal and spiritual, who finally nursed him through the long illness which terminated his life, and who survived him for more than a decade.

When Mr. Hackney moved to Aurora, in 1844, he took with him $20,000, and located on a farm, now embraced within the city limits, and which he afterward platted into town lots. He lived to see a house built on each of them, except several which he gave as sites for the erection of Churches. In 1847 he brought his family to Aurora, from which time he was intimately identified with the development and success of the city until his death. When the Galena and Chicago Union Railroad was projected, he became one of the projectors and incorporators of the Aurora Branch Railroad, from Turner's Junction to Aurora, the road from Chicago to the Junction, thirty miles, being then the only railroad in the State. Considerable difficulty was naturally experienced in starting this enterprise, he having to negotiate the bonds, which could only be done by his personal indorsement. "Benjamin Hackney may in truth be said to have been the original projector of the now famous Chicago, Burlington and Quincy Railroad." He was also its first General Superintendent.

Mr. Hackney acted as Superintendent of the road for a number of years, and might have continued in the position longer, had not his conscience, after his conversion, disapproved of the running of trains on the Sabbath. He expressed his convictions to the directors, who refused to heed them, whereupon he decided that he could not in honor longer hold his position, resigned the same, and immediately offered his stock for sale, declaring he would not become rich at the expense of obliging poor men to break the law of God.

Mr. Hackney was also one of the first movers in the founding of Clark [now Jennings] Seminary. He contributed $5,000 towards its erection, and later was compelled, through the financial failure of some and crookedness of others, to give enough more to make a total of $25,000, or $500 more than he had on moving to the State.

In 1859 the Rev. Seymour Coleman, of the Troy Conference, settled in Aurora; and, a vacancy having been made in the pulpit of the Methodist Church on the east side of the river, he was requested to fill the place for the remainder of the year, which would be about six months. He consented; and, as was his usual custom, he gave particular attention to the subject of entire sanctification, emphasizing the privilege and necessity of the experience on the part of all believers Mr. Hackney at this time was one of his parishioners, and had the privilege of the clear and safe teaching of this holy man of God. In the fall of that year a camp-meeting was held near the city of Aurora, under the direction of the Rev. Luke Hitchcock, Presiding Elder. It was a meeting of remarkable interest and great power. On Monday morning Mr. Hackney, under deep conviction for the experience of sanctification, met "Father Coleman," as he was commonly called, and said to him, "I have laid all at Jesus's feet; what next?" "Oh, just leave it there," said Father Coleman, and turned immediately away. Mr. Hackney was somewhat annoyed at being answered and left in this abrupt manner when he was undergoing such a soul struggle; but presently his better judgment prevailed, and he said to himself, "Yes, that is the way; if I have given all, I must leave it there;" and while he was thus meditating and trusting in Christ, suddenly the witness of the Spirit came that the work was done. He was accustomed to refer to this matter often as an illustration of Father Coleman's wisdom in dealing with seeking souls. Regarding his new-found experience he testified on this wise: "I have dealt in canal stocks, in railroad stocks, and in State stocks, but never received such returns as from the stock I have in Jesus."

The same fall many of the society desired Father Coleman to be placed in charge of the work another year; but, because of his preaching so plainly and thoroughly on the subject of holiness, he was regarded as being identified with "Redfieldism," for which cause the Presiding Elder and other influential persons opposed the plan, and another was appointed. In December came the separation at St. Charles, twelve miles away; the expulsion of the Bishop family of McHenry County followed in March; then the first Western Laymen's camp-meeting in June, immediately following the adjournment of the Methodist Episcopal General Conference at Buffalo, New York, where the last ray of hope for the redress of the expelled eastern preachers and their sympathizers died out, when their appeals were refused entertainment by that body. Mr. Hackney was at the camp-meeting with a large tent, boldly identifying himself with those who were persecuted for Christ's sake.

In August, 1860, Mr. Hackney and certain other laymen called another camp-meeting at Aurora, and invited Father Coleman to take charge of it, but he declined. The Rev. B. T. Roberts was then invited, and accepted. The meeting was largely attended not only by those who subsequently became Free Methodists, but by many Wesleyan Methodists as well; and from that meeting dates the revival of holiness among the Wesleyan people in Illinois.

Soon after this a Free Methodist society was organized in Aurora. Mr. Hackney became a member, and remained in the fellowship of the Aurora society, always aiding in the work by his fervent prayers, godly counsel, and liberal benefactions until his death. He subscribed $500 toward the erection of the Free Methodist Church building, which cost, together with the lot, something over $4,000; and in addition to the payment of this subscription he contributed more than $2,800 cash toward its total cost. He also built the parsonage, costing $1,311, at his own expense, and gave it to the society. Then in his will he provided that $5,000 should be given to the society as an endowment, the same to be invested, under direction of the trustees, on real estate worth double that amount, the income only to be used toward the support of such pastors as should be appointed to the charge by the Annual Conference. He likewise provided for leaving the Sunday-school $1,000 to be similarly invested, and the income to be used for books and other needed equipments; but as this was to come out of what remained of the estate after other provisions of the will, amounting to $50,000, were met, the funds appear to have fallen short, so that it was never realized by the school. It shows, however, that he was accustomed to devise liberal things.

The Rev. J. W. Redfield was appointed pastor of the newly formed society, and it was during his labors in that capacity that he was stricken with paralysis, which finally terminated his earthly career.

Mr. Hackney was a man of clear convictions, and of the courage which enabled him to avow them boldly and stand by them at any cost. His devotion to principle was well known, and could not be excelled. He was a man of calm and clear judgment, free from personal bias, and from everything that savored of rashness or inconsiderateness; but he would allow no influence of public opinion, popular favor, personal friendship, political relationship, or prospects of financial loss or gain to swerve him from his sense of right and convictions of duty.

As an evidence of his sound judgment he was chosen to represent his district in the State Legislature, and did so with credit to himself and his constituency. He was also chosen to represent the Illinois Annual Conference at every session of the General Conference so long as he lived, which position he always filled with much dignity, and with extraordinary wisdom. He was one of the strongest pillars of Free Methodism among the laymen of his day.

A chapter might be written regarding the beneficence and philanthropy of this good man; but suffice it to say that his faith in God and his devotion to the welfare of men amounted to a passion with him.

At his death the city papers each published an extended sketch of his life, one of them concluding thus:

"And so has passed away another of the founders of our city—a man, in his youth, of iron constitution; a man of nerve and commanding will—well fitted to cope with the obstacles to civilization and empire. He has gone in the ripeness of his years, crowned with the respect of his fellow-citizens."*

The thoroughness of Dr. Redfield's labors in Northern Illinois at length began to provoke opposition from superficial, false, and fashionable professors of religion. As is customary in such cases, this opposition first manifested itself among the ministry; and the first decided outbreak of it occurred at St. Charles, where certain changes had taken place since the Doctor first began his work there. Under his early labors there many were converted and sanctified. His preaching had stirred things to their profound depths, bringing to light some horrible hidden iniquities. Drunkenness, theft, adultery, and other gross iniquities were unearthed and confessed.

During the next two years the Rev. Charles French served the charge as its pastor. He invited the Doctor at various times to return and assist him in revival work, but such was the attitude of certain prominent members with regard to helping on the thorough work he felt called to do, that Dr. Redfield thought nothing could be accomplished, and so declined the invitations.

Mr. French was followed by the Rev. S. G. Havermale.

---

*The information in the foregoing was gleaned from an article by the Rev. J. G. Terrill in the Free Methodist of July 27, 1871, and an editorial of the Rev. B. T. Roberts in the Earnest Christian of 1871.

His spirit seemed to be such that it was thought by Mr. Redfield's friends that the two could work together harmoniously. A large majority of the members finally signed a petition and presented it to the official board, asking that Doctor Redfield be invited to return to St. Charles and hold another meeting. A fair majority of the official board voted to grant the request. But such was the determined opposition of the minority, that the decision of the matter was finally left to the pastor. He decided not to invite him, and so notified him by mail.

The Rev. D. C. Howard succeeded Mr. Havermale as pastor in 1859. Doctor Redfield had about concluded arrangements to go South, and as he was soon to leave, there was a great desire on the part of a large majority of the Church, and also on the part of the outside community, to hear him preach before he should leave. Accordingly Elisha Foote and J. M. Laughlin called on the pastor, and requested him to invite Doctor Redfield to preach. The pastor refused their request. Among his reasons for so doing, he said: "I have been sent here to guard this pulpit against Redfield and Coleman." On being asked, "What have you against them?" he replied: "Nothing; I believe them both to be good men; and they are doing good; but they must be sacrificed for the good of the Church."

As the Baptist Church was without a pastor, one of Dr. Redfield's friends suggested to them that they invite the Doctor to occupy their pulpit the following Sabbath. The invitation was given, and Dr. Redfield preached to a crowded house. Arrangements were then made for him to preach the next Sabbath. But during the week certain influences were at work which led the Baptists to cancel their part of the arrangement.

The Universalists then offered their Church; and, as it was too late to withdraw the appointment, the offer was accepted, and the Doctor preached there. Of course, a good many of the Methodist people went to hear him. On Monday, Pastor Howard appointed a committee to see the leading members of his Church who had attended the Redfield meeting, and inform them that it would be necessary for them to confess that they had done wrong, and pledge themselves to do so no more, if they desired to retain their membership in the Church. If unwilling to make such acknowledgement and promise, they could have their choice between two courses. They could take letters in good standing from the Church; or, declining this, they would have to accept expulsion.

These people did not feel that they had done any wrong to be confessed, nor did they wish to take letters of removal from the society. That day the pastor went away to counsel with one of the Bishops. It is supposed that he went to Evanston, to lay the matter before Bishop Simpson. On his return he reported having consulted a Bishop, who gave it as his opinion that the official board was competent to declare those members withdrawn who had been to hear Dr. Redfield preach. Acting upon this advice, on Wednesday evening, they declared fourteen persons withdrawn—"among them one who was not a member of the Church, and never had been, as the list of membership would have shown." That was a woman named Monroe, who had been dead for many years. Five of the thirteen members were members of the board of trustees, of which there were but nine.

Doctor Redfield preached, with freedom and power, on Monday and Tuesday evenings, and several souls were converted. But when he saw the trouble that was likely to ensue, he ceased his labors there, and the following week started on his contemplated journey to the South.

Thursday evening found those "withdrawn" members in their usual places at the weekly prayer-meeting. They were not allowed, however, to participate in the exercises. At the close of the services they were formally "read out" of membership in the Methodist Episcopal Church. Following this, about fifty more asked for their Church letters, but instead of granting their request the pastor offered them letters of withdrawal, which they refused. Believing that in due time the wrong inflicted on them would be rectified, these good people soon rented the dining-room of an old hotel as a place of worship. Joseph G. Terrill, a local preacher from Elgin, visited them about this time. He was the boy converted in the revival held by his own mother in her kitchen. They invited him to become their preacher. He consented, and, under his labors, the revival broke out to which mention has already been made in this chapter.

It was soon found necessary to form some kind of organization to care for the large number who had been converted. Accordingly a Band was formed, which adopted the General Rules of the Methodist Episcopal Church, with the exception of the rule on slavery. In the meantime the Methodist society had elected five new trustees to serve in place of those declared "withdrawn," which was in plain violation of the statutes of Illinois, the statutes making no provision for declaring vacancies in such a manner. Besides these persons, among those declared "withdrawn" were old, tried and worthy members of the society, men who had been chiefly instrumental in building up the Church property.

On the 27th of April, 1860, convinced that their grievances would find no redress from the General Conference, these persecuted "pilgrims" organized themselves into an independent Church, taking the name Free Methodist. At that time they numbered one hundred twelve. The five trustees "read out" of the Methodist Church as "withdrawn," were elected trustees of the new Church at its incorporation. Their names were Elisha Foote, John M. Sangle, Ira D. Tyler, Warren Tyler, Ephraim Collar.

A friend of the new society, who still belonged to the old Church, submitted the question regarding the method pursued in the expulsion of the "Redfieldites," as they were contemptuously called, to the next session of the Rock River Conference. The Conference approved the administration of Mr. Howard, but declared against the pursuing of such a course in the future.

Not far from Marengo lived the Bishop family, already referred to in this chapter. They numbered five—all members of the Methodist Church at a place called Franklinville. This place had been visited with a gracious revival in which many were both converted and sanctified. The work there continued to move on with power. Finally the Presiding Elder came out in plain terms and warned the people against the use of such dogmatic terms as sanctification, holiness and perfect love. Then the preacher in charge began to weaken, and finally took a decided stand against the distinctive work of holiness.

When the time came for the Annual Conference to hold its session, Father Bishop and others went, and urgently petitioned for a change of preachers; "for," said Father Bishop, "we will not pay Methodist preachers for fighting Methodist doctrine." Their petition appears not to have been heeded; for after the adjournment of the session both the senior and junior preacher returned. This indicated that the war against "Redfieldism," as the holiness movement was called in the West, was to be continued, in an effort to banish it from the Conference. So now the battle was set in array, and the conflict was renewed in good earnest.

Father Bishop opened his house for a Monday night holiness meeting, to which the holiness people rallied in large numbers from Woodstock, Queen Ann Prairie, South Elgin, Crystal Lake and the intervening country. This meeting was kept in the hands of laymen; and, though the preacher in charge came, proposed to lead it, and finally declared he would remove it to the Church, all his plans to capture the meeting in the interest of the opposition miscarried. The work went steadily forward, and souls were converted and sanctified at nearly every service.

The sequel to the story is told as follows by Bishop

E. P. Hart, son-in-law of Father Bishop, and who was personally familiar with the circumstances:

Living two miles east of Father Bishop was a family by the name of Best, and, as their name indicates, they were to be classed among the superlatively good. The family consisted of father, mother and four boys. The boys were young, but were being carefully taught and trained by the mother, who was a woman of superior intelligence as well as of superlative piety. Outside of this family the neighborhood was wild and reckless. There had been no preaching there for years, and many of the young people had never heard a Gospel sermon. The place later became favorably known as "The Brick Schoolhouse." I. H. Fairchilds, the local preacher spoken of before, sent an appointment to this schoolhouse and a series of meetings was held. Many of the holiness people attended, among them the Bishop family, and as a result of the meetings floods of mercy broke on the community and fifty or more were saved. If I remember aright a Methodist Episcopal class of forty was organized on an adjoining circuit as a fruit of this meeting. * * * A good work was going on, and for a few Sabbaths Father Bishop and family felt they ought to attend meetings at the schoolhouse and did so. This served for a pretext, and they were soon cited to trial for not attending public worship and class at Franklinville Church where they belonged. There were persons whose names were on that Church book who had attended neither public worship nor class for years, and some of whom were avowed Mormons, and others who gloried in being Universalists; but they were not troublers in Israel.

The day for the trial arrived and these people who were stanch Methodists, and who had come from Methodist stock a century old, appeared at the Church. But they had hundreds of sympathizers, for they were well and favorably known throughout all that region. So on the day of the trial, to the dismay of the preacher, the Church was filled. Finally the preacher came in and informed the accused that he had concluded to have a private trial and to hold it in the parsonage across the street. Father Bishop, who knew something of Methodist law, quoted Baker on the Discipline and said, "A trial should be private only at the request of the accused, and we demand a public trial; for," said he, "if we have done anything worthy of bonds or of death, we refuse not to be bound or to die." But the preacher took his committee and went over to the parsonage to go on with the trial, and the saints went on with a love-feast. As one after the other their heads went off, ecclesiastically, the preacher would come into the Church and announce the fact.

William, the eldest son, in preparation for the ministry, had been attending the theological school at Evanston. When he went he took a Church letter, but concluded not to put it in at Evanston, so on his return home had it with him. When the preacher declared him expelled, William said, "Brother W., you can't expel me: I hold a letter." "Let me see it," said the preacher. William feeling a little suspicious, held up the letter, when the preacher, as if to get a better look at it reached up, and, taking hold of the corner where his own name was signed, with a sudden jerk tore his name from the certificate. At this a young woman by the name of Sponable, with a piercing shriek, fell in a burden at the feet of the preacher. It was getting uncomfortably warm for the pastor, and he started for the door; but a stalwart saint stood against the door and refused to let him out. He then rushed into the pulpit and with loud and earnest protestation, declared he did not tear the letter. The saints looked on him with pity and prayed the Lord to have mercy on him.

A copy of the original bill of charges against W. D. Bishop, and also of the Church letter from which the preacher in charge who gave it tore off his name and then denied doing so, is herewith subjoined. First, the bill of charges:

"William D. Bishop: You are hereby charged with neglect of duty and disobedience to the order and Discipline of the Church,

"1. Specification. In neglecting the public worship of God at the Franklinville Church where you belong.

"2. Specification. In neglecting to meet your class.

"FRANKLINVILLE, March 20, 1860. A. C. Coquillett, C. L."

"Bro. Wm. D. Bishop, you are notified hereby to appear at the Church in this place next Friday at 2 o'clock P. M. for trial on the above. L. WHIPPLE, Pr. in Charge.

"FRANKLINVILLE, March 20, 1860."

The following is the Church letter:

"The bearer, W. D. Bishop, has been an acceptable member of the Methodist Episcopal Church in Crystal Lake charge, Rock River Conference.

"FRANKLINVILLE, Aug. 20, 18 L. W

"P. S.:

"Bro. Bishop has license to exho

The author of these pages copied the foregoing documents from the original papers, which were loaned him for the purpose by W. D. Bishop's brother, Dr. M. F. Bishop. The preacher who gave the foregoing letter was L. Whipple, whose name is signed to the citation to trial on the bill of charges. In attempting to tear off his signature from the Church letter, he succeeded in tearing off all but the initials, "L. W" These, with the handwriting, which is the same as that of the citation on the bill of charges, which is signed by "L. Whipple, Pr. in charge," is evidence as to who gave the letter, and at the time of this writing there are a number of living witnesses to the fact that they saw him tear his name from the letter in question. If this matter appears to any as of trifling significance, let it be remembered that the case is cited here as illustrative of the spirit and methods employed against Methodists of that time in Northern Illinois who manifested sympathy with the reform movement sneeringly termed "Redfieldism."

Having been most unrighteously excluded from the Methodist Episcopal Church, to which they had long been devoted, the Bishops were at a stand for a season as to what course to pursue. Finally Father Bishop drew up articles of association to which they and many of those who sympathized with them, subscribed, thus forming themselves into an Earnest Christian Band.

The foregoing instances are samples of the general spirit of opposition to spiritual religion prevailing at that time in the West as well as in the East. They are also illustrations of the unjust and cruel methods by which it was sought to rid the Methodist Church in Illinois of "Redfieldism," which was a synonym for the work of holiness in the West, as "Nazaritism" was in the East. Great blessing had uniformly attended Dr. Redfield's labors in the West, hundreds having been clearly converted (as many as five hundred in a single meeting), and also hundreds having received the sanctifying baptism with the

Holy Spirit. The Churches had been greatly quickened, and a loftier standard of righteousness had been lifted up for the people generally. "Could the Methodist Church have been persuaded to take care of the work," wrote Dr. Redfield in a private letter to a friend, "rather than to contend against it, it might have spread farther, and a more glorious harvest have been reaped." They failed to recognize their opportunity, however, failed to know their day of gracious visitation, and so the spiritual harvest that might have been for their enrichment was allowed to be gathered by others, though not without great sacrifice, and experiences of much anguish.

CHAPTER XXIX

THE THIRD LAYMEN'S CONVENTION

This was the last of the Laymen's Conventions held before the General Conference at which it was expected that the appeals of the expelled brethren would be heard. In some respects it was the most important of them all. It reaffirmed the declarations of the preceding Conventions. It also provided that from each district in the Conference laymen should be appointed to coöperate with the ministers in the direction and management of the Bands, maintaining that in the formation of these Bands they were introducing no innovation antagonistic to the Methodist Episcopal Church, but that they were acting in full harmony with its established policy.

It was this Convention that memorialized the General Conference, to meet the following May, to the effect that the judicial action of the Genesee Conference in the various expulsions which had occurred should be carefully investigated by that body, and also for such an amendment of the judicial law of the Church as should secure to both ministers and laymen the right of trial by an impartial committee. This Memorial was finally signed by more than fifteen hundred of the laymen of the Conference before its presentation to the General Conference.

The Convention also petitioned the General Conference to the effect that a new chapter should be inserted in the Discipline, such as would exclude from membership all persons guilty of holding, buying or selling, or in any way using a human being as a slave. These and several other actions passed by this Convention had a very important bearing upon the ultimate formation of the Free Methodist

Church. Hence it is important to give an account of its proceedings here.

The following partial report of this third Convention is gleaned from a copy of the Olean *Advertiser,* which published quite an extended and accurate account of it:

PROCEEDINGS OF THE LAYMEN'S CONVENTION

Of the M. E. Church, Genesee Conference, held in the Presbyterian Church, Olean, Wednesday and Thursday, Feb. 1st and 2nd, 1860.

A Convention of the Laymen of the Methodist Episcopal Church, of the Genesee Conference, assembled, pursuant to a call, which we published, at the Presbyterian Church, in this village. The Convention was large, every charge or congregation in the Conference being represented. It was at first intended to hold the Convention in the Methodist Church in this village; but Judge Green, upon the application of a member of the Church, granted an injunction restraining and forbidding the Trustees to open their edifice for this purpose. With a commendable liberality, the Trustees of the Presbyterian Church tendered the use of their house for the holding of the Convention.

At 10 o'clock, on Wednesday morning, Abner I. Wood, President of the Laymen's Convention, called the delegates to order, and S. K. J. Chesbrough, Secretary, assumed the duties of his office.

The Convention opened with prayer by Mr. S. C. Springer, of Gowanda; after which the Secretary, Mr. Chesbrough, read the call of the Convention. He also read a letter from D. W. Tinkham, expressing the strong sympathy of that gentleman with the object of the Convention.

Mr. Chesbrough presented a lengthy Memorial to the General Conference, upon the subject of the expelled ministers, which was read, and laid upon the table for the present.

Later the Memorial which was read by Mr. Chesbrough at the opening of the Convention was discussed, and the following finally substituted:

"PETITION

"*To the Bishops and Members of the General Conference of the M. E. Church, to be held in Buffalo, N. Y., May 1, 1860.*

"REVEREND FATHERS AND BRETHREN:

"We, the undersigned, members of the Methodist Episcopal Church, in the bounds of the Genesee Conference, respectfully represent to your Reverend body, that a very unpleasant state of things prevails in the Church throughout this Conference. This difficulty has grown out of the judicial action of the Conference. Many honestly believe this action to have been wrong and oppressive. We, therefore, ask your Reverend body to give to the judicial action of the Genesee Conference, by which six of the ministers, to wit: B. T. Roberts, J. McCreery, J. A. Wells, Wm. Cooley, L. Stiles, Jr., and C. D. Burlingham, have been expelled from the Conference and the Church, a full and careful investigation, trusting you will come to such decision as righteousness demands. We also ask your Reverend body so to amend the judicial law of the Church, as to secure to the ministers and members the right of trial by an impartial committee."

A motion was adopted, authorizing the chair to appoint a committee of five, to procure a sufficient number of copies of the Memorial to be printed for circulation in the Conference. W. J. Colgrove, S. K. J. Chesbrough, S. C. Springer, Rev. J. A. Wells, and Rev. B. T. Roberts, were appointed such committee.

The following petition to the General Conference was read and adopted:

"*To the Bishops and Members of the General Conference of the M. E. Church, to be held in Buffalo, N. Y., May 1st, 1860.*

"Reverend Fathers and Brethren:

"Inasmuch as there are now known to be, in the Slave States, many members of the Methodist Episcopal Church who hold their fellow-beings, and even their brethren in Christ, as slaves, contrary to natural justice and the Gospel of Christ; and

"Whereas, We believe the buying, selling, or holding of a human being as property, is a sin against God, and should in nowise be tolerated in the Church of Christ: therefore,

"We, the undersigned, members of the Methodist Episcopal Church in the ——— charge, Genesee Conference, would earnestly petition your Reverend body to place a chapter in the Discipline of the M. E. Church that will exclude all persons from the M. E. Church or her communion, who shall be guilty of holding, buying or selling, or in any way using a human being as a slave."

Rev. B. T. Roberts said that his opinions on slavery were not changed. He had always been an anti-slavery man; and the first speech he had ever made was an anti-slavery speech. He was opposed to its being in the Church; it had no more right there than the devil had. He said it had been reported that he had reported that he had received a letter from a Presiding Elder, stating that he had better drop the hobby of Holiness, and take up the Slavery Issue. He had never received any such letter. He also said:

"The Genesee Conference, in former days, was thoroughly anti-slavery. It seems, by the returns of the last Conference, that there is a change somewhere. The report on slavery was permitted to get into the hands of the committee; and it seems they were either afraid or ashamed to publish it in their minutes."

The Reverend gentleman proceeded at some length, and declared that if the Church would only take hold of the matter in the right way, and in the right spirit, slavery would soon be extirpated from the land. He declared his determination to labor for such a result as long as he should live.

Rev. J. McCreery, and others, followed in a similar strain, and hoped that the Church would do her duty. [Resolution adopted].

The following resolution was also adopted:

"*Resolved,* That we are highly pleased with the appearance of the *Earnest Christian.* The articles, thus far, prove it to be just what is needed at this time, when a conforming and superficial Christianity is prevailing everywhere. We hail it with delight among us; and we pledge ourselves to use our exertions to extend its circulation."

At the afternoon sitting the following resolution was offered and finally adopted:

"*Resolved,* That we reiterate our unfaltering attachment to the M. E. Church, while we protest against, and repudiate its abuses and iniquitous administration, by which we have been aggrieved, and the Church scandalized. Our controversy is in favor of the doctrines and Discipline of the Church, and against temporary maladministration. And we exhort our brethren everywhere not to secede, or withdraw from the Church, or be persuaded into any other ecclesiastical organization; but to form themselves into Bands, after the example of early Methodism, and remain in the Church until expelled."

There seems to have been a Committee on Resolutions, and that Committee presented the following report:

"PREAMBLE. God deals with us as individuals. No man or body of men can take the responsibility of our actions. It is a Bible doctrine, very clearly taught, that 'every one must give account of himself to God.'

"Ministers cannot take into their hands the keeping of our consciences. The right of private judgment lies at the foundation of the great Protestant Reformation. It forms the basis of all true religion. No person who does not act and think for himself can enjoy either the sanctifying or justifying grace of God. When John Wesley was told that he could not continue in the Church of England, because he could 'not in principle *submit to her determinations*,' he replied, 'If that were necessary, I could not be a member of any Church under Heaven; for I must still insist upon the right of private judgment. *I cannot yield either implicit faith or obedience to any man or number of men under heaven.*'

"This is equally true of every honest man. In our Church, the government is vested exclusively in the ministry; the Bishops appointing the preachers to whatever charges they please, and thus having the power to influence them to a great extent, if not to absolutely control them, by the hope of obtaining preferment, if they are submissive, and the fear of being placed in an obscure position, if they do not carry out the will of their superiors. They are elected by the ministers, and are responsible alone to the men who are thus completely dependent upon them for their position in the Church. The General Conference, possessing all the power to make laws for the Churches, is composed exclusively of ministers, elected by ministers. The Annual Conference, which says, who shall preach and who shall not, is made up of ministers. The Book Agents, wielding a mighty, pecuniary influence, are ministers. The official editors, controlling the public sentiment of the Church, are ministers. The same principle is carried out in the administration upon our circuits and stations. The preacher sent on—it may be, in opposition to the wishes of a large majority of the members—appoints all the leaders, nominates the stewards, and licenses the exhorters. If he wishes to expel a member, he selects the committee, and presides over the trial as judge. He goes out with them, and sees that they make up their verdict as he desires.

"The only check to this immense clerical power—without a parallel, unless it is in the Church of Rome—consists in the right of the laity to refuse to support those ministers who abuse their trust, and show themselves unworthy of confidence. This only remedy in our power against clerical oppression we have felt bound to apply.

"The course of those members of the Genesee Conference, known as the 'Regency party,' in screening one another when lying under the imputation of gross and flagrant immoralities; and in expelling from the Conference and the Church devoted ministers of the Gospel, whose only crime consisted in the ability and success with which they taught and enforced the doctrine of Holiness, and the fidelity with which they labored to secure the exclusion of slaveholders from the Church,—this course, so contrary to the spirit of the Gospel, as honest men going to judgment, we felt called upon to discountenance. We dare not give these ministers Godspeed in their bloody work, lest we be partakers in their evil deeds. We accordingly voted, in our Conventions, that we could not sustain these preachers who were putting down the work of God.

"These efforts of ours to correct great evils have been met by persecutions worthy of the priests of Rome in her darkest days. Men of approved piety of long standing, whose prayers and efforts and money have been freely given to promote the interests of the Church, have been expelled from the communion of their choice for having dared to act according to their convictions; therefore,

"*Resolved*, That we heartily indorse the sentiments contained in the Preambles and Resolutions passed at the Albion Conventions (December, 1858, and November, 1859). The position then taken, we this day unhesitatingly affirm, in our estimation, to be right. Convinced more than ever, that we need to act as one body in this matter, we hereby pledge ourselves unflinchingly and uncompromisingly to stand by the principles then laid down; and to sustain, by our sympathy and our aid, our brethren in the ministry who have been the subjects of a heartless and wicked proscription.

"*Resolved*, That we heartily condemn the practise pursued by many of the Regency preachers, in reading out members as withdrawn from the Church, without even the form of a trial, or without even laboring with them. We deem it an act of outrage upon our rights as members of the Church, contrary to the Discipline, and in direct opposition to the Spirit of Christ. We truly extend to our brethren and sisters who have thus been illegally read out of our beloved Zion, the right hand of fellowship. We rejoice that the 'Lamb's Book of Life' is beyond the reach of human hands. And while they continue faithful followers of Jesus, whether in or out of the Church, we hail them as members of the body of Christ."

The preamble was unanimously adopted.

The resolutions were discussed at considerable length, those who spoke, however, being of the same mind; then they were adopted unanimously.

At the second day's proceedings the following resolution was offered by S. K. J. Chesbrough:

"Whereas, The wants of the cause of God demand the holding of Camp-meetings, General Quarterly Meetings, and other general gatherings of our people, in the several Districts, demanding judicious and general counsel and coöperation, in appointing and conducting the same; therefore,

"*Resolved*, That the following laymen and local preachers, together with the traveling preachers appointed by this Convention, be an executive council in each District respectively, to appoint and superintend all Camp-meetings, General Quarterly Meetings, and such other general meetings as they may judge proper; and in the interim of the sessions of this Convention, to take the general oversight of the work within the bounds of their respective districts."

Adopted and appointments made.

The following resolution, introduced by S. K. J. Chesbrough, was also unanimously adopted by a rising vote:

"*Resolved,* That we look with lively interest on the denominational position of the Free Methodist Church of Albion, under the pastoral care of Rev. L. Stiles, Jr.; that we rejoice in her prosperity; that we hail her as a welcome co-laborer in the vineyard of our common Master, and as a worthy member in the sisterhood of Evangelical Churches."

After a few other motions and resolutions of a less important character had been finally adopted the Convention adjourned.

CHAPTER XXX

THE GENERAL CONFERENCE AND THE APPEALS FROM GENESEE

The General Conference of the Methodist Episcopal Church met in Buffalo, New York, May 1, 1860, and remained in session during the entire month. Great expectations were entertained by many respecting its action in case of the appeals from the Genesee Conference. It was fondly hoped and believed that this august body, with its constituency from all fields occupied by the Methodist Episcopal Church, would give proper respect to the appeal cases, and would so thoroughly sift the administration of affairs in Genesee, by which so many preachers and laymen had been unjustly excluded from membership, as to result in the disapproval of that administration, and in the reversal of the Conference action in case of the expelled preachers, who had appealed to this the Supreme Court of the Church.

They were the more hopeful because of the fact that fifteen hundred lay members of the Church within the bounds of the Genesee Conference had signed memorials and petitions which were to be presented to the General Conference, respectfully urging that body to give the Genesee Conference difficulties a full, fair and impartial investigation, and apply such remedies as in their wisdom might be judged proper.

While many were thus hopeful as to the final issue, there were others who seemed to have sized the situation up more accurately, and who predicted that the same influences which had wrought so disastrously and cruelly in Genesee, would also be present in combined force at the General Conference, to blockade and turn aside the course

REV. W. B. M. COLT
(Deceased)
First General Conference Evangelist
1886-1890

REV. S. K. WHEATLAKE
General Conference Evangelist since
1907

REV. C. W. STAMP
General Conference Evangelist since
1903

REV. A. D. ZAHNISER
General Conference Evangelist since
1911

[Plate Twenty]

of justice, and that those influences would ultimately prevail. Perhaps this class was in the minority, but theirs was the clearer vision and the surer judgment. The results at the General Conference fulfilled their predictions most fully.

When the petitions from Genesee Conference were presented, the delegates from that Conference professed much anxiety to have the matters sifted, by a thorough examination of all the facts connected with the Genesee Conference administration. "We have done right," said the Rev. James M. Fuller, "and are not afraid to have our conduct looked into. We want the troubles probed to the bottom." Having thus prepared the way, he then moved that the petitions be referred to a special committee of nine, to be appointed by the chair.

The friends of the petitions regarded this as virtually a move to forestall an impartial investigation, and so opposed and defeated it. The matter was then referred to a special committee to be composed of one from each Conference, each delegation to select its own member. The Committee was duly appointed, and all the memorials and petitions relating to the case were referred to it. This committee was generally regarded as able and impartial, and this inspired the confidence that right would triumph, and that justice would prevail at last.

Matters went on quietly for a few days. Then the Rev. William Reddy presented a resolution authorizing the committee appointed to consider the Genesee Conference difficulties to investigate fully the nature and origin of those difficulties, and, in order to this, giving them access to all the official papers, and the power to avail themselves of any reliable information, at their discretion. The delegates from Genesee stoutly opposed the resolution. James M. Fuller insisted that the General Conference would be transcending its constitutional powers in undertaking to overhaul the papers of Genesee Conference, or to appoint a special committee to pry into the proceedings of that body. He declared his Conference "would not submit, unless compelled to it, to any Star-chamber investigations!" His attitude was directly the reverse of what it had been a few days before, when these matters were under consideration. Why, it is difficult to explain on any other ground than that then he had hope of getting a committee more suitable to his purposes. He finally moved that the special committee be discharged, saying that in politics he was a State's Rights man, and in religious matters a Conference Rights man! The expression sounds like a covert appeal to the pro-slavery sentiment of the body to aid him in the defeat of the purpose for which the special committee had been appointed.

The Rev. Henry Slicer, of the Baltimore Conference, was soon on his feet, and "supported Mr. Fuller's motion, in a violent speech, of the plantation style." He talked glibly, echoing what Mr. Fuller had said about "Star-chamber proceedings," and contending for the right of Genesee Conference to be let alone. F. G. Hibbard, W. H. Goodwin, W. Cooper, of the Philadelphia Conference, and G. Hildt, of East Baltimore Conference, indorsed Mr. Fuller's position, and spoke in favor of discharging the special committee.

Dr. Peck then moved the previous question, which carried, thus cutting off debate and inflicting what is sometimes coarsely but appropriately called, "gag rule," and that before any representative of the petitioners from Genesee had been permitted to speak a word in favor of continuing the committee. The committee was then discharged.

The same influences had evidently been secretly at work in the General Conference, since the appointment of the special committee, that had operated for several years past in the Genesee Annual Conference to thwart the ends of fairness and justice. These influences had operated in the direction of turning delegates in favor of the ruling majority of the Genesee Conference, thereby practically effecting a prejudgment of the case. At least suspicions of corrupt combinations were engendered in many minds. The confidence which had earlier been inspired that justice would be done was shaken. The memorials and petitions which had already been referred to the special committee, were now referred to the committee on Itineracy. This committee had about all the routine business to look after for which there was time; and it is probable that the chief memorial was not even read before that body. Nothing like the full, fair and impartial investigation asked for was had. Instead of such a proceeding, the matter was passed over in the same farcical manner as had characterized the so-called administration of Discipline under the "Regency" power during the whole period of the Genesee Conference difficulties. This seems to have been what was intended, on the part of the Genesee Conference delegates, from the beginning.

The conflict that had been raging in Western New York was well known throughout American Methodism generally. That this conflict had now reached a crisis in which the determinations of the General Conference were to decide whether the Methodist Episcopal Church should thenceforth stand committed to the uncompromising principles of spirituality which Methodism was originally raised up to promote, or whether it should become an apostate type of Methodism, "having the form of godliness, but denying the power thereof," was clearly perceived by the spiritually-minded in various parts of the Methodist Episcopal Church. Many were the members in all the various Conferences who awaited the decisions of this august body, on the appeals that were to come before it and the issue involved therein, with gravest apprehensions.

It soon became apparent, however, after the General Conference had got under way far enough to manifest its true temper and spirit, "that the spirit of early Methodism had departed from that venerable body, and another spirit than that of the fathers—the spirit of a worldly, ambitious, temporizing policy—ruled the hour." It became more and more manifest that the secret-society delegates from the North and those of a pro-slavery character from the South were making common cause, whereby the former were to help the latter in side-tracking the *Rule* against slavery, by substituting therefor an excellent but powerless advisory paragraph in the Discipline; and the latter were to help the former in their final effort to dispose of "Nazaritism." At all events appearances indicated that, by some kind of understanding between them, Baltimore delegates were helping delegates from Genesee, and Genesee delegates were helping those from Baltimore, to carry their respective points.

"The action of the General Conference in an appeal case that came before it, from one of the Ohio Conferences," says the Rev. B. T. Roberts, "weakened still further confidence in its integrity, as a body. A member of that Conference had been expelled, the daily papers said, for licentious conduct with nine young ladies of his congregation. When a knowledge of his guilt came before the public, he left that part of the state, and went into business. His Presiding Elder wrote to him to come back and stand a trial. He did so. Both were high Masons. This Presiding Elder was elected a delegate, we believe. Such was the reputation of this expelled preacher for his profligate manners, that though he had formerly been stationed in Buffalo, it was said that not a Methodist family was willing to receive him. His appeal was heard, and he was promptly restored!

"Meeting Brother Purdy soon after this decision was announced, we said to him, 'There is hope for us. A. W. has been restored.'

" 'Oh,' said he, in his peculiar way, 'That won't help your cases any. A. W. has been loyal! He has not even had family prayer or asked a blessing since he was turned out. He has been loyal!' "

We have heretofore stated that Messrs. Roberts and McCreery, after being expelled, united with the Methodist Episcopal Church again on probation. As their action in this particular is one of the grounds on which the General Conference based its final action in the appeals, it is proper that it should receive further consideration in this connection.

The question, "What shall we do in the meantime?" was pressing heavily upon those young men who had been expelled, as their appeals could not be considered until the General Conference should meet two years hence. They were comparatively young men, full of life and vigor, feeling clearly their call to preach the Gospel, and deeply anxious to do all they could to win men for Christ. To the day of their death they avowed that they had no thought or idea of forming a new Church. They were lovingly devoted to Methodism, and had unfaltering confidence in the integrity of the Church as a whole. They believed the General Conference would disapprove and rectify the administration of the Conference which had expelled them. But they did not wish to stand idly waiting for two years, nor could they feel at liberty to engage in secular employment. They sought advice from men of age and experience, in whom they had confidence, before deciding upon their course of action.

As Mr. Roberts left the Conference after his expulsion, Bishop Janes cordially shook hands with him and said: "Do not be discouraged, Brother Roberts—there is a bright future before you."

Later he received a letter from the Rev. Amos Hard which contained the following:

> At the session of the Genesee Conference held at Perry, October, 1858, while the character of several brethren was under arrest, I had with Bishop Janes substantially the following conversation:
>
> "Would the joining of another Church by an expelled member invalidate his appeal?"
>
> He replied: "I would prefer not to answer that question tonight, as I do not call to mind the action of the General Conference in the case of John C. Green."
>
> I then asked, "Would it affect his appeal if an expelled member should join our Church on probation?"
>
> He replied: "I do not think it would."

The Rev. William Reddy, who was at that time a prominent minister of the Methodist Episcopal Church, who had served as Presiding Elder with marked success, and had also served several times as delegate to the General Conference, and was highly esteemed for his piety and judgment wherever known, also wrote Mr. Roberts, advising him concerning this matter. The following is a copy of his letter:

GENOA, Oct. 29, 1858.

DEAR BROTHER ROBERTS:

Let me freely speak to you. The General Conference will not be under such an inflammation as was the Genesee Conference, and I think they will judge righteous judgment. At all events, I am glad you exercise your rights and have appealed; and I am glad you appealed from last year's sentence, because this year's is founded on the last.

But now as to your course until General Conference: I think I would do one of two things—either join on trial at, say Pekin, where you labored last year; or not join at all until after General Conference. It occurred to me since reading your letter, that you had better not join or attempt to join even on probation; but as to relation, remain where you are until the appeal is decided.

Then, as to labor, you feel, and others believe, that God has called and commissioned you to *preach the unsearchable riches of Christ.* The Genesee Conference has said you should not preach under their authority; but you have not lost your Christian character, nor has their act worked the forfeiture of your commission from God. I would then go on and *preach* and labor for souls, and promote the work of the Lord, under the *avowed declaration* that you do it, not as by the authority of the M. E. Church, but by virtue of your divine call. Then, whoever invites your labor or comes to hear you, they alone are responsible. You violate then no Church relation, because you have none. You violate no Church order, for you are not now under Church authority. You are simply God's messenger. I would not exercise the functions of a *minister*, for that implies Church authority and order, and that you have not. I would not officiate at meetings nor administer the Sacraments, *as a minister.* But I would preach because God calls—I would receive the Sacrament of the Supper, if invited and *permitted*, because *Christ commands.* I would forego the other points for the sake of your appeal, and to show that you are not so very contumacious. This very course, I doubt not, will increase sympathy for you, and *increase your influence*, and if you are restored, will put you on higher ground than ever. Meantime I would avoid reference as far as possible to your *opposers* and oppressors, as though you were fighting *them.* "Contend for the faith once delivered to the saints." "Let them that suffer according *to the will of God* commit the keeping of their souls unto Him in well-doing, as unto a faithful Creator."

I do not see why you may not in that way promote the work of real *holiness*, and the salvation of sinners. Go where you are invited, and where the door opens, *not in the name of the M. E. Church,* but simply as *a man of God to preach the Gospel.* Who shall forbid your doing this?

But keep yourself from appearing to set yourself in array against the authority and order of the M. E. Church, *while you claim the constitutional rights* of an expelled member. I believe God will bring you out like gold, tried in the fire.

Dear Brother, excuse my liberty. These are but suggestions coming spontaneously from a brother's anxious heart. I praise God that He keeps you.

Yours faithfully,

WILLIAM REDDY.

After duly considering the matter Mr. Roberts and his friends generally thought he had better join the Church again on probation. As they viewed the case this would show loyalty to the Church. Furthermore, it would be almost impossible for him to hold meetings without worshiping now and then with some of those preachers in the Conference who were in sympathy with him, and, as he viewed it, his holding a relation to the Church would shield them from censure. He says:

We could not, in conscience make confession for what we had been expelled—for we felt we had done no wrong. So we adopted Bishop Baker's construction of the Discipline:

"When a member or preacher has been expelled, according to due form of Discipline, he can not afterward enjoy the privileges of society and Sacrament, in our Church, without contrition, confession, and satisfactory reformation; but if, however, the society become convinced of the *innocence* of the expelled member, he may again be received on trial, without confession."

The Church at Pekin was the one he served last. The members there were so fully convinced of his innocence that they unanimously received him on probation.

Mr. McCreery was also received on probation, almost unanimously, by the society at Spencerport.

Having been received into the Church on probation, they each received from the societies they had respectively joined, license to exhort. Under the authority of these licenses they went out into the work of God, holding meetings wherever there were providential openings. Deep religious interest attended their labors wherever they went. Many souls were led to Christ, many believers were quickened and sanctified, and a general awakening occurred among the people. All these things were regarded as against them, however, in the consideration of their appeals.

The following paragraphs regarding the appeal cases are from "Why Another Sect?"

> We endeavored to have our appeals come before the Conference as a body. We knew that in the selection of a committee, our opponents would have every advantage. They knew how the members in general stood affected in relation to the issues that were between us. We did not.
>
> A Court of Appeals was organized. It consisted of one delegate from each Conference, selected by the respective delegations. The right of challenge for cause was awarded to both parties. At least two-thirds of the whole must hear each case, a majority of whom should decide it. Their decision in all matters coming before them was to have the same force as the decision of the General Conference, as a body.
>
> Before this tribunal our appeal cases were presented.
>
> My first case, in which I appealed from the decision of the Genesee Conference, reproving me for saying, in my article entitled, "New School Methodism," what I do not say, was entertained. After hearing the documents read and the case presented, the committee were equally divided on the question of affirming the decision of the Genesee Conference! They stood evenly balanced in judgment whether a Methodist minister should, or should not, be held responsible for the perversion which his enemies might put upon his language! In civil Courts the Judge instructs the jury to give the prisoner the benefit of a doubt. In this religious Court the Bishop decided that a failure to acquit was a conviction, and therefore the sentence of the Genesee Conference must stand affirmed!

When the next appeal case came up, I began to exercise my right of challenging for cause members of the committee. Two were set aside. I was not then allowed to challenge any farther, though I assigned as the cause that those objected to had published hostile articles against me in the papers. My objections were overruled. I have been credibly informed that it was the evident unfairness of the committee towards me in the outset that made one Bishop vacate the chair, because he did not wish to be a party to the wrong. A Bishop of strong pro-slavery proclivities took his place.

Our opposers evidently felt that so great was the lack of evidence to sustain the charges on which they expelled us, that even this committee could not be depended upon to sustain their verdict. Notwithstanding all their professions of a desire to have the action of the Genesee Conference reviewed by the General Conference, they directed all their energies to prevent the appeals from being entertained. They had already secured the discharge of the special committee appointed to investigate Genesee Conference affairs. If now they could shut out the appeals, their action would stand unexamined and unrebuked by the highest authority in the Church. *For every one that doeth evil hateth the light, neither cometh to the light, lest his deeds should be reproved.*—John 3:20.

The efforts at suppression were successful. The majority voted not to entertain my appeal from the verdict of the Genesee Conference, sentencing me to expulsion from the Church. Why the same committee should hear my appeal from the sentence of reproof, and, a few days later, refuse to entertain my appeal from the sentence of expulsion, remains among the unsolved mysteries.

As their final decision was announced, I said, "I APPEAL TO GOD AND THE PEOPLE."

As the appeal cases came up one after another, the committee voted *not to entertain them*, with the single exception of the appeal of Mr. Burlingham.

Whatever may have been thought regarding the merits of "New School Methodism" at the time of its original publication, does not the action of the General Conference of 1860, regarding the appeals from the Genesee Conference, fully justify, at last, the contents of that article? Did not that body, by its action in these cases, virtually commit itself and pledge its patronage to "New School Methodism?" Its action affected the whole Church. It produced "an epoch indeed in the history of Methodism; since it involves nothing less than a radical change in the system: a change which supersedes the Methodism of Wesley—'Christianity in earnest'—and replaces it with a smooth, formal, fashionable religion, whose very insignia and watchword is popularity."*

It seems, too, that the historians of the Methodist Episcopal Church have felt under the necessity of veiling the action of the General Conference in the appeal cases under statements that are either absolutely untrue or decidedly misleading. Bishop Simpson is especially at fault in this respect. He took an active interest in the proceedings, and must have known that the plainest canons of the Church were ignored, and that justice was defeated by its professed friends. Yet in referring to those who had appealed from the action of the Genesee Conference, in his "Cyclopedia of Methodism," he says: "As they had declined to recognize the authority of the Church, and had continued to exercise their ministry and to organize societies, the General Conference declined to entertain the appeal."

In this quotation there are several statements that are not true. In the first place, the appellants had never "declined to recognize the authority of the Church." Nothing of the kind was ever proved against them. The very fact of their appealing to the General Conference was a recognition of the Church's properly constituted authority. The same may be said of Roberts and McCreery in their act of uniting with the Church on probation after their expulsion. The statement of the Bishop is a sweeping one, yet no instances are given, and for the reason that well-grounded instances were absolutely wanting. In no single particular had they failed of properly recognizing the authority of the Church.

Moreover, it is not true that "they continued to exer-

*Bowen's "Origin of the Free Methodist Church," p. 227.

cise their ministry." It was never shown, and can not be shown, that they ever performed a single function peculiarly belonging to a Christian minister pending their appeals. They refrained from marrying people, from baptizing, from administering or helping to administer the Sacrament of the Lord's Supper, and from exercising any of the rights formerly belonging to them in virtue of their ordination either as Deacons or as Elders. They labored in public meetings, and that with great success, but they did it as any layman of the Church might do, and in accordance with the Discipline, which, in the General Rules, says, "It is expected of all who continue in these societies that they shall continue to show their desire to flee from the wrath to come, by doing good" to the souls of men, "by instructing, reproving, or exhorting all with whom they have any intercourse." That is what they did, and all they did. This is all the Bishop or others could ever point to as instances of their "declining to recognize the authority of the Church." Hence the action of the General Conference practically declared it to be a crime for a minister who has been expelled from the Church, and has appealed, to engage in honest efforts to save lost men and build up believers in the faith, pending his appeal.

As to the Bishop's statement that they continued "to organize societies," it is at least misleading. One who did not know otherwise would naturally suppose from this statement that these brethren, pending their appeals, had either organized regular Methodist societies, or rivals to the Methodist societies. Neither case is correct. They organized "Bands," as was originally provided for by the Discipline of the Methodist Episcopal Church, and quite similar in most respects to "Holiness Bands" and "Holiness Associations" that have become quite common in the Church in later times. These "Bands" were not "societies" in the Disciplinary sense of that term, and yet they were associations for conserving and promoting the essential principles of original Methodism. Nor were they rivals of the Methodist "societies," but simply organized "Bands" of earnest Christians, whom the Methodist Church had proscribed, organized with a view of keeping them from being scattered, until such time as the administration under which they had been thus proscribed should be reviewed and passed upon by the General Conference.

When Mr. Roberts went to Buffalo to labor, there was a Free Methodist Episcopal Church, in which the seats were neither rented nor sold, located on Thirteenth street. The building in which they worshiped was owned by Mr. Jesse Ketchum, of the Congregational Church, who allowed the Methodists to use it gratis. The society at this place was merely a mission—few in numbers and weak in influence. Mr. Edward P. Cox, an intelligent Englishman of considerable means, had charge of the building by Mr. Ketchum's direction. He invited Mr. Roberts to hold a meeting there one week night, when the Methodists had no appointment with which it would interfere. The invitation was accepted. Mr. Cox was at once informed, by the Presiding Elder and some of the preachers, that if Mr. Roberts was allowed to speak there, the preacher would be removed, and the missionary appropriation withheld. Mr. Cox, who was not a man to be turned from his course by threats, especially when confident that he was in the right, replied that "they might do as they liked; the house would be open for Mr. Roberts at the time." The appointed service was held, and, good as their word, the Presiding Elder and ministers saw that the preacher and the missionary appropriation were both taken away.

Mr. Roberts then continued to look after these sheep without a shepherd. Would common humanity have dictated that he do less? He held meetings in the Church, which were blessed to the salvation of many souls. A Church with the free-seat system had been started there, and was much needed in Buffalo at that time; and, had the appeal of Mr. Roberts been entertained and he restored to membership in the Methodist Church, in all probability the Thirteenth street society would have returned to the fold with him. Owing to the appeal being turned down, the final result was otherwise.

In the meantime Mr. Stiles had organized a Congregational Free Methodist Church at Albion, but as he had taken no appeal, he had an undoubted right to organize, where, when and what he pleased, his action could not properly be included in the Bishop's charge.

"But even if Bishop Simpson's statements were true, they would not constitute a valid reason why our appeals should not be heard upon their merits," says Mr. Roberts. "We were only claiming the rights that were solemnly promised us by the M. E. Church in its book of Discipline when we united with it. In the very Constitution of the Church is an article which says of the General Conference:

"THEY SHALL NOT DO AWAY THE PRIVILEGES *of our ministers or preachers, of trial by committee and appeal.*

"This prohibition is general. It does not say they shall not do it in some particular way, but they shall not do it at all. It does not say they shall not do it under some pretexts—but they shall not do it under any pretext whatever. They shall not do it by hostile enactments, or by precedents, or by arbitrary refusals to hear appeals.

"The only condition contained in the Discipline was in these words—'Provided, nevertheless, that in all the above mentioned cases of trial and conviction, *an appeal to the ensuing General Conference shall be allowed if the condemned person signifies his intention to appeal, at the time of his condemnation, or at any time thereafter when he is informed thereof.*' There is only one condition here expressed. No one claimed that this condition had not been met. If there is any meaning in language then a General Conference administering these laws had no right to refuse to allow an appeal. In doing it, they violated, in the interest of wrong, the *plainly expressed written* Constitution of the Church.

"This law did not give a General Conference original jurisdiction over preachers. They had no right to *try us*, but our *appeal* cases. The question for them to decide was: Were those men fairly tried according to the Discipline? Did the law and the facts justify the verdict of the Genesee Conference in these several cases?

"If we had violated the laws of the Church after our expulsion,

20

then the Genesee Conference could, if we were restored, try us for such violation.

"Nor should our appeals have been injured by our joining the Church again on probation. A few years previous to these difficulties, the Chautauqua Presbytery deposed a minister. He joined the Methodists; after a while was licensed, and preached among them several years. The Presbytery afterwards becoming satisfied of his innocence, restored him to his ministerial standing, though he was at the time an accredited minister of another denomination. They told him they wished, as far as they could, to repair the wrong they had done him and he was at liberty to remain in whichever Church he chose. He went back to the Presbyterians."*

To all unprejudiced minds who are acquainted with the polity of the Methodist Episcopal Church the foregoing argument will be conclusive. It matters not what crimes a man may have committed after his appeal from the decision of a lower to a higher Court, the Appellate Court has no jurisdiction in his case over anything but the appeal, and must try that on the merits of the case, the same as though the appellant had been perfectly law-abiding pending his appeal. For his later violations of the law the Court of original jurisdiction must initiate new proceedings, and prosecute according to statute. Otherwise appeals would be utterly useless.

*"Why Another Sect?" pp. 288-290.

CHAPTER XXXI

THE GENERAL CONFERENCE AND THE APPEALS FROM GENESEE—CONTINUED

Of the various reviews of the General Conference action on the appeal cases, none has more ably and fairly presented the case than has the Rev. William Hosmer, who wrote and published the following, in the *Northern Independent:*

The General Conference *assumes powers* which *do not* belong to it, when they make the right to have an appeal heard depend upon anything the appellant has done since the decision from which he appeals.

In doing this, they must first try the appellant upon his general conduct since his trial from the decision on which he appeals, in order to determine whether his appeal shall be entertained or not! But the Discipline does not give the General Conference original jurisdiction over any of the ministers except the Bishops. They have no more right than Judge Lynch has to try a preacher unless his case comes before them on an appeal, and then they must be confined to the testimony taken in the lower Court.

If the conduct of an expelled preacher pending his appeal has not been correct, let him, if unjustly deposed, be restored, and then he is responsible to his Conference for his actions while suspended. The General Conference is authorized to try appeal cases, but not preachers. For them to undertake to do that, is an unwarrantable and odious assumption of power.

What does the right of appeal amount to, if the security of its exercise depends upon the prejudice or caprice of a majority of a committee!

The appeal of Mr. Roberts should have been heard, *because the majority was committed against him* BEFORE ANY COMPLAINT WAS MADE OR CHARGE PREFERRED.

There is nothing guarded with greater jealousy by the common law, than the impartiality of juries. A person put on trial before its tribunals may challenge all day "for cause." Let it be shown that the jury had, by any acts, committed themselves before the trial, and the verdict would be set aside.

The necessity of an impartial jury is as great in ecclesiastical as in criminal trials—when character, as when life is at stake. The credit of religion as well as the security of the individual, demands no less. A verdict obtained by connivance, or by partisan excitement, is none the more to be respected because it was rendered under religious forms, by men professing godliness.

It is well known that at the time of these trials, the Genesee Conference was divided into two parties;—that this partisan feeling, which has existed for years, was wrought up to the greatest intensity—that at the Conference which instituted the first of these trials, the party opposed to the appellant for the first time became a majority, several of the opposite party having been transferred to other Conferences—and that it was by this accidental, excited and thoroughly partisan majority that Mr. Roberts was tried. This being the case, and the trial resulting as it did, if there ever was an instance where the corrective agency of an Appellate Court was needed, that case was the one under consideration.

If there is any analogy between an Ecclesiastical Court and a Civil Court, then the necessity was even greater than we have stated, and so far from not entertaining the appeal, the Court should have annulled the previous trial, and sent the case back for a new investigation, if a trial was judged to be necessary. But, admitting the validity of the action of the Court below, we see not how it was possible for this Appellate Court to refuse to entertain the appeal. The hearing of cases is not optional with such a Court—an appeal always lies if the party appealing gives due notice of his intention, and is on hand to prosecute his claims. Not to entertain an appeal is, therefore, a palpable dereliction from duty; and, in this instance, it was equivalent to saying that, so far as these expelled brethren were concerned, there should be no Appellate Court in the M. E. Church—thus practically annihilating one of the most important branches of our judiciary, and rendering it forever impossible to correct the errors of the Court below.

Well might the appellant stand aghast at such treatment, and make his appeal to God and the people. The judicial infatuation which has rendered it necessary to transfer this and other like cases, from an earthly to a heavenly tribunal, we deplore, but cannot help. The deed is done, and, with all its appalling consequences, the record must go up to God. We have the satisfaction of knowing that we have not been awed by authority, nor terrified by threats, into silence in the presence of such wrongs. The senseless, shameless cry of "Nazaritism," we fling back with the hearty contempt which it merits. Those who indulge in this low style of abuse, should remember that there are people in the world who are not afraid of slang, and who will not desert the innocent because malice, for the accomplishment of its own purposes, heaps upon them disparaging epithets. To defend the injured should be regarded as a virtue, not as a crime; and whatever the meaning or the madness of persecution may inflict, we had far rather share it with the oppressed, than betray them to the clutches of a relentless tyranny.

Brave words of a brave man! When half a century and more has passed since the events to which they refer occurred, any man may utter his sense of righteous indignation at such travesties on justice in the name of Christianity, and display no very great moral heroism in doing so. But in those days, and under those conditions, to have written as William Hosmer did, in registration of his protest against the crooked administration of the Genesee Conference and the unrighteous support of that administration by the General Conference, required and exhibited a degree of moral courage which should class him with the Reformers of the sixteenth century for moral courage and noble doing.

We have already seen that the General Conference made an exception in the case of the Rev. C. D. Burlingham, and entertained his appeal. The final action of that body in his case, however, was such an insult to justice and common sense as to merit universal condemnation. The case was remanded for a new trial. Mr. Burlingham admitted, on his trial, the facts alleged in the bill of charges, but pleaded certain other facts in justification of his conduct. Thus, it will be seen, the General Conference took no action regarding the merits of his appeal, but dodged the issue by sending it back for a new trial, *when there was absolutely nothing to try!* Here again we quote the editorial comments of the *Northern Independent* as *apropos* to the situation:

That the Court of Appeals, constituted by the last General

Conference, did not do its work so as to secure either divine or human respect, is a conclusion forced upon us by every view we have been able to take of the subject. Gladly would we pass by these judicial proceedings without further notice, if it were allowable, but they are of too serious a character, and will be found too far reaching in their consequences, to admit of silent acquiescence. Ecclesiastical Courts are not famous for liberality and justice, but we believe the Courts of Methodism have not generally sunk to the level indicated by the trial of these appeals.

First in order, was the case of Rev. C. D. Burlingham. He was expelled from the Genesee Conference, and from the M. E. Church, for doing three things:

1st. Admitting B. T. Roberts into the Church on trial.

2nd. Licensing him to exhort.

3rd. Officiating with expelled preachers at a General Quarterly Meeting held in a Wesleyan Church, at the same time that his Presiding Elder was holding a regular Quarterly Meeting in the same charge, about three miles distant. Mr. Burlingham admitted the facts alleged, but pleaded other facts in justification.

These were the only offenses with which Mr. Burlingham was charged.

After his expulsion, he waited silently for the General Conference. He did not preach, nor lecture, nor exhort—did not attend meetings held by expelled preachers—but did *penance* up to the session of the General Conference. He should have been restored on the ground of having expiated his guilt, if he were guilty of any ordinary offense, if on no other. When his appeal came up, Mr. Fuller, who has been chief prosecutor in all these trials, challenged several of the committee who had manifested a desire to have Genesee Conference matters fairly investigated. Though the General Conference, in constituting the committee, or Court of Appeals, had given to parties the right to challenge *for cause,* yet Mr. Fuller, after the first instance, was not required to give *cause,* but challenged as many as he chose, *and they were set aside.* He simply said of the challenged, that "he considered them prejudiced."

Mr. Olin, of the Oneida Conference, managed the case for Mr. Burlingham with consummate tact, and great ability. His plea was a masterly effort, and carried conviction to the minds, we believe, of all who heard it, except the committee. *They sent the case back to the Genesee Conference for a new trial.* This we regard as a remarkable decision. Neither party asked for it. We never heard before of a case being remanded for a new trial, unless there was some alleged informality in the Court below, or defect in the record, or unless one or the other of the parties claimed to have new testimony which could not be introduced into the first trial. But nothing of the kind was intimated in this case. There can be no new testimony, for Mr. Burlingham admitted all the facts with which he was charged.

Do these facts, mentioned above, constitute a crime, for which an able minister, of spotless reputation, who has served the Church for over twenty years, devoting the vigor of his manhood's prime, in self-sacrificing efforts to promote her interests, should be expelled? Then let the General Conference say so, that all who henceforth enter the Methodist ministry, may understand that they are expected to lay their manhood in the dust, part with the right of private judgment, and yield a servile, unquestioning obedience to all the behests of their ecclesiastical superiors.

Was Mr. Burlingham, through party malignity, treated unjustly? Was he wrongfully deposed from the ministry, and excluded from the Church? Then the General Conference should have restored him. This was due to him; it was due to outraged justice—it was due to the M. E. Church, whose Discipline, confessedly more susceptible of abuse than that of any other Church in this country, has been used for the purpose of inflicting ecclesiastical oppression without a parallel in the nineteenth century.

But the General Conference, through its committee, or Court of Appeals, after gravely listening to the testimony and pleadings, sent the case back for a new trial, without a motion to that effect, from either party. *What*, we ask, is there to try? There can be no issue on the facts—these are admitted.

But Mr. Burlingham contends that these facts do not constitute a crime for which he should be deposed from the ministry, and excluded from the Church.

The Genesee Conference has said that they do. Here is the issue—who shall decide? The Discipline vests the power in the General Conference—the body to try appeals. The case was properly brought before them, and they have sent it back, for the Genesee Conference to decide over again. What an absurd decision! What an insult to Mr. Burlingham, and to common sense! Suppose the views of law and justice entertained by the Genesee Conference remain unchanged, and the same sentence be again pronounced against Mr. Burlingham, and he again appeals. After waiting four years for another General Conference, if he still survives, there will not only be the same reason for sending the case back for a new trial as now, but the additional one of precedent. Thus, this mockery of justice may continue *ad infinitum.*

This looks more like the tiger playing with the victim he intends to devour, than like a body of Christian ministers, bound by every consideration that can influence to right action, to "judge righteous judgment."

Another fact is worthy of especial notice. Though the decision in the case was not asked for *in Court* by either party, yet it is precisely what partisans of the Regency party of the Genesee Conference have been endeavoring for months to persuade Mr. Burlingham to consent to. These efforts were continued up to the morning of the day on which the appeal was heard. Yet neither in their pleadings, nor at any time while the appeal was being heard, did the counsel for the Conference signify their wish that the case might be remanded for a new trial. At whose suggestion was it done? When was the suggestion made? Was there any collusion in the matter? It is impossible for us to answer these questions. View it in whatever light you may, the whole case has a dark and suspicious aspect.

Perhaps some clue to an explanation of the strange proceedings in relation to the Genesee Conference appeal cases may be found in the action had upon the slavery question.

The Genesee Conference has heretofore been one of the strongest anti-slavery Conferences in the connection. The proscribed party have, from the first, been uncompromising in their hostility to slavery in the Church and in the State.

The Genesee delegates to the late General Conference were once regarded as anti-slavery; what they are now their votes will show. We asserted last fall that the Conference had become pro-slavery, and gave as proof the fact, that while it condemned this paper, it refused to take any action against slavery. The truth of our inference was denied by some, but the recent course of their delegates has made our words good. When the important question was decided in the General Conference upon a change of Constitution, so as to prohibit slave-holding in the Church, the delegates of the Genesee Conference voted against a change, *and their vote turned the scale.* And when the Genesee Conference matters came up, *the border pro-slavery delegates voted solid with the representatives of the majority of the Genesee Conference.* This may be all fair. It may be that men who, four years ago took the stump to keep slavery out of the territories, have suddenly become convinced that it should be nestled and fostered in the bosom of the Church! We should like to know by what arguments they were converted, and when it was done! Was this a part of a scheme to keep slaveholders in the Church? Did the border delegates understand that if they voted as desired by the

Genesee delegates, they would reciprocate the favor, and assist them in their extremity? Or did this strange coincidence come about by chance?"

If the foregoing comments appear to be somewhat caustic, we ask, Does not the case deserve the stinging rebuke therein given? Could timidity and tameness be more out of place anywhere than in an editorial review of such action on the part of a General Conference? Were not those brave words of the *Northern Independent* worthy of general commendation? And were not the men who dared to speak and write thus plainly in defense of righteousness, and in condemnation of wrong, even though that condemnation was necessarily a reflection upon the Church and likely to incur ecclesiastical wrath, the salt that preserved the Church itself from moral putrefaction?

The question will naturally arise, What were the reasons why the General Conference took such unwarrantable action in dealing with the appeal cases. This question has been so clearly answered in "Why Another Sect?" that we reproduce the answers here:

1. The charge of doing any specified wrong is not met by claiming or conceding general respectability for the body which did it. The Congress which passed the Fugitive Slave Law was a highly respectable body. President Fillmore, who signed it, was a highly respectable man. Yet that law made every free man at the North liable to become a slave-hunter or a law-breaker.

2. This General Conference had in it a large number of Masons and Odd-Fellows. When it is known beforehand that the Secret Society question is to be made an issue it is an easy thing for those belonging to these societies in the various Conferences of the M. E. Church to send an unusually large proportion of their friends to a General Conference.

3. In the Discipline of the M. E. Church are important rules which the preachers not only openly disregard, but teach the people to disregard. On dress, their rule forbids "the putting on of gold and costly apparel;"—in practise they generally put on both,—often beyond their means,—and many preachers defend the practise. In Church building, the rule required them to be plain and cheap;—the practise was to build as expensively as credit,—and means not infrequently obtained by pew-selling and Church-

gambling, would permit. The result of "holding the truth in unrighteousness" is the demoralization of the conscience. The law of present expediency comes to be the rule of conduct. Policy takes the place of conscience.

4. The General Conference at Buffalo was held just before the breaking out of the Civil War. The Nation and the Church were greatly agitated on the Slavery question. With many, it was the great question before the General Conference of 1860. The Genesee Conference had for years been classed as a radical Abolitionist Conference. The Baltimore Conference was considered on the point of religious experience committed to old-fashioned Methodism, but was at the same time the champion of the slaveholders in the M. E. Church. At the General Conference at Buffalo, the delegates from Baltimore and the delegates from Genesee, when these issues came up, talked and voted lovingly together. Herod and Pilate became friends. Baltimore helped Genesee to dispose of the "Nazarites;" and Genesee helped Baltimore to substitute for the *rule* against slaveholding, some good, but powerless advice. We do not *say* there was any bargain to this effect—we have no proof of it—but we do not believe that at that late day the Genesee delegates were really converted to pro-slavery doctrines. Nor do we believe that the border delegates were converted to the religious theories of the Genesee delegates. They still invite Fay H. Purdy, who was called the ring-leader of "the sect called Nazarites," to labor in that section.

The appeal cases were referred to a committee. Thomas Carlton had visited the Conferences as book agent, and was acquainted with the delegates generally. That he *could* exercise an influence in the selection of the Committee of Appeals is easily seen. That he would not scruple to do it is evident from the case mentioned by Dr. Bowen, in which Thomas Carlton bore a prominent part, as counsel for a so-called Regency preacher, accused by one of the members of the Church of gross, intentional dishonesty. Before the trial commenced, Mr. Carlton had the parties agree to abide by the decision of the arbitrators. Each party was to choose two, and the four were to choose the fifth. Mr. Carlton selected two preachers; the other party, two highly respectable laymen. They could not agree upon the fifth. At length Mr. Carlton suddenly remembered that he had seen on the hotel register (it was at Niagara Falls), the name of a preacher from New York. He would help them out. All agreed upon him. The case was heard and the preachers gave a most unrighteous verdict against the laymen. *This fifth man was afterwards found out to be*

Thomas Carlton's brother-in-law, whom he had brought there on purpose.

Of the truth of what is here affirmed there can be no question. Yet, in that case there was nothing like the inducement to unfairness that there was in the cases appealed from the decision of the Genesee Conference.

In the absence of any other solution of the problem, the foregoing furnishes a key to its solution. At all events it is evident that the delegates from Genesee were afraid to have the appeals come before the General Conference for a hearing. It is also equally evident that no stone was left unturned by them to defeat their entertainment, as also the measures by which it was sought to have a full and impartial review of the Genesee Conference difficulties with a view to correcting the administration by which so many worthy members had been unjustly proscribed. Moreover, judging from their past record, are we not warranted in believing that those same delegates resorted to most unrighteous measures for the accomplishment of their ends, whereby the majority of the General Conference were influenced, either wittingly or unwittingly, to unite in such action as can by no means be justified?

It will readily be seen that the slavery question must have figured largely in the final determination of the appeal cases. It should not have done so, but it did. As touching the far-reaching effect of this action of the General Conference of 1860 on the slavery question, the *American Wesleyan* of March 27, 1861, contained the following eminently pertinent criticism:

OFFICIAL EXPOSITION OF LAW.

In the Baltimore Conference, recently in session, the following questions were proposed to Bishop Scott, and answered by him. We are glad that after so much evasion as has filled up the history of the M. E. Church upon the anti-slavery attitude of this body, we are at last in possession of an official decision, too plain to be misunderstood. Here are the points—look at them! A slaveholder can be admitted a member of the Church, ordained, and hold slaves for *gain*, and there is no Discipline in the Church by which to arraign him, or object to him. Can anything be more abhorrently plain than this?

The following questions were presented to the chair, and promptly answered:

1. Is there anything in the Discipline which, in your judgment, would be a bar to the ordination of a local preacher holding slaves? Answer—No.

2. Anything in the Discipline which, in your judgment, would operate against the admission of a slaveholder into the Church? Answer—No.

3. Anything in the Discipline that would justify an administrator in arraigning a slaveholder? Answer—No.

4. Is there any process authorized in the Discipline by which a member can be brought to trial who holds slaves for gain? Answer—I know of no such process.

Corrupt as was the action of the General Conference regarding these cases, God in His wise providence overruled it for good in the end, causing to issue therefrom a stream of "living waters"—a river whose onward flow should broaden, deepen, increase its momentum and bless the world to the end of time. "The so-called 'Nazarites,' who never thought of a separate existence before, now losing all hope of reconciliation with the old Church, resolved upon an independent organization. They felt they were shut out from all sympathy on the part of a Church which had thrust many from her bosom—their leaders in particular—with such illegal and malignant violence; and that they had no alternative left them but to provide for themselves."*

*Bowen's "Origin of the Free Methodist Church."

CHAPTER XXXII

THE FREE METHODIST CHURCH ORGANIZED

We have already seen the important part the Laymen's Conventions played in those providential steps which prepared the way for the formation of the Free Methodist Church. The Laymen also were largely instrumental in its final organization. The Rev. A. A. Phelps, who was present and participated in the proceedings, has given the following brief account:

"In accordance with the provisions of the last Laymen's Convention, a Delegated Convention was called at Pekin, Niagara County, N. Y., August 23rd, 1860, to confer as to the best mode of extending the work which God had so graciously begun among them. The Convention was called to order, and opened with devotional exercises. Isaac M. Chesbrough, of Pekin, was elected Chairman, and Rev. A. A. Phelps, Secretary. The body, duly organized, was composed of sixty members—fifteen preachers, and forty-five laymen. [B. T. Roberts, in an editorial account of the Convention in the *Earnest Christian,* gives the number as "eighty laymen and fifteen preachers"—W. T. H.] Most of the business was transacted on the camp-ground—a spot newly consecrated by the outpouring of God's Spirit and the salvation of precious souls. The deliberations of the Convention resulted in the organization of the Free Methodist Church, and the adoption of their first Discipline."*

The call for this Convention read as follows:

A Convention will be held at Pekin, for the purpose of adopting

*Bowen's "Origin of the Free Methodist Church," p. 229.

a Discipline for the Free Methodist Church, to commence at the close of the camp-meeting, August 23rd. All Societies and Bands that find it necessary, in order to promote the prosperity and permanency of the work of holiness, to organize a Free Methodist Church on the following basis, are invited to send delegates:

1. Doctrines and usages of primitive Methodism, such as the witness of the Spirit, entire sanctification as a state of grace distinct from justification, attainable instantly by faith; free seats, congregational singing, without instrumental music in all cases; plainness of dress.

2. An equal representation of ministers and laymen in all the councils of the Church.

3. No slaveholding and no connection with secret, oath-bound societies.

Each Society or Band will be entitled to send one delegate at least, and an additional one for every forty members.

There were grave doubts in the minds of some who participated in this Convention as to the expediency of proceeding to organize a new Church at that time. The matter was freely discussed, however, after which a considerable majority voted in favor of proceeding with the work of organization. The Rev. S. K. J. Chesbrough, who had hitherto taken a prominent part in the Laymen's Conventions, has expressed his attitude at that time in the following statement:

"At the time of the Convention I was not clear in my own mind that the time had come for us to organize, and, therefore, I refused to be a delegate to that Convention. I took no part whatever in the proceedings. In fact, I was not present at the Convention on the camp-ground. All I remember of it is this: Before the Convention was called, B. T. Roberts and several others—I can not remember distinctly who they were, but they were the principal preachers and laymen who were active in the matter—came together under an apple tree right back of our kitchen. I sat in the kitchen door looking at them. They were nearly all seated on the grass under the tree, and it was voted that they proceed to organize the Church. They then arose and went over into the grove, where the

HOME OF S. K. J. CHESBROUGH AT PEKIN, N. Y.
At rear of which it was decided to organize the Free Methodist Church

CAMP GROUND AT PEKIN, N. Y.
Where the Free Methodist Church was organized, timber partly cut away

[Plate Twenty-one]

Convention was held and the child was born and named. This will account for my want of recollection in the matter. It was but a little while afterward that I felt the wisdom of the brethren was better than mine, and I joined the organization in a few weeks."*

Elsewhere Mr. Chesbrough says: "I well remember the Sunday after the organization, when my wife and eighteen others answered the questions in the Discipline, which Brother Roberts had written on a piece of paper, and formed the first Free Methodist class ever formed under the Discipline."

A further account of the differences of opinion existing between brethren at this Convention regarding the expediency of proceeding to organize at that time, and as to the result as well, has been given by the Rev. M. N. Downing, who was present, but who finished his earthly course in 1913. Mr. Downing says:

> I was a delegate to the Convention at which the Discipline was decided upon at Pekin, N. Y. At this Convention Rev. Joseph McCreery, W. Cooley, Alanson Reddy, and, I think, a Rev. Mr. Farnsworth, and several laymen opposed the immediate organization of a new denomination, on the ground, as they believed, that it would be premature; but it would come [later] in a greater swarm from the M. E. Church. They would in the meantime substitute Bands.
>
> Dr. Redfield was present to represent the West. He arose and said, "Brethren, when fruit is ripe, it had better be picked, lest on falling it bruise. In the West we are ready for an organization. If in the East you are not ready, wait until you are." Mr. Roberts arose and remarked: "We are ready, and the West and the East should move in the matter simultaneously." The majority prevailed, and the organization was effected, taking the name, The Free Methodist Church.
>
> The minority withdrew, and were after that known as the Nazarite faction of the salvation movement, though the name Nazarite was well known among us before that crisis came. [The author understands that those who withdrew *chose* to accept the name, "Nazarite Bands".] The Nazarite faction went to seed completely at a camp-meeting in East Shelby, N. Y. Rev. W. Cooley

*Life of B. T. Roberts, pp. 230, 231.

and wife were at this meeting, and seeing the fanaticism in some of its wildest features coming in, fled to the Free Methodist Church for refuge, and were useful workers therein. Afterwards Brother McCreery joined on probation; but never seemed to be fully in sympathy with the Church.

Brother L. Stiles desired a clause inserted in the Discipline favoring a gradualistic as well as the instantaneous view of entire sanctification. Dr. Redfield arose and remarked substantially as follows: "Brethren, I would not make a threat, but unless we go straight on the question of holiness in the Discipline, we had better halt where we are. The gradualistic theory is what has made so much mischief. We are John Wesleyan Methodists. We must not dodge that point." This view prevailed.

The organization of the Free Methodist Church having been effected, the Convention proceeded to elect the Rev. B. T. Roberts as General Superintendent of the same. The following from his private journal is of interest, because of certain light which it throws on the proceedings in addition to the statements in the foregoing quotations:

August 23rd, 1860.—Convention at Pekin to form a Free Methodist Church. There were present delegates from Genesee Conference: one, Daniel Lloyd, from St. Louis, and Dr. Redfield, from the West. Rev. J. McCreery was very much opposed to forming a close organization of a Church. He said that many of the sheep in the Methodist fold had been so starved by the Regency preachers that they were unable to jump the fence, and he wished to remain in a position where he could salt them through the rails. Brother William Cooley was also opposed to organizing a formal Church; but a majority of the delegates thought that the interests of the cause of God required an organization. The vote stood forty-five for organizing and seven against it. I felt, for the following reasons, that it was best to organize a Church:

1st. We had been—six preachers of us—wickedly expelled from the M. E. Church, and two other preachers had been located in the same way. Many pious members had been expelled and read out for sympathizing with us. The General Conference, though petitioned by fifteen hundred members, refused to grant us any redress, or even to investigate our grievances.

A. W., who was expelled for licentious conduct with several young ladies, was restored by the same General Conference, though his character for fourteen years at least has been regarded as bad.

In nearly every place in which he has preached within that time similar reports of licentious conduct have followed him.

Mr. ——, of New York East Conference, who admitted that the husband of one of his members—coming home unexpectedly—found him hid away under the bed, and the brother's wife was in the room, was also restored. But the General Conference would not hear our appeals.

A memorial stating our grievances was presented to them, but was not, as far as we can ascertain, even read. This memorial was signed by Rev. Asa Abell, John P. Kent, and other members of Genesee Conference.

2nd. The M. E. Church has gone so far from its original position, and has become so involved in formalism, secret-society influence and pro-slaveryism that there is no hope of its recovery.

3rd. There is no existing Church that makes the salvation of souls its prominent and main work. We had to form a new Church or live outside of any and have no place to put those that God converts through our instrumentality.

The form of Discipline which I had prepared under, as I believe, the influence of God's Spirit, was adopted with but slight alterations. I proposed to have a Standing Committee who should have the general oversight of all the interests of the Church. But the Convention judged best to have a General Superintendent. To my surprise the choice fell on me. Lord, give me heavenly wisdom to guide me! It was a heavy cross to accept the appointment, but I did not dare to decline, because of the conviction that God called me to this labor and reproach and responsibility. Yet, oh, to what calumny it will subject me! Lord, I will take the cross and the shame. Let me have Thy presence and help, O God of power.

Had Mr. Roberts's proposition for a Standing Committee to supervise the affairs of the Church at large prevailed, doubtless the history of the Free Methodist Church would have been very different from what it has been, in various particulars. He appears to have been thoroughly convinced at last that the decision of the Convention was wisely made.

From the foregoing chapter it appears that, for a year or two prior to the General Conference, those members who were "read out" or expelled from the Methodist Epis-

---

*Life of Roberts, pp. 233-235.

copal Church because of their sympathy with the proscribed ministers, had been forming themselves into either Bands or independent Churches. Bands were formed in numerous places, and Churches had been organized at Albion, New York, St. Charles, Illinois, St. Louis, Missouri, and possibly at two or three other places. These persecuted ones, excluded from the Church they so dearly loved, were passing through a transition state, as to Church membership, though TO what they did not know. They went forth cheerfully "without the camp, bearing His [Christ's] reproach;" and, having no surety of an abiding Church home, they became fond of referring to themselves as "Pilgrims," a name quite common among them, even in their denominational capacity, to this day. The organization of these small societies seems to have been providentially ordered, as well for their own preservation in unity, as for the better advantages it gave them to labor effectively for the salvation of others, and for the general promotion of the work of God.

Those who formed independent Churches took to themselves various names, but into several of these the words Free Methodist Church entered. As to who originated this name we have been unable to ascertain. The reader will recall, however, that the little society which Mr. Roberts found in Buffalo, N. Y., after his expulsion, worshiping in a building on Thirteenth street, the use of which was granted them by a Congregational brother, was then known as the Free Methodist Episcopal Church. It was a Church in which the seats were all free, and which stood for freedom in several other respects. Presumably the name Free Methodist Church is an adaptation from that of the Buffalo Free Methodist Episcopal Church, the word Episcopal being omitted, because of the Democratic rather than the Episcopal form of government having been adopted. Mr. Stiles had also organized a Congregational Free Methodist Church at Albion, New York, a year or two before the new denomination was formed. Two hundred members of the Methodist Episcopal Church followed him into the new organization.

As finally characterizing the new denomination the name, Free Methodist Church, is significant. In the first place, the term Church indicates that this people from the beginning believed in Church organization, and were no mere anti-sect society, reform organization, or holiness association. They were organized as a permanent branch of the Church militant, and proposed, so far as possible, to honor both the name Church and that for which it stands.

Then the name Methodist was assumed because they claimed to be Methodists—of the original type—in doctrine, usages, experience and practise. They were and are John Wesley Methodists.

Finally, as to the prefix Free, it signified freedom from Episcopal domination, from which they had suffered in the Church which cast them out; freedom from Lodge rule or interference, which had wrought so disastrously in the troubles which led to their expulsion; freedom from those discriminations in favor of the wealthy and aristocratic in the house of God, which are engendered by the renting or sale of pews; the freedom of the Spirit in personal experience, accompanied by freedom on the part of all, in the public worship of God, to give such outward expression to deep religious emotion as the Holy Spirit may inspire or prompt.

A little over a year after Mr. Stiles organized his Church at Albion, New York, the Rev. C. D. Brooks withdrew from the Genesee Conference of the Methodist Episcopal Church, and one hundred sixty of his members with him. Later they united with the Free Methodist Church. This was the largest number that ever joined the Free Methodist Church at one time except when Mr. Stiles and his newly organized Church united in a body.

Since next to the foregoing paragraph was written the following letter has been received from Mr. Brooks, which throws additional light on the origin of the name Free Methodist Church:

GENEVA, N. Y., May 19, 1913.

DEAR BROTHER:

I have been thinking lately that I ought to write you, and mention a matter of fact about the organization of the Free Methodist Church. As I suppose you purpose to bring out a history of our Church, you may wish to give the item of which I now write you.

I am now nearly eighty-eight years of age, and the only minister still living of the old Genesee Conference of the M. E. Church, who passed through those unrighteous trials that prepared the way for the organization of the Church that is still doing faithful work and seeing many souls clearly saved every year.

Now for the item, the name given, etc. The second year of expulsions, at Brockport, in 1859, Rev. Loren Stiles was the first one of the four that was excluded. In fact one hour after the Masonic party of the Conference voted him out of the Conference and membership of the Church, that noble man, of precious memory, proclaimed publicly, with great emphasis, "I'll take my appeal to God and the people." He soon left and went back to Albion, where he had been pastor two years. I then foresaw that he would probably organize a new Church; and after thinking the matter over for a day or two, I wrote him, in case he organized a new Church, *a good name* for it would be

THE FREE METHODIST CHURCH.

And I further suggested that I hoped the position of the new Church would embody the following principles, viz.:

Free from slavery,

Free from secret societies,

Free seats in all Churches.

Free from the outward ornaments of pride, and

Free in Christ.

I soon learned that Brother Stiles at once organized a new Church in Albion, and nearly 200 people joined it, and that the *name* and *principles* were indorsed, as I had given them.

And, further, when nearly a year later, in 1860, at Pekin, N. Y., the general Church was organized, August 23, the same name and principles were embodied in the Discipline of the Church; and one chapter of the Discipline, as adopted at Pekin, was in my handwriting, though I was still a member of the Genesee Conference of the M. E. Church.

HOME OF I. M. CHESBROUGH
At Pekin, N. Y.

REV. C. D. BROOKS
One of the pioneers of Free Methodism in Western New York

REV. MOSES N. DOWNING
A member of the Convention at which the Free Methodist Church was organized

[Plate Twenty-two]

Perhaps you had never previously known that your humble servant had such a share in shaping things in those strenuous times.

Your fellow-laborer of many battles during the fifty years past, still after souls, C. D. BROOKS.

No sooner was the infant organization born and christened than the scattered remnants of Methodism—scattered by the hand of ecclesiastical tyranny and despotism—began to turn toward the new Church as a place of refuge from oppression, and as an organization specially committed to the work for which John Wesley said the early Methodist societies were raised up—"to spread Scriptural holiness over these lands." One after another the Bands, Societies, and Churches which had been organized here and there as a temporary expedient, united with the new denomination by the adoption of its Discipline, no longer to be mere fragmentary and isolated groups, but societies of a regularly constituted Christian Church, united in one body, laboring together for the advancement of the kingdom of God under one and the same ecclesiastical organization.

The Discipline adopted was based largely on the Discipline of the Methodist Episcopal Church. All but four of its "Articles of Religion" were adopted. Articles xiv., xix., xxi. and xxiii. were appropriately omitted, and two others were added—one on "Entire Sanctification," and the other on "Future Rewards and Punishments."

As the M. E. Church borrowed her "Articles of Religion," in the main, from the Church of England, which had so lately broken away from Romanism, says Dr. Bowen, it is not strange that she should have guarded against the errors of Popery, in imitation of the mother-creed, by retaining the "Articles" on "Purgatory," "Works of Supererogation," the "Marriage of Ministers," and the like; but who is not surprised that she should have omitted to introduce the doctrine of "entire sanctification," and of "future rewards and punishments," which she has always at least until lately, deemed fundamental? These doctrines, so clearly taught in the standards of the Old Church, and made to enter into the confession of her ministers—the former especially—upon their admission into full connection, the Free Methodist Church has most appropriately incorporated into her creed—her life and teaching eminently corresponding thereto.*

The Free Methodist Church also at its organization adopted the "General Rules" of the parent denomination unmodified, except that, where the Rule on slavery in the Methodist Episcopal Discipline was absurdly ambiguous, the Rule on the subject in the Free Methodist Discipline distinctly forbade "The buying, selling, or holding of a human being as a slave." This it should be remembered was adopted while American slavery was still in existence. "The 'Rule,' as adopted by the Free Church, is too full and explicit in language to be evaded in any way; and is, in fine, as it was intended to be, the very synonym of anti-slaveryism in all its moods and tenses."

At an early period following its organization, the Free Methodist Church also modified the rule against "softness and needless self-indulgence" by the addition of a clause making it apply especially to "the use of tobacco for the gratification of a depraved appetite;" and at a still later period it was again further modified so as to make it forbid "the growth, sale or manufacture" of the commodity.

Another feature of the Discipline of the new Church which differentiated it from that of the parent Church was that of the conditions of membership. Persons have always been received on probation in the Methodist Episcopal Church on profession of "a desire to flee from the wrath to come." As a result vast multitudes have thus entered the probationary relation who, if they ever had such a desire, failed to manifest it for any length of time by keeping the General Rules and pressing on until thoroughly converted; but at the expiration of their probationary period they have been recommended for membership in full connection, and accordingly received. In this way the Church has become largely filled with uncon-

*"Origin of Free Methodist Church."

verted members—with those who are as much in love with worldliness and sin as they ever were, who ignore the restraints of ecclesiastical rules, and propose to have their fill of pleasure at the card-table, in the ball-room, at the theater, or wherever else they please, and in any and all kinds of worldly-conformity that is to their liking.

Warned by this, the Free Methodist Church from the beginning has received persons on probation only upon their giving affirmative answers to the following questions: 1. "Have you the assurance of sins forgiven?" 2. "Do you consent to be governed by our General Rules?"

The object has been to keep unconverted persons from becoming members of the Church. Unless the bars are kept up at this point, there is every likelihood that sooner or later some of the Churches, if not the Church at large, will fall entirely under the control of unsaved men, and be conducted merely as clubs or social centers, with little or no regard to spiritual things. Who of us have not seen the practical out-working of this principle repeatedly in those bodies which receive probationers on a mere profession of "desire to flee from the wrath to come"?

It may be asked, however, "Did not Mr. Wesley receive persons on probation on this condition?" We answer, Yes, into his "United Societies," but not into the Church. The "societies" of early Methodism did not compose a Church, in the technical sense, but were "societies" *within the national Church,* designed to help such as were desirous of escaping the wrath of God in finding peace and assurance, and then to build them up in that "holiness without which no man shall see the Lord." Mr. Wesley did not recognize the Methodism of his time as a Church, but simply as a union of "societies" within the Church of England, in which he himself was a regularly ordained priest, and from which he never separated. Nor did the Methodist "societies" separate from the Church of England until some time after Mr. Wesley's death. It should also be borne in mind that those who continued in these societies under Mr. Wesley's superintendency were *expected and required* to keep the General Rules as an evidence of their desire to "flee from the wrath to come." Under this régime they either experienced genuine conversion, or soon ceased from their relation to the Methodist "societies."

Members were to be received into full connection in the Free Methodist Church only upon giving affirmative answers to the following questions, and upon consent of at least three-fourths of all the members present at a society meeting:

1. Have you the witness of the Spirit that you are a child of God?

2. Have you that perfect love which casteth out fear? If not, will you diligently seek until you obtain it?

3. Is it your purpose to devote yourself the remainder of your life wholly to the service of God, doing good to your fellow men, and working out your own salvation with fear and trembling?

4. Will you forever lay aside all superfluous ornaments, and adorn yourself in modest apparel, with shamefacedness and sobriety, not with broidered hair, or gold, or pearls, or costly array, but, which becometh those professing godliness, with good works?

5. Will you abstain from connection with all secret societies, keeping yourself free to follow the will of the Lord in all things?

6. Do you subscribe to our articles of religion, our General Rules, and our Discipline, and are you willing to be governed by the same?

7. Have you Christian fellowship and love for the members of this society, and will you assist them, as God shall give you ability, in carrying on the work of the Lord?

It will be seen from the foregoing that candidates for full membership in the Free Methodist Church must publicly declare that they have the witness of the Spirit to the fact of sonship in the family of God; that they have experienced perfect love, or entire sanctification, or will diligently seek until they do experience it; that they will conform to the apostolic advice regarding dress; and that they will abstain from connection with all secret societies;

four things not substantially covered by the conditions of membership in the Methodist Episcopal Church.

It was venturing much for the infant Church to erect such a standard of membership, and such a course would never have been dictated by worldly policy. Those who were instrumental in starting the new movement were led to the adoption of such measures by the things they had seen and experienced under the more liberal policy of the mother Church. They had learned much by the things they had suffered. The wisdom of their measures was problematical at the time, and multitudes there are who question the saneness of such a policy to-day. For fifty-five years, however, the Free Methodist Church has maintained this standard in the face of fearful odds, and though her growth has been slow, it has been constant, and her influence for good has extended in manifold ways far beyond her own pale, having been largely felt by practically all ecclesiastical bodies in the country.

The following editorial *resumé* of the doings of the Convention at which the Free Methodist Church was organized, and which appeared in the *Earnest Christian* of September, 1860, shows that the adoption of a Discipline was not inconsiderately done, and also furnishes some of the reasons that determined the brethren in favor of some of the new provisions adopted:

About eighty laymen and fifteen preachers met in Convention, at Pekin, Niagara County, N. Y., on the 23rd of August, to take into consideration the adoption of a Discipline for the "Free Methodist Church." Quite a discussion took place as to the propriety of effecting, at present, a formal organization. When the vote was taken, all but seven—five preachers and two laymen—stood up in favor of organizing immediately.

In considering the provisions of the Discipline presented by the committee, every new feature was scanned most closely and critically. The deep interest and close scrutiny of the intelligent laymen who were present as delegates must have convinced any-one that that Church is a great loser which excludes them from her counsels. After a careful examination, item by item, the Discipline as agreed upon was adopted with singular unanimity.

It was as surprising as delightful to notice the similarity of views entertained by men who think for themselves coming from different parts of the country.

The doctrines agreed upon are those entertained by Methodists generally throughout the world. An article on sanctification, taken from Wesley's writings, was adopted. As a difference in views upon this subject is one cause of the difficulties that have occurred in the Genesee Conference, it was thought best to have a definite expression of our belief.

The countenance given of late by Methodist ministers in this region to Universalists, by affiliating with them, supplying their pulpits, and going without rebuke to their communion, rendered it necessary, in the judgment of the Convention, to have an article, drawn from the Bible, on future rewards and punishments.

The Annual and Quadrennial Conventions are to be composed of an equal number of laymen and ministers. The Episcopacy and Presiding Eldership are abolished. Class-leaders and stewards are chosen by the members, and the sacred right of every accused person to an impartial trial and appeal is carefully guarded.

Several searching questions relating to personal experience, and the purpose to lead a life devoted to God, must be proposed to every individual offering to join the Church; and, upon an affirmative response, he is to be admitted with the consent of three-fourths of the members present at a society meeting.

It is not the intention to try to get up a secession. On the contrary, as much as in us lies, we shall live peaceably with all men. The wicked expulsion of several ministers for no other crime than simply trying to carry out their ordination vows, and the cruel refusal of the General Conference to grant us the hearing of our appeals, guaranteed to us in the most solemn manner by the Constitution and Laws of the Methodist Episcopal Church, and the violent ejection from the Church of many of its pious and devoted members, whose only offense was that of sympathizing with us, as we are trying to endure "the affliction of the Gospel," have rendered it necessary to provide a humble shelter for ourselves and for such poor, wayfaring pilgrims as may wish to journey with us to heaven.

We are very firm in the conviction that it is the will of the Lord that we should establish free Churches—the seats to be forever free—where the Gospel can be preached to the poor. We have this consolation, and it is a great one, that if our effort is not for the glory of God, and does not receive His approval, it cannot succeed. And if it is not for His glory, we most devoutly pray that it may fail in its very incipiency. We would rather be covered with any amount of dishonor than have the cause of God suffer. We have no men of commanding ability and influence to help on the enterprise—no wealth, no sympathy from powerful ecclesiastical, or political, or secret societies; but all these against us—so that if we succeed, it must be by the blessings of heaven upon our feeble endeavors. We can not avail ourselves of any popular excitement in favor of a reform in Church government—or against slavery; but we are engaged in the work, always unpopular, and especially so in this age, of trying to persuade our fellow men to tread the path of self-denial—the narrow way that leadeth unto life.

That the founders of the Free Methodist Church were devotedly attached to Methodism is evident from the fact that the Articles of Faith adopted by them were all borrowed from those of the Methodist Episcopal Church, except two,—that on Entire Sanctification, which is a reproduction of the words of Wesley, and reiterated in the chief doctrinal works of the Methodist Church, and that on Future Rewards and Punishments, which also is in full accord with the teaching of Methodism's doctrinal standards—as also from the fact that they adopted most of the usages of early Methodism, and so much of the polity of the Methodist Episcopal Church as could be utilized consistently with their purpose to conserve more fully the rights of laymen in their ecclesiastical proceedings. The life tenure of the Bishopric was discarded, but an elective Superintendency, limited to four years, unless extended by reëlection, was substituted therefor. The Presiding Eldership was not retained, but a District Chairmanship, which included the same idea of district supervision, though with less authority attaching to it, was adopted in its stead. The term District Chairman was changed to District Elder by the General Conference of 1894. The power of the ministry in the General Conference, and also in the Annual Conferences, was abridged by the adoption of lay delegation, thus anticipating by nearly fifty years the action of the Methodist Episcopal Church in regard to the admission of laymen to its General Conference. The Free Methodist Church from the beginning admitted lay delegates to the Annual Conferences, as well as to the General Conference, and that in proportion of one lay delegate to each regularly stationed preacher or supply. In respect to their admission to the Annual Conference the mother Church has not yet followed the example set by her offspring, though the call for it is in the air, and may yet materialize.

In the Free Methodist Church, as in the parent body, there is a General Conference, which meets quadrennially; there are also Annual Conferences, Quarterly Conferences and Official Boards; and the various Church officials are in the main called by the same names. For the ministry the two ordinations—as Deacons and as Elders—are retained. Also the Free Methodist Church retained the Methodist system of local preachers, exhorters, class-meetings and class-leaders. Its methods in its Judicial Proceedings are much the same as those of the Methodist Church, except that it is somewhat more simple, and that the effort has been made to guard more sacredly and securely the rights of individual members. In regard to Temporal Economy, Educational matters, Ritual, and other things of less importance, the new Church has been largely modeled after the pattern of that from which she sprang. These differences have characterized it from the beginning, however: free seats in all its Churches; simplicity and inexpensiveness in the erection of Churches; no kind of entertainments allowed for the purpose of raising funds for religious purposes; neither instrumental music nor choir singing permitted in public worship.

It will readily be seen, therefore, that the founders of the Free Methodist Church were much more anxious to build up a Church of earnest, humble, self-denying and devoted souls than to bid for the patronage of the rich, or to secure the following of the multitudes who, while professing godliness, fall under the apostolic classification—"lovers of pleasures more than lovers of God."

CHAPTER XXXIII

FORMATION OF THE GENESEE CONFERENCE

The first local society of the Free Methodist Church in its denominational capacity was organized at Pekin, New York, by General Superintendent B. T. Roberts, August 26, 1860, three days after the adoption of the Discipline by the Pekin Convention. From that society as a nucleus the Free Methodist work has since spread in all directions, until it now embraces thirty-seven conferences in the United States, four in the Dominion of Canada, and one in South Africa, besides extensive missions in India, China, Japan and the Dominican Republic. It also embraces a fine publishing plant in Chicago, Illinois; two colleges, one located at Greenville, Illinois, and one at McPherson, Kansas; four seminaries doing preparatory and junior college work; three seminaries doing preparatory work; several schools of lower grade; and a number of prosperous benevolent institutions.

It was frequently predicted in the beginning that the Free Methodist work would "soon run out." The foregoing indicates that it has been running out these many years, though in a different sense from that which its enemies prophesied. God, who planted this vine, has watered it, nourished and protected it, and caused it to grow and spread abroad its branches in various directions and to extensive limits, in spite of all the agencies and powers that have conspired for its destruction.

The society organized at Pekin in 1860 was composed of nineteen members. All but two of these have been gathered to the Church Triumphant. Ripe for their translation, the Rev. L. E. Chase, a local Elder, of Jackson, Michigan, and Mrs. Cornelia Castle, of St. Johns, Michigan, await their change from the mortal to the immortal state as the weary watcher awaits the coming of the dawn.

It was noted in a previous chapter how the wholesale excommunication of members from the Methodist Episcopal Church resulted in the formation of "Bands," "Societies," and "Independent Churches," as a means of preserving the persecuted sheep from being scattered and devoured. These various local and independent organizations now began to ally themselves with the newly organized denomination. This was done by voting as a whole to adopt the Discipline of the new organization, and then by each member of the respective organizations answering the disciplinary questions.

Quite naturally after becoming thus identified with the larger organization, these local "Bands" or "Societies" began to call upon the leaders of the new movement for some one to have pastoral oversight of them. While there were but few societies to be thus provided for, the problem was a simple one; but as they multiplied, and the demand for spiritual guidance increased, it became more difficult and perplexing. The logical outcome of this condition of affairs was the organization of Conventions (later called Conferences), with authority to decide upon those who should be regarded as suitable for meeting this demand, and to fix their pastoral relations from year to year.

The first one organized was what is now known as the Genesee Conference of Western New York. At its organization it was known as the Eastern Convention. All the preliminary gatherings of a deliberative character had been designated as Conventions, and quite naturally the name was adopted by the new denomination as designating its annual deliberative gatherings, until it was found that the name Conference was better suited to the character of the business done and to the way of doing it. After the first few years the term Convention was abandoned, and Conference took its place—a change for the better surely.

The first session of the Eastern Convention (Genesee Conference) was held at Rushford, Allegany County, New York, beginning November 8, 1860. Sixteen preachers and thirteen lay delegates were enrolled.

The following were received in full connection: B. T. Roberts, Loren Stiles, Jr., Hanford Colborn, A. F. Curry, John W. Reddy, Ephraim Herrick. Those admitted on probation were: Daniel W. Sinclair, Moses N. Downing, Russell Wilcox, Arthur King, J. B. Freeland, A. A. Phelps, Judah Mitchell, James Mathews, T. W. Read, and Henry Spear.

The lay delegates to this first session of the Free Methodist Conference formed were as follows: Dewey Tefft, Gilbert Eggleston, Jonathan Handly, J. R. Annis, Edward P. Cox, P. Hartshorn, George P. Rose, Isaac Williams, G. W. Holmes, Lyman Parker, Charles P. Greenman, George Worthington, and James Doty, Jr.

The Convention authorized the employment of the following persons as supplies on circuits: Otis O. Bacon, Isaac Foster, A. B. Matthewson; also Charles P. Greenman, S. K. J. Chesbrough, Isaac Williams, and A. C. Leonard, provided they be duly licensed.

The preachers were all appointed to circuits or stations, and the District Chairmen were authorized to employ ten more, as supplies, and still the places calling for preachers could not all be filled. The following appointments were made by the Stationing Committee:

Genesee District—Chairman, ——; Holly, to be supplied; Albion, L. Stiles, Jr.; Kendall, M. N. Downing; Rochester and Chili, Daniel M. Sinclair; Buffalo (Thirteenth Street), James Mathews; Buffalo (Second Free Methodist Church), supplied by S. K. J. Chesbrough; Carey and Shelby, J. B. Freeland; Asbury, to be supplied; Carlton and Yates, supplied by A. C. Leonard; Alden, to be supplied; Pekin, Tonawanda, Porter and Wilson, Russell Wilcox, Judah Mitchell, Arthur King and Isaac Williams.

Allegany District—Chairman, A. F. Curry; Wales and Spring

Brook, Ephraim Herrick; West Falls, supplied by Levi Metcalf; East Otto, supplied by Otis O. Bacon; Rushford, J. W. Reddy; Gowanda and Collins, to be supplied; Chemung, T. W. Read, H. W. Spears; Perry, A. A. Phelps; Cadiz, supplied by A. B. Matthewson.

B. T. Roberts, General Superintendent.

A. F. Curry, one of the preachers who was received into full connection at the organization of this Conference, was formerly a Doctor of Medicine, but had given himself to the work of the ministry at the call of God, and had served in that capacity for some time in the Methodist Episcopal Church. During the latter part of the time the Genesee Conference agitation was in progress which led to the formation of the Free Methodist Church, he was stationed as pastor at Allegany, New York. He was a strong sympathizer with the despised and persecuted brethren called "Nazarites," and openly espoused and defended their cause.

At last, as a matter of duty, and in order to clear himself of complicity with the oppressive measures of the Conference, he withdrew from the Methodist Church, and formed a Congregational Free Methodist Church at Allegany. Nearly all of the members of the Church he had been serving as pastor went with him. This so reduced the Methodist Episcopal society in that place that the appointment was given up, no Methodist services being held there for a number of years afterward. The Congregational Free Methodist Church used the Methodist Episcopal Church property, which, after the formation of the Free Methodist Church in 1860, was also used by the Free Methodist people for a number of years.

When the Genesee Conference of the Free Methodist Church was organized, Mr. Curry offered himself to that body, and was received into the Conference in full connection. He was elected Chairman of the Allegany District. He continued to serve in the ranks of the Free Methodist ministry, though chiefly in the Susquehanna

BENJAMIN TITUS ROBERTS, A. M.
General Superintendent of the Free Methodist Church from 1860 to 1893

[Plate Twenty-three]

MRS. ELLEN LOIS ROBERTS

[Plate Twenty-four]

Conference, so long as he lived. He was District Chairman (or District Elder as the office was later called), for many years, and represented his Conferences in the General Conference repeatedly. He was a man of much dignity, but of great geniality and sociability; an able and at times an eloquent preacher, his favorite theme being the Atonement of Christ. He was also a valuable counsellor and a faithful friend. He had considerable to do with the early legislation of the Free Methodist Church, and was one of the honored builders of primitive Free Methodism.

Another man who became connected with the Genesee Conference at this, its first session, and who was prominently identified with the Free Methodist movement for more than fifty years, was J. B. Freeland. He was received on trial. He was a young man of noble parts and of unusually deep and clear religious experience. His home was in Allegany, New York. A. F. Curry was his pastor in the Methodist Church of that place. Not only did they come into the Free Methodist Church at the same time, but in the providence of God they were fellow-workers in the same Conferences for many years, and their acquaintance and fellowship remained unbroken until death summoned Mr. Curry to the other world.

Some time after E. E. Chambers was sent as Presiding Elder to the Olean District in place of C. D. Burlingham, by the Regency power, the Official Board at Allegany attended his service on Saturday at 2 o'clock, p. m., but on Sabbath they attended services at the Five Mile, a neighborhood five miles north of Allegany, in a body. This was a sort of protest against the action of the Regency power in having removed Presiding Elder Burlingham, an anti-Regency man and an advocate of holiness, and appointing Mr. Chambers, a very strong Regency devotee, in his stead. The meeting at the Five Mile was in charge of Mr. Freeland and George Fuller, exhorters on the Allegany circuit, and G. C. Sheldon and others,

Class Leaders. The meeting was held in the deserted Ball-room of Cornell Wiltse, who had also become affected with "Nazaritism," and the room was well filled.

True to the pledge made at the first Layman's Convention, and reiterated at later ones, these brethren had refrained from paying the new Presiding Elder anything, because of his having been a participant in the expulsion of Roberts, McCreery, and others, and having shown no signs of repentance. "Doctor Curry," as he was commonly called because of his having been an M. D., being their pastor, and the Official Board being favorable to them, Dr. Chambers was unable to dispose of their cases by having them read out as withdrawn, and so they were not put to the ignominy that many of their brethren were.

The pastor and Official Board saw that the licenses of those who were Exhorters were duly renewed. Hence Mr. Freeland was enabled to unite with the Free Methodist Church by letter, duly given from the Methodist Episcopal Church—a very rare occurrence in those days. Before going to the Rushford Conference he had been laboring for some three months as an Exhorter among those who had been "read out" of membership in the Methodist Church, in Niagara County, prior to the Brockport Conference. He was present at the tent-meeting held by Fay Purdy at the time of that Conference. From the time when he united with the Genesee Conference of the Free Methodist Church on trial, he ever proved a true servant of God and the Church. His work will come before us for further consideration as we proceed with our narrative.

Of those who composed the membership of this, the first Conference of the Church, at its formation, all have gone to their long home except J. B. Freeland. In the calm expectancy of advanced age he awaits the summons to cease from toil and enter into rest.

It will be noticed that the name of the Chairman of the Genesee District is not given in the foregoing list. The office appears to have been left to be supplied later by appointment of the General Superintendent. The *Earnest Christian* for March, 1861, contains an editorial account of a General Quarterly Meeting at Albion in February preceding, from which the following is reproduced, as throwing light upon the appointment that was finally made:

One of the most thrilling scenes we ever witnessed took place in the Quarterly Convention when the

REV. ASA ABELL

JOINED THE FREE METHODIST CHURCH

For forty years he has been a traveling preacher in the M. E. Church. He has been a delegate to four General Conferences, and for eighteen years he filled the office of Presiding Elder. He is generally known and deeply beloved. There was scarcely a dry eye in the Convention when he announced his conviction that the time had come when he must change his Church relations. We cannot hope to do justice to his remarks, but they were in substance as follows: "I have long been a member of the Methodist Episcopal Church. It is with great reluctance that I leave. I owe my salvation under God to the M. E. Church. She is my mother. I cannot turn against it. It is not in my heart, and I trust it is not in the hearts of any of us to make war upon it. My sympathies are with those brethren who have been branded as Nazarites. The heel of oppression has been placed upon them. Some of them have been, as I believe, unjustly excluded, and all redress denied them. It has been thought that they could be easily annihilated. I thought otherwise. The great revival of holiness in Genesee district was branded as fanaticism. I believed it to be a genuine work of God. My sympathies have been with this class of persons. I must go with one or the other. I have made up my mind to cast in my lot with you. I could sit down and cry for an hour. I wish there had been no occasion for this step. But we are sundered in feeling. The fellowship is gone. So I must come among you if you will take me." We need not add that he was received with open arms. He is to fill the station of Chairman of Genesee District.

At this session of the Conference, A. A. Phelps was received in full connection and elected to Deacon's Orders. General Superintendent Roberts ordained him on the

Sabbath. He continued to labor in the Free Methodist ministry for a number of years with much acceptability, and was also a frequent contributor to the *Earnest Christian.* Mr. Phelps was a scholarly man, a college graduate with the degree of Master of Arts, an able preacher, an excellent pastor, and a writer of ability. He finally became tinctured with materialistic Adventism, left the Free Methodists, labored among the Adventist people for some time, then united with an independent Church of the Restorationist persuasion, finally returned to an orthodox fold, and spent the closing period of his life conducting a training school for Christian workers in Boston, Massachusetts.

The matter of starting a weekly paper was also introduced at this first session of the Genesee Conference, or Convention. The proposal elicited considerable discussion, which finally resulted in a majority vote to the effect that such a project was at that time inopportune and unwise. The great argument in favor of such a periodical was the need that existed for some medium through which the Church might correct the frequent and damaging misrepresentations continually being made by those who had been instrumental in forcing the split in the Methodist Episcopal Church which necessitated the new organization.

On this point Superintendent Roberts said: "A weekly paper at this time would almost unavoidably involve us in controversy. Those who are leaving no means untried to destroy us have put so many weapons into our hands that might be employed to our advantage and to their discomfiture, that the temptation would, we fear, be irresistible. But to beget and foster a controversial spirit among the people of God would be a great calamity. What we most need is, *a general, deep, and thorough revival of religion.* A rehearsal of the wrongs we have suffered, and of the misdeeds of others, will not be very likely to save souls. If we stick to this, the Lord will be our defense. 'Salvation will God appoint for walls and bulwarks.' "

The financial embarrassment it would involve was another consideration urged against the project by Mr. Roberts, and one which had its weight in determining the Conference to defer decisive action on the matter. The Conference did, however, appoint a committee of laymen and three ministers who were instructed to raise $1,000 during the year, if possible, toward the purchase of type, press and other fixtures, preparatory to starting a paper at a later period. The committee was composed of the following named gentlemen: A. W. Perry, D. E. Tyler, George Worthington, G. W. Holmes, J. Handly, W. H. Doyle, E. S. Woodruff, Charles Denny, and Seth M. Woodruff, laymen; and A. F. Curry, J. W. Reddy, and T. W. Read, ministers. The members generally throughout the Conference were requested to coöperate in this undertaking.

Having adopted these measures the brethren finally decided to abandon the project for the time being; and, committing their cause to Him who said, "No weapon that is formed against thee shall prosper, and every tongue that shall rise in judgment against thee thou shalt condemn," they went forth from this first session of the Conference unmindful of the wrongs suffered in the past, and hopeful for a year of revival and salvation. Nor did they indulge this hope in vain.

Revival fires were kindled on most of the circuits during the year, and even in the "regions beyond" the Conference bounds. Great refreshings were enjoyed at Wales; showers of blessing fell on the Parma charge; Buffalo was aflame with revival interest, the work going thoroughly at the Free Methodist Church, and also having broken out among the Swedes in a settlement out about four miles, and a good work being accomplished on the Dock, where the Rev. D. M. Sinclair and some of his members regularly held Sabbath services among the boatmen;

at Allegany, Rochester, Rushford, North Chili, Lyndonville, Collins, and many other points revivals were also carried on and many souls were gathered unto the kingdom of God; camp-meetings were held in various parts of the Conference, which were attended with marvelous manifestations of divine power, and resulted in many conversions and in the sanctification of many believers. The Bergen camp-meeting in particular was a time of great uplift to the work within and even beyond the Conference bounds. The *Earnest Christian,* in an editorial account of it, said: "The results will be felt all over the land. A large number obtained the blessing of pardon, and a still larger number, we trust, that of purity of heart. The members generally were quickened, and went home encouraged and resolved to labor with greater diligence than ever for the salvation of souls. Some of the ministers also felt anew the life-giving power of the Holy Ghost, and went out to scatter more than ever the holy fire."

The General Quarterly Meetings were also seasons of remarkable interest and power. These were not merely official gatherings, but gatherings of the "Pilgrims" from every circuit within each district, for purposes of fellowship and mutual encouragement, and to spend a few days in earnest service for the promotion of the genuine work for God. From one hundred to two hundred would frequently be present from abroad, and as the firebrands came together the wind of the Holy Spirit blowing upon them would kindle them into a regular blaze of revival fire, in which many of the scenes of ancient Pentecost were repeated. These services were a great means of promoting unity and brotherly love, and of spreading and deepening the work of God within the infant Church. The revival flame was well-nigh continuous.

The following action was taken by the Conference at its second session, held at Perry, New York, October 24-28, 1861, which is in marked contrast to what has been the general policy of the Church for many years, and to what became the policy of the Conference which passed it not many years afterward:

Ques. 1. Do we, as a Church, approve of female labors?

Ans. *Most heartily.* It is the duty of Christian women to exercise in social and public meetings, by way of prayer, personal testimony, or exhortation, according as their abilities may warrant or the occasion may offer.

Ques. 2. Do we approve of female preaching?

Ans. We do not. And for the following reasons:

1. We do not find it authorized in the Old Testament.
2. We do not find it authorized in the New Testament.
3. On the contrary, it is clearly intimated in the Word of God that woman is not designed for the office of the holy ministry.
4. It clashes with the ordinary duties and relations of the female sex.
5. It tends to awaken prejudice, and produce confusion in carrying on the work of God.
6. It is contrary to the usage of the Church in all ages; the Methodist Church forming no exception. That the practise is anti-Wesleyan may be seen from the following language of John Wesley in his advice to Mrs. Crosby: "The Methodists do not allow women preachers. * * * In public you may properly enough intermix short exhortations with prayer; but keep as far from what is called preaching as you can: therefore never take a text; never speak in continued discourse, without some break, above five or six minutes. Tell the people, 'We shall have another prayer-meeting at such a time and place.' If Hannah Harrison had followed these directions, she might have been as useful now as ever" (*Works, Vol. VII., pp.* 28, 29).

Notwithstanding the drastic character of the foregoing action the Conference that passed it was one of the first (possibly *the* first) to license women as local preachers. In 1873 "The following paper, presented by C. D. Brooks, of Genesee Conference, was referred at his request to the General Conference, as a suitable form of license to be granted to women whom a Quarterly Conference may judge called to preach the gospel:"

"This certifies that we, the members of the.................. Quarterly Conference, being acquainted with the gifts and graces of Sister .... do gladly state our entire confidence in her integrity, and also prize her ability to expound and teach the Scriptures of Divine truth; and that she may have encouragement to use her gifts, we cheerfully recommend her as a public laborer, for the upbuilding of the cause of Christ.

"Voted by the Quarterly Conference held at..................
18..... ....Chairman.
..................................Secretary."

Action was also taken at this second session of the Conference looking toward the establishment of a denominational school, and the following regarding the matter was passed:

Resolved, That a committee of two preachers and two laymen be appointed to take measures to secure, if possible, during the coming Convention year, a suitable edifice and grounds to be devoted to school purposes, either as a Seminary or an Academy; *provided* such purchase come within the bounds of $2,000.00, and provided, also, that no purchase be made which shall involve this Convention in any financial responsibility.

REV. ASA ABELL,
REV. L. STILES, JR.,
G. W. HOLMES,
T. B. CATTON,
Committee.

This shows that in the very beginning of the Church's history its founders recognized the need of educational equipment for one's life work, and also the necessity of the Church establishing schools of her own, if she would have her children and young people educated under such Christian influences as make for strong Christian character. Nothing appears to have come of this Conference action, however, the printed minutes not even showing that the committee ever reported. It was several years later before anything definite took shape in the direction of starting a school, and then it was upon the initiative of General Superintendent Roberts, who piloted the matter through to successful completion, rather than by the action of any Conference.

The first statistical report of this Conference appearing in the printed minutes was in connection with its third session. From that report it appears that the Conference had ten preachers in full connection, and twelve on probation; 1,421 lay members, and 278 probationers, making a total of 1,699; and Church property valued at $31,850. Its ministry now numbers fifty in full membership, and four on probation; its lay membership aggregates 1,823, including a few probationers; and its Church property is reported as amounting to $116,700, with parsonages valued at $66,050. It should be remembered, however, that the Oil City and Pittsburgh Conferences were later formed of territory the most of which at one time was occupied by the Genesee Conference, and at the time Genesee was divided to form the Pittsburgh Conference, its membership was much reduced by the division.

There are few Conferences in the denomination that have raised up and sent out so goodly a company of able and godly men to preach the Gospel as has the Genesee. It has furnished the Church with three Bishops—Roberts, Coleman, Hogue; with three Editors of the *Free Methodist*—Wood, Roberts, Hogue; with one Publishing Agent—Chesbrough; with two Treasurers of the Church funds—Chesbrough and Sully (the latter a layman); all of whom were raised up within its territory and elected from within its bounds to their respective offices. Others who began their ministry within its bounds have also filled some of the more important offices of the Church, but first united with other Conferences and then were elected from within those Conferences to their respective offices, as W. A. Sellew to the office of Bishop, D. S. Warner to that of Editor of the Sunday-school Literature, and J. S. MacGeary to that of Missionary Bishop. Still others who were raised up in other Conferences have, after uniting with the Genesee, been chosen to fill prominent positions in the Church—William Pearce being chosen to the Bishopric, and J. G. Terrill and B. Winget as Missionary Secretaries.

It is a pleasure also to recall the names of others who contributed to the upbuilding of the cause in early years, and some of whom are still strong factors in Free Methodism. There was A. G. Terry, a saint of God, remarkable for his faith and devotion; Henry Hornsby, notable for his knowledge of Church history and ecclesiastical jurisprudence; J. W. Reddy, the silver-tongued orator of the Conference; William Manning, the sweet singer of Genesee; C. D. Brooks, in his early days a man of revival tact and power; Otis O. Bacon, a man in whom there was no guile; T. B. Catton, one of the strong pillars of Free Methodism; A. A. Burgess, in his prime a man of evangelistic tact and zeal; C. C. Eggleston, a veteran of the Civil War, modest genial, interesting, and loyal to God and the Church; A. H. Bennett, always faithful, yet kind and loving to all, the St. John of Genesee; John O'Regan, converted from Romanism, a remarkable trophy of Divine grace; E. A. Taylor, whose years of discipline in the school of vexatious trial developed him into a man of much usefulness; and C. W. Bacon, the weeping prophet, and a true son of Free Methodism. These were all good, able and useful men, an honor to the Church and to the cause of God.

A score or more of others might be mentioned who labored with ability and zeal for the upbuilding of Free Methodism, some of whom long since went to their heavenly home, others of whom are at the borders of the spirit world, and still others of whom are faithfully bearing the burden and heat of the day, but it would make the record of unwarrantable length. Undoubtedly their names appear upon "the Lamb's Book of Life."

Moreover, it would be difficult to find in any Church more stanch, noble, consecrated and godly laymen than Abner I. Wood, Seth Woodruff,* Philander H. Curtis,

*Seth Woodruff was a remarkably good and useful man—a sort of William Carvosso in the Free Methodist Church. He was a miller by trade, and had a good business. He finally told the Lord that as soon as he became possessed of $5,000 he would give his entire time to work for the advancement of His kingdom. He soon was the owner of $5,000, and true to his word he at once arranged to devote all his time thereafter to the Lord's work. He was one of the most faithful of men in exhorting sinners to repentance. On one occasion his horse became unmanageable and ran away. The animal was tearing through country like the wind, with its owner in constant danger and expectation of being killed; and, while in this wild ride, Mr. Woodruff met an unconverted man, and, feeling that he desired to warn one more sinner to repent before he should be killed, he shouted, "Flee from the wrath to come!"

ORIGINAL ROBERTS HOME AT NORTH CHILI, N. Y.
Now Pioneer Hall of the A. M. Chesbrough Seminary

REV. C. H. SAGE
Veteran of the work in Canada

REV. ALBERT SIMS
Veteran of the work in Canada

[Plate Twenty-five]

Bailey Burritt, G. C. Sheldon, Cornell Wiltse, S. B. Lane, Thomas Hogg, Hiram Snell, Franklin Smith, Lorin Hill, Abram Castle, J. R. Annis, A. K. Bacon, N. S. Bennett, G. W. Holmes, Thomas Sully, George W. Johnston, Dewey Tefft, J. Cady, Henry Swanson, Tristram Corliss, Simon Witmer, the Metcalf brothers and the Worthingtons, of Rushford, New York, and Alexander Leonard. These are names of only a few samples of the laymen that have ever helped to make Free Methodism a success in the Genesee Conference and even in "the regions beyond." They were a noble band; and, with their consecrated and heroic wives, spared neither toil nor sacrifice in the interest of the cause they had espoused. There were hundreds more of like faith and devotion, and to the wise counsels, earnest labors, heroic sacrifices and munificent gifts of its noble laymen and their equally noble wives, the work in the Genesee Conference has ever been largely indebted for its success.

At an early period in its history the Genesee Conference lost one of its strongest pillars in the untimely death of the Rev. Loren Stiles, Jr. This eminent preacher was one of the makers of Free Methodism in the beginning, and the infant Church hoped for great things from him in the interest of God's kingdom for the future, which hope doubtless would have been realized could he have been spared to labor, as many others were, during the first generation of the Church's history. But God called him from earthly toil to the higher service of His heavenly kingdom in the very prime of his manhood. His ways are inscrutable and mysterious, and it seemed especially so in this instance.

At the time of Mr. Stiles's death, General Superintendent Roberts, referring to the melancholy event in the *Earnest Christian,* said: "One of the great discouragements we have had to meet with in trying to promote spiritual religion, has been the early removal from the scene of conflict of those who seemed to be most necessary for the advancement of the cause." He then instanced the deaths of Bishop Hamline, William C. Kendall, Dr. Redfield and others, in addition to Mr. Stiles, and added: "We feel alone; we feel sad. What does it mean? Is God displeased with our efforts to promote pure religion, that He thus lays by those who are doing most for its advancement? It can not be. He takes away His workmen, but carries on His work. He would have His Church—the Church of the First-born—lean on Him alone, and so He takes away its pillars, and sustains, by His unseen, almighty power, the trembling edifice whose downfall, to human appearance, seems inevitable and near at hand."

Mr. Stiles was an extraordinary man. He was not made on the narrow plan, but was characterized by breadth and symmetry of character. Physically he was tall, broad-shouldered, erect, but with slightly stooping head. He had a high forehead and waving hair, the fore-lock of which would keep falling over his forehead when he was speaking, making it necessary for him repeatedly to brush it back with his hand. He was in every sense of the word a man, a gentleman and a Christian. He was modest and retiring, but never so much so as to shirk responsibility. He had strong and positive convictions, and was neither afraid nor ashamed to avow them anywhere or at any cost. He was devout, pious, spiritual, and preached with heavenly unction. He possessed all the qualities of the orator, and these, fired by the baptism of the Holy Spirit, made him not only an intensely interesting man to hear, but a very popular man in the better sense of the word. He was called by many "*the* orator of Western New York Methodism."

He died at his home in Albion, New York, on the 7th of May, 1863, from typhoid fever. At the time of his death he was filling the position of District Chairman of the Northern District.

Since the foregoing part of this chapter was written Mr. Thomas Sully, one of the laymen mentioned on page

349, has died. He was one of the laymen who attended the second Laymen's Convention to protest against the proscription policy in the Genesee Conference of the Methodist Episcopal Church. This was in 1859. He also participated in the Delegated Convention at Pekin, New York, where the Free Methodist Church was organized. As soon as the Free Methodist Church in Buffalo was formed he connected himself with it; so that he was one of the early makers of Free Methodism. He ever remained true to the primitive ideals of the Church he helped to form. He was ever ready, too, to support the cause, not only financially, but with all the weight of his influence and with all the efficacy of his prayers. For many years he was Secretary and Treasurer of the Pitts Agricultural Works, of Buffalo, New York, and later became a stockholder in the corporation; and during all those years he was recognized by all who knew him as a man of the strictest integrity. During the last six years of his life he served as Treasurer of the General Missionary Board of the Free Methodist Church, and also as Treasurer of all the other general funds of the Church. In this relation he was faithful to the last. He spent the day before his death in his office as usual, and did a full day's work. He was in his eighty-third year, and about the spryest man in the Publishing House. He did not miss a day from illness during his six years as Treasurer of the Church funds. His death was most befitting such a life as he had lived. He fell into a gentle slumber, and awoke no more.

CHAPTER XXXIV

FORMATION OF THE ILLINOIS CONFERENCE

While the foregoing events were occurring in the east, the work was also developing in Northern Illinois. There, as in Western New York, those who had been ruthlessly excommunicated from the Methodist societies which they had helped to maintain for years had formed themselves into "Bands" and independent "Free" Methodist Churches, as a means of preservation from becoming scattered, as also for the more effective promotion of the work of holiness, and for greater success in securing the conversion of sinners. When apprized of the fact that the Convention at Pekin, New York, had voted to organize the Free Methodist Church as a new denomination, and had adopted a Discipline, they hailed the tidings with delight; and soon, one after another, these "Bands" and "Churches" sought and found a home therein, adopting the Discipline, and becoming societies within the newly organized denomination. By this means, as also by the spreading of the work of revival and the raising up of new societies from among the converts, the work in this region rapidly increased in proportions, until, in June, 1861, the Western Convention (now the Illinois Annual Conference) became a necessity in order to the proper supervision of the multiplied societies.

This Convention (Conference) was organized and held in connection with a camp-meeting in Mr. Laughlin's grove near the village of St. Charles. The camp-meeting was largely attended, and was productive of most gracious results. The late Rev. J. G. Terrill wrote concerning it: "Many at this meeting entered into the experience of perfect love," and "about thirteen united with the Free Methodist Church." He also further says: "The Convention held its sittings on a pile of rails, across the road from Mr. Laughlin's house. There were twenty preachers and an equal number of laymen enrolled. Judah Mead was elected Chairman of the [St. Charles] District. Joseph Travis and J. W. Redfield were elected to Deacon's Orders, and Judah Mead and Joseph Travis to Elder's Orders. The last named was elected to both Orders because of his appointment [as missionary] to St. Louis with no ordained men to assist him."*

This was really the second session of the Western Convention, though it was the first since the adoption of the Discipline of the Free Methodist Church. From an editorial report of it which appeared in the *Earnest Christian* for September of that year we extract the following:

> Ten preachers were admitted to the traveling connection. All the preachers profess and we believe enjoy the blessing of entire sanctification. They are devotedly pious, laborious young men, capable of doing a great deal of service in the cause of Christ upon a very small salary. One of them during the year walked sixteen hundred miles, visited and prayed with a thousand families, and received thirty dollars. Such men are not easily to be put down when engaged in spreading holiness, with the Holy Ghost sent down from heaven.

The following list of appointments was arranged by the Stationing Committee, each appointment being a circuit, and supposed to have at least six different preaching places:

St. Louis District.—Joseph Travis, Chairman. St. Louis, Joseph Travis, and one to be supplied.

St. Charles District.—Judah Mead, Chairman. St. Charles, Thomas LaDue; Clinton, I. H. Fairchilds, W. D. Bishop; Aurora, J. G. Terrill, Erastus Ribble; Marengo, E. P. Hart, J. W. Dake, and one to be supplied; Crystal Lake, R. M. Hooker, E. Cook; Newfield, G. L. Shepardson, supply; Ogle, G. P. Bassett; Sugar Creek, Wisconsin, D. F. Shepardson, C. E. Harroun; Geneva, P. C. Armstrong; Belvidere, J. W. Mathews; Elroy, J. Collier; Rensse-

*History of the St. Charles Camp-meeting, p. 22.

lear Mission, A. B. Burdick; Norwegian Mission, J. Oleson; General Missionary, J. W. Redfield.

Most of these noble men have passed to the great beyond; and those who remain at the time of the present writing are on the retired list, and, in the calm confidence of Christian faith and hope, they await the coming of the Lord, or, if He shall delay His advent, the descent of the chariot that shall bear their redeemed spirits to His celestial presence.

Several from among the foregoing list of preachers were ultimately advanced to highly distinguished positions in the Church. E. P. Hart became General Superintendent in 1874; Joseph Travis was elected editor of the *Free Methodist* in 1882; and J. G. Terrill was chosen as Missionary Secretary by the Executive Committee in 1893, to fill a vacancy occasioned by the resignation of W. W. Kelley, whose failing health necessitated his retirement from the position. In 1894 he was again chosen to the same position, from which he was soon removed by death.

A question has been raised as to the historical accuracy of the statement that the Free Methodist Church was organized at Pekin, New York, August 23, 1860. The question has risen from the fact that there is still extant the original of a preacher's credential issued by the Western Convention of the Free Methodist Church in June, 1860, bearing the signature of B. T. Roberts as President. It is asked, "Is not this evidence that the Free Methodist Church was an organized body as early as June, 1860, even though the historical account dates its origin at Pekin, New York, in August, 1860?" The solution is this: A number of local "Free" Methodist Churches had been organized in Northern Illinois prior to June, 1860. In connection with a camp-meeting held in Mr. Laughlin's grove at St. Charles, Illinois, in June, 1860, "a Laymen's Convention was held * * * under the trees in Mr. Laughlin's yard." B. T. Roberts was in attendance at the camp-meeting, and also at the Laymen's Convention,

REV. CHARLES B. EBEY
Editor of the "Free Methodist"
1903-1907

REV. WALTER W. KELLEY
Missionary Secretary 1890-1893

HON. BENJAMIN HACKNEY

MR. JAMES H. PORTER

[Plate Twenty-six]

and, being present at the latter, was quite naturally "called to the chair."*

This is the Convention which gave the credentials referred to in the foregoing, and Mr. Roberts, as Chairman of the Convention, of course signed the same. This, however, was a *Laymen's* Convention, representing individual "Bands" of "Free" Methodist Churches, without organic unity, and none of which had as yet adopted the Discipline of the Free Methodist Church, as that was not framed and adopted as a basis of the new denomination until it was done by a delegated Convention of Laymen and Ministers at Pekin, New York, August 23, 1860. This first Western Convention of June, 1860, elected the Rev. J. W. Redfield and Daniel Lloyd as its delegates to the Pekin Convention, where the Free Methodist Church was organized, and Mr. Roberts made its first General Superintendent.

No statistics of the earlier sessions of this Conference are available as to lay membership or as to Church and parsonage property. In 1864, however, there were 982 members, of whom 141 were probationers, with value of Church property given as $13,953. At present the Conference has forty-one preachers, of whom two are probationers; 1,043 lay members, and 127 on probation; Churches valued at $136,900; and parsonages at $67,300. The Illinois has also been one of the mother Conferences from which several others have sprung. The personnel of the ministers composing this body has generally been considerably above the average for preaching and administrative ability, and a number of the strongest men of the denomination have come from their ranks.

*Terrill's "History of the St. Charles Camp-meeting," p. 15.

CHAPTER XXXV

THE SUSQUEHANNA CONFERENCE ORGANIZED

The incidents heretofore related concerning the early developments of Free Methodism occurred in Western New York and Northern Illinois. Similar conditions, however, existed in other places, though somewhat less aggravated in their manifestation. In the central and eastern portions of New York State, as also in Eastern Pennsylvania, many were becoming thoroughly tired and sick of worldly-conformed Methodism, and were deeply desirous for something to occur which would afford them relief from their bondage to formalism and spiritual death and open to them a congenial Church home in which they could enjoy freedom and participate in spiritual worship. Hearing of the organization of the Free Methodist Church, and hoping to find it conformed to the original type of Methodism instead of partaking the "New School" characteristics, they corresponded with General Superintendent Roberts, and others prominent in the new movement, extending to them the Macedonian cry for help. Letters were received from strangers in distant regions like the following from the East to Mr. Roberts:

I see in your March number of the *Earnest Christian* an account of Brother Asa Abell's joining the Free Methodist Church. His convictions of leaving the M. E. Church and joining the Free Methodist Church are the convictions of my heart, and doubtless those of a great many; and when, oh! when can we have the opportunity of breathing free air? His opportunity came. O Lord, give us an open door, is our prayer. I know of many that never will be satisfied until they are free. This panting to be free is like unto the soul panting for full salvation, and cannot any more be satisfied without having its freedom. For a good reason Jesus has made them free, and they must be free, indeed. Many in these far off regions would be glad to get into your meetings and enjoy freedom with you in worshiping God in spirit and in truth. We are like other bondmen down South, in one sense of the case: they have an idea of the land of freedom, they long to be free, but cannot tell when or how they shall obtain it. So in regard to many out here. We hear of your freedom and of your joys and of your people, but as yet we have no opportunity of tasting of freedom. But our trust is in God. We do believe the time will come when God's free ones will be known all over the land. God hasten the time.

Superintendent Roberts, William Cooley and Zenas Osborne appear to have pioneered the way for the introduction of Free Methodism into the region now embraced within the Susquehanna Conference. During 1860-1861 Mr. Roberts "held many meetings in New York, Binghamton, Union, Syracuse, Utica, Rome, Rose and Clyde, besides being present at grove-meetings and camp-meetings elsewhere in that part of the State that lay east of the bounds of the Genesee Conference. One who knew him well writes of these services, that "his preaching, his praying, his manner of conducting meetings, was very acceptable, and made a deep and lasting impression upon his hearers. This was especially true at Binghamton."*

The first Free Methodist society in this region was organized by Mr. Roberts in a stone schoolhouse near Rose Valley, Wayne County, New York, December 2, 1860. It was composed of the following members: Josephus Collins, John Glen, Mr. and Mrs. William Glen, Mr. and Mrs. Harrison Holcomb, Mr. and Mrs. John Barrett, Leonard Mitchell, Sarah Mitchell, Mr. and Mrs. William Sherman, Margaret Nusbickel, Elizabeth Finch, John Weeks. On February 12, 1861, he organized a second society at the home of Aaron Winget, in the town of Huron, same County, of which the following were the members: Mr. and Mrs. Aaron Winget, Benjamin Winget, Lovilla

*Biography of B. T. Roberts, p. 273.

Winget, Mr. and Mrs. John B. Stacy, Hervey Perkins, Sophia Perkins. Among those who composed these two societies three later became itinerant preachers in the Free Methodist Church—John B. Stacy, and John Glen, both of whom witnessed a good confession and finished their course triumphantly some years ago, and Benjamin Winget, who for about twenty years has been the honored, faithful and efficient Missionary Secretary of the denomination.

From these points the work gradually spread abroad in various directions under the faithful labors of such men as William Cooley, Zenas Osborne and others, until finally those engaged in developing the field, believing the interests of the work could be better conserved and promoted thereby, began to urge upon Superintendent Roberts the importance of organizing the work into a Convention (or Conference), similar to the Eastern and Western Conventions already organized.

Accordingly, on April 10, 1862, Mr. Roberts organized what was then known as the Susquehanna Convention (now the Susquehanna Conference) of the Free Methodist Church, with a membership of six ministers. Like the Eastern and Western Conventions at their organization, this was an out-of-doors deliberative body, holding its sittings upon a rail-pile in an apple orchard. The following list of appointments was made:

Union circuit, James Guion; Madison and Otsego, J. Olney; Rose, W. Cooley; Hudson River Mission, A. B. Burdick; Susquehanna, T. F. Johnson; White Haven, to be supplied.

The organization of this small Conference later became a source of much unpleasantness within the infant denomination, which apparently came near effecting a division. The circumstances which led to the unpleasantness were as follows:

The Book of Discipline which had been adopted at the organization of the denomination made no specific provision for the organization of new Conferences in the intervals of the General Conferences. It did, however, specifically state that the General Superintendent was to travel through the connection at large, and labor for the advancement and upbuilding of the work. Regarding it as his right and duty according to this Disciplinary requirement, Mr. Roberts, in response to the call from those directly interested, organized the Susquehanna Convention. There appears to have been some previous dissatisfaction on the part of a few who had regarded the organization at Pekin as premature, as also with others who evidently felt a measure of disappointment with the action of that Convention regarding the General Superintendency. A respectable minority were opposed to any General Superintendency, preferring the election of a President each year, as is the case with the Wesleyan Church of England, and with the Wesleyan Methodist Connection of America. Moreover, this was the year that had been designated for the first General Convention to hold its session, and it may have been that some were anxious to accomplish what they had failed to accomplish at the Pekin Convention—the defeat of the General Superintendency—and that they regarded the formation of the Susquehanna Convention as rendering their success in that direction less probable than it otherwise would be.

Being aware that this feeling existed to some extent regarding the Superintendency, Mr. Roberts had studiously refrained from any reference in the *Earnest Christian* to his advancement to that office, as also from everything that could reasonably be construed as regarding himself in any sense superior to the humblest of his brethren. He published accounts of the Conventions, without the slightest reference to himself as presiding over them, lest he should give offense to any that might be sensitive over the decision of the Pekin Convention.

His having organized the Susquehanna Convention was destined, however, to make him considerable trouble in the near future, and to give him an appreciating sense of the fact that advancement to office, even in ecclesiastical bodies, is no security for an easy passport through life. The question as to whether he had a legal right under the Discipline to organize an Annual Convention or not, was one about which equally good men might differ. But when some assumed that he had transcended his authority as overseer of the denominational interests, and began to talk about the exercise of "one man power" invidiously, though their number was small, it grieved him to the quick. It was a serious disappointment to him to lose in any degree the confidence and sympathy of brethren whom he loved, and with whom he had suffered in the fiery trials which came to him in the Methodist Episcopal Church. He did not allow this to deter him, however, from what he conceived to be his duty as an administrative officer in the Church, nor to chill or sour his spirit toward those who differed from him, nor to damp his zeal toward the work of God. He pressed on in his work with all possible earnestness, and with a holy cheerfulness prosecuted the manifold duties of his calling as the Church's chief administrative officer, as editor of the *Earnest Christian,* and as a preacher of the gospel, with his heart on fire with zeal for the conversion of sinners and for the sanctification of believers. He found the work prospering wherever he went within the newly organized denomination, and saw numerous new charges raised up and added to those already existing, while the preachers and members were greatly strengthened everywhere under his ministry as the result of his simple, pointed and earnest proclamation of the truth.

At the fall Conventions of 1862 delegates were elected to the ensuing General Convention, to be held in St. Charles, Illinois, beginning October 8. Hence the Susquehanna Convention, which was organized in April, held its second session in September, and regularly elected delegates to the General Convention. In a brief report of this gathering in the *Earnest Christian* Mr. Roberts said, "There are nine preachers belonging to the Convention—all of whom we believe are wholly devoted to God and His work, enjoying the clear witness of entire sanctification. We trust that through their labors a great impetus will be given to the cause of holiness in all the region where they travel."

The General Convention was one of much disharmony, due chiefly to the delegates from the Eastern (or Genesee) Convention opposing the admission of the delegates from the Susquehanna Convention, on the ground that the Susquehanna Convention had been irregularly and illegally organized, and therefore had no proper standing, and was not competent to elect delegates to the General Convention. The purpose of the Genesee delegates was to refuse the Susquehanna delegates admission, and the feeling was so intense over the matter for a time, and the contention was so sharp, that serious results were threatened. In the Biography of B. T. Roberts his version of the case is given, from his own handwriting, as follows:

> The delegates appointed by the several Annual Conventions of the Free Methodist Church met at St. Charles on the 8th of October, 1862. We were called together at two o'clock. One of the delegates from the Illinois Convention, B. Hackney, was absent on a jury, and could not be present at the General Convention until the next day. It was proposed on that account to organize temporarily, and defer a permanent organization until all the delegates could be present. Rev. L. Stiles opposed an adjournment. He said that the mere matter of organizing was not of sufficient importance to occasion any delay. We should organize, he urged, and be ready for business when all the delegates are present. Other of the Genesee delegates said their time was precious, they were anxious to get through as soon as they could. An attempt was made at organizing. When the credentials of the delegates from the Susquehanna Convention were read, Rev. A. Abell said that at the proper time he would object to their admission. An issue being raised, an adjournment was made until ten o'clock the next day, that all the delegates might be present. In the evening, O. P. Rogers, the reserve delegate of the Western Convention, arrived.
>
> In the five o'clock morning prayer-meeting, all the delegates,

except the Genesee, being present, it was thought best, to accommodate them, to call the service at half-past eight. A preacher was accordingly dispatched to them by seven o'clock, informing them of the change of time. Word was brought back that they said: "We have adjourned to meet at ten, and we will not meet till then. One man has not the power to call this Convention together." At ten we met. The Genesee delegates wished to have the delegates from one of the Conventions admitted by virtue of their credentials, and regarded as the nucleus, and then they vote in the rest. The President decided that all who came with proper credentials were *prima facie* members, and should be so regarded for the purpose of organizing. After we were organized, if any one held a seat improperly he could be deprived of it by the General Convention. Every organized body must be a judge of the qualifications of its own members. In this view of the case the Western delegates concurred. They urged that if there was any good reason for excluding the Susquehanna delegates, once organize and they would then exclude them. They pressed this point. They said repeatedly and emphatically: "Come in with us and organize, and then if the Susquehanna Convention is not a legal Convention, or if there is any personal reason why the Susquehanna delegates should not have a seat, we will help you put them out." But the Genesee delegates refused to organize, though on the vote for secretary two of them put in ballots. After the secretary was elected and the General Convention organized, Rev. L. Stiles whispered to G. W. Holmes, a lay delegate from the Genesee Convention, and Mr. Holmes moved, "That the Susquehanna delegates be admitted." The President decided "That the delegates have already been admitted by virtue of their credentials," and that the proper form of the motion would be to move, "That they are not entitled to seats as delegates." They refused to make the motion in that form. They talked the matter over at length. They said the only thing that divided us was the formation of the Susquehanna Convention. When the president remarked that that was not the main difficulty, that there were other things that lay back of the Susquehanna Convention that were the real cause of the difficulty, Mr. Stiles resented the remark, and asked, with a good deal of spirit, "if their veracity was called in question." He said that the only thing that divided us was the Susquehanna Convention. Mr. Hartshorn also said the same thing. The Western delegates urged that they should take their seats, and then make a motion to exclude the Susquehanna delegates, and if there was any good reason for excluding them, they, the Western delegates, would help them out.

The following papers were offered and adopted on the 10th and 11th of October:

"The Free Methodist Church as a body, as well as this General Convention, is organized on the basis of the Discipline adopted at Pekin, August 23rd, 1860, and printed at Buffalo in 1860, under the title of 'The Doctrines and Discipline of the Free Methodist Church.' This Discipline is the outward, visible bond of union among us as a people.

"The delegates from the Genesee Convention are dissatisfied with the admission of the delegates from the Susquehanna Convention and refuse in consequence to participate in our action, and have expressed an intention to leave and go home.

"Therefore, we propose that inasmuch as we have come together on the basis of the Discipline that we act together on the same basis, make such changes as can be agreed upon by all, and where all cannot agree upon any change, then no change shall be effected.

"Adopted October 11th, 1862."

"Whereas, the delegates from the Genesee Annual Convention handed in the book of records of said Convention certifying to their election as members of this body; and whereas a part of them subsequently voted for secretary, and after we organized made a motion and speeches; and whereas they subsequently declared that they were not members of this body, and have accordingly absented themselves, and continued to absent themselves; and whereas they have withdrawn their book of records; therefore,

"Resolved, that we, the General Convention of the Free Methodist Church, consider them as withdrawn from this body, and that we proceed to the discharge of the duties assigned us by the Church, whose representatives we are."*

After having continued in session from October 8th to October 16th, at St. Charles, Illinois, the General Convention adjourned to meet at Buffalo, New York, on the 4th of November following. At the adjourned session, inasmuch as some of the Genesee delegates who were in attendance at St. Charles were absent, the reserve delegates were allowed to take their places. The Rev. Levi Wood was thus seated in the place of Loren Stiles, Jr., and Titus Roberts in place of George W. Holmes.

The Rev. Moses N. Downing was at the time pastor of

*Pages 276-280.

the Free Methodist Church in Buffalo, and from his pen the following account of this adjourned session of the General Convention appears in the Life of B. T. Roberts:

A number of delegates of the Genesee delegation declined to take their seats unless the General Convention would organize without the Susquehanna delegation, inasmuch as they believed the latter delegation was illegal, maintaining that the Superintendent had no right to organize the Susquehanna Convention, stipulating, however, that if the General Convention would thus organize without the Susquehanna delegation they would consent that the legality of the organization of the Susquehanna Conference should be passed upon by the General Convention. Benjamin Hackney, delegate from the West, a man of prominence who had been a member of Congress, arose and said that much as he loved the Free Methodist Church, he would see it split in two in its infancy before he would compromise on a principle of righteousness. He maintained that the delegates from the Susquehanna Convention were legally elected, and that in the absence of any specific law governing the organization of Annual Conventions, the General Superintendent had the right to organize the Susquehanna Convention, and that the Susquehanna delegates on presenting their credentials should be admitted. Thereupon, Rev. Loren Stiles and Asa Abell, ministerial delegates, and the lay delegates withdrew, the reserve delegates taking their places.*

The foregoing action caused decidedly intense feeling, which was destined to manifest itself in very positive form at a period some time subsequent to the adjournment of the General Convention.

[This body met under the designation of General Convention, but before its final adjournment it wisely changed its name to that of General Conference. Following the example of the General Convention the Annual Conventions also soon changed their names to Annual Conferences, and they will be thus designated henceforth in this volume.—AUTHOR].

The sequel to the story of the trouble occasioned by the organization of the Susquehanna Conference is thus told in the Life of B. T. Roberts, by his son, B. H. Roberts, A. M., and chiefly in his father's own words:

*Pages 277, 278.

THE LAST OF THE SUSQUEHANNA QUESTION

The Genesee Annual Convention, that was held at Albion, the 18th and 22nd of September, was a somewhat stormy time; the principal occasion being with reference to the admission of some to the Convention. Because of the dissatisfaction, emanating largely from the Susquehanna matter, confined, however, to a small minority, an attempt was made to call a second session of the Genesee Convention, to meet at Perry, 4th of November. This call was issued by Rev. Loren Stiles, Asa Abell, G. W. Holmes and H. Hartshorn. The evidence in hand as to its existence is the copy of the following letter, addressed to these brethren, which reads as follows:

"To the Ministers and Members of the Free Methodist Church, convened at Perry, November 4th, 1862, at the Call of Rev. L. Stiles, Jr., and Rev. A. Abell, G. W. Holmes and H. Hartshorn.

"*Dearly Beloved Brethren:*

"I should have been glad to have met with you, and should have made arrangement to do so, had I known in time that you had been called together. I was in the same village with the brethren who called you together at the time when, I suppose, they decided to do so. They said nothing to me about their intentions; nor did I learn that they had issued a call until one week ago last Saturday. I learned the fact incidentally. My engagements are such—the General Convention having adjourned to meet at Buffalo the same day—that, very much to my regret, I cannot meet with you. From what I have heard, I gather that the object of those who have called you together is to procure a condemnation of my official action. If such is the case, it appears to me that I should have been consulted in reference to the time. 'Doth our law judge any man before it hear him, and know what he doeth?'—John 7:51. Does Christian candor require any less than that you should suspend, not only any formal decision bearing upon my official acts, but even the formation of your own private opinion, until you hear what explanations I have to make? Could common candor, to say nothing of brotherly love, ask you to form and express your judgments upon matters affecting deeply the interests of our infant Church upon one-sided representations? I am aware of the successful efforts that have been made among you to excite prejudice against me; but you owe it to yourselves, as well as to the cause of God, to lay aside all prejudice as far as possible, and to defer all action in the premises until I can have a fair and full hearing.

"Precipitous measures will sensibly injure the cause of God, whereas no possible harm can come by your waiting until the regular session of our Convention, acquainting yourselves in the meantime, as far as possible, with all the facts of the case. 'He that believeth shall not make haste.' I have endeavored to perform all my official duties as Superintendent of the Free Methodist Church with fidelity and love, in meekness and humility. I have studiously avoided everything that could excite envy or jealousy in any one. I have never published myself in any of the periodicals as occupying an official position, and have been careful not to injure the feelings or reputation of any among you.

"In organizing the late General Convention, I took the only course that, as it seems to me with my limited knowledge of parliamentary usages, it was proper for me to take. The Discipline (Chap, 2, sec. 2, par. 1, p. 34) prescribes how the General Convention shall be composed. Persons coming with credentials duly certified are, as it appears to me, entitled to a seat until an organization can be affected. Then, if any one holds a seat to which he is not entitled, the General Convention can deprive him of the seat improperly held. I so decided. In this decision I am sustained by the highest authority on parliamentary usages. The Constitution of the United States says: 'Each shall be the judges of the election returns, and qualification of its own members (Art. 1, sec. 5, par. 1).' The president does not say who shall have a seat in the Senate; nor the Senate who shall sit in the House. The representatives from New York do not, in their local capacity, say whether the representatives from Illinois shall be admitted or not, but all who hold certificates of election are enrolled, and the house is organized, and then after the organization is effected, if any one hold a seat improperly, he is excluded. I am charged with 'an usurpation of power, such as was never exercised by any Bishop, or by any number of Bishops, in the history of Methodism,' whereas the real ground of complaint is my refusal to usurp the power belonging to the General Convention alone, and on my own prerogative exclude from their seats persons whose credentials as delegates from an Annual Convention had been presented and read. This power, I believe, belongs to the General Convention alone; but because I did not usurp this power I am held up in an odious light, and charged with unprecedented usurpation. After we were organized, Brother Stiles whispered to Brother Holmes, and the latter made a motion: 'That the delegates from the Susquehanna Convention be admitted.' The motion I decided to be out of order in this form, as they had already been admitted by virtue of their credentials. I stated that a motion to the effect that the delegates from the Susquehanna Convention are not entitled to seats would be in order. But no one would make it. The Genesee delegates argued the case at length, but failing to carry their points they left. Before they left, however, I presented to them in open Convention the following proposition: 'The Free Methodist Church as a body, as well as the General Convention, is organized on the basis of the Discipline adopted at Pekin, August 23rd, 1860, and printed at Buffalo, in 1860, under the title of "The Doctrines and Discipline of the Free Methodist Church." This Discipline is the outward visible bond of union among us as a people. The delegates from the Genesee Convention are dissatisfied with the admission of the delegates from the Susquehanna Convention, and refuse in consequence to participate in our action, and have expressed their intention to leave and go home. Therefore, we propose that, inasmuch as we have come together on the basis of the Discipline, we act together on the same basis, make such changes as can be agreed upon by all, and where all cannot agree upon any change, then no change shall be effected.' The Genesee delegates took no notice whatever of this proposition. If they had desired the preservation of the Free Methodist Church, essentially as organized, would they not have accepted this proposal? Any small, needful changes would, no doubt, have been acquiesced in unanimously by men of piety and love of peace. But under this proposition an attempt to revolutionize the Church could not have succeeded.

"The 'usurpation of power' complained of may refer to the organization of the Susquehanna Convention. But was this any usurpation? The first to be settled is this: 'Had the Superintendent, prior to the meeting of the first General Convention, the right to organize any Annual Convention? The Discipline does not in express words make it the duty of the Superintendent to organize Conventions. Nor does it say he shall not. Nor does it make it the duty of any one else to organize Annual Conventions. In the M. E. Church Annual Conferences are made by the General Conference. But this usage could not obtain in our case, for we had no General Convention, nor could we have any until Annual Conventions were formed, as the General Convention is composed of delegates elected by the Annual Conventions. The General Convention could not organize Annual Conventions in the first instance. Who, then, should do it? The Discipline does not say in express terms, but it makes it the duty of the Superintendent to preside over the Annual Conventions. It is a maxim in the interpretation of law, that a requirement to do anything carries with it the right to do everything that is essential to the doing of the thing required. This is common sense and common law. A command to a general to lead an army across a river implies the right to bridge over if there is no other way of crossing.

"The Discipline says (Chap. 3, sec. 1, par. 2, p. 46) that it shall be the duty of the Superintendent to preside at the Annual Conventions. But how can he preside over an Annual Convention until it is organized? It seems plain, then, that in the absence of any other provision for organizing an Annual Convention, the Superintendent has an unquestionable right to do it. Nor can this with any fairness be said to be setting a dangerous precedent, for the first General Convention could, and undoubtedly would, make provisions for organizing Annual Conventions in the future. The Superintendent organized the Genesee Convention in the same way. Some brethren presented credentials as delegates from Free Methodist Societies, or from persons who desired to be organized into Free Methodist Societies. By virtue of their credentials they were organized as members. They then by vote admitted the preachers. The Western Convention and the Susquehanna Convention were organized in the same way. In no case did the Superintendent say what preachers should, and who should not, belong to an Annual Convention; nor, as we judge, has one Annual Convention the right to say what preachers shall belong to another Annual Convention. Some have assumed that when the Discipline was formed, it was contemplated by those adopting it to have only two Annual Conventions until after the General Convention. But this is mere assumption without the shadow of proof. Nothing of the kind is in the Discipline. Nothing of the kind was said in the Pekin Convention. The Discipline plainly implies that there might be more than two. It says (Chap. 2, sec. 2, p. 34) : '*Each Annual* Convention.' Had only two been meant it would have read 'both' Annual Conventions. The small number of delegates of which the General Convention would be composed, on the supposition that there are to be but two Annual Conventions, plainly shows that in the judgment of those who formed and adopted the Discipline, there would be more than two Annual Conventions prior to the first General Convention.

"The Susquehanna Convention was formed in good faith for the purpose of spreading the work of God, and for good and sufficient reasons, as I believe I can satisfy any unprejudiced mind. But suppose there had been any irregularity in forming this Convention, is it not fully justified by the fact that we are in a formation state? Many irregularities have been tolerated among us, and justified on this ground. The Church at Albion was formed without asking of those received as members the questions required by the Discipline (Chap. 1, sec. 3, p. 32). The delegates to the General Convention elected by the Genesee Annual Convention were elected contrary to the express provisions of the Discipline. The Discipline (Chap. 2, sec. 2, par. 1; p. 341) requires that the ministerial delegates should be elected by the ministers in full connection. But probationers and supplies were allowed to vote. The Discipline says that the ministers should elect their delegates and laymen theirs. But all voted together. If the plea that we are in a formation state may cover in the administration at Albion, and in the action of the Genesee Convention irregularities, that were not necessary, and that are in conflict with express provisions of the Discipline, shall the benefit of that plea be denied to me when I organized Annual Conventions in the only mode in which under the circumstances they could be organized? Will you justify others in violating plain provisions of the Discipline when there is no necessity for it, and then in order to procure my condemnation, have recourse to the usages of another Church which has long been in existence? Where is the justice, the charity, of such a course? Can men of God act thus inconsistently and uncharitably?

"I have only touched upon a few leading points bearing on this matter. I have written in great haste, surrounded with company and crowded with cares; but I trust I have said enough to lead you to pause in your verdict until you have heard the matter presented on both sides.

"May the Lord bless you and lead you aright, and send peace and prosperity in our midst.

"Yours affectionately in Jesus,

"B. T. Roberts."

This clear and courteous presentation of the case had weight. The matter of a Convention was dropped. Surely the infant Church had no quiet birth, nor gentle cradling; foes without and dissensions within must alike be met, and in a Christlike spirit, exemplifying the grace that was preached.

This disturbing Susquehanna matter was not, however, allowed to drop just yet. One more trial must be had before this question was settled. The Genesee Convention in 1863 met at Parma, N. Y. Because the Discipline had been amended at the General Convention in the year preceding, in which the delegates from Susquehanna had a seat, a minority headed by John W. Reddy, objected to having the Superintendent preside over its sittings. But how to organize legally they did not know, for he was present. It was a curious sight, doubtless, to see him sitting quietly by and submitting in meekness to have his position canvassed publicly. Finally John W. Reddy ventured the astounding request: "Would he not permit the Convention to do its work without him in the chair?" A gentle, but firm, "No, sir," made it manifest that meekness and strength are not incompatible. To appease the minority he consented to a compromise, as he knew how to do when there was no principle at stake. He soothed their ruffled feelings by consenting to use the Discipline as originally adopted, not as amended by the General Convention, of which the obnoxious Susquehanna delegates were a part. This action, I believe, ended this incident.*

One more reference to the case is on record, however; and that is in the printed minutes of the Genesee Conference of 1864. The Conference record says:

The following document was presented and adopted:

TO THE MEMBERS OF THE ILLINOIS AND SUSQUEHANNA ANNUAL CONFERENCES:

Dear Brethren: At our last session the points of difference between us were candidly considered. We were willing to accord to you the most perfect honesty, and claimed the same for ourselves. Acting on this basis, we unanimously agreed to concede half the ground, and requested you to make an equal concession and meet us at the middle point. We felt that this would be mutually just and generous. But as you refused to accept our proposition, we still desire to be "of one heart and one mind." Therefore, maintaining the same view of our case as before, we agree to give up the whole ground of controversy, and to adopt the new edition of the Discipline.

Adopted, 35 to 2.

*Pages 284-291.

CHAPTER XXXVI

THE SUSQUEHANNA CONFERENCE—PROMINENT ACCESSIONS

The Susquehanna Conference in 1869 was honored by the accession of the Rev. Elias Bowen, D. D., who said upon joining that he had been a Free Methodist for over fifty years (meaning that the Free Methodist Church he was now joining was the same in character and spirit as that he originally joined); that they were the people with whom he originally united; that he could not run the risk of losing his soul by even seeming to countenance the anti-scriptural innovations which had become so firmly in-trenched in the Church to which he originally belonged.

He was too much advanced in years to take regular work, although his faculties were unimpaired. Accordingly he was granted a superannuate relation. His stay among the people he had newly joined was not permitted to be long, however, as on October 25th, 1870, he closed his eyes to mortal scenes, and passed within the veil.

Although a member of the communion but for a brief time, he was so associated with and influential in the organization of the Free Methodist Church that the history of the movement would not be complete without a sketch of his life and character.

Dr. Bowen was indeed a remarkable man. He was converted when a child of thirteen years, but lost his hold on Christ for a season. He was graciously reclaimed, however, at twenty, and began to preach the Gospel at the age of twenty-two. Soon after this he united with the Oneida Conference of the Methodist Episcopal Church, in which he labored with great acceptability and efficiency.

He was prominently before the Methodist public for

over fifty years. He filled prominent appointments, even at an early period in his ministry, not by his own choice but against his will. For twenty-four years he served as Presiding Elder, and would have been elected to the office earlier than he was but for his vigorous protest against it. He was seven times elected delegate to the General Conference, and at one time was strongly urged to become a candidate for the Bishop's office.

Dr. Bowen was an out-and-out Abolitionist when Abolitionism was a most unpopular issue in American Methodism. He preached, and wrote, and labored zealously to save the Methodist Church from complicity with slavery, "that sum of all villainies," but in vain. He was one of eleven against one hundred twenty-two members of the General Conference of 1836 to vote against the resolutions censuring Orange Scott and another brother for lecturing against slavery, and condemning the Anti-slavery movement generally, at their first reading; and one of fourteen against one hundred thirty to oppose the same resolutions at their second reading.

When those persecutions which led to the expulsion of Roberts, Stiles and others from the Genesee Conference and from the Church began, he openly avowed his sympathy for the persecuted brethren, rebuked the policy of the Buffalo Regency courageously and strongly, and wrote and spoke in no uncertain terms in defense of those brethren who were the objects of ecclesiastical wrath. After the Free Methodist Church was formed he wrote a "History of the Origin of the Free Methodist Church," the first elaborate statement of the case ever given to the public. He was also the author of a volume entitled "Slavery in the Methodist Episcopal Church," which was published in 1859.

As a preacher Dr. Bowen is said to have been "strong, clear, forcible and thoroughly evangelical. He was quiet in his manner, yet he often manifested in the pulpit deepest feeling. He was bold and fearless. His semi-centennial sermon preached before the Oneida Conference [which the Conference never did him the justice to publish], affords one of the best specimens of pulpit courage and fidelity that we have ever met with. The Conference had treated him with most marked kindness and consideration, yet he pointed out to them, with the greatest of plainness, their departures from God and from Methodism."*

Although unsparing in his denunciation of sin, Dr. Bowen was far from being harsh and uncharitable. He was the personification of tenderness and kindness, both in the pulpit and in his daily life. He was a man greatly beloved by those with whom he lived in closest relations. His piety was deep, uniform, and consistent. He was fully prepared for the end when it came. "The last day of his life was one of great peace, and he often, during the day, praised God aloud." He fell asleep in Jesus at the ripe age of seventy-nine years.

At the same time that Dr. Bowen united with the Susquehanna Conference another veteran minister of the Methodist Church also cast in his lot with that body. That minister was the Rev. Epenetus Owen. Though past middle age, he was still sufficiently strong so that he rendered more than twenty years of effective service to the Church. He was somewhat tall, with slightly stooping shoulders, and a prominent countenance, which beamed goodness from its every feature. He was intellectual, spiritual, genial to all, characterized by a quaint and unstudied humor in ordinary conversation, and even in his preaching, which made him very interesting to converse with or to listen to, and ever gave a pleasing originality to his public discourses.

"His sermons were always evangelical, awakening, interesting, instructive and edifying. * * * His services were sought for by our best appointments, and his labors

*Editorial in "Free Methodist" of November 10, 1870.

were always successful." He was of that amiable, quiet, and peaceable disposition that enabled him to make warm friends everywhere; and yet withal he was a man of positive and strong convictions, and also of the courage to avow them and to stand by them with the firmness of Gibraltar. But, strong as he was in his convictions, it was hard for those who differed from him to quarrel with him.

Mr. Owen was an admirable writer, as well as an able and eloquent preacher. He corresponded frequently for the columns of the Church periodicals, and was elected editor of the *Free Methodist* at the General Conference of 1882, but resigned the position in the afternoon of the same day. He was also the author of "Things New and Old," and "Struck by Lightning," two volumes that proved a blessing to many souls.

He several times represented his Conference at the General Conference, and always with ability and dignity.

He had preached the Gospel at the time of his death about fifty-two years, having preached his semi-centennial sermon at Conference in Rome, New York, September, 1888, and his last sermon at the Susquehanna Annual Conference at Binghamton, New York, September 6, 1889. He died of pneumonia, terminating in consumption, at Spring Hill, Pennsylvania, where he had gone to visit his brother, January 10, 1890.

At an early period in the development of the work within the bounds of the Susquehanna Conference the Free Methodist Society of Syracuse was organized, and in connection therewith was brought into the Church Mr. Charles T. Hicks, a layman, who subsequently became an important and influential factor in the work of Free Methodism. The Third Methodist Episcopal Church of Syracuse had become much dissatisfied with spiritual conditions in the denomination of which it was a part, and had determined to undertake securing some one to preach for them who would proclaim the Gospel in its purity and fulness. They were worshiping in a building known as "The Hemlock Church," because built cheaply with hemlock siding, placed in an upright position, and then battened. The members had belonged to other Syracuse societies, but had withdrawn, banded themselves together, and formed the Third Methodist Episcopal Church, as a means of securing such preaching as they believed needful to their spiritual growth. Different preachers supplied them for some time, among whom was G. W. Henry, a blind Virginian, better known to survivors of early Free Methodism in Western New York as "Blind Henry," author of "Shouting in All Ages," who was a great favorite among them.

Among the leading members of this Church was Mr. Charles T. Hicks, a man who used to have his name lettered inside his hat, followed by the words, "Death on rum, tobacco and slavery," and also another man of prominence named Gordon. When the Free Methodist movement began, the members of this Third Church naturally sympathized with it, and some of them attended the old Bergen camp-meeting. About the time the Free Methodist Church was organized the Rev. B. T. Roberts visited them, accompanied by his devoted wife, Mrs. W. C. Kendall (later Mrs. T. S. LaDue), Ellen Fuller (afterward wife of the Rev. James Mathews), another sister who later became the wife of Rev. A. B. Burdick, and Mrs. Esther Preston, the only one of the company now living (1914).

At this time the Rev. William Gould, who later figured prominently for many years in the Free Methodist movement, was acting as pastor of an Independent Methodist Church, which had swarmed from the First Methodist Episcopal Church under his leadership, on account of the pro-slavery principles and practises of its pastor. He attended the services held by Mr. Roberts and his company in "The Hemlock Church," and invited Mr. Roberts to preach for him, which he did, the service being held in a hall which the society had hired as a place of worship, at which time Mr. Roberts also dedicated the hall for the Independent Church people.

About this time a sort of rivalry sprang up between Mr. Hicks and Mr. Gordon of the Third Church, known as "the Hemlock Church," and some of the members drew out with Mr. Hicks, presumably intending to form themselves into a Free Methodist Society. Mr. Gordon, as leader of those who remained, proceeded to organize them into a Free Methodist class. Mr. Roberts soon visited Syracuse again, but declined to recognize the followers of Mr. Gordon as Free Methodists, and on the other hand did recognize those who followed Mr. Hicks. These formed the nucleus from which the Free Methodist Society of Syracuse was developed. Mr. Gordon and his followers finally connected themselves with the Methodist Protestant Church.*

Mr. Hicks became one of the most influential laymen of the Susquehanna Conference. He was born in New Jersey, and early in life removed to Buffalo, New York, where he engaged in trade. In 1830 he removed to Syracuse, in the same State, and soon afterward entered the County Clerk's office, in which he remained as Deputy Clerk and County Clerk about forty years. He was elected County Clerk in 1840, and reëlected in 1843. He was also admitted to the practise of law in the Court of Common Pleas, and at the last city election before his death he was elected to the office of Justice of the Peace for the city at large. He was a man of unbending integrity, and enjoyed the confidence of his fellow citizens in a high degree. All who knew him understood full well that he was a man who could not be bought at any price.

Mr. Hicks was converted in 1835, and soon after united with the First Methodist Episcopal Church of Syracuse. He filled the position of class-leader in this Church for many years. Under the labors of Dr. Redfield and Fay H.

*The facts here given have been gleaned from a personal letter from the Rev. William Gould and from his private Journal.

Purdy he was finally led into the experience of entire sanctification, and openly declared what God had done for him in this experience. His was an experience much beyond that of the fashionable holiness(?) of the time, and his testimony regarding it and its fruits was an occasion of annoyance to the rank and file of worldly conformed professors in the Church. Finally, feeling that he could not countenance the pride and worldly popularity of the Church to which he belonged, now that his eyes had been opened to its sinfulness, by remaining in its fellowship and contributing of his means to its maintenance, he, together with others of like convictions and spirituality, had severed connection with the First Church and formed the Third Methodist Episcopal Church of Syracuse.

As soon as the Free Methodist Church was organized, Mr. Hicks united with it, and continued a faithful and devoted member until summoned to the Church on high. His influence did much toward building up the Free Methodist Church in Syracuse and in the Susquehanna Conference. He was a warm supporter of B. T. Roberts in the early struggles of Free Methodism, and was also generous and hospitable in the entertainment of the preachers and "pilgrims" generally.

He was gradually failing for about two years before his end came, but he kept on his feet until about two weeks before his death. His resolute will made a brave fight against disease until its long continuance finally overpowered him. A little before his departure he told his wife he was going home to glory. His sky was clear, and he passed victoriously to his reward on Thursday, November 2, 1871.

One of the most unique and interesting characters in the Susquehanna Conference for many years was Moses N. Downing. He was what in colloquial phrase would be called "a live wire." He was a man who always made things lively around him—a man who could not and would not live in atmosphere of spiritual death. He was one of those who attended the Convention of Preachers and Laymen at Pekin, New York, in 1860, at which the Free Methodist Church was formed, and helped in its formation. He joined the new denomination but a few days prior to the session of the first Annual Conference, and remained in full fellowship with it to the close of his life. He was a preacher and writer of more than ordinary ability, and at times was decidedly eloquent in the pulpit. He served the Church faithfully for thirty-eight years, and much precious fruit of his labors remains. His work was chiefly in the Susquehanna, New York, Genesee and Southern California Conferences, where those who knew him hold his memory dear. He was a number of times a delegate to the General Conference. He died in the triumphs of faith in Christ at his home in Whittier, California, June 30, 1913. One of his last utterances was, "Tell all the people I am bound for glory."

REV. WILLIAM B. ROSE
Assistant Publishing Agent, 1896-1907
Publishing Agent since 1907

REV. J. T. LOGAN
Editor of the "Free Methodist" since 1907

REV. WILLIAM GOULD
A pioneer of early Free Methodism

W. B. BERTELS
Local Elder

CHAPTER XXXVII

FORMATION OF THE NEW YORK CONFERENCE

Although the New York Conference was not organized until fourteen years after the Pekin Convention at which the Discipline was adopted and the denomination formed; and although in chronological order the Michigan Conference preceded it by eight years, and the Minnesota and Northern Iowa by two years; yet because of its having been so long a part of the Susquehanna Conference, and because of its first society having been raised up by a minister of the Genesee Conference, this has been deemed the logical place to sketch its origin and progress.

In the early part of 1861, the Rev. Loren Stiles, Jr., at the urgent and repeated request of many devout souls who had suffered like treatment from the Methodist Church to that of those excommunicated in Western New York and Northern Illinois, went to White Haven, Pennsylvania, and spent some time preaching the Gospel of full salvation. The condition in which he found matters, and the results of his labors, are set forth in the following letter which he sent for publication in the April number of the *Earnest Christian:*

BROTHER ROBERTS: I am in White Haven, Luzerne County, Pennsylvania, about forty miles from the New Jersey line, encouraging the hearts and strengthening the hands of God's little ones here. On arriving here I found a noble little band of earnest Christians, who had been for years, while yet in the M. E. Church, earnestly contending for the faith once delivered to the saints. Such, however, has been the oppressive policy of the powers that be, that for the glory of God and the salvation of souls, they were forced to the choice of either giving up their convictions of duty, and tamely submitting to a relinquishment of their rights as

Methodists and Christians, or to establish separate meetings where they could labor and pray for souls, and follow their convictions of duty. They chose the latter course, and by their request I have organized thirty-six of them into a Free Methodist Church; and a few others, enough to increase their number to between forty and fifty, will soon give in their names. Relatively to their number, I think I have not found anywhere more clear and distinct witnesses for entire holiness than among these brethren, who have grown up here by themselves in this wild mountain region, all alone, with no ministerial help, living by faith, and working for God in the real old-fashioned Methodist way.

Had I come here blindfolded, and gone into their meetings, and heard them talk, and pray, and sing, and shout, I might easily have imagined myself on the Genesee battle-ground, surrounded by some of our best, tried, and most skilful veterans of Western New York, in this glorious war. Some of them are slightly scarred by Baltimore Regency weapons. Two have suffered expulsion on like frivolous charges, and by similar sham-like trials to those that have characterized Genesee Conference administration, and rendered it immortal in infamy. About twenty joined us from the M. E. Church.

They have for weeks been holding their prayer and exhortation meetings in private houses, where souls have been converted and sanctified. This Friday evening, the last evening of my labors with them, eleven went forward for prayers, seeking the pardoning favor of God.

Since I have been among them our Presbyterian brethren have very kindly granted us the use of their Church, where I have preached several times to large and attentive congregations. Our Free Methodists here are erecting a Church edifice for themselves, and expect soon to ask us to supply them with a preacher. So very like are these earnest Christians of Eastern Pennsylvania to our Free Methodists in Western New York, and so similar is the opposition with which they have met, and so very like is the path in which they have been led, that I can account for it in no other way than that they have the same Lord and the same devil here that we have there. L. STILES, JR.

This work was ultimately taken under the charge of the Susquehanna Conference, and at the session held in New York, in September, 1863, A. B. Burdick was sent to White Haven, Pennsylvania, as preacher in charge. In 1864 another circuit had been raised up, and two preachers were sent into that region. The work in these parts continued to grow, and in 1865 there were six preachers appointed to circuits in this territory. In 1867 a lay membership of 175, including probationers, was reported from this section of country, and the number of circuits remained the same. By 1879, however, the membership had increased to about 300, and nine preachers were required to supply this work. There continued to be a steady, healthy growth until, in 1874, it was judged best to organize the work into a separate Conference.

The Susquehanna Conference of 1873 having voted to request it, and the Executive Committee having acted favorably on the request, General Superintendent Roberts called a session for the organization of the New York Conference, to be held in Brooklyn, New York, September 2-6, 1874. When the Superintendent took the chair and had conducted devotional exercises, he "announced that all preachers who had charge of circuits within the aforesaid bounds [prescribed as the territory of the New York Conference] would be considered as members of the new Conference, unless they wished to retain their membership in the Susquehanna Conference; and that any other members of the Susquehanna Conference would be considered members of the new Conference if they [so] desired, and stated their desire to this Conference. The president read the names of preachers who had labored within the said bounds,—each responded, and his name was placed upon the new Conference roll."

The ministers who became charter members of this body numbered sixteen in all—thirteen of whom had been members of the Susquehanna Conference in full connection, and one of whom had been in full connection in the Genesee Conference. The following are their names: A. G. Terry, William Jones, William Gould, James Mathews, M. N. Downing, M. D. McDougall, W. M. Parry, S. H. Bronson, John Glen, G. E. Ferrin, W. W. Warner, R. Coons, O. V. Ketels, F. J. Ewell. In addition to these H.

Hendrickson, George Eakins and J. E. Bristol were continued on probation, and Andrew Ahgreen was received on probation.

The stationing committee unanimously recommended the dividing of the Conference territory into three districts—the New York, Wilkes-Barre, and Philadelphia—and that the two former be under a traveling Chairmanship and the latter be supervised by a stationed Chairman. The Conference approved the recommendation, and William Gould was elected Chairman of the New York and Wilkes-Barre districts, and James Mathews was stationed at Philadelphia and elected Chairman of the Philadelphia district.

The statistical record shows the lay membership at this time to have been 617, including ninety probationers, and the value of Church property to have been $57,035.

At the time of its organization the New York Conference embraced "all parts of the States of New York and Pennsylvania not included in the Genesee and Susquehanna Conferences, and all that territory lying due east." Later it was made to "embrace all parts of the States of New York and Pennsylvania not included in the Genesee, Oil City and Susquehanna Conferences, and the States of New Jersey, Maryland, Delaware and Virginia." Among its present appointments are Newark, Dover, Phillipsburg, Flemington and Vineland, in the State of New Jersey; at Baltimore, Hampstead, Alesia, Fairmount, Spencerville, Rockville, Avery, Lay Hill, etc., in the State of Maryland; and at Alexandria, Virginia. The work in Maryland has nearly all of it been raised up within recent years, and is very promising. The work at Alexandria, Virginia, was started much earlier, as was also that at most of the points in New Jersey.

The work in the New York Conference has ever been favored with some of the best ministerial talent of the denomination. In its early period it was blessed with the services of such men as William Gould, James Mathews,

M. N. Downing, John Glen, Joseph Travis, T. S. LaDue, A. F. Curry, William Jones, M. D. McDougall, W. M. Parry, S. H. Bronson, J. E. Bristol—men of strong ability, deep piety, unconquerable courage, and holy aggressiveness, and whose influence for good still survives. Later such men as A. G. Miller and J. T. Michael came to the front. Both were men of marked ability. When Mr. Michael was received into full connection in the Newark Methodist Conference a number spoke in his favor. An ex-presiding elder, M. E. Ellison, spoke very highly of his work on the circuit, and Dr. Hurst, then President of Drew Theological Seminary (afterward bishop), said that Bishop Foster had stated that Mr. Michael had the best mind of any student who had attended the seminary during his (Foster's) presidency; Dr. Hurst added that "he [Brother Michael] was the second Watson." George Eakins, J. T. Logan and W. B. Rose should also be mentioned among the foregoing list, the latter two of whom have for a number of years past served the Church as General Conference officers—Mr. Logan as editor of the *Free Methodist,* and Mr. Rose as denominational Publishing Agent.

Free Methodism in the New York Conference has experienced more than the ordinary amount of testing and sifting, and at times it has seemed as though in some of the more important centers it would be wholly destroyed; nevertheless, it has kept its head above the billows, and seems destined still to survive and be a blessing to the world. At the present time (1914) it has thirty-two preachers in full membership, with five on trial; lay members numbering 1,338, inclusive of 219 probationers; Church property valued at $118,500, and parsonage property to the amount of $28,750.

The early growth and progress of the work in the New York Conference owed much to the devotion, integrity, wisdom, and liberality of such laymen as W. B. Bertels, of Wilkes-Barre, Pennsylvania, a manufacturer of tinware; C. O. Schantz, of Allentown, Pennsylvania, who was engaged in the banking business; Joseph Mackey, of New York City, editor and publisher of a railroad Guide, and of "The United States Economist and Dry Goods Reporter;" James Gray, also of New York City, a general printer; James Dickson, of Philadelphia, a hardware merchant; his wife, Mrs. Emily Dickson, a woman gifted with rare abilities, who preached frequently with great acceptability, and who chiefly raised up the work at West Philadelphia; John Gray, an ordained local preacher of general acceptability; Lucien Woodruff, Justice of the Peace, a very devoted and influential man of God; and Noah Patrick, another influential man of God, whose memory is precious to all who knew him.

Also there were several other women deserving of special mention among the laity prominently identified with early Free Methodism in the New York Conference: Mrs. Maria Rose, who was gifted with evangelistic ability, and who assisted in raising up the society at Dover, New Jersey, and labored effectively in other fields; Mrs. Jane Dunning, for many years Superintendent of Providence Mission, New York, raised up and maintained by Dr. Sabine; and Mrs. Calista Fairchild, a talented evangelist, identified with the origin of the work at Alexandria, Virginia, and Washington, D. C., and who is still living within the bounds of the Conference. To these, and to other "elect ladies" whose names can not be mentioned in this connection but are in the book of life, the progress and prosperity of the work in the New York Conference territory was largely indebted in its primitive days.

Some of the laymen named in the foregoing list also finally became prominently identified with the more general work of the Free Methodist Church. Joseph Mackey was for a time editor and proprietor of the *Free Methodist;* this of course before the Church had assumed proprietorship of the paper. C. O. Schantz served for two quadrenniums as denominational Auditor, and that with remarkable efficiency. His final resignation was because of failing health. W. B. Bertels, though a layman, is an ordained local Elder, and has repeatedly represented his Annual Conference as delegate to the General Conference, in which he has ever acquitted himself with much wisdom, dignity, and spirituality. James Dickson, who with his wife gave generous aid to the Church in Philadelphia, West Philadelphia and Brooklyn. It is seldom that any Conference is favored with a nobler and more intelligent and devoted class of laymen than have generally graced the New York Conference.

www.ingramcontent.com/pod-product-compliance
Lightning Source LLC
Chambersburg PA
CBHW020904100426
42737CB00043B/128

9781621714736